Analysis and Integration
of Behavioral Units

Analysis and Integration of Behavioral Units

Edited by

Travis Thompson
Department of Psychology
University of Minnesota
Minneapolis, Minnesota

Michael D. Zeiler
Department of Psychology
Emory University
Atlanta, Georgia

LEA LAWRENCE ERLBAUM ASSOCIATES, PUBLISHERS
1986 Hillsdale, New Jersey   London

Lawrence Erlbaum Associates, Inc., Publishers
365 Broadway
Hillsdale, New Jersey 07642

Library of Congress Cataloging-in-Publication Data

Analysis and integration of behavioral units.

Based on a conference in honor of the 65th birthday
of Kenneth MacCorquodale, held in 1984 in Minneapolis,
Minn.
Includes bibliographies and index.
1. Behavior assessment—Congresses.   2. MacCorquo-
dale, Kenneth.   I. Thompson, Travis.   II. Zeiler,
Michael, D.   III. MacCorquodale, Kenneth.   [DNLM:
1. Behavior—congresses.   2. Learning—congresses.
3. Psychology, Experimental—congresses.
BF 121 A532 1984]
BF698.A55   1986   150   86-2039
ISBN 0-89859-577-0

Printed in the United States of America
10   9   8   7   6   5   4   3   2   1

CONTENTS

CONTRIBUTORS

Baer, Donald M.
Department of Human Development
University of Kansas
Lawrence, Kansas 66045

Cerutti, Daniel T.
Department of Psychology
Temple University
Philadelphia, Pennsylvania 19122

Catania, A. Charles
Department of Psychology
University of Maryland Baltimore Co.
Catonsville, Maryland 21228

Dews, Peter B.
Department of Psychiatry
Harvard Medical School
Boston, Massachusetts 02115

Falk, John L.
Department of Psychology
Busch Campus
Rutgers, New Jersey 08903

Harzem, Peter
Department of Psychology
Auburn University
Auburn, Alabama 36849

Hineline, Philip N.
Department of Psychology
Temple University
Philadelphia, Pennsylvania 19122

Lubinski, David
Department of Psychology
University of Minnesota
Minneapolis, Minnesota 55455

Marr, M. Jackson
School of Psychology
Georgia Institute of Technology
Atlanta, Georgia 30332

Meazzini, Paolo
Psychology Department
University of Rome
Rome, Italy

Meehl, Paul E.
Department of Psychology
University of Minnesota
Minneapolis, Minnesota 55455

Ricci, Carlo
Psychology Department
University of Rome
Rome, Italy

Schnaitter, Roger
Department of Psychology
Illinois Wesleyan University
Bloomington, Illinois 61701

Sidman, Murray
Department of Psychology
Northeastern University
Boston, Massachusetts 02116

Thompson, Travis
Department of Psychology
University of Minnesota
Minneapolis, Minnesota 55455

Zeiler, Michael D.
Department of Psychology
Emory University
Atlanta, Georgia 30322

PREFACE

This volume grew out of a conference in honor of the 65th birthday of Kenneth MacCorquodale, an exceptionally eloquent spokesman for the field of the experimental analysis of behavior. Plans for the conference began in 1982 with a casual conversation between the editors. As the possibility of the conference and this volume became a reality, it seemed only fitting that the meeting be held near the University of Minnesota where Professor MacCorquodale had taught for 37 years. Financial support provided by the College of Liberal Arts, the Department of Psychology and the Nolte Center for Continuing Education (all of the University of Minnesota) made it possible to assemble 16 of the foremost scholars in psychology and the analysis of behavior. Gordon Amundson, Associate Director of the Nolte Center for Continuing Education, and Paula Sanders, Program Associate, were instrumental in bringing together the remarkable group of scientists who contributed to this volume. They expended extraordinary efforts to make the event successful, and no simple statement of gratitude adequately expresses our appreciation. Among the others who made invaluable contributions were Dean Fred Lukerman of the University of Minnesota, College of Liberal Arts, and Jack Burton, Editorial Vice President, Lawrence Erlbaum Associates, Inc.

Numerous University of Minnesota staff and students contributed in large and small ways to both the conference and to preparation of the manuscripts in this volume. To our friend and colleague Celia Wolk Gershenson, who selflessly devoted vast numbers of hours working both on the conference and resulting volume, goes our deepest thanks. Her dedication to Professor MacCorquodale is manifest in her assistance with countless editorial details throughout the volume. Those who must be singled out, however, and to whom the most credit belongs, are Peggy Boden and Marit Gladem. It was they who prepared every manuscript page, every reference, and every square pixel of layout that made this volume possible. It was their diligence and dedication that helped transform a confederation of manuscripts into a finished published product. It is to them that our most heartfelt thanks is extended.

TT, Minneapolis
MDZ, Atlanta
10-22-85

FOREWORD

Every academic discipline has its iconoclasts, superstars, and entrepreneurs. If we are very fortunate, we may also come to know a precious few scholars who more adequately idealize the academic endeavor. In the C.P. Snowian world of internecine academic departmental politics and bloodless (or nearly so) coups d'état, these men and women rise above the quarreling. They are the comportmental as well as intellectual standard by which a true academician is judged. The present volume is dedicated to such a man: Professor Kenneth MacCorquodale.

Born on June 26, 1919, Kenneth MacCorquodale attended both undergraduate and graduate school at the University of Minnesota, completing his doctorate in experimental psychology under the tutelage of Professor William Heron in 1946. During his tenure as a graduate student at Minnesota, MacCorquodale's contemporaries included William Estes, Norman Guttman, Howard Hunt, Keller Breland, George Collier, and of course, Paul Meehl. One says, "Of course, Paul Meehl," because during the halcyon days of their closest professional association, Kenneth MacCorquodale and Paul Meehl published several of the era's most important papers for psychological theory. Their partnership produced "On a Distinction Between Hypothetical Constructs and Intervening Variables" (*Psychological Review*, 1948) and "Edward C. Tolman," published in Estes et al., *Modern Learning Theory* (1954). The prophetic "Excursis: The Response Concept," contained in the latter paper was the conceptual wellspring for the present volume.

Kenneth MacCorquodale has been preoccupied with fundamental units of analysis of behavior as long as I can remember. He taught that there were two such behavioral units; elicited and emitted units - and that all else was composed of permutations and combinations of these. When we taught together he occasionally vacillated about the possibility of adjunctive behavior being a third class. Whether there are two or three types of fundamental units, the problem still remains as to how these basic units are combined to form the natural stuff of behavior which we see around us on a moment to moment basis. We spent many hours in our joint seminar, "Readings in the Analysis of Behavior," wrestling with that problem.

The present volume grew directly out of the issues raised by MacCorquodale and Meehl in their "Excursis: The Response Concept" paper and which MacCorquodale posed so often when he taught. It is a fitting tribute to the man on his 65th birthday that a group of scholars whom he holds in highest regard convened in one place to think out loud about two of the thorniest problems facing behavioral science, namely, the nature of the units of analysis of the subject matter and the mechanisms responsible for their integration.

Kenneth MacCorquodale's academic upbringing was unorthodox. Though William Heron was his doctoral advisor, Richard M. Elliott was his closest counselor and colleague among the faculty during his graduate student days. MacCorquodale wrote of Elliott, "He was wise, determined, unfailingly kind and courteous, full of personal charm and life. He was a gentleman." MacCorquodale learned his lesson well at Elliott's knee, for Kenneth MacCorquodale embodies those qualities himself. While Elliott provided MacCorquodale with one of the most important influences of his career, his intellectual mentor was unquestionably B.F. Skinner. Skinner was on the faculty at Minnesota from 1936-1945 and exerted a profound influence on the group of graduate students in training during that time. MacCorquodale had flirted with Clark Hull's hypothetico-deductive theory, attracted by its formal properties and the possibility of direct quantitative tests of theoretical predictions. The truth was, however, that MacCorquodale was always more attracted to Tolman's purposive behaviorism than Hullian theory. That MacCorquodale and Meehl chose to analyze Tolman's theory at the Dartmouth Conference in the summer of 1949 was no accident. However, when it came to a fundamental intellectual commitment, Skinner's behaviorism won hands down with MacCorquodale.

Elliott invited MacCorquodale to join the faculty on his return from military service in 1946. MacCorquodale set about teaching a course called "Advanced General Psychology," a course with contents very similar to Keller and Schoenfeld's text *Principles of Psychology* which was published a few years later. MacCorquodale devoted much of his first few lectures each term to philosophical underpinnings of modern behaviorism so as to provide a foundation for the rest of the course. In 1952, MacCorquodale began teaching a second course called "Verbal Behavior," the content of which was very similar to Skinner's book by the same title. Kenneth MacCorquodale was, in a very real sense, Skinner's first and one of his most intellectually influential students. Yet MacCorquodale never refers to himself as a "Skinnerian." To Kenneth MacCorquodale one does not follow a woman or man, one assimilates an intellectual tradition. MacCorquodale has always paid Skinner the highest honor by teaching his students that Skinner's contributions belong in the intellectual tradition of Claude Bernard, Ernst Mach and Edward Thorndike, and are of a comparable order of magnitude.

Most first generation behavior analysts know of Kenneth MacCorquodale's editorial contributions to the most influential series of books in the history of modern psychology. When Richard M. Elliott retired as editor of the *Century Psychology Series*, Kenneth MacCorquodale assumed the mantle of leadership of that distinguished series with grace, if a little discomfort (at least in the beginning). Mr. Elliott (as MacCorquodale always refers to him) was a tough act to follow. The *Century Psychology Series* had been unequaled in the history of psychology as the repository of major psychological writings. During MacCorquodale's editorial tenure, the series continued to publish significant volumes by such people as Berlyne, Bijou and Baer, Campbell, Church, Gibson, Honig, Lofquist and Dawis, McGuigan, Reese, Skinner, and Tyler, to name only a few. MacCorquodale was and is a gentle, but incisive editor. T.S. Eliot once remarked that an editor should tell the author that his writing is better than it is. Not a lot better, but a little better. MacCorquodale is a master of the technique. His skill in helping the author rise above him or herself is uncommon.

Psychologists trained in the tradition of the experimental analysis of behavior of B.F. Skinner chafed at the beating Skinner's book *Verbal Behavior* took in many academic circles following publication of Noam Chomsky's critique. Other psycholinguists joined the attack like so many chickens attracted to blood on an adversary's comb. Several psychologists operating within the behavior analytic tradition replied to Chomsky's attack on Skinner's interpretation of verbal behavior, but they seemed to be largely ineffective in quelling the hue and cry. In 1969 MacCorquodale published his retrospective review of Skinner's *Verbal Behavior* and in 1970 published his "Reply to Chomsky," which laid the matter to rest. These two papers generally are viewed as the definitive analyses of the functionalist-structuralist disagreement, coming down strongly on the former side of the issue. They are the sine qua non of scholarship to which most aspire, but which few achieve.

For all of Kenneth MacCorquodale's scholarly accomplishments, those of us who had the good fortune to sit through one of his classes as students at the University of Minnesota owe our greatest intellectual debt to him as teacher. To note that he was an excellent teacher would be a significant understatement. He brought a truly unique combination of scholarship and rhetorical excellence to bear each time he stood before a room full of students. The quality of MacCorquodale's pedagogical style is virtually impossible to describe, but is instantly recognizable. If there were a Nobel Prize for University lecturers, Kenneth MacCorquodale would have been the recipient of at least three. One could not sit passively through his course in "Analysis of Behavior" (originally "Advanced General Psychology") or "Verbal Behavior." The course "took." Once you completed MacCorquodale's "Advanced General Psychology" course, it was in your bones the rest of your life. Nearly every fall quarter when I am about to begin teaching my "Analysis of Behavior" course, I dig out my yellowed typewritten lecture notes from Kenneth

MacCorquodale's course (Fall, 1957) and take a strong swig of intellectual reassurance.

As remarkable as the quality of Kenneth MacCorquodale's teaching was (he was granted the Distinguished Teacher Award by the College of Liberal Arts of the University of Minnesota in 1965) his quantitative contribution to the teaching of psychology is equally extraordinary. Figure 1 shows a cumulative record of the number of students enrolled in the "Analysis of Behavior" (or "Advanced General Psychology") and "Verbal Behavior" courses from 1946 to 1982. Figure 2 shows a cumulative record of the students MacCorquodale taught in his general psychology courses (some jointly with Charles Bird, Richard Elliott, James Jenkins and David LaBerge). Figure 3 shows the cumulative number of students taught by Kenneth MacCorquodale by the

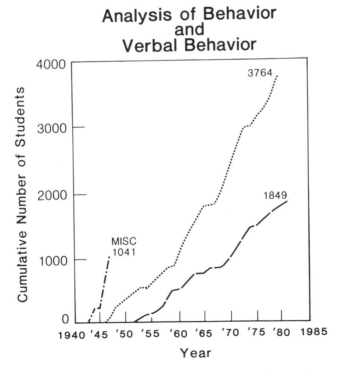

Fig. 1. Cumulative Number of Students in Analysis of Behavior and Verbal Behavior

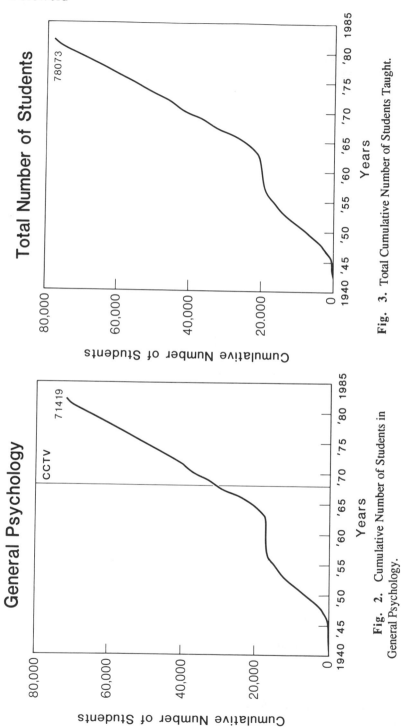

Fig. 2. Cumulative Number of Students in General Psychology.

Fig. 3. Total Cumulative Number of Students Taught.

time he retired from the University of Minnesota in the spring of 1982. The total exceeds over 78,000 students, which defies conventional adjectival description.

I still remember seeing 600 students in an overcrowded Burton Hall auditorium rise to their feet in applause as Kenneth MacCorquodale completed the final sentence of his final lecture in the "Introduction to Psychology" course in which I was enrolled in the spring of 1956. He had thanked the students for their attention and forebearance, then turned, drew a large smiling face on the chalkboard in acknowledgement of their approbation, turned back to the lectern, picked up his 4" by 6" cards from which he always lectured, straightened them with a firm "clunk" on the edge of the reading desk, turned, and walked briskly off the stage without looking back. Those of us who participated in preparing manuscripts for this volume have done so with this quality of man in mind.

Travis Thompson
Minneapolis
April 8, 1985

Postscript: As this volume goes to press, it has been learned that Professor Kenneth MacCorquodale died at his home in Coronado, California on February 28, 1986. We are reminded of a remark by Henry Brooks Adams, who wrote, "A teacher affects eternity; he can never tell where his influence stops."

Travis Thompson
Minneapolis
February 28, 1986

PART I

BACKGROUND

CHAPTER 1

Behavioral Units: A Historical Introduction

MICHAEL D. ZEILER

The successes of atomic theory and cell theory are indisputable evidence for the value of discovering proper units in a science. A well-defined unit clarifies the way phenomena are conceptualized and thereby guides research and theory. Isolation of a unit brings order to otherwise discrepant phenomena; invalid units easily lead to confusion as to the meaning and significance of data.

Biology provides an excellent example of the importance of units. Prior to the development of cell theory, what we now call biology was a collection of disciplines that seemed to share little more than a common interest in living organisms. The structure of life was the subject matter of anatomy and embryology, function was the province of physiology, animal activity was the interest of zoology, plants were the focus of botany, and none of these shared a common conceptual foundation. However, cell theory changed all this. According to the theory all living organisms are composed of cells; the cell describes the fundamental structural components of living matter. Although cells are of different types and are comprised of still smaller components, they constitute the smallest level having the complex of properties that define life. (Units always are defined at a particular level of analysis; rarely are they irreducible.) The cell, then, is the unit of life.

The bearing of cell theory reaches, however, well beyond matters of simple structural description. The ramifications of cell theory are abundant . . . For the cell, while always an architectural element of prime importance, is also the critical unit of organic function above the molecular level. The cell is thus the site of metabolism and energy exchange; it is the basis of nervous and secretory activity and therefore the foundation of harmonious, integrative, organic behavior; the cell, as manifested in the reproductive products, ensures, finally, the very continuity of life across the generations. (Coleman, 1971, p. 17)

Cell theory integrated all the biological sciences into one unified field because recognition of a common fundamental unit combined areas whose differences otherwise seemed more compelling than did their similarities. "The cell theory is the most important tectonic generalization in the whole of biology" (Medawar and Medawar, 1983, p. 51).

If, as occurs in complex systems, units are constituents of the whole, a complete picture requires not only unit specification but also explication of the integration rules. Within psychology, the most straightforward program of unit analysis and integration appeared in the Wundt-Titchener approach to mind. The units were the mental elements - sensations, images, or emotions - to be determined by painstaking experimental introspective analyses. These are the smallest events that are conscious mental entities. Psychology was to proceed by first analyzing into elements and then by synthesizing those elements into ordinary complex mental experience.

As psychology shifted from mentalism to the study of behavior, the nature of units became less obvious. Pavlov - who really was to shape behavioristic thinking - brought neurophysiological concepts into the picture because of his commitment to psychical reflexes as the way to study brain physiology. He, like Sherrington, thought of the nervous system as structural chains of receptors, conductors, and effectors. This, of course, is the Sherringtonian reflex arc. The reflex - the mechanism by which neural units were believed to be integrated - itself is the basic unit of integrated behavior. Sherrington viewed the reflex as a mechanism of communication among nerve cells; with conditioned reflexes

Pavlov moved to the reflex as the mechanism of communication between input (stimulus) and output (response). The reflex had expanded its role as the basic unit of integrated activity.

Thorndike certainly was not a physiological reflexologist, but his position was compatible with the notion that learned behavior involved the integration of basic units. For him, like Pavlov, stimuli and responses were the structural units, even though Thorndike's stimuli and responses were more molar than were Pavlov's. For Thorndike, the organization of units was based on associations rather than on reflexes. The structural view of stimulus and response is apparent from Thorndike's belief that educators should first teach students those stimuli and responses that occur most often, because transfer is based on commonality of elements. Elements of this sort, like cells, have a definite architectural significance.

The mechanical connotations of reflexology appealed to hard-headed behaviorists. Watson was interested both in expanding the concepts of stimulus and response to include complex situations and activities and in explaining how simpler reflexes became chained together to produce extended sequences. Skinner, more than any other psychologist of his era, expanded the reflex concept until he arrived at a definition of units that remains current to this day. His 1931 paper extended the reflex to all of the behavior of intact organisms. By defining stimuli as total situations and responses as complex activities, and by relating the two by the reflex, behavior could be treated in purely mechanical terms. Skinner gave the reflex the general definition, $R = f(S)$, where S is a stimulus and R is a response. This definition was not intended as a vague generality, but carried with it the necessity of finding the relations between particular stimuli and particular responses. At this point, stimuli and responses were independently defined structural units that could be combined into reflexes. However, in 1935, Skinner redefined stimuli and responses as functional classes rather than as immediately observable events. Coleman's (1984) provocative discussion explains how Skinner's unequivocal determinism necessarily committed him to the generic interpretation of stimulus and response.

The importance of the 1935 paper was in its redefinition of stimuli and response as classes of events described in terms of commonality of effects. Stimuli are defined not only in terms of physical energy but by the correlation with a particular class of responses; responses are defined not by their topography but rather as a class of events subject to control by particular stimuli. Thus, the old units of stimulus and response now have no independent definition. The entire relational complex of events is referred to as a reflex. Coleman (1984) points out that: "His complex argument for generic concepts of stimulus and response in no way counseled abandonment of the concept of reflex, but only argued against the use of extremely restricted preparations in the study of behavior, a fault which he placed against Pavlovian preparations" (p. 492). Units now are defined functionally rather than as structural entities, although the persistent, albeit liberated, reflexology still produces a structural undertone. These units, defined in terms of what they do, are welded together by the reflex.

The reflex and its psychological relative, the conditioned reflex, still were tied to an eliciting stimulus. However, Skinner soon used conditioned reflex to refer to all learned behavior. The several types of conditioned reflex now were differentiated by procedure. Operant behavior was response (R) followed by stimulus (S) (behavior that has a certain consequence) rather than behavior following the reflex pattern of stimulus followed by response. The unit of operant behavior is the R-S functional relationship; the unit of respondent behavior is the S-R functional relationship; the unit of stimulus control was the S-R-S functional relationship. When these distinctions are combined with generic definitions of stimulus as the class of events that maintain the same response, and response as the class of behavior correlated with a stimulus, integration and structure become identical. Given the totally relational definitions of the terms, units of structure and units of integration are inseparable, and the intact functional relationships become the fundamental units of behavior.

Much is gained by this approach. The fundamental units (operants, respondents, discriminative operants) are the smallest entities that display the full characteristics of adaptive behavior. The previous structural entities (stimuli and responses in isolation) now become components of the basic units, analogous to nuclei and cytoplasm as components of cells. Research can involve the variables determining how generic classes are constructed and the factors responsible for particular forms of coordinated behavior, but never is it necessary to move to a nonbehavioral level of analysis. To pursue the analogy to cells, behavioral units are the smallest bit of integrated behavior, just as cells are the smallest living structure. They can be observed with appropriate methodology, just as cells can be seen with a microscope. They have components; cells do as well. Indeed, experimental analyses of these components can serve as a primary focus of behavioral research, just as intracellular study can be a major emphasis in contemporary biology. Whether or not component analysis - the analysis of factors producing discriminative and eliciting stimuli, reinforcers, effective responses, etc. - proves to have an impact equivalent to that of molecular biology and sub-atomic physics, at least the parent units of the various sciences are parallel. The foundation of the science of behavior is in good order.

One might wish that the various behavioral units would be types of one basic unit in the way that neurons, muscle cells, and the like all are types of cell. The best we can offer to date in this regard, however, is to organize them in terms of the rather programmatic $R=f(S)$ relationship. No more substantial commonality between operants and respondents has been forthcoming as yet. We have, however, questioned whether Skinner's list of units is complete. As behavioral research has developed, the list seems to require more entries than just operants, discriminative operants, and respondents. This matter is explored in the present chapters by Sidman, Falk, Lubinski and Thompson, Hineline, Marr, Catania and Cerutti, and in a rather unique way, Meehl.

The relational definition of a unit means that each represents an integrated coherent sequence of events (see Thompson's brief chapter for further discussion). However, a major problem of integration involves relations between units rather than relations within a given unit. Biologists display a similar concern when trying to understand how cells become differentiated into tissues and organs. Research and theory in embryology focuses on these morphogenetic processes, and it has had some success in describing the processes by which cells become organized into higher order structures. How are we to consider complex behavior such as temporally and spatially organized sequences or behavior determined by a series of stimuli? How are we to know whether such behavior actually represents compounded simple units or should itself be deemed a unit? If units are compounded, what are the integrating principles? Of course, proponents of simple chaining hypotheses must deal with the sorts of considerations raised by Lashley (1951) in his penetrating discussion of the problem of serial order in behavior. The Gestalt psychologists also firmly maintained that complexes rarely if ever are composed of intact smaller elements, but themselves are fundamental units. Actually, these criticisms are most applicable to a simple summative process, and they may be less compelling if the interaction rules are of some other form. Note, however, that Skinner's scheme imposes no restrictions on the size or extent of either stimulus or response, nor does it require that complex behavior be composed of smaller units. Any behavior, no matter how extended in time and space, could itself be a unit. If an extended behavioral sequence meets all of the rules for a generic response class, it then has equal footing with any other response and integration processes need not be of any concern. One might be intrigued by how such extended classes are constructed, and this "biochemistry of behavior" is likely to begin with specification of the operations required to have the sequence function as an operant. The possibility that extended sequences do in fact have unitary properties is explored in the chapters by Baer, Marr, and Zeiler, each taking a different behavioral phenomenon as their reference point.

But an orderly sequence of behavior may not meet the definition of a unit. Surely, the smooth sequential transitions that mark our typical working day or even an hour of tennis or of teaching a class are not likely to show the characteristics of a generic response, barring a definition so loose as to render the entire concept ridiculous. Sequential progression over long time periods, then, entails understanding of how units communicate with each other. Among the authors who deal explicitly with this concern are Lubinski and Thompson, Marr, Schnaitter, Dews, and Harzem.

Given the historical context suggested by the preceding discussion, it was predictable that a conference on units and integration could take many directions. To no one's surprise, the prediction was confirmed.

The broad picture of the development of contemporary views of units as reviewed here shows the change from a model derived from the classic reflex of neurophysiology to one defined in terms of inextricable relationships between events. Thompson provides another introduction to the relational interpretation by offering a rather unique historical perspective. He points out some surprising antecedents of both the initial reflex concept and Skinner's final relational version. Meazzini and Ricci provide a historical overview of behaviorism, largely from the perspective of the changing conception of basic units. The history of behaviorism involves a number of interrelated themes, many of which have not been well understood previously.

Sidman's chapter stands out as one of the clearest, most penetrating, and provocative analyses of units in the contemporary psychological literature. It is a conceptualization that takes a giant step forward in dealing with complex behavior. After tracing the development of the integrated unit through Skinner's two and three term contingencies, Sidman goes on to systematically analyze more complex organizations. His elucidation of four and five term contingencies and equivalence and transitivity relations existing among the components provides a sophisticated and logically coherent model that permits understanding highly complex activity. The analysis promises an experimental entrée into creativity as well as into much of what now comprises cognitive function.

Even multiple levels of the operant contingency together with the S-R arrangement of Pavlovian conditioning may not exhaust the list of functionally defined units. Falk's pioneering work indicated that adjunctive behavior does not fit comfortably into either an operant or a respondent mold. Instead, it appears to represent a unique arrangement in which complex situations develop either the power of eliciting certain kinds of behavior or result in stimuli gaining unusual reinforcing ability. Falk now takes adjunctive behavior further by discussing its adaptive role with respect to conserving some other essential behavior: Adjunctive behavior may be an adaptively neutral laboratory manifestation of truly adaptive displacement activity. This approach leads to speculations about the causes of human rituals, an area hitherto primarily of interest to anthropologists.

Three chapters - Marr's, Catania and Cerutti's, and Harzem's - deal with verbal behavior. Marr is very much concerned with understanding the organizational units of mathematical activity, which certainly is high order verbal behavior. The traditional concept of the operant emphasizes reinforcement contingencies as part of the defining attribute, but it is not evident what may be reinforcing mathematical behavior. Even expanding the notion of operant to include rule-governed behavior may not be sufficient. What processes are implicated in describing mathematical principles? Indeed, what is the response? In short, the full spectrum of the unit problem - structure and integration - appears anew.

But can verbal behavior be cleanly separated from nonverbal activity? Catania and Cerutti now have converted some earlier thought experiments into hard procedures and data. In these experiments, pigeons deal with conditional discrimination procedures (Sidman's four-term contingency) in ways that seem analogous to language use. Although no verbal behavior is involved, parallels to language emerge.

Harzem's thoughtful analysis points out that meaningful human behavior simply does not usually occur in continuous sequences. Instead, it occurs in fits, starts, stumblings, interruptions, and re-starts. Unitary properties exist at the verbal level, not in the form of smooth behavior emitted over real time. So "working" or "being a good husband" are not sequences, and it is a mistake to assume that they can be studied directly. How, then, do the linguistic labels arise if, in fact, they have no consistent referent? As they do indeed refer to certain sets of actions in that we can agree that one is working or is a good husband, they may indeed be units composed of temporally non-contiguous components. The integration into units is another candidate for analysis in terms of Sidman's higher level contingencies.

Hineline believes that the verbal behavior of psychologists is the source of inappropriate conceptualizations of central issues. These problems, he believes, can be resolved by carefully maintaining the Radical Behaviorist view that the agent of behavior is the environment and not the behaving organisms. The organism does not produce behavior; the environment is the source, and the organism serves as the context for the environment-behavior interaction. This position leads to strictly procedural distinctions between types of behavioral unit: Operant refers to behavior affected by its consequences; nonoperant is orderly behavior occurring when events happen independent of responses. The nonoperant category, then, contains respondents, adjunctive behavior, and presumably, superstitious responses, even though the latter can be shown in many cases to result from adventitious reinforcement. Although Skinner eliminated the eliciting stimulus from operant behavior, he retained it for the other type of unit (respondents). Now, Hineline takes the further step of removing it from the definition of nonoperants as well.

The study of personality has not been a favorite of behavior analysts, and indeed some think that the very concept is unpalatable. Meehl shows that trait language is perfectly appropriate, rigorous, and scientifically desirable. As he develops his argument, it becomes evident that traits are closely related to generic responses. They are composed of topographically dissimilar events that have content similarity in the same way as a generic response class involves topographically different events. These different events covary in the same way as do the components of a generic response class. Particular theoretical problems appear when covariation is not accompanied by detectable content similarity: It is as if certain response topographies that did not have the same environmental effect increased and decreased in probability together. This may be a promising arena for theoretical integration, because in fact related observations appear elsewhere. Adjunctive behavior covaries with operant behavior even though the two have no apparent content similarity. Also, Sidman has shown that equivalence and transitivity relations established by higher-order contingencies can result in covariation in responses that would seem totally unrelated to the onlooker unaware of the experimental history.

When psychologists thought of basic units structurally, it seemed reasonable to also think of them as the bricks for constructing larger pieces of behavior. The functional perspective, however, is less straightforward in this regard. A combinatorial approach to integration is offered by Lubinski and Thompson. They consider the integrity of response of sequences in time as the product of specific discrete discriminative, eliciting, evocative, and reinforcing events occurring at appropriate temporal intervals. The result is to regulate the sequence of elicited, adjunctive, and operant response classes. Here is an answer to how smooth extended sequences can occur even when units occurring in series each maintain their individual properties.

Dews' tour of the history of behavioral pharmacology is an account of how the experimental analysis of behavior has proven useful in understanding drug action. Unit issues are left implicit. The rates and patterns of responding generated by schedules of reinforcement have proven most useful in analyzing drug effects. The ability of a pharmacological agent to affect one aspect of schedule performance but not another provides support for the notion that behavioral sequences are composed of smaller intact units, each of which can be influenced separately.

Any discussion of integration of components confronts the philosophical problems of reductionism. Reductionism tends to get a bad press, yet: "Reductive analysis is the most successful research strategem ever devised: it has been the making of science and technology" (Medawar & Medawar, 1983, p. 227).

Even when we do not change levels of analysis, we still face the problem of reducing one phenomenon to others presumed to be more basic. Schnaitter offers a thoughtful discussion of reductionism, as do Meazzini and Ricci in their historical review of behaviorism. Schnaitter also deals with the matter of physical versus psychological definition of critical events. Stimuli and responses must be defined in terms of organism-environment interactions and not in terms of physical properties alone. This is an exceedingly important point within behavioral analysis, and it clarifies the notion inherent in the concept of generic stimuli and responses.

Zeiler describes experiments indicating that extended sequences of behavior themselves can be unitary instead of being composed of smaller response classes. All operant behavior appears to be interchangeable with respect to laws of temporal control. If, in fact, principles of operant behavior truly are independent of the particular conditionable responses, the operant as a basic unit of analysis gains substantial credibility. Not only does it suggest that so-called complex operants are fundamentally identical to simpler ones, but it also indicates that apparent anomalies may stem from incomplete theoretical analyses rather than from any core limitations in the general approach to behavior.

When integration refers to the establishment of new units rather than the concatenation of old, Baer's argument that the unit is whatever emerges when a contingency is applied seems compelling. If behavior is infinitely shapeable, it has no essential structure and may be relatively free from stimulus control. This again is the idea that operant units can involve any number of stimuli and responses. Units of measurement of behavior also are a problem in that different generic units must be measured in different ways.

The chapters do not take issue with the general view of behavioral units developed by Skinner in the 1930s. Despite the comfortable sense of good fellowship provided by such consensus, the close of this essay on historical development seems an appropriate place to verbalize some qualms. Why is it, given the apparent acceptance of this approach, that no one has described this particular theory of behavioral units in the glowing terms invariably applied to cell theory and to atomic theory? Actually, many psychologists join the scientific world at large in their failure to recognize this theory of units as a major contribution to knowledge. Could they be right? Even another science dealing with animal behavior - ethology - apparently does not consider our units compelling or even very interesting. Unfortunately, we may have the same reaction to their preferred unit, the episode, because it appears to have no more content than the old R=f(S). Maybe our view of operants, respondents, and their relatives as units, which represents a reflexology so liberalized that it would be unrecognizable to a reborn Sherrington or Pavlov, is purely a product of the historical roots of behaviorism combined with the equally strong positivistic bias of our immediate intellectual ancestors. Have we confused technology for studying behavior in the laboratory and orderly observable effects of variables with a unit? At the very least, the conference and papers serve to stimulate thinking about these fundamentals of a science of behavior.

REFERENCES

Coleman, S. R. (1984). Background and change in B.F. Skinner's metatheory from 1930 to 1938. *The Journal of Mind and Behavior, 5,* 471-500.

Coleman, W. (1971). *Biology in the nineteenth century: Problems of form, function, and transformation.* New York: Wiley.

Lashley, K.S. (1951). The problem of serial order in behavior. In L.A. Jeffress (Ed.), *Cerebral mechanisms in behavior.* New York: Wiley.

Medawar, P.B. & Medawar, J.S. (1983). *Aristotle to zoos: A philosophical dictionary of biology.* Cambridge, Massachusetts: Harvard University Press.

Skinner, B.F. (1931). The concept of the reflex in the description of behavior. *Journal of General Psychology, 5,* 427-458.

Skinner, B.F. (1935). The generic nature of the concepts of stimulus and response. *Journal of General Psychology, 12,* 40-65.

CHAPTER 2

The Problem of Behavioral Units

Travis Thompson

The search for structural order in behavioral phenomena is not unique, of course. In pre-Newtonian times, scholars struggled with the problem of action at a distance and less than a century ago physicists puzzled over the wave versus corpuscular nature of light. The billiard ball model of the atom in fixed time was an appealing metaphor, but created more problems than it solved. The nature of the units of analysis in modern physics was changed by the theory of relativity and quantum mechanics.

The search for fundamental units of psychological phenomena began with the Greeks who divided the causes of behavior into the four elements, earth, water, air and fire. This was a view adopted by Leonardo da Vinci who, in the late 15th Century, wrote:

> I affirm that the said force of movement [of man] is based upon different points of support [*poli*]. Force is produced by the lessening and contraction of the muscles which draw back and by the nerves which reach as far as the stimulus [*sentimento*] communicated by the hollow nerve dictates. (Keele's translation, 1983, p. 159)

Da Vinci further suggested that the afferent sensory stimulation conducted sensation to the soul, located in the third ventricle of the brain, which then directed the efferent motor impulses down the nerves to the muscles which then contracted (Keele, 1983). Da Vinci's anticipation of the Cartesian automaton and the concept of the reflex arc laid the foundation for the first unit of behavioral analysis.

Both da Vinci's and Descartes' models of the unit of human action were structural, not functional. The Sherringtonian (1906) reflex arc became a metaphor for the process underlying the development of associations, which Pavlov (1904) and his students, and Thorndike took to heart. Though Pavlov (1904) first described the conditioned reflex and the laws governing its development, he thought of the conditioned reflex in structural terms. Pavlov's colorful imagery replete with hypothetical constructs is reminiscent of pre-Newtonian physicists' attempts to explain the forces holding the solar system together, and modern cognitive psychologists' accounts of memory (another case of action at a distance). That a conditioned reflex could be best described *as a relationship* would have made as much sense to Pavlov as the notion that Eddington's (1929) table was actually nearly all empty space, would have made to a typical student of physics in early 20th Century. In both cases, common sense belies reality.

Thorndike (1898) was indifferent to the units comprising the behavior of his pole-tilting cats. The fact that there was an orderly relation between the number of exposures to the task and the length of time required to escape from the puzzle box was all that mattered to him. He believed he had arrived at a better understanding of the *process* of development of associations, which was sufficient for Thorndike. It was for John B. Watson, unfairly the object of derision in the popular press as well as the scientific literature, to seriously suggest that a *unit of behavior*, per se, could be a suitable subject matter for scientific analysis. Watson had no telephone switchboard models of nerve function nor hyperspatial conceptions of psychic forces driving the machinery of human behavior. His problem was not so much with the basic reflex unit, since Watson was more or less on the right track, but his inability to conceive of a way in which individual units could become integrated to form smoothly articulated behavior sequences was his scientific albatross. Nonetheless, Watson gave behavioral science a *functional unit*, which B.F. Skinner wisely recognized for what it was.

The operant concept (Skinner, 1935, 1938) changed all of that, and provided behavioral science with a more flexible functional unit permitting the construction and analysis of complex behavioral repertoires (cf. Findley, 1962). The mechanisms permitting successive responses to be bound together in an organized way began to be spelled out in *Schedules of Reinforcement* (Ferster and Skinner, 1957). The functional unit of behavior analysis is the relationship between a class of environmental events and a class of movements of an organism. The concept is at one and the same time functional and structural, for the fundamental unit is functionally defined, but forms building blocks for construction of larger response classes (i.e. structural).

Correlational psychologists concerned with normative individual difference variables have been more interested in predispositional antecedents of behavior than in behavior and its proximal causal variables, per se. As a result, it comes as no surprise that the question, "What are the fundamental units of behavior?" has been of limited interest to them. Two kinds of behavioral units and response classes can be distinguished, one having to do with the arrangement of response sequences in time, and the other which organizes response classes contemporaneously independent of time. The integrity of response sequences in time comes about largely through the arrangement of specific discriminative, eliciting, evocative and reinforcing events at appropriate temporal intervals, regulating the local probabilities of elicited, adjunctive or operant response classes. Which of several members of a given response class is observed at a given moment in time is determined not only by such environmental variables, but is also regulated by the probability structure of members of that class (e.g., through response induction, stimulus equivalence). As response classes become larger and more diverse, which member of a given class (several topographies sharing a common controlling variable) will be observed at a specific moment approaches randomness. Statistically across many occasions, however, the relative probabilities of the various members of such a class can be estimated, but on any given occasion, that is impossible.

Whether such structural arrangements (some of which are undoubtedly of genetic origin) are of interest to correlational investigators is unclear, though one would think such relations ought to be of considerable concern (Lubinski and Thompson, 1986).

Our preoccupation with arriving at an understanding of the units of which behavior is constructed and their organization is of a familiar type. In 1940 Albert Einstein wrote:

> . . . from the very beginning there has always been present the attempt to find a unifying theoretical basis for all these single sciences, consisting of a minimum of concepts and fundamental relationships, from which all the concepts and relationships of the single disciplines might be derived by logical process . . . For the time being, we have to admit that we do not possess any general theoretical basis for physics which can be regarded as its logical foundation. (p. 487)

Whether the behavioral sciences are any closer to such an analysis remains to be seen.

REFERENCES

Eddington, A. S. (1929). *The nature of the physical world: The Gifford Lectures.* Cambridge: Cambridge University Press.

Einstein, A. (1940). Considerations concerning the fundaments of theoretical physics. *Science, 91,* 487-492.

Ferster, C.B. and Skinner, B.F. (1957). *Schedules of reinforcement.* New York: Appleton-Century-Crofts.

Findley, J.D. (1962). An experimental outline for building and exploring multi-operant behavioral repertoires. *The Journal of the Experimental Analysis of Behavior, 5,* 113-166.

Keele, K.D. (1983). *Leonardo Da Vinci's elements of the science of man.* New York: Academic Press, Inc.

Lubinski, D. and Thompson, T. (1986). Functional units of human behavior and their integration: A dispositional analysis. In T. Thompson and M. Zeiler (Eds.), *Analysis and Integration of Behavioral Units.* Hillsdale, New Jersey: L.E. Erlbaum Associates.

Pavlov, I.P. (1966). On conditioned reflexes, (W. Horsley Gantt, Translator). In R. J. Herrnstein and E.G. Boring (Eds.), *A source book in the history of psychology.* Cambridge: Harvard University Press. (Original work published 1904).

Sherrington, C.S. (1906). *The integrative action of the nervous system.*

New Haven: Yale University Press.

Skinner, B.F. (1935). The generic nature of the concepts of stimulus and response. *Journal of General Psychology, 12*, 40-65.

Skinner, B.F. (1938). *The behavior of organisms*. New York: Appleton-Century Co.

Thorndike, E.L. (1898). Animal intelligence: an experimental study of the associative processes in animals. *The Psychological Review Monograph, 8* (2, Pt. 4).

CHAPTER 3

Molar vs. Molecular Units of Analysis

PAOLO MEAZZINI AND CARLO RICCI

Despite its relatively long history, no satisfactory definition of behaviorism has been set forth as yet. To be sure, there was a definition that gained some popularity years ago. It was proposed by Mace (1948) who made a distinction between metaphysical, methodological, and analytical behaviorism. According to Mace, metaphysical behaviorism included all the ideological and philosophical premises on which most behavioral thinking seemed to rest; methodological behaviorism consisted in the choice of objective vs. subjective methodology; whereas analytical behaviorism made reference to the language (mainly operational) used by behavioral psychologists to describe the domain of events in which they were interested. Gradually, however, this definition lost much of its appeal. In fact, few behaviorists accepted the view that untestable beliefs lie at the basis of their theoretical and scientific efforts (Fraisse, 1967; Naville, 1963; Tilquin, 1950). In fact, Eysenck (1972) pointed to objective methodology as the only distinguishing feature of behaviorism when compared with other psychological approaches.

In our opinion, the latter definition does not do justice to the richness of behaviorism. Behaviorism is viewed not only as a methodological approach but also as a well articulated and dynamic network of closely connected cultural and scientific subsystems, continuously affected by epistemological, scientific, psychological, and social events taking place outside. In addition, should behaviorism be considered only as a methodological approach, it would lose its cultural identity, since most experimental psychologists have adopted the objective methodology that was and still is emphasized by behaviorists. "Behind any experimental psychologist lies a behavioral consciousness" [sic] (Meazzini, 1977, p. 47).

An attempt at making clear the rich interconnections among the various behavioral approaches and outer cultural and scientific events is shown in Figure 1 (Meazzini, 1983; Meazzini & Ricci, in press).

Since its very beginning, behaviorism was affected by events taking place in other psychological approaches, in sciences such as physics and in disciplines such as philosophy. A few examples will help in clarifying this issue. Let us consider the first generation of behaviorists, i.e., Dunlap, Kuo, Hunter, Weiss, Holt, Lashley, and obviously, Watson. They were not a homogeneous group, apart from some features shared by all of them such as the rejection of introspection as a research methodology and the belief that animal research would help in discovering basic nomothetic laws. As a matter of fact, Holt (1915, 1931) was affected by Freudian and Gestalt theories, whereas Lashley (1951a) gradually abandoned the rigid Watsonian explanatory model in favor of a holistic approach that was very fashionable at that time, thanks to Gestalt psychologists such as Koehler and Koffka.

The second generation included some of the most representative behaviorists such as Hull, Spence, Guthrie, Tolman, and Skinner, revealing an even richer exchange with other cultural and scientific models. In fact, Hull, Spence, Guthrie, and Skinner were deeply affected by the operational approach of Bridgman (1927) and by the neopositivistic school of philosophy, whereas Tolman (1932, 1938) was attracted by the molar approach typical of Gestalt psychology. In addition, Tolman was not only sensitive to some of the most relevant psychodynamic concepts but also was in strong opposition to the mechanistic S-R theories of his contemporary neobehaviorists (mainly Hull and Spence). According to Tolman, the issue at stake was the role of cognitive events that were necessary to explain most behavioral phenomena.

Coming to present day behaviorism, split into at least five different approaches (radical, social, S-R, social learning

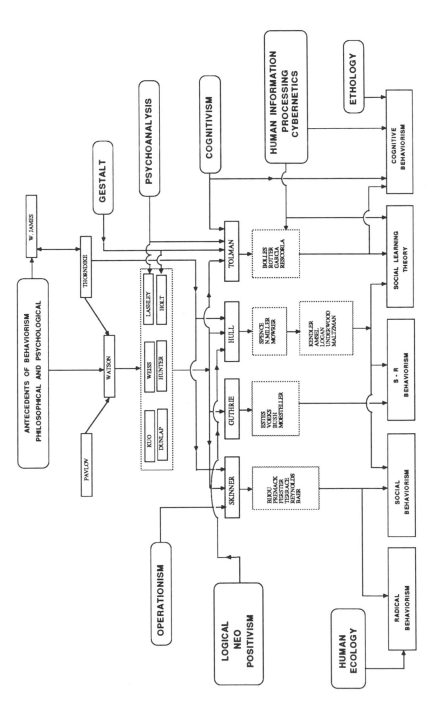

Fig. 1.   Historical view of Behaviorism

theory, and cognitive behaviorism), one can see once again how deeply it has been affected by outer forces. To be more precise, radical behaviorism seems to be closer and closer to ecological system theory, whereas cognitive behaviorism (Mahoney, 1974, 1980; Meichenbaum, 1977) has been influenced to a very large extent by information theory and modern cognitive psychologies. Moreover, it must be admitted that psychoanalysis appears to have gained some appeal once again, so much so that a reconciliation between the two approaches seems to be plausible, at least according to some cognitive behaviorists (Meichenbaum & Gilmore, 1985). In short, behaviorism has defied any precise definition because it works as an open system continuously receiving and evaluating new data that gradually change its theoretical structure and methodology.

BEHAVIORISM AS A CULTURAL SYSTEM

Contrary to the expectations of most behaviorists, past and present, our view is to consider behaviorism not only as an array of more or less reliable and valid scientific theories and technologies but also as a broader cultural system (Rachlin, 1970). As a matter of fact, most behavioral innovations regarding theoretical issues and methodology have their roots in past philosophical schools, such as British empiricism, French materialism, Darwinian biology, positivism, and pragmatism. Let us take some examples. The emphasis placed by behaviorists on learning as the basic psychological process is but a continuation of Locke's conception, according to which man is not bound by any hereditary constraint. Man is the result of experience, i.e., of the continuous interchange with the physical and social environment in which he lives.

The view of man as a very complicated and subtle machine subject to the laws of nature was first proposed by the French philosopher de La Mettrie (1748/1927) in a very detailed and challenging fashion. Of course, the kind of machine one thinks of now is quite different from de La Mettrie's. Nowadays, the inspiring model is the computer; at the time of La Mettrie it was a mechanical device.

As for the impact of Darwinian biology on behaviorism, there is no doubt that it has affected the Skinnerian conception of reinforcement that is viewed as a factor shaping both ontogenetic and phylogenetic development. Finally, positivistic and pragmatic philosophies are at the basis of two distinguishing features of most behavioral approaches: objective methodology and the use of theory as a tool in solving relevant individual and social problems. As a result of this philosophical heritage, behaviorism has a much broader and richer structure than might have been expected, as can be shown in Figure 2.

Although never explicitly stated by most representative behaviorists, behavioristic thinking is made up of different layers, namely, metatheoretical assumptions, attitudes, theories, and methodology. Let us briefly take each into consideration. Metatheoretical assumptions mean the set of beliefs that guides the theoretical and scientific research of all behaviorists, although these beliefs cannot be empirically checked. They lie beyond theory. The first of the main assumptions is *determinism*, either strong or weak, linear or circular. Its core is the belief that nature is an orderly set of events subject to universal laws that have to be gradually unfolded. Within behaviorism no exception can be found to this basic belief, although there are some differences. Skinner, for instance, can be seen as the representative of a strong and circular deterministic assumption whereas Guthrie, Hull, etc., may be located close to the weak and linear pole of the strong-weak determinism continuum.

Second, the *environmentalist belief* is shared by most behaviorists, with the notable exception of Eysenck. As a result of this belief, behaviorists choose to investigate learning and motivation which are viewed as the main processes making possible the continuous adjustment of man to his environment. This belief has a very strong liberal and optimistic flavor, as the blame for social or personal failures or weaknesses is not put on the individual but on the environment. The environment makes up the most relevant class of stimuli from which continuous demands stem and to which humans have to adjust. The result is that through careful social planning environment can be altered, so much so, that social and psychological problems should be

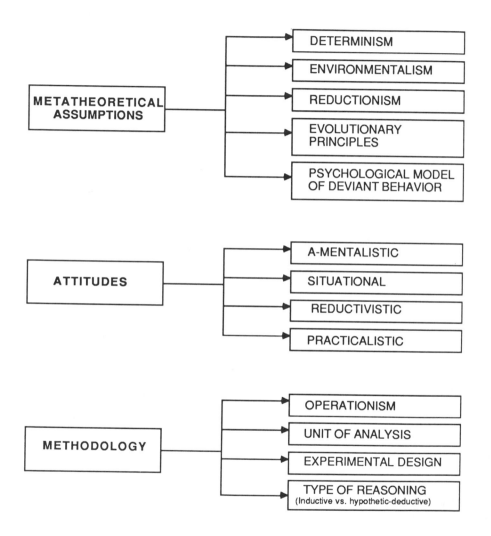

Fig. 2.   Metatheoretical assumptions, attitudes and methodology of Behaviorism

entirely prevented.

The third assumption, *constitutive reductionism* , that is, a belief in a hierarchy of sciences in which all physical matter, living and non-living, is all composed of the same physical entities and follows common physical laws. *Theoretical reductionists*, moreover, believe in the possibility of completely reducing laws, empirical generalizations, concepts, and languages from the surface sciences into those of the bottom ones. While some behaviorists hold a theoretical reductionist position, most (e.g., Skinner and his followers) do not, opting instead for a "constitutive reductionist" position.

The fourth assumption, the belief in the *continuity of species* (a cornerstone of Darwinian biology) was strongly supported by behaviorists. The core of this assumption can be seen in the possibility of extending behavioral laws from phylogenetically lower species to higher ones, man included.

The *psychological model of deviance* (the fifth assumption), used by later behaviorists (Bandura, 1974; Staats, 1975; Ullman & Krasner, 1969) to oppose the more usual medical model, the logical inconsistency of which was emphasized when applied to the description and explanation of behavioral problems.

Let us now consider so called *attitudes*, which concern more practical aspects than metatheory implies. Whereas a belief has mainly theoretical relevance, an attitude is an effective modus operandi, by means of which the relevant domain of events is approached and tackled. Three out of the four attitudes we discuss are not shared by all behaviorists. Therefore, they must be viewed as a continuum with two opposing poles, rather than a consistent unipolar modus operandi, on which there is full agreement.

The *amentalistic* attitude has two different meanings. The first implies that behavior is not an epiphenomenon but a phenomenon that has its own relevance and scientific dignity. As regards this meaning, there is no controversy among behaviorists. The second meaning, however, is much more controversial. The issue at stake is the role played by and the nature of cognitive events. Do they play a causative role, as many psychologists would say, or are they to be considered as an epiphenomenon as Skinnerians are inclined to assume? Do they comply with the same laws as do overt behaviors (principle of continuity, Mahoney, 1974), or are they subject to different and more specific laws? According to the different answers supplied to these two questions, a wide divergence can be found among the various behavioral approaches. At one pole (the amentalistic one) we can safely place radical behaviorism; at the other, cognitive behaviorism.

Let us next consider the *situation vs. trait* attitude. Once again the controversy is far from quieted down. Radical behaviorists are to be placed very close to a pure situational pole (Baer, 1973; Catania, 1974; Skinner, 1953) whereas one can safely place Eysenck on the other pole. Between the two poles one can find social learning theory and social behaviorism.

The controversy, whether real or fictitious involving the so called *global* or *holistic* attitude will be described later.

The *pragmatic* attitude, which refers to the special sensitivity shown by many behaviorists to the practical and technological aspects of their scientific and theoretical efforts. When compared with Gestalt or modern cognitive psychology, no one can deny that behaviorists have always been much more inclined to set forth explanatory models suitable not only to deepen our knowledge of human behavior but also to solve relevant individual and social issues (Baer et al., 1968). The pragmatic attitude has become so strong that behaviorism (the radical one, in particular) risks turning primarily into technology (Meazzini & Bauer, 1984).

As regards *theories*, it must be emphasized that within behaviorism there was never a single dominant theory, apart from the early years of Watson's research when there was no competing behavioral theory. In addition to other differential aspects, each theorist has coined a different language such as S-R (Watson, Guthrie, Hull, etc.), S-O-R (Woodworth, Eysenck, etc.), S-S (Tolman and cognitive behaviorists) and finally R-S^r (radical behaviorists). It is beyond the goals of this paper to deal extensively with this wide theoretical differentiation. Suffice it to say that behaviorists have always set forth conflicting theories in order to explain the same domain of events.

Finally, let us take *methodology* into consideration. This term refers to four different components. The first is the *language*, by means of which empirical and conceptual events are described. There is no doubt that weak operationalism is the dominant language within behaviorism at present. The second one concerns the *unit of analysis*, i.e. molar vs. molecular. More will be said about this issue in succeeding paragraphs. The third deals with the *way of reasoning* and *type of constructs* that may be either inductive or hypothetico-deductive. To be accurate, however, there has never been a purely inductive way of reasoning nor a purely hypothetico-deductive one. Even Skinner (1938), who advocated the inductive method, could not avoid proposing at least one hypothetical construct, the reflex reserve. On the other hand, Hull and Eysenck employed hypothetical constructs extensively. Despite their methodological leaning, however, they were unable to get rid of inductive reasoning. Therefore, the difference among the various behaviorists is more quantitative than qualitative. In other words each behaviorist works along both inductive and hypothetico-deductive paths, the difference consisting in the proportion existing between these two ways of reasoning in the single scientist.

As for the *experimental design* (the fourth component), once again one finds a differentiation between two opposing groups: those who favor experimental control and those who prefer a statistical approach. Radical behaviorists support the single subject experimental design, as it is more suitable for analyzing the continuous impact of environmental stimuli impinging on a subject (Sidman, 1960), whereas some other behaviorists stand in favor of control group design. While they fulfill different functions under some circumstances, in many instances the choice of one or the other experimental design is based primarily on the experimenter's preference.

HOLISM, MOLARISM, MOLECULARISM, REDUCTIONISM, AND REDUCTIVISM

Much more than most sciences, psychology has shown a propensity to react to concepts as if they were good or bad.

Conceptual and theoretical fashions have been very popular in psychology, so much so that being Field-oriented or molecular sounded good or bad in different periods, according to the dominant scientific models. It is no wonder that to a certain extent " . . . new theories are but a leap from one set of affects to another" (Littman & Rosen, 1950, p. 58). This state of affairs has not disappeared because psychology, more than most sciences, is closely connected with one's ideology and *Weltanschaung*.

One of the main results stemming from this state is the coinage of ill-defined terms, charged with such intense connotative meanings that the denotative ones seem to have been lost. Therefore, we find it necessary to attempt to clarify some basic terms. Let us begin with *holism*. Despite some differentiations, holism implies the following assumptions (Phillips, 1976): *a*) analytical or mechanical approaches are unsuitable for the investigation of living and social organisms; *b*) the whole is more than the sum of its parts; *c*) the whole determines the nature of its parts; *d*) parts cannot be understood, if they are detached from the whole; and *e*) parts are closely and dynamically interlocked.

Of these basic assumptions, *a*) is empirically unfounded, since analytical approaches did show effectiveness in investigating living and social organisms (Phillips, 1976); *b*) is beset with the problem of emergence and the definition of the term 'sum': The theoretical problems connected with the emergence of new features as a result of the aggregation of the subordinate parts of the whole will be dealt with later. Here, suffice it to say that the term 'sum' has no definite meaning. Does it refer to an additive sum, an algebraic sum, or a physical one? Of course each of these three definitions entails different results; *c*) is logically untenable. It is at least paradoxical to assume that the whole can cause itself; *d*) and *e*) can easily be accepted by all scientists, irrespective of their epistemological and methodological leanings.

As regards the terms *molar vs. molecular*, the following usages have been traced (Allport, 1963; George, 1963; Littman & Rosen, 1950):

a) *Interaction*. Molar was the term used when referring to

experiments where multiple variables were manipulated and a factorial or multivariate experimental design was used accordingly. On the other hand, molecular was used to make reference to very simple experiments, where one independent variable was manipulated and a dependent one was measured. This usage generally has been dropped nowadays.

b) *Action-unit*. This usage has become more and more prominent and is still in force today. It refers to the space and time dimension of a behavioral unit. Articulated and long-time units are said to be molar and simple and short-time ones molecular. The problem with this kind of distinction has to do with the difficulty in finding the exact space and time parameters, according to which one may classify an action-unit as molar or molecular.

c) *Levels of investigation*. Psychology deals with molar units, whereas physiology and neurology deal with more molecular ones. This distinction, set forth by Tolman (1938) does not hold any longer. In fact, physiology and neurology may deal with very complicated and long-term molar units, whereas psychology may deal with very simple and short-term ones, as it happens in the shaping of various behaviors in the handicapped persons (see Figure 3).

Let us now consider the concept *reductionism*. Generally speaking, the core of the reductionistic assumption consists in the following beliefs (Hamlyn, 1967; Jessor, 1963):

a) Sciences are ordered within a hierarchial structure. The bottom and most basic science is physics. All the other sciences, such as chemistry, biology, psychology, and sociology depend on physics. The connection between sciences lying at different levels is mediated by bridging disciplines, such as biochemistry or social psychology;

b) The language, models, empirical generalizations, and theories typical of any surface science can be translated into the language, models, etc., of the bottom ones. What is emphasized is the possibility of such a translation, which de facto may not be possible at the present time;

c) The most satisfactory explanations are to be found at the bottom level.

These beliefs, that are typical of the neopositivistic

philosophy (Kolakowski, 1972) are still widely held among psychologists, although some differences can be found among them, the main one being the distinction between hard and soft reductionists. Hard reductionists, such as Bechterev, Watson, Lashley, etc., held the view that psychical events are epiphenomena without any real explanatory power as regards behavior. The basic events, by which the so called psychical events are to be explained, are biological and better still biochemical. Hence, psychology, qua science, should be short lived and replaced by hard and bottom sciences before long. On the other hand, soft reductionists, such as Tolman (1938), Hebb (1949), etc., believed in the usefulness of psychological lanugage and theorizing as far as it helps in ordering and classifying behavioral events. Hence, psychology is granted only descriptive power, the explanatory one being attributed to the bottom sciences once again.

The final term to be defined is *reductivism* which very rarely has been distinguished from reductionism, so much so that the two terms have been considered interchangeable. As a matter of fact, reductivism differs from reductionism in that it does not imply any kind of translation from one surface science to one located below in the hierarchy. On the contrary, reductivistic psychologists' explanatory terms are within the same domain of events. The objective is to unfold the basic units of behavior and discover the composition laws by which molecular units can be aggregated and form molar units. A fine example of a reductivistic approach is Guthrie's, where actions are reduced to movements, which in turn are considered to be the basic behavioral units (Guthrie, 1935). In doing so, Guthrie remained within the boundaries of psychology, restraining himself from physiological theorizing.

Finally, there is no necessary connection between and among all these theoretical choices. One may hold a holistic reductionistic view at the same time, as was the case with Lashley (1951a,b) and Tolman (1932, 1938). One may hold a reductivistic and reductionistic view, as was the case with Guthrie (1933, 1935), Hull (1934, 1935, 1942), and Logan (1956), or finally, one may hold an areductionistic and areductivistic one, as is the case with Skinner (1938, 1969,

1974). Although Skinner does not deny reductionism, he agrees it is more profitable for psychologists to work within the observable overt behavioral domain and theoretical boundaries. In other words, Skinner argues it is not the psychologist's task to discover the physiological or biochemical mechanisms underlying behavior. As regards reductivism, Skinner is interested in a functional analysis of behavior, which may apply both to molar or molecular behavior units.

THE MOLAR VS. MOLECULAR CONTROVERSY IN THE HISTORY OF BEHAVIORISM

The First Generation of Behaviorists: Watson, Hunter and Weiss

It is a widely held belief (Bagnara et al., 1975; Chaplin & Krawic, 1969; Koch, 1964; Tolman, 1928, 1932) that Watson's brand of behaviorism was 'muscle-twitch psychology' aimed at discovering the laws governing molecular events, such as muscle twitches and glandular secretions. This interpretation, warmly accepted by Gestalt psychologists such as Koffka (1935), and Koehler (1947), etc., does not do justice to Watson's view. In fact, Watson seldom tackled the problem of defining behavior and when he did so, the definition was vague. According to him, behavior was "anything the organism does . . . such as turning toward or away from a light, jumping at a sound, and more highly organized activities such as building a skyscraper, drawing plans, etc." (1930, p. 6), as well as "the total striped and unstriped muscular and glandular changes which follow upon a given stimulus" (1919, p. 14). Following an already established usage, the first definition of behavior refers to molar units, whereas the second to more molecular ones.

The apparent contradiction, however, disappears when one takes into account the strong reductionistic assumption held by Watson. In his view molar behavior was completely reducible to molecular movements, so much so that the purpose of psychology was to find out the laws by which molecular movements are integrated and shape behavior. ". . . The behaviorist is interested in the integration and total activities of the individual" (1919, p. 40). In other words, it was up to physiologists to study the individual movements of the various body parts, whereas the task of psychologists was to study the integrated movements of the whole man, that is, his actions. However, actions which are purely physical phenomenon are not equivalent with movements, although they can be totally reduced to them. In fact, composition laws have to be added which make possible the integration of molecular units and determine the final form of behavior. Therefore, there is no new emergent difference when passing from molecular to molar units. Integration occurs in a mechanistic way.

This issue was to become a battleground of the second generation of behaviorists (Tolman, Hull, Guthrie, etc.). It does not concern emergence and reduction as much as the nature of the integration processes: mechanistic or holistic?

According to Watson, psychology may be either molar or molecular in its methodology. Psychologists need not "reduce the total activity to muscle twitches. We can do it if necessary and we do it at times when it becomes necessary to study the various part reactions" (1919, p. 40).

This pragmatic attitude, however, was soon to be dropped as a result of the establishment of the grand behavioral theories of the 1940s. Hunter and Weiss followed strictly the Watsonian lead, so that few and rather superficial were the issues on which there was disagreement. One of these had to do with the definition of behavior and its reduction to molecular movements. Hunter (1925) never equated behavior with mechanical movements. On the contrary, behavior qua behavior has two distinguishing properties that do not belong to molecular movements: *vicarious functioning* and *response equivalence*. " . . . such behavior as language, typing, and maze solution may at one time involve responses of the right hand while at another time other parts of the body may exercise these functions" (Hunter, 1932, p. 18). Should the right hand fail to accomplish its task, the other hand will work to reach the same goal. Thus the path was opened to the concept of *functional response class*, which still plays a very important role in Skinnerian psychology. According to Hunter, molar units are endowed with new emergent qualities, so that it is not feasible to completely reduce them to a mechanical integration of molecular units.

Weiss (1917,1924) couched his theoretical system within a physical monistic framework, in which everything, behavior included, was theoretically reducible to physical movements between electron-proton systems. Behavior was said to be made up of two different response classes, i.e., biophysical and biosocial. Biophysical responses are muscular contractions and glandular secretions (hence molecular movements), whereas biosocial responses ". . . are biophysical reactions, but the responses are not classified according to the contractile effects . . . but according to the response in other individuals" (Weiss, 1930, p. 303). Therefore, "A response is a biosocial one just in case some other individual is affected by it and categorizes it in one of a variety of ways" (Kitchener, 1975, p. 21). Although Weiss was not directly concerned with the molecular or molar nature of behavior, he thought of behavior as a set of goal-directed response classes, a description very close to Hunter's point of view.

The Second Generation:
Guthrie, Hull, Tolman, and Skinner

At the basis of Guthrie's theory (1933, 1935, 1959) lies the distinction between acts and movements. A behavioral act is a response defined in terms of end results, such as playing a tune, driving a car, etc. A movement, on the other hand, is the actual physical behavior displayed on any occasion. Therefore, acts are equated with molar units, whereas movements are equated with molecular ones. In addition, acts are wholly reducible to movements and their integration is made possible by a single principle: contiguous association of a stimulus pattern (cue) and a set of movements.

Is there any qualitative difference, i.e., emergent property, between the two kinds of units? The answer is equivocal. In fact, in Guthrie's view, both kinds of units were goal oriented and purely physical at the same time. Therefore, there was no necessity to assume that new properties differentiated molar from molecular units. This point of view, however, completely disappeared in his revised system.

> . . . the hope that response could be treated as movements in space which was the crude interpretation of behaviorism failed to carry us very far toward the understanding of behavior. The reason for this is that we cannot reduce the classes of psychological facts which make up the data we must deal with to component movements in space. (Guthrie, 1959, p. 165)

An outcome stemming from this deep revision was the necessity of resorting to a psychological language suitable to describe psychological facts. As one can see, Guthrie's point of view changed dramatically, moving from a strong physicalistic or reductionistic assumption to the opposite one.

More consistency is found in Hull's theory (1930, 1934, 1935, 1951, 1952), in which behavior is a physical event, made up of different kinds of responses: molar and molecular. The term 'molar' refers to grossly observable behavioral phenomena, whereas the term 'molecular' refers to ". . . the behavior of the ultimate molecules upon which this behavior depends, such as the constituent cells of nerve, muscle, gland, and so forth. The term molar thus means coarse or macroscopic as contrasted with molecular or microscopic" (1943, p. 17). Therefore, molar behavior is completely reducible to molecular events.

An obvious result of this theoretical point of view is to consider behavior-as-molar a derived concept, whereas behavior-as-molecular is the primitive event, the hard core of any scientific model. Did this point of view imply a de-emphasization of the peculiar characteristics of molar behavior, such as goal directedness? Not at all. On the contrary, Hull attempted to explain the emergence of molar units mechanistically, doubting any brand of emergentism.

> Some writers believe that there is an impassable theoretical gulf between mere muscle contractions and the attainment of goals: that the latter are 'emergent.' This doctrine of despair grows naturally out of the doctrine of teleology. The present treatise accepts neither teleology nor its pessimistic corollary. Goals, intents, intelligence, insight, and values are regarded not only as genuine but as of the first importance. Ultimately, an attempt will

be made to derive all of these things objectively as secondary
phenomena from more elementary objective conditions, concepts
and principles. (1943, p. 29)

Hull maintained this view until the end of his career (1951).

A very different scenario qualifies Tolman's theory and
his conception of behavior. According to him behavior is a
molar phenomenon that cannot be reduced to molecular
movements. In fact, behavior is an emergent event and has
descriptive and defining properties of its own. Therefore,
moving along Holt's path, behavior is more than and different
from the sum of its physiological parts. Its descriptive
properties are purpose and cognition, that prima facie cannot be
explained only in terms of molecular events. Hence, they need a
language suitable to describe them in which mental terms are
required, unlike what Hull had attempted to accomplish.
Although vague, Tolman seemed to assume each level of unit
had its own set of laws. After discovering intra-level laws, one
can search for bridging laws connecting the different levels.
These bridging laws would explain events such as expectancies,
demand, and so forth, and as a result cannot be equated with the
composition laws, to which Watson, Guthrie and Hull made
reference. Mechanical integration of molecular events is not the
kind of answer that appealed to Tolman. Therefore, it was not
surprising that Tolman gradually moved from a hard
reductionistic position to a soft one, in which the possibility of
translating psychological concepts and facts into those of
physiology was denied. At the same time, however, he
maintained the old positivistic conception of a hierarchy of
sciences, so much so that sociology was viewed as ancillary to
psychology and in its turn psychology ancillary to physiology.
Tolman's theory was firmly anchored on the concept of
behavior as molar, which is the primitive and basic unit of
analysis for psychologists. Molecular units, on the other hand,
should be of no concern to psychologists, according to Tolman,
as they are not useful in explaining global behavior, unless some
mysterious bridging laws are discovered.

Far from this heated controversy connected with the molar
vs. molecular attitude is Skinner's operant behaviorism. Its

core consists of the notion of response as a class concept (Skinner, 1935) and a functional analysis of responses (Skinner, 1938, 1953, 1969). According to Skinner, behavior is made up of a constant flow of response instances, each of which is a unique spatiotemporal event that cannot be repeated. Under these conditions, however, psychology could never become a science, as it would be unable to predict behavior. To be predictable, response instances are subsumed under well defined response classes, the members of which possess at least some properties in common, differing rather freely in other aspects. The one and only property any such response need have is an effect such as bar pressing, turning left or right, etc. Such a class is a 'functional class.' "The number of distinguishable acts on the part of the rat that will give the required movement of the lever is indefinite and very large. They constitute a class, which is sufficiently well-defined by the phrase 'pressing the lever'" (Skinner, 1938, p. 37). A functional class can be defined in terms of two different kinds of properties: intrinsic and extrinsic. The first does not require any reference to a result or effect and may include qualities such as latency, amplitude and rate of response. The second kind of property makes explicit reference to a result. Therefore, a functional class is relational, since it involves both the individual members of the class and the effect produced.

According to Skinner and other behavior analysts, e.g., Catania (1974), and Thompson and Lubinski (1986), the membership of a response in a functional class is defined exclusively in terms of extrinsic properties and not in terms of intrinsic ones. Therefore, responses may differ widely in their topography and quantitative parameters and still belong to the same functional class, provided all of them produce the same kind of effect. The structural aspects of responses are of little concern, since emphasis is on the effects of certain movements (i.e., the controlling consequences).

THE PRESENT STATE OF THE MOLAR VS. MOLECULAR CONTROVERSY

The molar vs. molecular controversy has been of little

concern to modern behaviorists (Bandura, 1974; Rachlin, 1970; Staats, 1975). The reasons for the declining interest are manifold. The first is the decline of Gestalt psychology. Gestalt psychologists strongly opposed Watson's behaviorism. One of their favorite attacks was the assumed *elementarism* backing the behaviorist approach. With the fading of Gestalt psychology, the controversy lost its virulence. The second reason is connected with the rise of Skinnerian psychology and the emphasis laid on the functional response class. The focus shifted from structural or intrinsic to functional or extrinsic properties. Based on this concept, a very useful functional taxonomy of responses has been set forth, by means of which " . . . behavior can be divided into at least three main categories: *elicited* behavior, *emitted* or operant behavior and a derivative of the former two classes, *evoked* behavior" (Thompson & Lubinski, 1986). The third reason for decline of interest in the molar-molecular controversy is connected with the clash between hard and soft cognitive psychologists and hard and soft behaviorists, regarding the scientific status and the therapeutic relevance of cognitive events. The virulence of the polemics, probably triggered by different metatheoretical assumptions and attitudes, was and still is so strong that any other important theoretical issue such as the molar vs. molecular controversy is belittled.

In our opinion, however, the most important factor is the practical irrelevance and sterility of this controversy. Apart from the actual impossibility of specifying the space-time properties of any unit, molar and molecular, most behaviorists hold a pragmatic view regarding the basic unit of behavior. Their goal is to discover functional units having a scientific significance, meaning by that "the extent to which the unit enters into a wide range and number of lawful relations . . . To qualify as scientifically significant, a unit must reliably relate an array of phenomena" (Thompson & Lubinski, 1986). Therefore, significant units may be molar or molecular according to the goals set by the scientist. Once the goals and the task have been defined, there is no restraint as to the number and degree of molarism or molecularism. An example will help to clarify the issue.

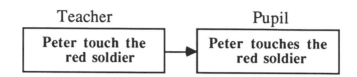

Fig. 3a

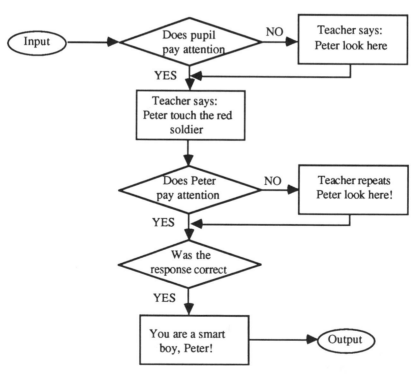

Fig. 3b

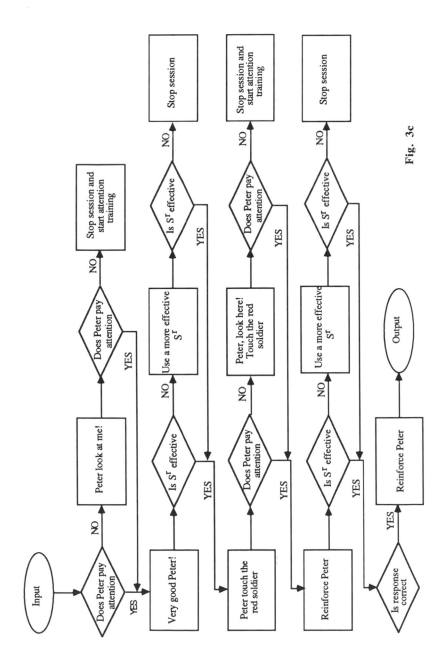

Fig. 3c

Let us suppose that a teacher wishes to teach a child to touch a red soldier among three other soldiers. S/he can resort to at least three different kinds of analysis. The first, suitable for normal children, is global as there is no necessity to be more analytic (Figure 3a). A normal child will fulfill this task easily. On the other hand, should the teacher try to teach the same task to a learning disabled or more severely handicapped child, a more subtle analysis is required (Figures 3b and 3c). In this case, the teacher's analytical behavior is controlled by the intellectual skills of his/her pupils. The lower they are, the more analytical his/her approach should be.

To conclude, time is ripe for getting rid of this kind of controversy that beset many behaviorists of the second generation. Scientific and technological activities should not be controlled by ideological S^Ds but by the effect one wishes to accomplish.

REFERENCES

Allport, G.W. (1963). The emphasis on molar problems. In M.M. Marx (Ed.), *Theories in contemporary psychology*. New York: MacMillan.

Baer, D.M. (1973). The organism as a host. Paper presented at the meeting of the Eastern Psychological Association, San Francisco.

Baer, D.M., Wolf, M.M., & Risley, T.R. (1968). Some current dimensions of Applied Behavior Analysis. *Journal of Applied Behavioral Analysis, 1*, 91-97.

Bagnara, A., Castelfranchi, C., Legrenzi, P., Minguzzi, G., Misiti, R., & Parisi, D. (1975). Per una discussione sulla situazione della psicologia in Itali. *Giornale Italiano di Psicologia, 2*, 285-321.

Bandura, A. (1974). Behavior theory and the models of man. *American Psychologist, 28*, 859-969.

Bridgman, P.O. (1927). *The logic of modern physics*. New York: MacMillan.

Catania, A.C. (1973). The concept of operant in the analysis of behavior. *Behaviorism, 1*, 103-116.

Catania, A.C (1974). The psychologies of structure, function and development. *American Psychologist, 28*, 434-443.

Chaplin, J.P., & Krawic, T.S. (1969). *Systems and theories of psychology*. New York: Holt.

Eysenck, H.J. (1972). Behavior therapy is behavioristic. *Behavior Therapy, 3*, 609-613.

Fraisse, P. (1967). La evolucion de la conception del comportamiento. *Revista de Psicologia General y Aplicada, 22*, 849-901.

George, F.H. (1963). Molar to molecular. In M.M. Marx (Ed.), *Theories in contemporary psychology*. New York: Macmillan.

Guthrie, E.R. (1933). On the nature of psychological explanation. *Psychological Review, 40*, 124-137.

Guthrie, E.R. (1935). *The psychology of learning*. New York: Harper.

Guthrie, E.R. (1959). Association by contiguity. In S. Koch (Ed.), *Psychology: A study of a science* (Vol. 2). New York: McGraw-Hill.

Hamlyn, D.W. (1967). Behavior. In V.C. Chappel (Ed.), *The philosophy of mind*. Englewood Cliffs, NJ: Prentice-Hall.

Hebb, D.O. (1949). *The organization of behavior*. New York: Wiley.

Holt, E.R. (1915). *The Freudian wish and its place in ethics*. New York: Holt.

Holt, E.R. (1931) *Animal drive and the learning process*. New York: Holt.

Hull, C.L. (1930). Knowledge and purpose as a habit mechanism. *Psychological Review, 37*, 511-526.

Hull, C.L. (1934). The concept of the habit-family hierarchy and maze learning. *Psychological Review, 41*, 33-54, 134-152.

Hull, C.L. (1935). The mechanism of the assembly of behavior segments in the novel combinations suitable for problem solution. *Psychological Review, 42*, 219-245.

Hull, C.L. (1942). *Principles of behavior*. New York: Appleton-Century-Crofts.

Hull, C.L. (1951). *Essentials of behavior*. New Haven: Yale University Press.

Hull, C.L. (1952). *A behavior system*. New York: Wiley.

Hunter, W.S. (1925). General anthroponomy and its systematic problems. *American Journal of Psychology, 36*, 286-302.

Hunter, W.S. (1932). The psychological study of behavior. *Psychological Bulletin, 39*, 1-24.

Jessor, F.G. (1963). The problem of reductionism. In M.M. Marx (Ed.), *Theories in contemporary psychology*. New York: MacMillan.

Kitchener, R.F. (1977). Behavior and behaviorism. *Behaviorism, 5*, 11-71.

Koch, S. (1964). Psychology and emerging conceptions of knowledge as unitary. In T.W. Wann (Ed.), *Behaviorism and phenomenology*. Chicago: The University of Chicago Press.

Koehler, W. (1947). *Gestalt psychology*. New York: Liveright.

Koffka, K. (1935). *Principles of Gestalt psychology*. Routledge and Kegan Paul: London.

Kolakowski, L. (1972). *Positivistic philosophy*. Harmondsworth: Penguin Books.

La Mettrie, J.O. de (1748). *L'homme machine,* (Leiden). Translated by G. C. Bussey & M.W. Calkins (1927) as *Man a machine*. Chicago: Open Court Publishing House.

Lashley, K.S. (1951a). *Brain mechanisms and intelligence*. Chicago: The University of Chicago Press.

Lashley, K.S. (1951b). The problem of serial order in behavior. In L.A. Jeffress (Ed.), *Cerebral mechanisms in behavior*. New York: Wiley.

Littman, R.A, & Rosen, E. (1950). Molar and molecular. *Psychological Review, 57*, 58-65.

Logan, F.A. (1956). A micro-molecular approach to behavior theory. *Psychological Review, 63*, 63-73.

Mace, C.A. (1948). Some implications of analytical behaviorism. *Proceedings of the Aristotelian Society, 49*, 1-16.

Mahoney, M.J. (1974). *Cognition and behavior modification.* Cambridge, Ballinger.

Mahoney, M.J. (1980). *Psychotherapy process: Current issues and future directions.* New York: Plenum.

Meazzini, P. (1977). *Watson.* Bologna: Il Mulino.

Meazzini, P. (1980). *Il comportamentismo: Una storia culturale.* Pordenone: ERIP.

Meazzini, P. (1983). *Watson: Uomo e scienziato. Prefazione a Watson J.B. Il comportamentismo.* Firenze: Guinti-Barbera.

Meazzini, P., & Bauer, B. (1984). La Terapia del Comportamento: Una rivoluzione mancata? *T.C. Giornale Italiano di Scienza e Terapia del Comportamento, 1.*

Meazzini, P., & Ricci, C. (in press). Antinomies in behaviorism and behavior therapy and modification: Historical perspective and possible future scenario. *Annals of Theoretical Psychology, 4.*

Meichenbaum, D. (1977). *Cognitive behavior modification.* New York: Plenum Press.

Meichenbaum, D., & Gilmore, J. (1985). The nature of unconscious processes: A cognitive-behavioral perspective. Unpublished manuscript.

Naville, P. (1963). *La psychologie du comportement.* Paris: Gallimard.

Phillips, D.C. (1976). *Holistic thought in social science.* Stanford: Leland Stanford Junior University.

Rachlin, H. (1970). *Introduction to modern behaviorism.* San Francisco: Freeman.

Sidman, M. (1960). *Tactics of scientific research.* New York: Basic Books.

Skinner, B.F. (1935). The generic nature of the concepts of stimulus and response. *Journal of General Psychology, 12*, 40-65.

Skinner, B.F. (1938). *The behavior of organisms.* New York: Appleton-Century-Crofts.

Skinner, B.F. (1953). *Science and human behavior.* New York: MacMillan.

Skinner, B.F. (1969). *Contingencies of reinforcement..* New York: Appleton-Century-Crofts.

Skinner, B.F. (1974). *About behaviorism.* New York: Knopf.

Staats, A.W. (1975). *Social behaviorism.* Homewood: Dorsey Press.

Thompson, T., & Lubinski. D. (1986). On the kinetic structure of behavioral repertoires. Unpublished manuscript.

Tilquin, A. (1950). *Le behaviorisme.* Paris: Vrin.

Tolman, E.C. (1928). Purposive behavior. *Psychological Review, 35*, 524-530.

Tolman, E.C. (1932). *Purposive behavior in animals and men.* Chicago:

The University of Chicago Press.

Tolman, E.C. (1938).   Physiology, psychology and sociology. *Psychological Review, 45*, 222-241.

Ullmann, L., & Krasner, L. (1969). *Psychological approaches to abnormal behavior.* Englewood Cliffs: Prentice-Hall.

Watson, J.B. (1919). *Psychology from the standpoint of a behaviorist.* Philadelphia: Lippincott.

Watson, J.B. (1930). *Behaviorism* (2nd ed). Chicago: University of Chicago Press.

Weiss, A.P. (1917).   Relation between structural and behavioral psychology. *Psychological Review, 34*, 301-327.

Weiss, A.P. (1924). Behaviorism and behavior. *Psychological Review, 31*, 32-50, 118-149.

Weiss, A.P. (1930). The biosocial standpoint in psychology. In C. Murchison (Ed.), *Psychologies of 1930.* Worshester, MA: Clark University Press.

CHAPTER 4

The Language Trap and the Study of Patterns in Human Action

PETER HARZEM

It is generally good practice to pay some attention to the critics of one's work. Even when it is known that they are mistaken, one may learn from criticism the points that may need development in more detail, the questions that should be but have not yet been raised, and so on. By the same token, there is an old criticism of the discipline of Psychology that has been ignored, probably because it is both superficial and over-general, but which, nevertheless, psychologists would do well to consider seriously. It is that in Psychology rigorous research deals with trivia, and interesting research lacks rigor. Now, of course, what counts as interesting is open to debate, and to regard as trivial the careful, detailed research published in journals of experimental psychology is objectionable. On the other hand it is difficult to defeat the proposition that human actions such as working, spending and saving money, child-rearing, making love, and voting are more interesting than human acts such as button-pressing. And it is undoubtedly true that the last-mentioned is scientifically documented in far more detail than any of the former. This contrast is, of course, unfair; button-pressing is studied with such intensity not because it is regarded, in itself, especially significant, but because the resulting findings are thought to have implications for the other, more important human actions.

Some of us, steeped in the established dogma of Psychology,

might take this at face value; but others will see the obvious question to be asked here: Why not, then, study these more significant actions directly? The answer will, in part, depend on the theoretical and conceptual persuasion of the psychologist being questioned. In terms of actual data gathered and processed (rather than theoretical divisions as to what such data might mean) research in contemporary psychology falls into two broad divisions: data obtained through the administration of questionnaires, and data obtained through experiments that entail the observation and recording of some act of the subject. Though not always, in most instances the act that is studied is the pressing of buttons, telegraph keys, computer keyboards, and the like. Two broad areas of psychology have accumulated a wealth of data on such acts: "cognitive psychology" and "operant psychology." Because these two areas are theoretically and conceptually contrary, this similarity appears to have gone unremarked. Nevertheless, the contrary positions would readily emerge in the answers to the question posed above. Cognitive psychology is misled into holding the view that its subject matter is cognitive processes [*sic*] and not any particular behavior of people; the data obtained through the recording of specific acts are a means of studying "cognitive processes," almost a necessary evil. It follows, then, that for cognitive psychology the question, "why not directly study those actions of people that most would consider interesting, rather than button pressing?" is moot, since the interest of this approach is not, in the first place, in actions.

The answer that can be given from the perspective of operant psychology is quite different, because the understanding of human actions is the direct and central focus of this approach. Sustained patterns of action have proved, however, wholly resistant to experimental study and laboratory control, so that simpler acts such as button and bar pressing have served as substitutes in their place. It is implicit in operant psychology that the frequency and patterning of these simple acts represent corresponding features of the more extended and complex human actions. The reason those actions that might be regarded as particularly interesting and significant have not been directly investigated in operant research, is that there is no known technique of conducting such direct studies without losing an excessive degree of scientific precision. This leaves unresolved, however, at least two related issues. First, the necessity remains to develop methods to investigate complex action patterns, in order to confirm that findings arising from studies of simple acts are also true of the complex ones. Second, to that end, it would seem essential to understand, why the complex actions of people have remained resistant to rigorous investigation. The remainder of this paper is devoted to examining this last issue, and to suggesting some ways that, if adopted, might help to overcome the difficulty.

Let it be noted that the apparent difficulty of harnessing patterns of action for the purpose of scientific investigation is not a problem specific to operant psychology; on the contrary, it is universal within Psychology. Given this, it would appear that the difficulty does not lie in any specific method, or a set of theoretical assumptions utilized in a particular approach; it is more likely to be found in some of the characteristics common to all approaches in psychology and, possibly, in other disciplines, too. Human behavior has resisted scientific analyses of not only psychology but also of other social and biological sciences.

One feature all these sciences have in common is their endeavor to find constant, reliable correspondence between (a) the terms in which their findings and theories are expressed, and (b) the phenomena that are being studied. Since all sciences of human action are communicated in ordinary language, and since the words of ordinary language have meanings and connotations that vary according to the verbal context (no word in the language has only a single meaning) a significant problem arises on how to establish an accurate correspondence between language and phenomena. Obviously, without a measure of constancy in this correspondence, communication, whether scientific or ordinary, would be impossible. Moreover, a greater degree of such constancy might reasonably be expected of scientific than ordinary communication. In sciences, in order to insure this constancy, two devices have been used: the invention of technical terms, and the adoption of "operational definitions."

Technical terms are more precise than ordinary words in the phenomena to which they specifically refer. This is simply because the term is specially invented as a name for the phenomenon at hand, whether an object, a substance, or an event (e.g., microscope, hemoglobin, and osmosis). A technical term does not, therefore, have previously established connotations that might confuse its present usage. In some sciences, however, including psychology, a different practice is common, namely, that of taking words and phrases from ordinary language and using them *as if* they were technical terms. The new, technical meaning given to an already existing term of ordinary language is called "operational definition." The practice of operationally defining terms of ordinary language has remained widespread in psychology, although it has failed to prevent conceptual confusions that have arisen in psychological discourse. Bridgman himself, who first developed operationism and laid down the principles of its uses, was disenchanted with the excessive and inappropriate uses of operationism that came to be practiced in many disciplines (e.g., Bridgman, 1938, 1940).

The problem caused by the practice of operationism arises from the fact that the attribution of an operational definition to a word does not eradicate the many other usages already associated with that word. For example, to say that "stress" is defined by the operation of immobilizing a rat for 48 hours has not ensured that the researcher adopting this definition will confine the conclusions to be drawn from this research to situations of this sort. The more common practice has been to make assertions about, for example, marital stress, work stress, and the like. Note that as regards empirical observation the only connection between the experimental "stress" and marital stress is the sharing of a label. Through the medium of the word "stress," findings about what happens to a constrained rat are *smuggled* into statements about the nature, and even the prevention and cure, of marital stress. This kind of smuggling of meanings between concepts is, in psychology, the rule rather than the exception. As a result, the practice of operationalism has become yet another source of confusion instead of serving its intended purpose of reducing the incidence of confusion. To sum, operationism has stood in the way of accurately identifying and bringing under scientific scrutiny any extended pattern of human action in two ways; first, by creating the false belief that this had already been achieved through operational definitions, and second, by generating conceptual confusions of its own. (For a detailed discussion of operational definitions see, e.g., Harzem, 1985; Skinner, 1945; and extensive commentary in The Behavioral and Brain Sciences, 1985).

Although the problems previously described have troubled psychology for some 50 years, none of them are fundamental enough to account fully for the present limited state of the scientific study of human action. To bring patterns of human action within the range of scientific investigation, scholars, so far, have looked to two aspects of the language-phenomenon correspondence; either to constraining the terms to bring about a better match between language and phenomena (by the use of technical terms) or, to limiting the phenomena, (by the use of operational definitions). The main thesis of the present paper is that the crucial problem lies not in the phenomena, not in certain terms, but in a different general characteristic of ordinary language. We turn next to considering this point.

Ordinary language has words and phrases as names of behavioral phenomena that never occur in unitary, continuous sequences. Such names can be misleading by creating the false belief that the phenomena to which they refer are empirically identifiable events. Consider the fact that much of an individual's knowledge of the environment is acquired not through direct, personal experience but through language. Perhaps the simplest form of language-phenomenon correspondence is when a child learns the names of objects such as table, cat, television, etc. As language acquisition progresses, however, some names are learned for which there is no corresponding unitary object or event; for example, "working," "writing a book chapter," "child rearing," "making love," and "electioneering." Note that these are not all "abstract" concepts in the same way as, say, the word "animal" is. The word "animal" applies directly to each of the entities - cat, dog, tiger, etc. - that are included in the concept. In other words "cat" is not a part or segment of animals but it is an animal. On the other hand none of the components that might be included in, for example, "child rearing" can by itself be said to be child rearing. Reading aloud a story, changing diapers, hugging, saying "go to bed," purchasing a bicycle, and hiding Christmas presents under a bed are not individually "child rearing" although they may all go together to constitute child rearing. No one who repeatedly performs only one of the acts listed above and none of the others, would be said to be engaged in child rearing, although a person who owns only one cat is an animal owner. Many of the human actions that appear, through their names in ordinary language, particularly significant and interesting are not continuous sequences of actions, and they are not segments of actions temporally separated from each other, where the segments have fixed, identifiable forms.

Gilbert Ryle (1974, unpublished communication) in a different context concerned with "mental acts" has described the matter as follows:

> I remember how when I was a young man I was troubled - as I daresay you have been troubled - by the seemingly contemptible intermittentness or fleetingness of my thinkings. I fancied that real thinkers could go on wrestling with an issue continuously, perhaps for hours on end, without pauses, or switches of attention. They, I supposed, stuck to their intellectual tasks like plough horses moving unremittingly up and down their furrows. Yet there was I, meaning well, but just drifting, flitting, alighting, flapping, sipping, resting and taking wing again - a mere butterfly, instead of a plough horse. Of course, I did not then realize that the task of excogitating something is, like angling, a chain-undertaking, in which a considerable sporadicness or intermittency of the infra-acts or infra-moves is perfectly compatible with the prosecution of the total undertaking being cumulative, progressive and even sometimes successful. The housewife spring-cleaning her house works but with all manner of pauses, interruptions, telephonings, re-reading letters before throwing them away, watering the flowers, chatting to her neighbours, looking out of the window, and so on. Yet by the end of the day her house has been properly spring-cleaned. The wheat-farmer can take his seaside holiday in February without postponing or diminishing his September harvest.

> Puppy-training has to be a sporadic, intermittent and repetitive thing; yet it may result in a well-trained sheep-dog within a few weeks or months. There is a lot of sheer waiting in angling, and in pondering; but the angler and thinker do not have to make excuses for these spells of calculated un-business.

In summary, the reason it has not been possible to bring under rigorous experimental investigation the apparently interesting and complex forms of human action is that such actions do not exist in any consistent and unitary form to permit such scrutiny. It is, of course, perfectly appropriate to *talk* of actions such as child rearing, loving, gardening, etc. in the same way as it is perfectly correct to talk of the rainbow, sunrise, and the state of Mary's marriage. To take the last example, note that although one might visit Mary at her home and meet her husband James, nowhere in the house would one expect to find their marriage for the purpose of examining it - nor for any other purpose. And from that fact, one would conclude not that the marriage does not exist, but that marriage is not a matter that can be said to exist in the same sense as do Mary and James. Rainbows exist, and marriages exist, but it makes no sense to talk of developing scientific methods that might enable us to study them *directly*. Rainbows can be studied by investigating light waves, refracting properties of water droplets, etc; marriages can be studied through the actions of married individuals, of other people towards married individuals, etc. How, then, are patterns of human action to be studied?

In answer to that question, at least two possibilities arise. First, simple acts such as button pressing can be *theoretically* assumed to represent the more complex acts, and the behavior of button pressing under various experimental conditions can be *theoretically* related to statements about complex acts. As everyone knows, this is the established strategy of operant research; it is not a novel finding here that this strategy is in principle correct. It is, however, also an incomplete strategy, because there remains the question of how to assess the correctness of the theoretical assertions concerning the complex acts. Much of the theoretical and conceptual confusion of the past has arisen at this stage when, through the necessity of talking about ordinary actions of people, terms of ordinary language referring to those actions enter the picture. This is the point when the social scientist may be misdirected by the complexities of language that are termed here the "language trap." The language trap is apt to lead the scientist in search of methods to observe empirically phenomena that do not permit such observation. It is necessary to avoid taking that inviting path at this point, and to turn, instead, to a different approach. This is the strategy of moving outside the experimental situation to the ordinary environment, and to observe there the effects of manipulations that were experimentally investigated (with simple acts) and theoretically proposed. This is the sort of validation some examples of which are given by Baer (1986). Baer's account is particularly encouraging, because it outlines a rare but promising technique of circumventing the language trap that has been previously described.

But no device will avoid the confusions and difficulties that can be generated when ordinary language is artificially removed from its ordinary functions and its terms are treated as if they were technical terms. Ordinary language, which serves perfectly all aspects of human life extending from mundane talk to literary beauty, will mislead the psychologist and anyone else who seeks in it fixities of meaning. Ordinary language can be used in a science appropriately and without confusion, only if the skills of conceptual analysis are taken seriously (cf. Harzem & Miles, 1978). It is essential that psychologists, too, acquire these skills so as to avoid the misunderstandings and misdirections than can arise from ordinary language. Without such skills some are bound to continue seeking "directly" to study the rainbow, and lamenting that techniques do not exist for putting some of it in the test-tube.

ACKNOWLEDGEMENT

There is a standard joke in my family whereby my wife and I compete in claiming that our daughter first said "mama" and "dada" respectively. In the same spirit of high regard, when I began in psychology one of the first words I learned was MacCorquodale. I am specially delighted, therefore, to contribute to this volume honoring Kenneth MacCorquodale. I am, as so many others have been, grateful for the dignity and balance of his scholarship.

REFERENCES

Baer, Donald M. (1986). In application, frequency is not the only estimate of the probability of behavior units. In T. Thompson & M. Zeiler (Eds.), *The analysis and integration of behavioral units*. Hillsdale, New Jersey: Lawrence Erlbaum Associates.

Bridgman, P.W. (1938). Operational analysis. *Philosophy of Science, 5,* 114-131.

Bridgman, P.W. (1940). Science: Public or private? *Philosophy of Science, 7,* 36-48.

Harzem, P. (1985). Operationism, smuggled connotations, and the nothing-else clause. *The Behavioral and Brain Sciences, 7,* 559.

Harzem, P. and Miles, T.R. (1978). *Conceptual issues in operant psychology*. Chichester, England: John Wiley & Sons.

Skinner, B.F. (1945). The operational analysis of psychological terms. *Psychological Review, 52,* 270-277.

The Behavioral and Brain Sciences, 1985, 7, 553-581.

PART II

BASIC UNITS OF ANALYSIS

CHAPTER 5

Re-Tuning the Operant-Respondent Distinction

PHILIP N. HINELINE

In the early days of behavior theory, all basic units of behavior were characterized as reflexes, or as having reflex-like properties. To be sure, there was Thorndike's demonstration of trial-and-error learning, but construed as the strengthening of stimulus-response units, this seemed not inherently different from behavior based upon prototypical reflexive units. Skinner's early theoretical statements (1931, 1935a) addressed the reflex concept as applicable to all behavior. Even his initial statement of the operant/respondent distinction was an identification of "two types of conditioned reflex" (Skinner, 1935b); only as the distinction was elaborated in an exchange with Konorski and Miller (Skinner, 1937), did the category of operant behavior come to be viewed as distinct from the category of reflexes.

Over the years, three main bases have been offered for identifying operant behavior as distinct from reflexive behavior. The first of these is an identification by default, that being the absence of an immediate environmental precursor that could be said to elicit the behavior in question. The second basis concerns sensitivity of the behavior to its consequences, and thus whether it is interpretable in terms of reinforcement and/or punishment. The third basis concerns the possibility that distinct response systems are involved in the two types of behavior. Clearly, most skeletal behavior patterns are sensitive to their consequences, and the prototypical conditioned reflexes are those mediated by the autonomic nervous system.

These three general bases have been prominent themes of arguments in a long-standing dispute: It is accepted that there are two types of procedures, but need this imply two processes? A theorist whose answer is "No" could point out that a desk-calculator has a single set of well-understood processes, yet when exposed to characteristically differing procedures it gives characteristically differing results. Operating on common sets of data, the harmonic-mean procedure will always result in the calculator behaving in ways that differ from its behavior under the standard-deviation procedure. Why, then, should we conclude that the underlying processes for two different conditioning procedures must be different?

If the argument is engaged on this ground, the most compelling basis for distinguishing two processes would be an anatomically-based dissociation. Without that dissociation, plausible covert eliciting events can always be hypothesized in cases where external elicitors are lacking, and consequences that demonstrably control behavior can be construed as acting upon reflex units, as in Thorndikian "stamping in" or S-R connections, or as proposed by Konorski and Miller (1937). Thus if they were valid, differing anatomical bases would be handy for delineating the domains of separate processes; they would identify as out-of-bounds, any appeals to hypothetical features that were predicated upon the alternative process. However, the now-commonplace modulating of autonomic responses through use of biofeedback techniques, and the routine Pavlovian experimentation with pigeons' key-pecking both serve to undermine an anatomically based operant/respondent distinction. More than a decade ago, Black (1971a) presented an exhaustive analysis of procedures, data and potential artifacts in autonomic conditioning, and found such conditioning to be an insufficient basis for clarifying the operant/respondent distinction. To be sure, there are other bases for addressing the proposition of distinct underlying processes, the most notable being a whole range of differing functional relationships based upon intermittent reinforcement. However, considering the tangle of arguments and counter-arguments that have evolved, it might be more productive to consider the ground upon which the issue has been engaged.

TWO TYPES OF THEORIZING

It is an often overlooked fact that the relative weight given to each of the three types of considerations - indeed, their very relevance or irrelevance - depends upon one's type of theory. In particular, the key issues concern what one means by "process," as well as what one accepts as legitimate theory. Still, theories throughout this domain share some general features that can provide a context for understanding their key differences. For all of them, to theorize is to interpret, to systematically describe, to talk or write in explanatory ways - and in so doing, to make comprehensible many particular observed relationships (including those we call facts) by describing them in terms of fewer, and thus more general relationships. Quantitative expressions are highly regarded, but since these do not stand alone, the characteristics of interpretive prose remain important. In some sense, this prose must be about what organisms do - about behavior, or more properly, about *behaving*, since all forms of doing are verb-like. Whatever one's theoretical biases, one's interpretive talk is predominantly in the form of agent-action: cause-effect, independent variable-dependent variable (Hineline, 1980). Indeed, for the verbal community of our surrounding culture, if one does not talk in agent-action locutions one's talking about what people or animals do seems unfocused and ineffectual. Further, in most psychological theorizing and especially in vernacular "psychologizing," agency is attributed to the organism: Organism produces behavior, with the immediate environment as context.

But there is an alternative agent-action locution; it is that of environment-behavior, with organism as context or parameter. Given the bipolarity of interpretive prose, the relationships of behavior to both environment and organism are not easily captured without attributing agency, and thus giving emphasis either to organism or to environment. Thus, we live with the

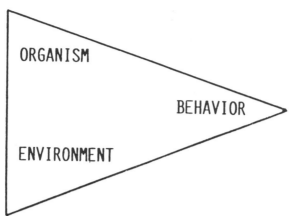

Fig. 1. Diagram schematizing the relationship between two types of interpretive locution. In both types, "behavior" is the action, in agent-action locutions. However, in one type, "organism" is the imputed agent; in the other, agency is imputed to "environment."

triangular relationship illustrated in Figure 1. There are two basic forms of interpretive locution: organism-action, with environment as context, and environment-action, with organism as context.

Both interpretive patterns occur normally within everyday speech. However, their normal circumstances of occurrence seem to be characteristically different. In particular, Jones and Nisbett (1971) have noted that within our culture, systematically differing interpretations of an action are given by the person who acts and by a person observing the action. The actor interprets his or her action in relation to environmental circumstances. The observer interprets the action in terms of characteristics of the person who acts, whether those characteristics are known from long acquaintance or are merely inferred from the act in question. The differing patterns of interpretation are found even in experimental situations where both actor and observer have equal access to the circumstances surrounding the action (Jones & Harris, 1967).

The viewpoint that developed from Skinner's elaborating the operant side of the operant-respondent distinction, is an account rigorously based upon environment-behavior locutions. Known philosophically as radical behaviorism, and known scientifically as behavior analysis, its axiomatic, perhaps defining principle is that of interpreting behavior through heavy emphasis upon environmental events, present and past. When an analysis encompasses an appreciable span of time it could describe a fairly symmetrical interplay between behavioral and environmental events. But in departing from agent-action conventions, such an account would come across as "merely descriptive." Furthermore, in the description of experiments asymmetrical, "controlling" relationships between experimenter's procedure and subject's behavior tend to be emphasized. Hence, behavior-analytic prose is couched in the vernacular pattern of agent-action, but that of environment-behavior rather than organism-behavior. These locutions would be conventional, perhaps noncontroversial interpretations of behavior *if they were offered from the standpoint of actor*. However, virtually by definition, *they are offered from the standpoint of observer*. In this respect, behavior-analytic prose is intrinsically counter-cultural. I wonder how much this subtle but consistent departure from cultural practice contributes to popular characterizations of behaviorism as sinister. Could it be the verbal equivalent of distorted facial features? ("I don't trust him; his eyes are too close together. They make me uncomfortable; they talk as if we were all controlled.")

COMPLEMENTARITY OF ORGANISM-BASED AND ENVIRONMENT-BASED THEORY?

Environment-behavior locutions versus organism-behavior locutions: As theorists we tend to insist upon one form to the exclusion of the other. Need we be so parochial? Aside from one of them requiring that a theorist speak or write as if he/she were actor rather than observer, could we not shift between the two modes of interpretation while retaining the stance of observer? After all, as citizens of the vernacular community we easily shift between those two roles. Unfortunately, I find that there are some fairly immutable reasons why the two flavors of theory do not blend (Hineline, 1984b). The reasons may be discernible in further elaboration of the triangular relationship.

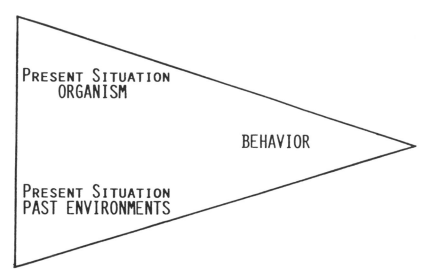

Fig. 2. Elaborated diagram of the relationship between two types of interpretive locution. The correspondence to "agent-action" locutions is the same as in Figure 1.

The radical behaviorist position is sometimes characterized as S-R psychology, implying that the environmental events of its environment-behavior locutions must be construed as events contiguous with the behavior. To be sure, behavior *is* to be understood partly in terms of its immediate context. However, as suggested in Figure 2, that is true of both the environment-based and organism-based accounts. The organism's actions are interpreted in the context of a "present situation." An environment-based account will appeal to a a present situation as well, typically characterizing it in terms of eliciting stimuli if the behavior is reflexive, or of discriminative stimuli in the case of operant behavior. However, this is not usually the key item in an environment-based interpretation of action; rather, there is an appeal to *past environments* - that is, to an environmental history, often denoted as a history of reinforcement. But even this fails to characterize the essential features of the environment-based account. What is involved in the history relevant to an action is not just past environments, but rather, a history of *behavior-environment interactions.* As Figure 3 illustrates, this makes things more complicated; the subtlety of the environment-based account is often lost when it is abbreviated in simple agent-action locutions. This is true even aside from the point indicated in Figure 3, that a complete environment-based account includes evolutionary history as well as ontogenetic history. Neither reflexes nor operants are well characterized as individual responses; both are classes of events arrayed over time and place (Skinner, 1931, 1935a; Catania, 1973), just as "species" is arrayed over time and place, but on a different scale (Skinner, 1981).

One can identify some point-to-point correspondences between features of the organism in the organism-based account, and features of the environment in the environment-based account. The evolutionary history of behavior-environment interactions is characterized as a genetic code, when one focuses upon the organisms. The ontogenetic history of behavior-environment interactions is characterized in terms such as representations, expectations, or physiological states, when one focuses upon the organism. Why, then can there not be direct translation between the two types of account? There appear to be two reasons, one relating to what constitutes process, and the other relating to the status of behavior within each of the two positions.

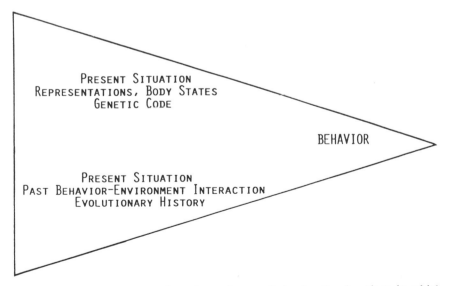

Fig. 3. Further elaboration of two forms of agent-action locutions in which behavior is interpreted.

In organism-based theorizing, behavior seems to be taken mainly as index, or evidence of what is going on inside the organism. Behavior is the basis for evaluating one's model; its status is that of "ambassador" for mind or brain (Wasserman, 1981). On the other hand, from the environment-based, behavior-analytic viewpoint, behavior is itself the focus of interest. That is the meaning of Skinner's often-repeated phrase, "a science of behavior," a meaning that differs from that of the less specific label, "behavioral science." This difference can also be understood in terms of operationism, for the two positions differ on the relationship of experimental operations to theory. In organism-based theory, the operations of an experiment are taken as attempts to reveal some property of the organisms, or as lending objectivity to definitions of inferred processes within the organism. On the other hand, for behavior-analytic theory, operations are attempts to efficiently arrange the effective characteristics of the environment as it interacts with behavior. This, then, leads to the differing meanings of *process* for the two viewpoints. For the organism-based position, process is what goes on inside the organism; process is said to mediate, or underlie behavior. From the behavior-analytic viewpoint, process is the very interplay between environment and behavior. Behavior-analytic theory is an attempt to characterize the effective environment in its interaction with behavior (for more detailed discussion of these differences, see Hineline, 1984a, b, c).

THE OPERANT/RESPONDENT DISTINCTION RECONSIDERED

I have gone to some lengths to characterize the difference between organism-based and environment-based interpretive positions because they differ profoundly regarding what counts as supporting the operant-respondent distinction. For organism-based theory, it seems unlikely that a clean version of the distinction will ever be established. On the other hand, if there can be discerned two distinct functional categories of behavior-environment interplay, those constitute two distinct processes as seen from the environment-based, behavior-analytic viewpoint. It is recognized that one cannot arrange a procedure for operant conditioning without stimulus-stimulus relationships being embedded therein, and thus the possibility of concomitant Pavlovian conditioning. Similarly, when one arranges the conditions of Pavlovian conditioning one cannot prevent the possibility of operant conditioning. Even central nervous system activity is directly susceptible to operant conditioning (Black, 1971b). Thus, while it may remain unspecified, *some* behavior is bound to occur during the interval between conditioned and unconditioned stimuli, and thus be reinforced or punished by the occurrence of the event that the experimenter supplies for the role of Pavlovian unconditioned stimulus. While the two processes occur concurrently they can occur quite independently even when they involve some of the same events (e.g., Marcucella, 1981); no unambiguous case can be made for one necessarily mediating the other (Black, 1971a).

Returning to the three bases for substantiating the operant/respondent distinction, differing physiological response systems would be crucially compelling for organism-based theory; for environment-based theory, such differences would be convenient but not crucial. If an organism-based account is predicated upon contiguous causation, as many seem to be, then the absence of an eliciting stimulus for the behavior in question could also be crucial. Wetherington (1982), in an excellent environment-based discussion of respondent behavior, also emphasized this feature. From my own viewpoint, the question of identifying an immediate precursor is only marginally important. Operant behavior, then, is not synonymous with emitted behavior, although much of emitted behavior is operant. As seen in the following, some instances of respondent behavior do not have immediately attendant environmental precursors. Given that respondent and operant conditioning procedures are inevitably embedded in each other, the question rests upon whether nontrivial, verifiable consequences can account for the observed variations in behavior. Thus, as an environment based theorist I favor defining operant behavior through its sensitivity to consequences, construed as reinforcement or punishment, and

I prefer to define the other category by default, rather than by appeal to eliciting stimuli. However, unlike Thompson and Lubinski (1986) I propose treating non-operant behavior as a single category.

What of this default category? Can it include *all* non-operant behavior? How are its patterns to be portrayed in relation to environmental events? What are we to take as *process* within the non-operant domain if it is not confined to the elicitation of reflexes? I propose that just as operant processes are defined by orderly relationships between behavior patterns and events they produce, respondent processes are orderly relationships between behavior patterns and events that typically occur independently of behavior. Some of these will involve stimuli that elicit, producing the familiar, phasic reflexive behavior patterns, and their delineation was well characterized long ago (Skinner, 1931, 1935a). But some behavior patterns will be better understood as involving *sequences* of events that proceed intrepidly, again independently of the behavior in question. This allows for inclusion of categories such as that of adjunctive behavior (Falk, 1966a), which often have been characterized as outside the operant/respondent domain, and which I discuss in detail later. My hypothesis is that behavior patterns such as these can be understood in terms of dynamic properties characterized in relation to those sequences. It is not an hypothesis about underlying process - although I could readily supply plausible physiological mechanisms if such were the nature of my theory. Rather, it is a hypothesis about properties of behavior patterns themselves.

RESONANCE AS A PROPERTY OF BEHAVIOR PATTERNS

A key notion is that behavior patterns can be well characterized by the property of resonance - that each pattern can be made to occur more easily at one frequency than at any other (Hineline, 1981). This property is readily demonstrated in the domain of physical systems, for it is ubiquitous there, and observable on dimensions ranging from microscopic to global.

Thus each vessel of water will slosh most readily at a particular frequency - quickly, if it is a glass- or cupful; more slowly, if a basin- or tubful; only twice daily, if it is the contents of the Bay of Fundy. Every bridge oscillates most easily at a particular frequency; scouts and army troops are instructed to break ranks when crossing, on the off chance that the resonant frequency of a bridge might coincide with their marching cadence, resulting in disaster. Electronic circuits are often resonant - indeed, the radio receiver is based upon that property - but here it is oscillations of voltage and current that are involved. Thus, it should be noted that applicability of the principle does not depend upon the stuff of which a system is made.

If this property were applicable to patterns of behavior, the most basic evidence for it would be a peaked function obtained when one measured the vigor of the behavior pattern while varying the frequency with which its inducing events were presented. Such bitonic functions are well known as properties of adjunctive behavior (Falk, 1966a). For example, when Falk (1966b) delivered food pellets on a fixed-interval schedule, and measured within-session water intake as a function of fixed-interval size, his rats ingested several times their normal daily intake within the experimental session, with a distinct maximum in the function, at 180 seconds for one animal (shown here in Figure 4), and at 90 seconds for another. Roper (1980) reported sharply peaked functions with maxima at either 30 or 45 seconds; his experiment included a number of measures and manipulations that verified that the bitonicity was not an artifact of measurement. Data from one of his animals are also shown in Figure 4. The two remaining curves shown in that figure were obtained by Allen and Kenshalo (1976). They are included here to illustrate the fact that the effect is not confined to rats' drinking. Allen and Kenshalo exposed Rhesus monkeys to a similar procedure, and also found bitonic functions for the behavior of drinking, with maxima at approximately 75 seconds and approximately 18 seconds, respectively. While lever-pressing was reinforced in each of these experiments, thus generating the various fixed-interval schedules, the effects on drinking were not attributable to operant relationships. First,

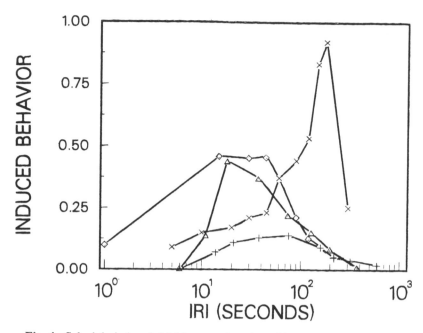

Fig. 4. Schedule-induced drinking as a function of inter-reinforcer interval (IRI), illustrating bitonic functions obtained in three different studies. The data plotted with "x" symbols are from Falk's (1966b) experiment with rats as subjects. The measure of induced behavior was amount of water ingested per session, re-plotted here in relative units. The data plotted with triangles are from one rat in Roper's (1980) experiment. Induced drinking was measured in ml/min. The plots with "+" and diamond-shaped symbols represent licks per second, re-plotted from Allen and Kenshalo (1976), who used rhesus monkeys as subjects.

measures of drinking have proved to be independent of rates of lever-pressing (e.g., Allen & Kenshalo, 1976). Second, imposing a negative contingency between drinking and food delivery failed to break up the pattern of drinking that was induced by approximately periodic delivery of food pellets (e.g., Segal & Oden, 1969). Third, it has been found that scheduled-induced drinking, including the bitonic function, is readily produced by sequences of food presentation that have no contingent relation to ongoing behavior (e.g., Segal, Oden & Deadwyler, 1965).

Just as the bitonic function is not limited to a single species, it also is not limited to a single type of behavior pattern. Flory

(1969) made a taxidermically-stuffed target pigeon available to live pigeons and delivered food to them periodically at various intervals while recording their pecks directed at the stuffed targets. The result for each of two birds was a sharply peaked bitonic function; their maxima were at 60 and 120 seconds, respectively, and one of them is shown in Figure 5. DeWeese (1977) used squirrel monkeys as subjects, measured biting by means of a conveniently-placed rubber hose, and delivered food periodically at various intervals. As shown in Figure 5 she, too, found for each subject, a frequency of food delivery that produced maximum amounts of biting. DeWeese also demonstrated that this bitonic function is not specific to food delivery schedules; she exposed the same monkeys to schedules of period shock delivery, and found similar effects to those obtained with food.

Patterns such as these occur in great variety (see Wetherington, 1982 for a review); they have been termed "scheduled-induced" or "adjunctive" behavior, and have not been satisfactorily incorporated within theory of whatever kind. Clearly, they are not attributable to selection by

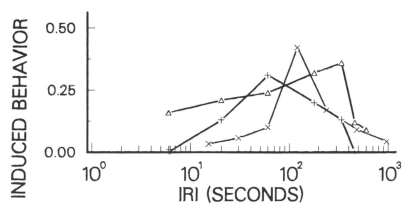

Fig. 5. Schedule-induced pecking and biting, as functions of inter-reinforcer interval (IRI), illustrating bitonic functions obtained in two different studies. The data plotted with "x" symbols were reported by Flory (1969); they show pigeons' attacks per minute (divided by three, for convenience of scaling). Points plotted with triangles and "+" symbols show hose-bites per second, from DeWeese's (1977) experiment using squirrel monkeys as subjects.

consequences, as in the case of operant behavior. There have been appeals to various types of motivational or emotional states (e.g., Staddon, 1977), but these have not been made integral with theory that accounts for other kinds of behavior as well. Since they are produced only by extended sequences of stimuli they are unlike the prototypical reflex, which requires only a single stimulus for its elicitation. However, Wetherington (1982) examined in detail some varied but often underemphasized characteristics of elicited behavior, and found that when one took into account the phenomena of repeated stimulation, such as habituations, sensitization, and the like, reflexive behavior seems not all that different from adjunctive patterns of behavior. The characteristics she identified are especially relevant here, for they suggest some additional properties of resonant physical systems.

One such property is the degree of damping, which describes the quickness with which the object or system comes to rest when external stimulation has been discontinued. Undamped systems will oscillate indefinitely after a single stimulation. Underdamped systems will continue for several oscillations, as in the case of a playground swing, or many, as in the case of a guitar string. Overdamped systems do not readily follow repeated stimulation - as in the case of a door with a pneumatic closing device. A special case is the critically damped system: It follows the stimulation exactly - one input, one output, and stop. An automobile with excellent shock absorbers (called "dampeners" in Britain), approximates this characteristic, with respect to externally applied vibrations. An automobile with faulty shock absorbers will oscillate a few times after a single perturbation.

Most reflexes could be described as slightly overdamped or slightly underdamped patterns of behavior. Damping, in combination with particular resonant frequencies, could perhaps account for refractory periods and temporal summation, as observed with conventional reflexes.

The other secondary property is the degree of tuning, which describes the degree of specificity to a specific resonant frequency. Tuning, then, corresponds to the sharpness of the bitonic function that is obtained when frequency of stimulation is varied. In the case of physical systems there is an inverse relation between degree of damping and degree of tuning. Thus the guitar string, which is only slightly damped, is sharply tuned; it is difficult to induce oscillation in the string at frequencies other than the resonant one or multiples thereof. Conversely, critically damped systems can be driven equally easily at any frequency; the prototypical example of this is a high fidelity audio speaker, whose output is proportional to the input, irrespective of frequency. Most physical systems lie somewhere along the continuum between these extremes.

The reader might wonder: If resonance is indeed a property of behavior patterns, why has this not been clearly evident? One reason might be that resonant systems are usually studied under the influence of analog, sinusoidal inputs (e.g., see McFarland, 1971); most behavioral effects of the type discussed here are studied under the effects of pulsed events - stimuli that are delivered in discrete pieces, or are turned on and off precipituously. Another reason for resonance not being an obvious property of behavior, is the unlikelihood that species would evolve with highly tuned behavior patterns. These would tend to be maladaptive, for such patterns would be underdamped, tending to persist long after their precipitating events had ceased, and thus long after the behavior was appropriate to the surrounding environment. For moderately damped systems the resonant property is less obvious. For example, the faulty shock absorbers in the front end of an automobile may not be evident to the prospective purchaser as he or she jumps upon the bumper, or drives around on rough roads within the neighborhood of the car dealership. However, on a smooth highway at some precise speed - say, 47 miles per hour - the vibration may be uncomfortable indeed, and compellingly obvious. Thus, for behavior patterns, the property of resonance may become evident only in special circumstances.

Some suggestive but inconclusive evidence for resonance in adjunctive behavior comes from assessments of the role of periodicity. Even Falk's initial demonstration showed that strict periodicity is not essential - that variable-interval schedules of food delivery can produce scheduled-induced polydipsia (Falk, 1961). However, Millenson, Allen, and Pinker (1977) noted that Falk had not used a constant-probability schedule, and thus that his sequences of food delivery entailed some degree of temporal regularity. Millenson et al., (1977) compared the effects of a traditional VI schedule such as the one Falk had used, with the effects of a constant-probability, random-interval schedule. They found that, as Falk had reported, a moderately aperiodic schedule induced substantial amounts of drinking. On the other hand, when the moment-to-moment probability of food delivery was constant, they found that the amount of induced drinking was greatly reduced. Lashley and Rosellini (1980) also found that use of a random-time schedule was less likely to induce polydipsic drinking than use of a fixed-time schedule. On the other hand, in both studies a minority of animals drank substantial amounts when exposed to the random-time schedules, and Allen and Weidinger (1980) and Shurtleff, Delamater, and Riley (1983) found both random-time and fixed-time schedules of food delivery to be effective for the induction of polydipsic drinking. However, a recent study by Plonsky, Driscoll, Warren, and Rosellini (1984) revealed that aperiodic patterns of food delivery do not necessarily produce aperiodic patterns of food-oriented behavior. Their time-sampling analysis of videotapes revealed that animals that engaged in excessive drinking also showed nonrandom distributions of time spent at the food cup. It may be that periodicity of food-consuming patterns interacts with that of drinking patterns, and that functionally, the delivery of food at random intervals does not ensure pure aperiodicity in its effects on behavior. This suggests the need to look at interactions between behavior patterns - and to consider food pellets not simply as stimuli, but as events that enable eating, much as has been done in studies of relativity or reinforcement (Premack, 1959, 1971; Timberlake & Allison, 1974; Timberlake, 1980). Also, as Keehn and Riusech (1979) have proposed, such effects may not be unidirectional, and drinking may modulate food-related behavior as well as vice-versa.

The consensus regarding necessary conditions for production of schedule-induced behavior, seems to be the occurrence of predictable/discriminable periods that are free of the inducing events. Most theorists interpret this in terms of time-based discrimination. In contrast, the present viewpoint emphasizes the temporal properties of behavior patterns, perhaps modulated by, but still distinct from discriminative processes.

OPERATIVE PRINCIPLES DERIVED FROM RESONANCE

To be powerfully convincing and useful in terms of environment-based theory, the resonance notion must translate directly into procedures that demonstrate orderly, environment-based relationships. For example, one of the compelling aspects of Skinner's early work was the demonstration of reinforcement in the direct shaping of behavior - direct demonstration of orderly behavior-environment interaction, not dependent upon inferential statistics or even group data. Crucial to this, although perhaps not universally noticed, was the arrangement whereby the subject's behavior shaped the experimenter's behavior on a moment-to-moment basis, as well as on a day-to-day basis (Skinner, 1956), instead of on the more traditional experiment-to-experiment basis. For traditional reflexes - those being responses close to critical damping - elicitation suffices as the principle that translates directly into orderly environment-behavior relationships. But for moderately-damped patterns, periodic induction is the operative principle. How does one find the circumstances that would be equivalent to driving the old automobile, noted previously, at 47 miles per hour? In collaboration with Thomas Tatham, I have undertaken to discover such a procedure, if it exists, with respect to rats' polydipsic drinking.

Our procedure resembles what have been called adjusting schedules and titration schedules, but the scheduled food deliveries are not contingent upon particular responses as in conventional schedules of reinforcement. Rather, particular food deliveries occur independently of behavior. A session begins with several food pellets delivered according to a fixed inter-pellet interval, while the rat's licking at a water-tube is recorded. Then the interval is incremented, and licking is again recorded for a block of several periodic food deliveries. At the end of that block of intervals, lick-rates before and after the change of interval are compared; if licking has increased, the interval is incremented further; if licking has decreased, the interval is decremented. These adjustments continue to be made at the end of each successive block of intervals.

In our initial attempt, the block size was seven (allowing 20 blocks per session), with comparisons based upon the final four inter-food intervals of successive blocks. The adjustments were five-second increments or decrements, and each session began where the preceding session left off. This procedure did not home in on particular intervals. Our second attempt used five-pellet blocks, and comparisons were based on licking in all five intervals. Adjustments were a constant proportion of the inter-pellet interval (12%), rather than a constant number of seconds. In addition, we started each session at the same value for at least five consecutive daily sessions, with session-starting intervals of 39, 62, and 154 seconds. Once again, the procedure failed to home in on particular values.

In a still more recent version, the starting point was again held constant over consecutive sessions, but this time within-session comparisons were made over blocks of ten intervals, and the inter-pellet intervals were adjusted by a larger proportion (approximately 18%). The results are more promising, as shown in Figure 6. The first increment of the session (indicated in the figure as a shift to the right) consistently produced an increase in drinking, indicated by the second adjustment being an increment as well. Thereafter, the sequences in two of the five-session groups homed in on one of two values. The third five-session group of sessions revealed less consistency. The procedure clearly requires refinement, not only to produce more consistent results, but also to include smaller adjustment intervals as an optimal interval is

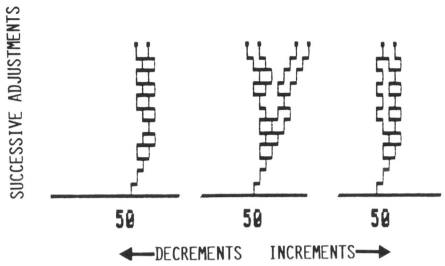

SUCCESSIVE ADJUSTMENTS

50 50 50

←—DECREMENTS INCREMENTS—→

Fig. 6. Paths of schedule adjustment based upon a rat's licking rates. Each tree-shaped plot is based upon five consecutive sessions in which the inter-pellet interval began at 50 seconds. After the 10th pellet, the interval was incremented by 18%. After every additional ten pellets, the interval was increased or decreased in 18% steps, depending upon comparisons of lick-rates in successive 10-interval blocks, and indicated by successive steps from bottom to top of the figure. The terminal point of each session is indicated by a dot; thus, in the first and third five-session plots all sessions terminated on one of two intervals. In the middle five-session plot, only two termination points coincided.

approached.

Conflicting with priorities of accuracy and stability, is the desirability of homing in quickly on an interval. It is possible that behavior patterns are resonant, but with resonant frequencies that shift over time as a function of within-session variables like satiation, or of uncontrolled variables that change over days. If so, our predicament would be analogous to that of attempting to identify the resonant frequency of a radio tuner by measuring its input/output relationships over a period of several minutes. At any moment, the tuner circuits have a precise resonant frequency; however, if unbeknownst to us someone is twiddling the dial out front, or if the capacitance in a circuit changes as the device heats up, evidence for resonance will be inconclusive. Should we succeed in developing an efficient adjusting procedure, the next step will be to attempt to induce drinking with inter-food intervals exactly double the optimal ones. This would be analogous to pushing a child's swing on alternate cycles; if a secondary peak in the function were obtained, it would be a result uniquely predicted by the present interpretation of adjunctive behavior. Of course, certain control procedures will also be required, such as starting with intervals somewhat smaller than the suspected optimal ones, so that the adjustments toward an optimal induction interval will entail reduced frequency of food delivery. This would be necessary to unequivocally rule out changes in lick-rate being reinforced by increases in frequency of food delivery.

The feasibility of the adjusting procedures described above depends upon induced behavior changing and re-stabilizing quickly when the food-delivery schedules are changed. Given that most experiments in this domain - including those that produced the bitonic functions - have followed the common practice of running a given procedure with its parameters held

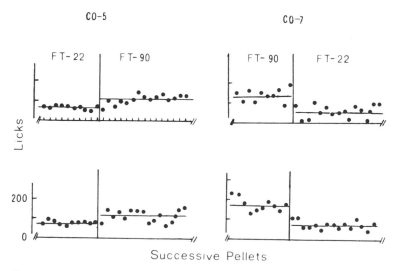

Fig. 7. Pellet-to-pellet licks for rats CO-5, CO-7, for the ten intervals preceding, and the fifteen intervals following mid-session changes of the interval separating food-pellet deliveries. Four individual sessions are shown: two with transitions from 22-second to 90-second inter-pellet intervals, and two with transitions from 90-second to 22-second intervals. Other than axes, the vertical lines indicate transitions; horizontal lines indicate median values for the corresponding pretransition or posttransition samples of data.

constant for several days or weeks, one might question whether behavior would track the frequent changes of our adjusting procedures. This possibility has been addressed by other experiments in my laboratory, in collaboration with Lynn Zakreski. Four inter-pellet intervals are used: 22.5, 45, 90, and 180 seconds, presented in an irregular order. However, each interval is used for six consecutive *half*-sessions of 30 pellets each, with interval changes occurring at mid-session. Pellet-to-pellet drinking is measured, and Figure 7 shows typical results for the ten intervals immediately before a change, and for the first fifteen intervals following a change. Clearly, the amounts of drinking shift systematically over the first few intervals after a change. Thus it appears feasible to track, within-sessions, the optimal intervals for inducing drinking. In addition to its supporting the feasibility of the adjusting procedures, the procedures with mid-session change may also be useful for exploring the property of phase-lag in schedule-induced behavior.

SCALES OF ANALYSIS AND BEHAVIORAL UNITS

The adjusting procedures are of special relevance to behavioral units, and to the organization of behavior. First, the reciprocal relationship between behavior and its environment is especially evident. In essence, while the computer is inducing particular behavior patterns through periodic food deliveries, the animal's drinking is reinforcing and punishing the computer's behavior. Adjustments that produce less drinking are less likely to occur in the future; adjustments that produce more drinking are more likely to occur in the future. Thus, the titration procedure may identify some special arrangement whereby, even though reinforcement and punishment are not the principles operative on the subject's behavior, that behavior selects its most relevant environment. The "fractures" between units are as much between sets of environmental events as between sets of responses. Also, it should be noted that the units are units of *process - in* and *of* behavior-environment interaction.

If we are to learn to identify such units, it will be through the experimenter's behavior being a flexible, adaptive part of the environment interacting with the subject's behavior. Also, the notion of resonance suggests how it is that even in the non-operant case, a single type of environmental event, such as brief shock or delivery of a food pellet, can produce the various types of adjunctive behavior that have been observed - drinking, attack, grooming, pica eating, or whatever.

One remaining unusual feature of this approach should be noted. Necessarily, if we are to understand units of behavior in terms of extended patterns of events over time, we must be flexible in our scale of analysis. Traditionally, compact patterns are seen as unitary, and we are most comfortable speaking causally in reference to contiguous events. However, units extended over time may be just as real as those that we easily view as tight and molecular. Morris, Higgins and Bickel (1982) have put this especially well, so I shall quote them, substituting the term "scale" for their term "level":

> Just as the power of a microscope must be adjusted as a function of the phenomenon under study, so, too does the scale of behavior analysis need to be adjusted to the functional unit of behavior-environment interaction. To be specific, when order is not apparent at a molar level, a more molecular analysis may be necessary . . . Conversely, if one fails to find an immediate stimulus that controls a response, perhaps the response is only an element of a larger functional unit which is controlled by currently operating variables not immediately attendent to that element. (pp. 119-120)

When one looks at the same object through a microscope using various magnifications one will see a variety of configurations, *and each of the orderly relationships is real and valid, irrespective of what is observed at other scales of magnification.* So, too, in exploring the domains of space and time that define behavioral units, we may encounter such boundaries on each of several time scales. Each of those time relationships can be real, and valid without necessary appeal to a different scale, if we can adequately delineate its features.

ACKNOWLEDGMENT

Research supported here was supported by a Grant-In-Aid of Research from Temple University. Reprints can be obtained from the author, Department of Psychology, Temple University, Philadelphia, Pennsylvania 19122. I wish to thank Thomas Tatham for his aid in preparation of figures.

REFERENCES

Allen, J.D., & Kenshalo, D.R. (1976). Schedule-induced drinking as a function of interreinforcement interval in the Rhesus monkey. *Journal of the Experimental Analysis of Behavior, 26,* 257-267.

Allen, J.D., & Weidinger, R.C. (1980). Truly random reinforcement intervals do produce schedule-induced polydipsia. Paper presented at meeting of the Psychonomic Society, St. Louis, Mo.

Black, A.H. (1971a). The direct control of neural processes by reward and punishment. *American Scientist, 59,* 236-245.

Black, A.H. (1971b). Autonomic aversive conditioning in infra-human subjects. In R.F. Brush (Ed.), *Aversive conditioning and learning* (pp. 3-104). New York: Academic Press.

Catania, A.C. (1973). The concept of the operant in the analysis of behavior. *Behaviorism, 1,* 103-116.

DeWeese, J. (1977). Schedule-induced biting under fixed-interval schedules of food or electric-shock presentation. *Journal of the Experimental Analysis of Behavior, 27,* 419-431.

Falk, J.L. (1961). Production of polydipsia in normal rats by an intermittent food schedule. *Science, 133,* 195-196.

Falk, J.L. (1966a). The motivational properties of schedule-induced polydipsia. *Journal of the Experimental Analysis of Behavior, 9,* 19-25.

Falk, J.L. (1966b). Schedule-induced polydipsia as a function of fixed interval length. *Journal of the Experimental Analysis of Behavior, 9,* 37-39.

Flory, R. (1969). Attack behavior as a function of minimum inter-food interval. *Journal of the Experimental Analysis of Behavior, 12,* 825-828.

Hineline, P.N. (1980). The language of behavior analysis: Its community, its functions, and its limitations. *Behaviorism, 8,* 67-86.

Hineline, P.N. (1981). Constraints, competing behavior, and the principles of resonance. In C.M. Bradshaw, E. Szabadi, & C.F. Lowe (Eds.), *Quantification of steady-state operant behavior* (pp. 153-164). The Hague: Elsevier/North-Holland Biomedical Press.

Hineline, P.N. (1984a). Editorial. *Journal of the Experimental Analysis of Behavior, 41,* 1-2.

Hineline, P.N. (1984b).   What, then is Skinner's operationism? Commentary, in *The Behavioral and Brain Sciences, 7,* 560.

Hineline, P.N. (1984c).   Can a statement in cognitive terms be a behavior-analytic interpretation? *The Behavior Analyst, 7,* 97-100.

Jones, E.E., & Nisbett, R.E. (1971).   *The actor and the observer: Divergent perceptions of the causes of behavior.* Morristown, New Jersey: General Learning Press.

Jones, E.E., & Harris, V.A. (1967). The attribution of attitudes. *Journal of Experimental Social Psychology, 3,* 1-24.

Keehn, J.D., & Riusech, R. (1979).   Schedule-induced drinking facilitates schedule-controlled feeding. *Animal Learning and Behavior, 7,* 41-44.

Konorski, J. & Miller, S. (1937).   On two types of conditioned reflex. *Journal of General Psychology, 16,* 264-272.

Lashley, R.L., & Rosellini, R.A. (1980). Modulation of schedule-induced polydipsia by Pavlovian conditioned states. *Physiology and Behavior, 24,* 411-414.

Marcucella, H. (1981).   Stimulus control of respondent and operant key pecking: A single key procedure. *Journal of the Experimental Analysis of Behavior, 36,* 51-60.

McFarland, J.J. (1971).   *Feedback mechanisms in animal behaviour.* London: Academic Press.

Millenson, J.R., Allen, R.B., & Pinker, S. (1977).   Adjunctive drinking during variable and random-interval food reinforcement schedules. *Animal Learning & Behavior, 5,* 285-290.

Morris, E.K., Higgins, S.T., & Bickel, W.K. (1982).   Comments on cognitive science in the experimental analysis of behavior. *Behavior Analyst, 5,* 109-125.

Plonsky, M., Driscoll, C.D., Warren, D.A., & Rosellini, R.A. (1984).   Do random time schedules induce polydipsia in the rat? *Animal Learning & Behavior, 12,* 355-362.

Premack, D. (1959).   Toward empirical behavior laws: I. Positive reinforcement. *Psychological Review, 66,* 219-234.

Premack, D. (1971).   Catching up with common sense or two sides of a generalization: Reinforcement and punishment. In R. Glaser (Ed.), *The nature of reinforcement.* New York: Academic Press.

Roper, T.J. (1980). Changes in rate of schedule-induced behaviour in rats as a function of fixed-interval schedule. *Quarterly Journal of Experimental Psychology, 32,* 159-170.

Segal, E.F., & Oden, D.L. (1969). Schedule-induced polydipsia: Effects of providing an alternate reinforced response and of introducing a lick-contingent delay in food delivery. *Psychonomic Science, 25,* 153-154.

Segal, E.F., Oden, D.L., & Deadwyler, S.A. (1965). Determinants of polydipsia: IV. Free reinforcement schedules. *Psychonomic Science, 3,* 11-12.

Shurtleff, D., Delamater, A.R., & Riley, A.L. (1983).   A reevaluation of the CS- hypothesis for schedule-induced polydipsia under intermittent schedules of pellet delivery. *Animal Learning & Behavior, 11,* 247-254.

Skinner, B.F. (1931). The concept of the reflex in the description of behavior. *Journal of General Psychology, 5,* 427-458.

Skinner, B.F. (1935a). The generic nature of the concepts of stimulus and response. *Journal of General Psychology, 12,* 40-65.

Skinner, B.F. (1935b). Two types of conditioned reflex and a pseudo-type. *Journal of General Psychology, 12,* 66-77.

Skinner, B.F. (1937). Two types of conditioned reflex: A reply to Konorski and Miller. *Journal of General Psychology, 16,* 272-279.

Skinner, B.F. (1956). A case history in scientific method. *American Psychologist, 11,* 221-233.

Skinner, B.F. (1981). Selection by consequences. *Science, 213,* 501-504.

Staddon, J.E.R. (1977). Schedule-induced behavior. In W.K. Honig & J.E.R. Staddon (Eds.), *Handbook of operant behavior.* Englewood Cliffs, New Jersey: Prentice-Hall.

Timberlake, W. (1980). A molar equilibrium theory of learned performance. In G.H. Bower (Ed.) *The psychology of learning and motivation, Vol. 14.* New York: Academic Press.

Timberlake, W., & Allison, J. (1974). Response deprivation: An empirical approach to instrumental performance. *Psychological Review, 81,* 146-164.

Wasserman, E.A. (1981). Comparative psychology returns: A review of Hulse, Fowler, and Honig's *Cognitive processes in animal behavior. Journal of the Experimental Analysis of Behavior, 35,* 243-258.

Wetherington, C.S. (1982). Is adjunctive behavior a third class of behavior? *Neuroscience & Biobehavioral Reviews, 6,* 329-350.

CHAPTER 6

Behavior Units and Optimality

MICHAEL D. ZEILER

The specific aim of this chapter is to describe the principles of temporally differentiated responding. These include the characteristics of behavior when it must have a specified duration in order to be followed by a reinforcing event, and the analysis of the variables that control that behavior. What emerges is a coherent set of principles that appear to be independent of particular responses, an approximation to a general law of temporally controlled responses, and a preliminary analysis of temporal control in terms of optimal foraging theory. The description of temporal control of response units serves as the starting point not only because it reveals a law of behavior, but also because it provides an example of how general behavioral principles can be.

RESPONSE UNITS

An organizing theme of the following discussion is that the effects of differential reinforcement on the duration of responses has been viewed from at least three different perspectives. Two of these have to do with response units, whereas the third has treated the procedures as psychophysical methods useful for showing the relation between experienced and physical duration.

The problem of response units is that of defining meaningful units of behavior. One sense of unit is that of building block for more complex systems: It is in this sense that one asserts that cells, proteins, molecules, or whatever are units. Psychology never has gotten very far in this respect. At one time, the reflex - later liberalized as the S-R connection - was thought to serve such a function, but such thinking no longer seems either widespread or influential. In contemporary behavioral research and theory the closest approximation is Shimp's (1979) hypothesis that interresponse times (IRTs) may serve as the functional components of extended behavioral sequences. In fact, the idea that interresponse time differentiation underlies operant behavior has a substantial history, and much experimental work on differential reinforcement of IRTs was motivated by this interest. The value of isolating a viable building block of behavior combined with Shimp's creative use of IRTs for this purpose certainly could revitalize the search. For present purposes, it is enough to recognize that one important source of interest in the effects of differentially reinforcing a temporal property of behavior has been that such behavior may serve as a fundamental unit.

A second sense of unit involves the definition of responses, and is reflected by the question of "what is learned?". In a paper that has become so well integrated in the way experimental psychologists think about responses that it is rarely cited, Skinner (1935) discussed the matter of defining responses (and the associated one of defining stimuli). Unit now is not considered as a building block, but refers to the definition of the response. Skinner proposed that a response unit was the generic class of behavior that showed orderly effects of an experimental manipulation. A fundamental unit is what is left when the irrelevant properties (those whose removal has no effect on orderliness) have been stripped away. This approach has led to the widely accepted strategy of defining as the same response any form of behavior that has the same effect on the environment, even though Skinner actually was not proposing such an inclusive definition of functional response units. So, for example, the unit is barpressing no matter whether the rat presses with nose or shoulder, but only if such lack of restriction is necessary to preserve the orderliness of data. The generic definition of stimuli has resulted in considerable research designed to determine the precise feature controlling behavior, but to my knowledge generic responses have not generated equal interest. Equivalent research on response units would require either detailed post hoc analyses to determine which value of which dimension could or could not be subtracted without disturbing the data, or else would entail first providing a reinforcing event following any behavior that had a certain effect on the environment, and then progressively restricting how the response could be executed in order to continue resulting in the reinforcer. Any restriction that changes the behavior means that the restricted property enters into the definition of the generic class, and whatever restrictions had no effect would be considered as involving properties irrelevant to the unit. In other words, differential reinforcement with respect to a dimension of behavior is the necessary operation for defining response units.

A related approach uses differential reinforcement to determine whether a feature of behavior can properly be called a response. If a property of behavior can be found that only could belong to a certain response and then that property can be controlled by differential reinforcement, the result would provide evidence that the response actually does exist as a unit. Sixteen years ago I became interested in determining whether extended sequences of behavior had unitary properties. Research had shown that whether a schedule of reinforcement was applied to a single response or to the entire sequence of responses established by some other schedule the effects were similar (Kelleher, 1966). These data implied that schedule-controlled sequences had the characteristics of individual responses. It seemed to me that added evidence for unitary sequences would be obtained if a property belonging only to the sequence could be controlled by differential reinforcement. For example, the duration of a 30-response sequence is a property that belongs only to the entire sequence and not to the individual responses. Experiments were conducted in which the time taken to begin and complete an entire fixed ratio had to meet a duration requirement. Not only did the sequence durations produced by the pigeons change in accordance with specific temporal requirements, but the most orderly effects occurred with respect to overall sequence duration rather than with respect to any more restricted aspect of the behavior (Zeiler, 1970, 1972). Here was temporal differentiation being used to analyze the nature of response units.

This research led to an interest in the generality of effects produced by temporal differentiation schedules. Generality is the problem of determining whether the laws relating to one response describe other responses as well. The "biological boundaries" literature argued that learning mechanisms were specialized and situationally determined rather than general across responses, but it later became evident that apparently special cases can be understood without reference to specialized mechanisms (Shettleworth, 1983). The temporal differentiation schedule readily lent itself to analysis of the generality of principles over a range of responses and species. Similar experimental paradigms have been used with different animals and a variety of responses, and the results are amenable to precise quantitative analysis. What better way to assess generality?

However, it is not difficult to look at temporal differentiation schedules in another way. All of these schedules require an animal to conform to a temporal requirement, and it seems natural to think of the task as involving time estimation. As soon as that occurs the response unit emphasis disappears or at least becomes secondary in favor of trying to describe properties of the time estimation process. Now the durations emitted by the animal under particular duration requirements become interpreted not as characteristics of the response, but rather as measures of the animal's perception of time. Variability in emitted durations is viewed readily as a measure of sensitivity to time intervals. What this means, then, is that temporal differentiation schedules become psychophysical procedures for studying the properties of timing. The study of response units becomes the analysis of time estimation.

From Responses to Psychophysics

Temporal differentiation schedules provide a good example of the dependence of data on theory. When differentiation schedules first were studied in detail (Skinner, 1938), they were seen as intimately related to the shaping of new behavior. Differential reinforcement could be used to mold behavior in a chosen way, and the effects were analyzed in terms of the joint roles of reinforcement and extinction in determining response characteristics. Reinforcement stereotyped behavior; extinction produced the variability necessary to generate novel responses. Skinner used differentiation as part of his argument for a basic difference between respondent and operant behavior: Response characteristics such as intensity and duration are measures of reflex strength in respondent behavior, but they are products of differential reinforcement in operant behavior. Response rate measures the strength of operant conditioning; response characteristics are part of what has been conditioned.

The importance of differentiation was enhanced with the development of IRT theory. This began with Anger (1956), was further developed by Morse (1966), and then by Shimp (1975). The central idea was that the particular IRTs that were reinforced were responsible for much schedule-controlled behavior. A great deal of research studied how differential reinforcement of IRTs shaped behavior. Extremely sophisticated use of differentiation in this way appeared with the development of percentile schedules (Platt, 1973), which provided an exquisite automated technique for the precise shaping of behavior. Percentile schedules consider some experimenter-specified characteristic of each response relative to the distribution of this characteristic over the last n responses, and deliver the reinforcer only when the current response falls in a certain segment of this distribution. These experimental arrangements showed the power and the limits of differential reinforcement.

Then, in the early 1970s, a new trend developed. Temporal differentiation schedules started being seen as a form of psychophysical procedure. This began with Catania (1970), who entitled his paper: "Reinforcement Schedules and Psychophysical Judgments: A Study of Some Temporal Properties of Behavior," and was soon followed by Platt, Kuch, and Bitgood (1973), with "Rats' Lever-Press Duration As Psychophysical Judgment of Time." The emerging view was that temporal differentiation provided a way of scaling duration with animal subjects. It was not long before the data were being used to describe the time sense and the internal clock (e.g., Church, 1978; Gibbon, 1977). The central issues now were seen as the nature of the internal representation of time and the validity of Weber's law. With some reservations (cf. Platt, 1979), the shift from schedule analysis and response characteristics to timing was complete.

TEMPORAL PSYCHOPHYSICS

According to the psychophysical approach, temporal differentiation schedules are one of several techniques for studying sensitivity to duration. These techniques fall into two general categories that differ with respect to whether the subject must evaluate the duration of an event presented by the experimenter, or whether the subject must emit behavior having some duration. In the first case, the duration is a stimulus under precise experimenter control. Just as an experimenter could give food for a response after presentation of one color and for a different response (or not at all) after presentation of another, the experimenter can give food for a response after presentation of one duration and for a different response (or not at all) after another. The duration of an event can be used as a stimulus, and one can determine whether or not it controls subsequent behavior. This type of arrangement is referred to as a *temporal discrimination schedule* or as a *stimulus timing procedure*.

In the second case, the experimenter does not control the critical duration directly, but only can provide different consequences depending on what duration the animal emits. So, food delivery might require that the animal depress a lever for at least 10 sec or wait 20 sec before responding. This type of arrangement is a *temporal differentiation schedule* or a *response timing procedure.*

Catania (1970) apparently was the first to point out the distinction, and he also showed the need to separate procedure from theory. Temporal discrimination or differentiation can be used to refer to an underlying process (it is even more natural to do so with stimulus and response timing), and then can be used to explain the results obtained with either procedure. For example, it might be asserted that animals are timing some unobservable aspect of their behavior when the experimenter requires them to judge the duration of an event. Or another kind of differentiation could be mediating behavior. This, then, is a differentiation account of performance in a discrimination schedule. Or, in a differentiation schedule, the animal might use elapsed time since the last bar press as a stimulus to control when the next bar press is emitted; this is a discrimination account of behavior in a differentiation schedule. Approaches to these procedures from a psychophysical perspective are likely to relate the effects of either procedure to inferred stimuli and to an underlying time sense. Because behavioral analyses of sensory systems are intimately related to familiar stimuli (e.g., activity in visual or auditory systems correlates very well with obvious external events), it is easy to infer that sensitivity to anything must involve a stimulus dimension. Yet, with respect to duration, no one as yet has identified a receptor system that is equivalent to any of those involving the senses, nor can it be shown that organisms even are sensitive to elapsed time in and of itself. As of now, process terminology has proven more confusing than useful and has provided little more than an exercise in verbal behavior.

Certain operant conditioning arrangements that display sensitivity to time do not qualify as either discrimination or differentiation schedules, because reinforcer delivery requires neither control by duration as an antecedent event nor as a property of behavior. A good example is performance under fixed-interval (FI) schedules. The reinforcer occurs only after a certain time period has elapsed, and behavior changes over the course of that period. Yet reinforcer delivery requires no control by time at all. The behavior could represent the time course of an arousal process (Killeen, 1979) rather than direct temporal control by duration operating either as a stimulus or as a functional dimension of a response.

TEMPORAL DIFFERENTIATION SCHEDULES

Temporal differentiation procedures are schedules of reinforcement that provide differential consequences with respect to a temporal property of behavior. Control of behavior occurs when the duration of the specified response changes with alterations in the temporal specification. They are procedures for studying the direct effects of temporal criteria on behavior.

Psychophysical Methods

As Platt (1979) has pointed out, it has proven tempting to consider temporal differentiation schedules as techniques for analyzing how animals scale time. Succumbing to this temptation means that reinforcement schedules become psychophysical procedures suitable for showing how psychological time or time estimation (the duration emitted) relates to physical time (the duration required for the delivery of a reinforcer). A potential commonality of effects in differentiation and psychophysical methods involving duration first was noted by Catania (1970), and, before long, researchers seemed to be treating them as identical. It should be noted, however, that differentiation schedules operationally are not the same as any standard psychophysical procedure, and if they are psychophysics at all, they are a unique method. Allan's (1979) list of methods used to study time perception shows the differences. The main division between procedures involves the distinction between duration scaling and duration discrimination methods. Discrimination includes the *method of comparison* (two durations occur sequentially, and the subject must indicate which was the standard); the *method of single stimulus* (one of two durations occurs, and the subject indicates whether it was the longer or shorter value); the *many-to-few version of single stimulus* (the total number of stimulus values is more than two, but one is presented on each trial and the subject indicates whether it was part of the longer or the shorter set); and the *identification method* (the number of stimuli and number of response alternatives are increased). None of these resemble the differentiation procedures employed with animals.

Duration scaling includes *verbal estimation* (the subject gives a verbal estimate in temporal units of the duration of a preceding event); *magnitude estimation* (the subject assigns a number rather than a temporal unit to the duration of the event); *category rating* (like magnitude estimation, except that the numbers are chosen from a scale determined by the experimenter); *production* (the subject produces a duration stated verbally by the experimenter); *ratio-setting* (the experimenter presents a reference interval, and the subject then generates an interval that is some judged proportion of the reference; if the proportion is 1.0, the procedure is reproduction; if it is less than 1.0, it is fractionation; if it is greater than 1.0, it is multiplication); and *synchronization* (the subject responds in synchrony with an event). Differentiation procedures resemble production, ratio-setting, and synchronization in that the dependent variable is the duration of a response. One difference is that the three standard timing procedures involve two stages, the first being presentation of a reference duration (presented verbally or displayed), and the second is occurrence of the timed response. Differentiation, in contrast, has no equivalent first stage: The subject generates a duration, and the experimenter arranges a consequence. Also, in studies of timing by humans, the subject usually is instructed to attend to the reference duration, but for animals no explicit instructions are possible. One might argue that the reinforcement contingencies serve as instructions, but even should that be so (how is one to know?), certainly the subject is not being instructed as to what duration is relevant. Therefore, differentiation schedules should be viewed with caution as direct scaling procedures, for even if they do involve time estimation, it is not obvious what time is being estimated. Similar ambiguity exists with respect to temporal discrimination procedures applied to animals.

The temporal differentiation procedure, then, involves a schedule of reinforcement applied to a temporally-defined response unit. The empirical issue is to describe the effects of these schedules, and the theoretical goal is to integrate the data in order to arrive at a law of temporal differentiation.

Temporal Differentiation: The Basic Data

Temporal differentiation schedules have been applied to a number of different response units and to several species. The most widely studied version has been the differential-reinforcement-of-low-rate (DRL) schedule, in which a reinforcer is given only when the subject produces an interresponse time (IRT) that exceeds the value specified by the experimenter. Other differentiation procedures have required that IRTs be shorter than a specified value, must fall between lower and upper limits, or have involved features of behavior other than IRTs. All have in common that a temporal property of behavior must meet a specification in order for a positive consequence to occur or for an aversive event to be avoided.

Although many experiments have involved temporal differentiation, present attention will be devoted only to those in which emitted duration must exceed a specified minimum, the consequence was a positive reinforcer, and the minimum duration requirement was varied parametrically so as to permit quantitative assessment of the function relating emitted to required duration. The response units considered range from individual responses to extended sequences of behavior.

Figure 1 shows the effects of these differentiation schedules. One experiment (Zeiler, Davis, & DeCasper, 1980) involved key-peck duration in pigeons, the second (Platt, Kuch, & Bitgood, 1973, Experiment 2) studied bar-press duration in rats, the third (Malott & Cumming, 1964) involved IRTs in pigeons, the fourth (Catania, 1970) studied response latency in pigeons, the fifth (DeCasper & Zeiler, 1977) involved the time from the first to thirtieth response in pigeons, and the sixth (DeCasper & Zeiler, 1974) entailed the time taken by pigeons to begin and complete a 30-response sequence. The data are

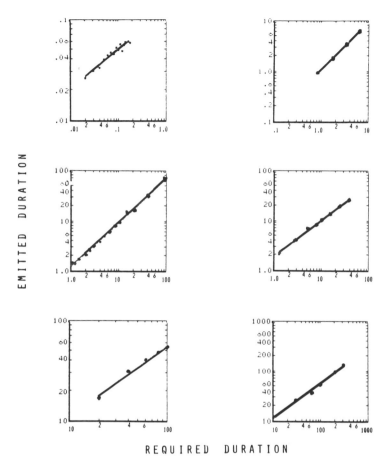

Fig. 1. Mean response duration in representative temporal differentiation experiments. Upper left: Zeiler, Davis, & DeCasper (1980); upper right: Platt, Kuch, & Bitgood (1973, Exper. 2); middle left: Malott & Cumming (1964); middle right: Catania (1970); lower left: DeCasper & Zeiler (1977); lower right: DeCasper & Zeiler (1974, Exper. 2). Diagonal lines are the best fitting power functions.

log-log plots of the mean emitted durations as functions of the minimum durations required for food delivery. All of the data yielded linearity on the double log scales and fractional-exponent power functions relating the dependent to the independent variables. The power function is: $T=kt^n$, where T is emitted duration, t is the duration requirement, and k and n (the coefficient and exponent of the function respectively) are the best-fitting parameters determined by the curve-fitting program.

Allan (1979) showed the danger of concluding that linear functions would not describe data well if power function exponents differed from 1.0. She reanalyzed 32 power functions, 29 of which had exponents less than 1.0 (median=.77), and found that for 23 of the 32, a simple linear function described the data more accurately. In contrast, analysis of the parametric differentiation data for individual animal subjects showed that all had fractional-exponent power functions, and that for 21 of the 33 the power function described more of the variance than did the linear. All these comparisons (both for humans and infrahumans) should be approached with caution, however. Power functions force the dependent variable through 0, which may or may not be reasonable. After all, requiring that emitted duration exceed 0 sec will maintain behavior very well, and the behavior certainly will have a nonzero duration. But does a 0-sec requirement really belong on the same continuum as do requirements that actually make contact with behavior? Yet, when the linear function has a positive intercept that predicts a nonzero duration at a 0-sec requirement, does that have any meaning when it does not actually correspond with what happens when such a requirement is imposed? A 0-sec requirement means that emitted duration must exceed 0 sec to be followed by the reinforcer, so it is the same as no requirement at all. The intercept obtained when a linear function is fit to a range of requirements that make contact with behavior has never to my knowledge corresponded with the duration emitted in the absence of a requirement. Or, when linear are superior to power fits as the power exponent nears 1.0, does that mean anything more than that the linear function has what amounts to an extra free parameter (the intercept)? No ready answer is apparent. Goodness of fit just is not a very good way of choosing between functions. In addition, differences in percent variance accounted for by the two functions usually are very small.

Perhaps the only justification for preferring one type of function to another is a viable theoretical rationale. Power functions at least have the theoretical legitimacy derived from

Stevens' (1975) power law, whereas linear functions had little apparent theoretical rationale prior to Gibbon's (1977) scalar expectancy theory. But this too can be misleading, because justification in terms of these theories virtually assures that temporal control will be considered as a psychophysical sensory phenomenon. One need only review the literature on differentiation in animals pre- and post-Catania's (1970) initial analysis in terms of power functions to see the shift from schedule analysis to a psychophysical conceptual framework. Temporal differentiation procedures no longer were viewed as schedules but rather as techniques for scaling durations, largely because the data fit a power function analysis.

In any event, all of the experiments reported since Catania's (1970) chapter reported power functions, thereby allowing quantitative comparisons of their results. DeCasper and Zeiler (1974) were impressed by the small range found in the power function coefficients and exponents across the different experiments, and they suggested that there might be one true set of values. It was not long before they changed their minds. The change began when DeCasper (1974) noticed that the coefficients (k) and exponents (n) were inversely related such that $\log k + n = 1.0$ (see Platt, 1979, Figure 1.5). Even more important was the discovery that k and n were related to an observable property of behavior. The initial procedure of the various experiments usually involved a baseline condition involving continuous reinforcement with no temporal requirement (nondifferential reinforcement with respect to duration). For example, rats received food following each bar-press or pigeons obtained food after each sequence of 30 responses. The durations of these response units later were to become critical, but they were irrelevant during the baseline phases. However, the response units did have durations, and these durations turned out to be related to the values of k and n obtained following the subsequent differentiation schedules.

The baseline response duration came to be viewed as the natural duration of the unit and was referred to as the *base duration*. DeCasper and Zeiler (1977) found that the best-fitting function relating the coefficient k to base duration d across experiments was the power function: $k = 1.6\,d^{.18}$, and that relating the exponent n to d was the log function, $n = .82 - .05\ln d$. (This is a conversion of the relation given in the original paper in common logs to natural logs.) These functions are depicted in Figure 2. Substituting these equations into the simple power function, $T = k\,t^n$, gave the new equation:

$$T = 1.6\,d^{.18}\,t^{.82 - .05\ln d}$$

The equation proved capable not only of dealing with the data from which it was derived, but Figure 3 shows how well it predicted the results of a later experiment involving a novel arrangement. Note that the equation explains behavior in temporal differentiation schedules without any curve-fitting parameters. The term T on the left side is the observed dependent variable (mean emitted duration of the response unit). Of the terms on the right side, one is observed directly in advance (d is the mean response duration occurring in the absence of temporal criteria), a second is the experimenter-specified independent variable (t is the minimum

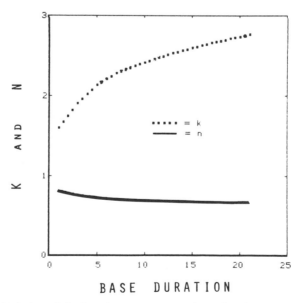

Fig. 2. Relation of the k and n parameters to base duration.

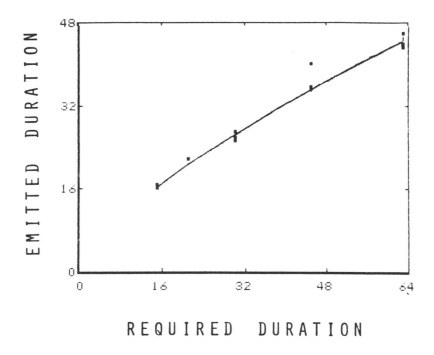

Fig. 3. Representative data from Zeiler (1983). The curve shows the durations predicted by the temporal differentiation equation.

duration required for food delivery), and all of the others are numerical constants. All that need be known to predict the effects of a specific duration requirement imposed on any conditionable response unit is the base duration of the unit for the particular subject. The equation is referred to as the *temporal differentiation equation.*

The Temporal Differentiation Equation and Response Units

The temporal differentiation equation implies that any chosen response unit can serve to illustrate the effects of duration differentiation schedules. Given that the equation applies equally well to bar-press durations, IRTs, individual response latencies, to various aspects of behavior sequences, and has been of heuristic value in understanding the operation of other variables in differentiation schedules (Zeiler, 1983), it seems to be a principle of some generality. Here is a case of a potential law of behavior, one that is independent of response unit, species, and individuals. All individual differences are reduced to variation in base duration, which operates as described by the equation. Such theoretical dilemmas as why DRL schedules produce different mean IRTs depending on the nature of the response (Hemmes, 1975) now can be understood as the inevitable consequence of response units having substantially different base durations. What appeared to be a biological constraint on a principle of behavior turns out to be the effect of different levels of a relevant variable.

Limitations on the Temporal Differentiation Equation

The temporal differentiation equation poses something of a dilemma. On the one hand, it has a precise predictive power that does not occur very often in psychology; on the other hand, it has no rational basis. Is it something that should simply be taken at face value, or is it something that itself demands explanation? If it in fact should perfectly describe and predict behavior, is it really of much interest given its paucity of psychological significance? It is not a new psychophysical law, because it offers nothing about the relation between physical and experienced events; it does not integrate temporal differentiation schedules with other research areas; it has no apparent implications beyond temporal differentiation schedules. It is at best an empirical generalization derived from an exercise in curve fitting. In short, the apparently powerful temporal differentiation equation seems to lead nowhere beyond the experimental situation that generated it. Although an alternative version which substitutes reinforced duration for the time requirement in the equation offers the advantage of coping with why adding upper limits to the duration requirement changes behavior (Zeiler, 1983), the alternative shares the other shortcomings of the original version.

A new perspective on the equation seems to offer more fruitful possibilities. It could be that the particular numerical constants and form of the equation really have no intrinsic meaning or significance, but actually only provide a shorthand approximation of what is going on. The equation indicates that time requirements interact with base duration to determine behavior. Perhaps the constants are as they are only because of the way the equation was derived and have no implications in and of themselves. Rather they are just a way of getting at the fact that behavior represents the lawful interaction between what the experimenter requires (the time requirement) and what the subject brings into the situation (base duration).

One possibility is that the subject is oscillating between presence and absence of temporal control. When such control is present, emitted duration is appropriate to required duration (whatever "appropriate" may mean, a question to be addressed shortly); when temporal control is absent, the subject produces durations corresponding to base duration. The combination of these two different forms of behavior, each occurring with some probability, is what yields mean emitted duration. Perhaps that is why d must appear twice, once as a multiplier and once as part of an exponent. Consideration of another aspect of performance - variability - fits with the notion that behavior is of two types.

Variability

Temporal differentiation schedules produce substantial variability in emitted response duration. As a result, researchers always have been careful to indicate that means or medians were not representative of individual durations. The relevant information was conveyed by providing either probability or conditional probability distributions, depending on which better suited the immediate purposes of the research. Examples of probability distributions appear in Figure 4.

The distributions of Figure 4 were chosen to illustrate the variety found in different experiments. It is not unusual to obtain the bimodality appearing in the first and third panels. In these cases, the left mode typically changes little over the range of duration requirements, but the right mode changes in the same direction as does the requirement. These data suggest two

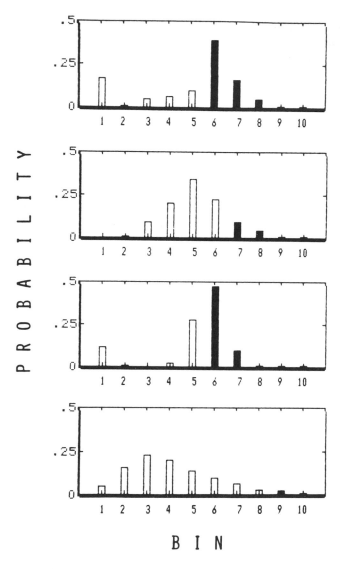

Fig. 4. Probability distributions of emitted durations. From top to bottom: Malott & Cumming (1964), 5-sec IRT requirement; DeCasper & Zeiler (1974, Exper. 1), 50-sec requirement on total time taken to begin and complete an FR 30 sequence; Kuch (1974), 2-sec requirement on bar-press duration with 2.5-sec upper bound; DeCasper & Zeiler (1977), 80-sec requirement on time to first response of a fixed-ratio sequence. Unfilled bars show durations not followed by food delivery; filled bars show durations followed by food delivery.

different sources of control over behavior, one temporal and the other by base duration. The other two distributions show the unimodality that sometimes occurs. Such distributions usually reveal different degrees of skewness depending on the particular duration requirement. All of the panels show how infrequently durations appropriate for reinforcer delivery can be emitted. It is common to find that the likelihood of emitting a reinforceable duration decreases with progressively longer requirements, yet responding is maintained as long as only a few reinforcers occur. Even under such conditions, it is the specific duration required for reinforcement rather than reinforcer density that controls behavior (DeCasper, & Zeiler, 1974, 1977).

After Catania's (1970) paper, researchers became interested in quantitative measures of variability. Catania had reported that the standard deviation of response durations divided by the mean was approximately constant over the full range of requirements. As the psychophysical perspective on temporal differentiation gained momentum, this statistic (the coefficient of variation) assumed increasing importance. The reason is that psychophysicists have treated the standard deviation as a convenient measure of sensitivity to the stimulus dimension under consideration: The smaller the standard deviation, the more sensitive is the subject to the dimension. This, in turn, lends theoretical significance to the coefficient of variation. Constancy in the coefficient across a range of conditions means that sensitivity is constant when expressed in relative terms, and Weber's law thereby is supported. Virtually all of the papers involving parametric manipulation of duration requirements in temporal differentiation schedules since 1970 have claimed that Weber's law fits the data, and an influential theory (Gibbon, 1977) has used its success in deducing Weber's law as one of its pillars of support.

More careful examination of the data, however, shows that Weber's law rarely holds for differentiation schedules. An alternative method of analysis is to plot standard deviations as a function of the means on linear coordinates (Platt, 1979). If Weber's law holds, the result will be a straight line with zero intercept and a slope representing the Weber fraction. (The slope would correspond to the coefficient of variation.) Determination of such functions for 31 individual animals showed that a linear function accounted for a higher percent of variance than did a power fit in 19 cases, but usually the intercept deviated noticeably from zero (it was greater than 15 sec in one case and was -14.8 sec in another; most of the time, it was negative). A nonzero intercept makes no sense: what could it possibly signify to have a standard deviation when the mean is 0.0? A negative standard deviation is totally bizarre. Given these considerations, a power function seems more viable in that it forces the value on the y-axis to be 0.0 when the x-axis value is 0.0. Now Weber's law requires an exponent of 1.0 (linearity), and the coefficient is the Weber constant (the coefficient of variation).

Figure 5 shows the plot of standard deviations against means and of coefficient of variation against means for three animals in different experiments. In every case visual inspection of the standard deviation curves suggests positive acceleration with an origin quite close to 0.0. Fits reveal that linear functions have negative intercepts, whereas power functions have exponents larger than 1.0. In contrast, visual inspection of the corresponding coefficient of variation plot for the top-most subject suggests random variation around a constant value. At the visual level only the bottom-most subject suggests identical conclusions no matter which measure is considered.

When considered in terms of the relation between standard deviations and means, much of the differentiation data obtained with animals show the decreasing sensitivity implied by these representative curves. As first emphasized by Cantor and Wilson (1981), the results of differentiation experiments do not support Weber's law. This disconfirmation is not peculiar to nonhuman subjects. Allan's (1979) review of temporal psychophysics in humans indicates that the simple version of Weber's law rarely holds. The more common result for very short time intervals is a decreasing coefficient of variation with either changing standard deviations, or, occasionally, constant standard deviations (determinacy). Weber's law can explain the

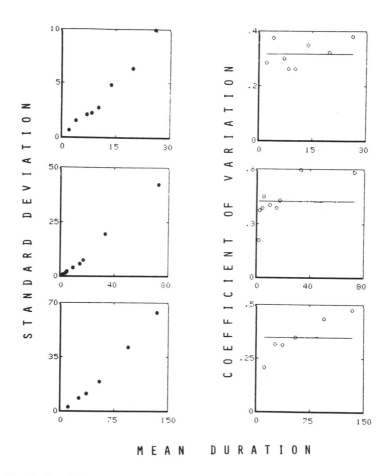

Fig. 5. Sensitivity. Left column is standard deviations plotted against means; right column is coefficients of variation plotted against means. The horizontal lines on the coefficient of variation graphs are the mean coefficients. From top to bottom: Catania (1970); Malott & Cumming (1964); DeCasper & Zeiler (1974).

decreasing coefficient with the assumption that nontemporal factors contribute a constant additional source of variance to the data (Getty, 1975). No extant version of Weber's law explains the increasing coefficient typically found with humans dealing with durations of 2 sec or longer in standard temporal psychophysical tasks (Getty, 1975) or with nonhumans in differentiation experiments. Experiments recently completed in collaboration with Gregory Scott using differentiation schedules with humans found that the exponents relating standard deviations to means resembled those found with nonhumans. Whether temporal discrimination data obtained with animals, which now are the only source of support of Weber's law, can survive critical reexamination has yet to be determined. One must view with skepticism any theory of temporal control that requires data supporting Weber's law.

If the bimodal probability distributions often found with temporal differentiation schedules could be viewed as the general case, the left mode approximates base duration and the right mode seems to track the duration requirement. This, then, supports the notion that temporal differentiation arrangements generate two types of behavior. If that is the case, an increasing coefficient of variation would be expected as the duration requirements are raised: The left part of the distribution remains constant, while the right part moves progressively further away, thereby increasing the standard deviation more rapidly than the mean. Weber's law would be expected to hold only with respect to the right segment (Zeiler, in press). In short, the two types of behavior implied by the temporal differentiation equation are also implied by the coefficients of variation. Further elaboration of this hypothesis into a model of temporal differentiation schedule performance will not be attempted here. A preliminary effort (Zeiler, 1981) had some success, but several problems show that it cannot be the right answer in the exact form that it was proposed. Adequate development requires the ability to specify exactly what is going on when behavior is under temporal control. Base duration behavior is easy to understand as the return to undifferentiated duration following from occasional lapse of temporal control, but now we need a clue as to what is happening when temporal control is active.

THE CONTROLLING VARIABLE IN
TEMPORAL CONTROL

A continuing puzzle faced by proponents of the psychophysical approach to temporal differentiation is that of understanding exactly what is being timed. The experimenter imposes a minimum duration requirement for a response to be followed by food, and responding changes in the appropriate direction. Does that mean that the animal is timing the requirement? Not likely, in that the only information given the animal about the relevance of response duration must stem from experiences of reinforcement and nonreinforcement. It seems more reasonable to assume that the animal abstracts the standard duration from the reinforcement history and is not directly sensitive to the requirement. Gibbon (1977) asserted that the fractional-exponent power relation between emitted duration and the time requirement was not an accurate representation of the correlation between the physical standard and experienced duration. The proper relation was the more linear one between emitted duration and mean reinforced duration.

In fact, the exponent of the reinforced-emitted power function approached 1.0 only for rats, which had exponents greater than .9 when the duration requirement was taken as the standard. With pigeons, where the original exponents were usually between .6 and .8 (and could go below .5), the exponent produced by considering reinforced duration still was below .9, and power fits continued to be better than linear. Gibbon's suggestion that the cause of the deviation with pigeons might be autoshaped keypecks is plausible in some cases, but it does not seem tenable when the response unit was a 30-response sequence. Yet the exponent is no closer to 1.0 for those experiments than for the others.

From Physical To Psychological Time And Vice Versa: A Psychophysical Puzzle

Before long researchers came to realize that the data would be puzzling even if the exponents were 1.0 or if linear functions fit better than power, as long as emitted duration did not match that of the standard. For temporal differentiation schedules to be direct scaling procedures, they must be tracking the relation between physical and psychological duration. Two durations, one past and one present, are critical, because the duration of some past event is controlling the duration of current behavior.

Whatever scaling transformation applies to previous durations should also describe current ones. How, then, could there be asymmetry between input and output durations?

Consider the following analogy (suggested to me by Ulric Neisser). Perhaps El Greco suffered from defective eyesight so that he actually saw people as elongated and simply was drawing them as they looked to him. Impossible. The picture could not then look to him like the actual person unless it was rendered so as to look to the rest of us like a normal person. The same is true of duration: Distortions in input must be balanced by distortions in output, so input and output must match exactly unless other processes are interfering. Either differentiation schedules are irrelevant to scaling, or we still are ignorant about the physical duration that is being scaled. Platt (1979) opted for the first of these alternatives, and he later was to offer the plea that they still were of interest as schedules even if they were irrelevant to an understanding of timing (Platt, 1984)! Psychophysics was becoming schedules once again!

The need to consider base duration is further evidence that emitted duration is more than the observable index of an underlying time sense. A possible solution, alluded to earlier, is to recognize that only some of the responses are under temporal control, so that mean emitted duration is not an appropriate measure of anything. If the animal only is timing some responses, only those should be used to study the correspondence between emitted duration and the standard. Unfortunately, however, this strategy does not pay off. Even when attention is restricted to the part of the duration distributions that are characterized by the second mode, behavior matches neither the time requirement nor mean reinforced duration.

The solution to the puzzle is that we are dealing with schedules of reinforcement and not with some version of the psychophysical procedures used with humans. Perhaps it is incorrect to view schedules as equivalent to sets of instructions used to inform the animals as to what the experimenter wants it to do. A focus on adaptation mechanisms rather than on analogies to sensory processes provides a clue about the source of temporal control.

OPTIMAL FORAGING THEORY
AND TEMPORAL CONTROL

The reasons for studying behavior in the laboratory are as many as there are experimenters. Some investigators just are intrigued with behavior and derive an almost aesthetic pleasure from imposing manipulations that mold behavior in an orderly predictable way. Others have a more theoretical interest. Some use laboratory behavior to model nonlaboratory situations. Few are interested in key pecks or bar presses or rats or pigeons for their own sake. These responses are taken as convenient representatives of behavior that are sensitive to manipulations, and these species hopefully are representative of living organisms in general at some level. The psychologist interested in operant behavior often is concerned with the way patterns of responses become organized in time and are sensitive to the contingencies of reinforcement. So, for example, food is taken as representative of the class of events and effects that define a reinforcing stimulus, and the results of the experiment presumably have general implications for the way contingencies shape and maintain behavior.

Temporal differentiation research fits comfortably within this conceptual orientation. Under the initial emphasis on response properties, temporal differentiation schedules had implications for schedule control in general, particularly with respect to the features of behavior operated on by reinforcement to produce a certain response rate. The later view of differentiation as a psychophysical method for studying timing by animals substituted the use of reinforcement as instructions for an interest in the dynamics of reinforcement itself.

Both of these views share a common failing, namely that either orientation takes behavior out of its biological context and fails to recognize what our experimental situations truly represent for the animal. Although students of conditioning hasten to claim that they are studying processes of adaptation, we tend not to treat the behavior as the outcome of environmental pressures imposed on a living animal. Instead, the interest usually is on the presumed psychological processes involved in learning or steady-state performance. The processes are viewed as having evolved, but we do not usually consider the behavior occurring in an experiment in terms of adaptation.

The research conducted by George Collier (1983) has played an important part in reinstating experimental psychology in evolutionary biology. The first thing to realize is that our experiments invariably involve commodities that are essential to survival, in fact they commonly involve food. Animals in the wild spend much of their time in food-oriented behavior: They search for, find, store, and ingest food during large portions of each day. The next point is that although we bring animals into laboratory environments that do not resemble their natural habitats, we then put them into situations that require them to perform certain activities in order to obtain food. The laboratory setting may be totally unlike the field, but it is where the animals spend much of their lives. In a sense, the laboratory has become their natural habitat. Furthermore, the behavior we study is food oriented, just as is most behavior in the field. Collier has argued persuasively that what we really are studying in the conditioning laboratory is foraging behavior: Schedule requirements can be viewed as models of environmental demands and constraints on fruitful foraging. He has shown that laboratory analysis can be used to study the full range of components of the feeding sequence, and at the same time has demonstrated the plausibility of viewing operant behavior of laboratory animals as foraging.

Food getting is crucial for survival, so it seems reasonable to assume that adaptive foraging mechanisms have evolved. In the past several years, a few experimental psychologists have joined with students of animal behavior in studying behavior from the perspective of optimal foraging theory (cf. Krebs, 1978). The key assumption of optimal foraging is that adaptation to the demands of the environment is perfect, that "natural selection acts as a maximizing process and penalizes individuals deviating from the optimal design for their environment" (Krebs, Houston, & Charnov, 1981, p. 4). The theory comes down to the view that in any foraging situation behavior is optimal with respect to some biologically significant process. The trick, of course, is to know exactly what it is that is being maximized, and then to determine whether the behavior truly is optimal with respect to that process. In a more colloquial sense, optimal foraging theory says that animals are always doing whatever is necessary to get the most out of a situation, and the task of the researcher is to discover what "most" refers to.

The approach would not be compelling if it rested at this verbal level, so it is exciting to find that optimal foraging theory goes well beyond such vague evolutionary pronouncements. The theorist must hazard a guess about what is being maximized, and then must derive the equation that relates the specific environmental demands and the dimensions of behavior to that property. By then differentiating the property with respect to the behavior, setting the derivative equal to zero, and then solving for the behavior, the optimal behavior can be found either analytically or through iterative routines. So, for example, Pulliam (1981) showed that maximum density of food availability occurs in concurrent VI VI schedules if the animal allocates responses among alternatives in the same proportion as reinforcers are allocated. The matching law turns out to be deducible from optimal foraging theory.

The application of optimal foraging to temporal differentiation leads to the view that the behavior is perfectly adaptive, but it raises the problem of specifying what the animal is maximizing. At first glance, the behavior seems glaringly nonoptimal, because it is not what it could be were the animal to be maximizing the availability of food. All the animal need do to maximize is to wait until just after the criterion duration has elapsed, and yet it does not do so after hundreds of sessions of exposure to the same requirement. The fractional-exponent power relation between emitted and required duration means that they are waiting too long with short requirements and not long enough with longer ones. In fact, with very long requirements, they may get food as infrequently as twice per week. This hardly seems optimal when the time requirement is 5 minutes.

Consideration of a novel form of duration differentiation schedule provides a good starting place for understanding how the behavior really is optimal. One form of the ratio-setting procedure used in temporal psychophysics is known as bisection, because the subject is asked to produce a duration that is one half that of the standard. Students of animal behavior who have taken the psychophysical approach to temporal discrimination and temporal differentiation schedules have devised ingenious procedures intended to study bisection of duration by rats and pigeons. The discrimination version has involved presenting animals with two or more durations. If two durations are used (Church & Deluty, 1977), the animal gets food for responding to one lever after the short duration stimulus and to the other lever after the long duration stimulus. Then, intermediate probe durations are introduced to determine the value that the animal is equally likely to classify as long and short. That is taken to be the duration that the animal views as lying halfway between the training values. Another discrimination version of bisection involves ten durations (Stubbs, 1968). One response yields food following the five shortest durations. A different response does so after the five longest. This procedure requires no probes, but allows plotting psychometric functions showing the probability of occurrence of one of the responses as a function of stimulus duration. The duration yielding $p = .5$ (usually by interpretation) is taken as the bisection point.

Bisection experiments can involve differentiation schedules rather than discrimination. Variations involve two (Platt & Davis, 1983) or ten (Stubbs, 1980) duration requirements, but all demand that the animal time a response in order to obtain food. For example, in Stubbs' experiment food delivery was correlated with each of ten durations, but it was available at only one of them at any one time. If assigned to one of the five shortest, food was delivered only if the animal pecked the left key; if assigned to one of the five longest, food required pecking the right key. The bisection point was the time at which the pigeons switched their responses from the left to the right key.

Analyses of the data from these four studies suggested that the bisection point corresponded to the geometric mean of the stimulus durations in discrimination and to the geometric mean of the duration requirements in differentiation. This conclusion was drawn because in three of the experiments the geometric mean corresponded more closely to the obtained bisection point than did the arithmetic mean, and in the fourth the geometric mean fit better than did either the arithmetic or the harmonic mean. Some additional data reported by Platt and Davis (1983) indicated that the geometric mean rule broke down if the durations were too widely separated. It has been pointed out, however, that the geometric mean was only a reasonable description of Church and Deluty's (1977) results. Zeiler (1985) showed that a more sensitive analysis of these data is obtained by considering them in terms of the power mean. Each duration is raised to the same power (a), and then the average of these values is determined. The exponent a is iterated until the average taken to the $1/a$ power corresponds with the bisection point obtained in the experiment. If the data fit the arithmetic mean, the exponent will be $+1.0$; if they fit the harmonic mean, the exponent will be -1.0; if they fit the geometric mean, the exponent has a very small but nonzero value. Only Church and Deluty's data resulted in an exponent near zero. The other discrimination experiment had a strongly positive exponent, and the two differentiation experiments yielded strongly negative exponents. Thus, the results appear uninterpretable theoretically. Despite the emphasis given to the geometric mean result - Gibbon (1981) and Gibbon and Church (1981) considered the finding to be one of the two definitive ones that an adequate theory must explain - the data are at best conjectural. Bisection at the geometric mean thereby joins the other "definitive finding" - the ubiquity of Weber's law - in being not generally true!

Now look at the experiments differently. A good starting point might be some skepticism as to whether the animals were bisecting duration at all. Does it really seem reasonable to assume that giving them food at different durations was instructing them to judge when elapsed time had reached a midpoint? I suspect not. What seems more likely is that the animals were trying to get as much food as possible out of a complicated situation, in short, that they were foraging optimally.

The optimal foraging theory analysis of the differentiation experiments was conducted by Mark Hoyert. It involved deriving the equation expressing the frequency of food delivery as a function of the time the animals switched their response, given that food delivery had been assigned to only one of the alternatives at a given instant, and recognizing that switching times have inherent variability. The equation allowed determination of the mean switching time that would maximize reinforcer frequency. Additional details of the equation appear in the Appendix. This solution gave the optimal time to switch between response alternatives.

Figure 6 shows that optimal switching time corresponded as closely with Platt and Davis' (1983) data as did the

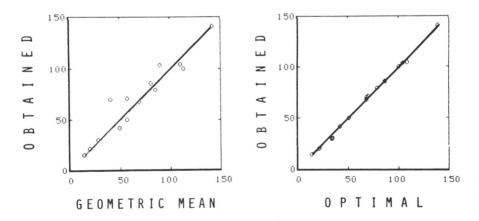

Fig. 6. Time of switching between two fixed intervals as function of the geometric mean of the intervals, and as function of the time predicted from optimal foraging theory. The diagonal lines show matching of switching time to the predictions.

geometric mean in most cases. Most striking was that the conditions that they concluded were beyond the bounds of the geometric mean account also fit the optimality predictions. In most cases, the geometric mean and optimal foraging predicted similar switching times. Most important is that when the predictions diverged substantially, behavior tracked optimality.

If one wished to maintain the psychophysical perspective on differentiation, conformity of behavior to optimal foraging predictions means that emitted time was veridical with respect to the temporal standard. This, of course, renders pointless any attempt to describe the psychophysical function for duration: Veridicality fits any type of function equally well. The problem now is not that differentiation is a poor scaling technique, it is that the scaling is much too precise! Veridicality also resolves the paradox of apparent input-output asymmetry in differentiation: The two match exactly when the physical standard is taken to be optimal duration.

The application of optimal foraging theory to the standard differentiation task remains to be accomplished. It will need to deal with the effects of base duration, so it probably will entail recognition of two kinds of behavior, one under and one not under temporal control. The present analysis suggests that a starting point for understanding temporal control is to consider it as veridical with respect to the optimal foraging theory prediction derived from the assumption that the maximized factor is reinforcer frequency. The variability inherent in temporal control will play an important role in determining the optimal response duration. If this program proves successful (first efforts have yielded encouraging results), a next step would be to try to understand why two types of response - one sensitive to time, the other not - are optimal in situations that produce temporal control. Optimal foraging is a powerful theory: Not only does it relate the experimental analysis of behavior to evolutionary biology, but it could be the heuristic and global integrating principle that at least some of us psychologists have been searching for.

APPENDIX

The optimal foraging analysis of the Platt and Davis (1983) experiment was conducted as follows. It involved the simplifying assumption that the animal began responding on the shorter FI and could make only one switching response per trial. Four possibilities exist on each trial:

(1) *Correct Short.* Food delivery is assigned to the shorter FI, and the animal does not switch from that component before the interval times out. Food delivery occurs.

(2) *Incorrect Short.* Food delivery is assigned to the shorter FI, but the animal switches to the long FI before the short interval times out. No food occurs, and the trial ends after 240 sec.

(3) *Correct Long.* Food delivery is assigned to the longer FI, and the animal switches to that component before the long interval times out. Food delivery occurs.

(4) *Incorrect Long.* Food delivery is assigned to the longer FI, but the animal does not switch to that component before the long interval times out. No food delivery occurs, and the trial ends after 240 sec.

Equations 1-4 yield the time spent at each of these alternatives.

$$\text{Time Correct Short} = x_s p_s S \qquad (1)$$

where x_s is the probability of reinforcer assignment to the short FI, p_s the probability of staying in the short FI until the interval times out with a given mean switching time, and S is the short FI value.

$$\text{Time Incorrect Short} = x_s (1-p_s) C_s \qquad (2)$$

where $1-p_s$ is the probability of switching out of the short FI before the interval elapses, and C_s is the trial length following incorrect short responses (240 sec).

$$\text{Time Correct Long} = x_L p_L L \qquad (3)$$

where x_L is the probability of reinforcer assignment to the long FI, p_L is the probability of switching to the long FI before it elapses with a given mean switching time, and L is the long FI value.

$$\text{Time Incorrect Long} = x_L(1-p_L) C_L \qquad (4)$$

where $1-p_L$ is the probability of not switching to the long FI component before the interval elapses, and C_L is the trial length following incorrect long responses (240 sec).

Equation 5 yields the probability of a correct response:

$$\text{Probability of Correct Responses} = x_s p_s + x_L p_L \qquad (5)$$

The sum of equations 1-4 divided by equation 5 yields mean time to reinforcement (T):

$$T = \frac{x_s p_s S + x_s(1 - p_s)C_s + x_L p_L L + x_L(1 - p_L)C_L}{x_s p_s + x_L p_L} \quad (6)$$

The probabilities of reinforcer assignment to each alternative are determined by the experimenter, and in this study, x_s and x_L both were 0.5.

The probabilities of staying or switching after a particular duration (p_s and p_L) depend on the mean time to switch (t) and the standard deviation of switching times. In the present derivation, the standard deviation was assumed to be a constant proportion of t and this proportion was taken as either .25 or .3, which corresponds with the average coefficient of variation typically found in temporal differentiation experiments with animals. Probabilities were determined from the normal distribution.

The next step was to find the value of t that produced the smallest T (shortest interreinforcer time) for each of the pairs of fixed-interval schedules. This potentially could be done by differentiating T with respect to t, however the result proved too complex to be manageable. Instead, a numerical solution was obtained by iterating t to determine which value would produce the smallest T. This obtained value of t was the optimal switching time.

ACKNOWLEDGMENT

Preparation of this chapter and the research now reported were supported by Grant BNS 83 - 15480 from the National Science Foundation.

REFERENCES

Allan, L. G. (1979). The perception of time. *Perception and Psychophysics*, *26*, 340-354.

Anger, D. (1956). The dependence of interresponse times upon the relative reinforcement of different interresponse times. *Journal of Experimental Psychology*, *52*, 145-161.

Cantor, M. B., & Wilson, J. F. (1981). Temporal uncertainty as an associative metric: Operant simulations of Pavlovian conditioning. *Journal of Experimental Psychology: General*, *110*, 232-268.

Catania, A. C. (1970). Reinforcement schedules and psychophysical judgments: A study of some temporal properties of behavior. In W. N.

Schoenfeld (Ed.), *The theory of reinforcement schedules*. New York: Appleton-Century-Crofts.

Church, R. M. (1978). The internal clock. In S. H. Hulse, H. Fowler, & W. K. Honig (Eds.), *Cognitive aspects of animal behavior*. Hillsdale, NJ: Lawrence Erlbaum Associates.

Church, R.M., & Deluty, M.Z. (1977). Bisection of temporal intervals. *Journal of Experimental Psychology: Animal Behavior Processes, 3*, 216-228.

Collier, G. H. (1983). Life in a closed economy: The ecology of learning and motivation. In M. D. Zeiler, & P. Harzem (Eds.), *Biological factors in learning*. Chichester, NY: Wiley.

DeCasper, A. J. (1974). Selectively differentiating temporal aspects of fixed-ratio sequences. Doctoral dissertation, Emory University.

DeCasper, A. J., & Zeiler, M. D. (1974). Time limits for completing fixed ratios. III. Stimulus variables. *Journal of the Experimental Analysis of Behavior, 22*, 285-300.

DeCasper, A. J., & Zeiler, M. D. (1977). Time limits for completing fixed ratios. IV. Components of the ratio. *Journal of the Experimental Analysis of Behavior, 27*, 235-244.

Getty, D. J. (1975). Discrimination of short temporal intervals: A comparison of two models. *Perception and Psychophysics, 18*, 1-8.

Gibbon, J. (1977). Scalar expectancy theory and Weber's law in animal timing. *Psychological Review, 84*, 279-325.

Gibbon, J. (1981). Two kinds of ambiguity in the study of psychological time. In M. L. Commons, & J. A. Nevin (Eds.), *Quantitative analyses of behavior: Discriminative properties of reinforcement schedules*. Cambridge: Ballinger.

Gibbon, J., & Church, R. M. (1981). Time-left: Linear vs. logarithmic subjective time. *Journal of Experimental Psychology: Animal Behavior Processes, 7*, 87-108.

Hemmes, N. S. (1975). Pigeons' performance under differential reinforcement of low rate schedules depends upon the operant. *Learning and Motivation, 6*, 344-357.

Kelleher, R. T. (1966). Chaining and conditioned reinforcement. In W. K. Honig (Ed.), *Operant behavior: Areas of research and application*. New York: Appleton-Century-Crofts.

Killeen, P. R. (1979). Arousal: Its genesis, modulation, and extinction. In M. D. Zeiler, & P. Harzem (Eds.), *Reinforcement and the organization of behaviour*. Chichester, NY: Wiley.

Krebs, J. R. (1978). Optimal foraging: Decision rules for predators. In J. R. Krebs, & N. B. Davies (Eds.), *Behavioural ecology*. Oxford: Blackwell Scientific Publications.

Krebs, J. R., Houston, A. I., & Charnov, E. L. (1981). Some recent developments in optimal foraging. In A. C. Kamil, & T. D. Sargent (Eds.), *Foraging behavior: Ecological, ethological, and psychological approaches*. New York: Garland.

Kuch, D. O. (1974). Differentiation of press durations with upper and lower limits on reinforced values. *Journal of the Experimental Analysis of Behavior, 22,* 275-283.

Malott, R. W., & Cumming, W. W. (1964). Schedules of interresponse time reinforcement. *Psychological Record, 14,* 211-252.

Morse, W. H. (1966). Intermittent reinforcement. In W. K. Honig (Ed.), *Operant behavior: Areas of research and application.* New York: Appleton-Century-Crofts.

Platt, J. R. (1973). Percentile reinforcement: Paradigms for experimental analysis of response shaping. In G. Bower (Ed.), *The psychology of learning and motivation* (Vol. 7). New York: Academic Press.

Platt, J. R. (1979). Temporal differentiation and the psychophysics of time. In M. D. Zeiler, & P. Harzem (Eds.), *Reinforcement and the organization of behaviour.* Chichester, NY: Wiley.

Platt, J. R. (1984). Motivational and response factors in temporal differentiation. *Annals of the New York Academy of Science, 423,* 200-210.

Platt, J. R., & Davis, E. R. (1983). Bisection of temporal intervals by pigeons. *Journal of Experimental Psychology: Animal Behavior Processes, 9,* 160-170.

Platt, J. R., Kuch, D. O., & Bitgood, S. C. (1973). Rats' lever-press duration as psychophysical judgment of time. *Journal of the Experimental Analysis of Behavior, 19,* 239-250.

Pulliam, H. R. (1981). Learning to forage optimally. In A. C. Kamil, & T. D. Sargent (Eds.), *Foraging behavior: Ecological, ethological, and psychological approaches.* New York: Garland.

Shettleworth, S. J. (1983). Function and mechanism in learning. In M. D. Zeiler & P. Harzem (Eds.), *Biological factors in learning.* Chichester, NY: Wiley.

Shimp, C. P. (1975). Perspectives on the behavioral unit: Choice behavior in animals. In W. K. Estes (Ed.), *Handbook of learning and cognitive processes, Vol. 2.* Hillsdale,NJ: Lawrence Erlbaum Associates.

Shimp, C. P. (1979). The local organization of behaviour: Method and theory. In M. D. Zeiler & P. Harzem (Eds.), *Reinforcement and the organization of behaviour.* Chichester, NY: Wiley.

Skinner, B. F. (1935). The generic nature of the concepts of stimulus and response. *Journal of General Psychology, 12,* 40-65.

Skinner, B. F. (1938). *The behavior of organisms.* New York: Appleton-Century-Crofts.

Stevens, S. S. (1975). *Psychophysics.* New York: Wiley.

Stubbs, D.A. (1968). The discrimination of stimulus duration by pigeons. *Journal of the Experimental Analysis of Behavior, 11,* 223-258.

Stubbs, D. A. (1980). Temporal discrimination and a free-operant psychophysical procedure. *Journal of the Experimental Analysis of Behavior, 33,* 167-185.

Zeiler, M. D. (1970). Time limits for completing fixed ratios. *Journal of the Experimental Analysis of Behavior, 14,* 275-286.

Zeiler, M. D. (1972). Time limits for completing fixed ratios. II. Stimulus specificity. *Journal of the Experimental Analysis of Behavior,*

18, 243-251.

Zeiler, M. D. (1981). Model of temporal differentiation. In C. M. Bradshaw, E. Szabadi, & C. F. Lowe (Eds.), *Quantification of steady-state operant behavior*. Amsterdam: Elsevier/North Holland.

Zeiler, M. D. (1983). Integration in response timing: The functional time requirement. *Animal Learning and Behavior, 11*, 237-246.

Zeiler, M. D. (1985). Pure timing in temporal differentiation. *Journal of the Experimental Analysis of Behavior, 43*, 183-193.

Zeiler, M. D., Davis, E. R., & DeCasper, A. J. (1980). Psychophysics of key-peck duration in the pigeon. *Journal of the Experimental Analysis of Behavior, 34*, 23-33.

CHAPTER 7

In Application, Frequency Is Not the Only Estimate of the Probability of Behavioral Units

DONALD M. BAER

Sometimes behavior is considered to have virtually no necessary structure of its own, because its essential characteristic is its responsiveness to environmental contingencies like reinforcement and its stimulus controls. In that case, the structure of behavior should be the structure of the environmental contingencies that operate on it, and its only units should be the units that characterize the construction of contingencies in the environment.

Sometimes only some behavior is considered to be that totally tractable by environmental contingencies. Skinner (1953), for example, having defined a class of behavior as *operant* to denote its sensitivity to consequent environmental contingencies, then characterized it as like a sculptor's clay:

> Operant conditioning shapes behavior as a sculptor shapes a lump of clay. Although at some point the sculptor seems to have produced an entirely novel object, we can always follow the process back to the original undifferentiated lump, and we can make the successive stages by which we return to this condition as small as we wish. At no point does anything emerge which is very different from what preceded it. The final product seems to have a special unity or integrity of design, but we cannot find point at which this suddenly appears. In the same sense, an operant is not something which appears full grown in the behavior of the organism. It is the result of a continuous shaping process. (p. 91)

Sometimes the behavior that Skinner labelled operant is doubted to be that completely manageable by environmental contingencies; instead, it is argued to have certain fixed characteristics (cf. Collier, 1981; Killeen, 1981; and perhaps Hineline, 1986; Falk, 1986). That kind of argument has been argued against in a variety of ways, most of them emphasizing the difficulty of proving that a class of behavior is *not* open to some specific modification (e.g., Baer, 1982; Staddon, 1984). That pattern of argument and counterargument suggests that *stable* resolution of the problem may not be possible at the level of data, but only at the level of postulate:

Postulate 1. There is a subclass of operant behavior completely open to construction and unitization by environmental contingencies; this subclass may be the entire class.

Postulate 2. All apparent cases of behavior with fixed characteristics are worth subjecting to an ongoing series of experimental contingencies designed to undo those characteristics, until some set of contingencies succeeds.

These are postulates, and probably will remain postulates, because every current failure in following Postulate 2 amounts to only a temporary inductive disproof of the reality of Postulate 1 for some case in point, just as every success in following Postulate 2 amounts to only a temporary inductive proof of the reality of Postulate 1 for some case in point. Thus, these two postulates could as easily have been stated obversely:

Postulate 1´. There is a subclass of operant behavior constrained by its necessary units and structure from being shaped by environmental contingencies into any organization incompatible with those units and that structure; this subclass may be the entire class.

Postulate 2´. All apparent cases of behavior open to arbitrary structure and organization are worth subjecting to an ongoing series of experimental contingencies designed to reveal the constancies and constraints within their environmentally modifiable forms, especially to experimental contingencies that should fail just because of those constraints and constancies.

Despite the logical parity of Postulate 1 and its transformation into Postulate 1´, it is Postulate 1 that has characterized a great deal of radical behaviorism since Skinner's 1953 metaphor of the clay (if not before). Its inductive base probably is the wealth of experimental analyses of behaviors subjected to experimental contingencies and found thoroughly constructible by those contingencies, just as Postulate 1 supposes should be the more general case. In those experimental analyses, it seemed that behavior would take on whatever shape the contingency applied to it required: Whatever aspect of behavior the functional events were contingent on showed increasing probability of occurrence, and so became a behavioral unit; and apparently arbitrary sequences of those units seemed easy to select thereby and chain together to construct a correspondingly arbitrary diversity of what could be called new behaviors. Thus it was an inductive form of Postulate 1 that was constructed in the experimenters' strategies: Behavior has few if any intrinsic units; its units are imposed on it by environmental contingencies, and if there are constraints on that process, they should be supposed to lie primarily in the experimenter's ability to see the necessary contingencies and manipulate them in the organism's environment, rather than in the behavior of the organism.

The very great majority of those experimental analyses used a certain class of behaviors: behaviors that meet some logical and inductively established criteria for sensitive experimental analysis. By and large, these are the behaviors that have clear and limited extensions in space and time: They have easy-to-determine onsets and offsets, and they minimally displace their organism in space, time, or further behavior[1] (cf. Johnston & Pennypacker, 1982; Ferster, 1953). Behaviors that

---

[1] A pigeon pecking a switch shows clean onset and offset, in that both the pigeon's response and the switch-closure mechanism have clean onsets and offsets. Pecking the switch displaces the head of the pigeon only a few millimeters, requires only a fraction of a second, and does not compel extensive further behavior. Human sneezing also has clean onset and offset per sneeze, displaces the head of the organism only a few centimeters, and requires only a fraction of a second. However, it quite often compels the socialized

meet those criteria and are relatively free from antecedent stimulus controls at the moment are called *free operants*. Apparently because of their defining characteristics, they prove extraordinarily sensitive to a wide range of experimental variables. That made them a choice medium for the program of experimental analyses that cumulatively have defined the discipline of operant conditioning. To some considerable degree, the fast-moving and systematic development of that discipline and its extension to the philosophy of radical behaviorism probably depended on the sensitivity of the free operant: Given its virtually inevitable realization in the Skinner box, almost any series of questions about the nature of environmental control of such responses was open to quick, steady, systematic, and consistent answers.

The obvious, almost inevitable measure of any free operant is its frequency. Clear onsets and offsets make the response easy to count. They also make it easy for the environment and the experimenter to program consequent events like reinforcers precisely contingent on either onset or offset. Then repetition of either onset or offset is exactly what the obvious reinforcement contingencies will accomplish, making response frequency over time, or rate, the natural derived measure. Since the response has minimally displaced the organism in time, space, or further behavior, the organism is ready to respond again almost immediately, and is almost free of any response-depressing stimulus changes that more displacement in either time, space, or further behavior might constitute. Furthermore, the relative absence of obligatory antecedent stimulus controls means that every moment is an opportunity

---

human to engage in further behavior, such as turning away, muffling the sneeze in a handkerchief, cleaning up afterward, disposing of the handkerchief, apologizing, and acknowledging the inevitable blessings of any audience. The pigeon's pecking is a good approximation to the ideal free operant; the human's sneezing is not, at least because of this last characteristic of displacing the human into extensive further behavior. We might also suspect that sneezing is respondent, not operant (although there seem to be no published accounts of attempts to control it by reinforcement or punishment, absent which we could hardly say that it is or is not operant); but even if that is so, the sneeze is not a good approximation of a free respondent, either.

for recurrence of the response. Thus, just as the operant is free, its rate is free to vary across a wide range of values. Of course it became the predominant measure of free-operant conditioning, and virtually the necessary measure of the analysis of free operants. But is it the necessary measure of the experimental analysis of behavior in general, as well as of the free operant?

Reference to Postulate 1 reveals a small paradox. According to Postulate 1, at least some operant behavior is open to whatever construction the environment can be made to impose on that behavior. Then the unit of that behavior will be whatever aspect of it the behavior-shaping process operates on consistently. The great majority of past experimental applications of behavior-shaping processes have operated consistently on repetitions of free operants and patterns of free operants; thus the rates of those free operants or the rates of those patterns of them were the correct first units of analysis. Dependence on the free operant as an experimental medium naturally created dependence on rate as its unit, as if rate were the only natural unit. But Postulate 1 implies that such dependence was unnecessary, even if reinforcing in its production of a cohesive and comprehensive discipline. That lack of necessity is perhaps nowhere more apparent than in the realm of application.

In application, behaviors are analyzed and changed because they constitute a problem for someone capable of changing them or getting someone else to change them. Behavior problems comprise both excesses of some behaviors and insufficiencies of others, but their essence as problems is that someone complains effectively enough about them to provoke a behavior-change program - neither excesses nor insufficiencies of behavior constitute problems in themselves[2] (cf. Baer, 1982; Baer, 1985). The nature of the complaint may be the current

---

[2]Sometimes it is argued that self-destructive behavior is intrinsically a problem, in that survival is an evolutionary value. Yet some of the people who make such arguments often prove willing to deliberately sacrifice their lives in some contingencies, such as in the rescue of their children from danger, and societies typically define contexts within which certain kinds of self-destruction are considered heroic (as in war), not problematic.

intolerability of some behavior, often because it is destructive or disruptive in the complainer's present environment; or it may be a prediction that the behavior, or its absence, if continued, will handicap the behaver in some future environment.

Such behaviors are rarely free operants. Apart from finger-squeezes on the trigger of a gun, finger-presses on the switch of a nuclear missile, and finger-misplacements on a keyboard, they are rarely like switch-closings. Their topography is not usually restricted to a small and invariant set; and the quite diverse and variable topographies that they usually comprise do not often have clean onsets and offsets. Furthermore, they quite typically do displace their organism in space, time, and further behavior, and they come already tied to some considerable set of antecedent stimulus controls that interfere with their flexibility of rate.

Consider as a prototypical example a preschool child's repertoire that the child's teachers and parents will complain is "aggressive," and the child's peers will complain is "bad." Studies of the indicated repertoire (e.g., Pinkston, Reese, LeBlanc, & Baer, 1973) show that: These complaints can easily refer to a response class of more than 30 identifiable topographies. These topographies are indeed a response class, in that operations applied to a subset of them can affect the entire set. Very many of all the possible different subsets of these topographies do occur as episodes at various times; and within each subset, these topographies occur in different sequences and concurrencies per episode. Many of these topographies have unclear, indefinite onsets and offsets, and their function rarely is to cause pain and damage to others, but more likely is to attract attention from adults or to drive away the other children, sometimes because they have become aversive in themselves, sometimes because their presence typically marks an occasion when adults are not likely to attend to the child, and sometimes only when the other children compete with the child for materials and space. These responses accomplish their function because they do indeed cause or threaten pain and damage, but that is usually coincidental with their function for the so-called aggressor (which is to be attended to maximally by the adults present, or to control space and materials in the absence of competition from other children).

Note that functional consequences of this complex and variable set of topographies are not simple events, either. They are a variety of behaviors by other people: mainly attention from adults and leaving-alone by other children. A topographical account of the ways in which adults attend to a child will easily prove as large, as complex, and as variable in their subsets, sequences, and concurrencies as the topographies that the adults and children consider this child's aggression. The ways in which other children leave this child alone or cease competition also will be found to contain a variety of topographies, again complex and variable in their subsets, sequences, and concurrencies.

Thus, the essence of this behavior class's function is a contingency between constantly variable subsets of sequences and concurrencies from the numerous topographies that are called aggression in this child, and constantly variable subsets of sequences and concurrencies from the equally numerous topographies that are called attention in adults and leaving-alone or noncompetition in the other children.

Consider a particular case in which it is adults' attention that will prove to be the functional contingent consequence. If we let the upper-case letters A to Z represent the various topographies of the child's so-called aggression, and the lower-case letters a to z represent the various topographies of adults' attention to those episodes, then sometimes that contingency will look like the first example of Figure 1, sometimes the second, sometimes the third, etc.

Figure 1 only begins to exemplify the variety of contingencies possible when constantly varying subsets, sequences, and concurrencies from one class of topographies somewhat systematically follow constantly varying subsets, sequences, and concurrencies from another class of topographies. And it only begins to exemplify the variety of remedial contingencies that the adults may well use when they discontinue their attention to this response class and transfer it to another, more desirable class such as positive peer interaction, the acceptable topographies of which can be made to greatly exceed those of this so-called aggressive class. The maintenance of the undesirable class and the shaping of the desirable class can both be shown to comprise reinforcement contingencies. But they are not reinforcement contingencies in which some reinforcer is contingent on a clean onset or offset of some response, such that the *rate* of that response should increase. Instead, they are reinforcement contingencies in which various clusters from a class of reinforcing topographies are contingent on almost any clustering of almost any subsets of rates, durations, inter-response intervals, sequences, and concurrencies of the topographies that make up the reinforced class. In effect, the reinforcement contingency is on filling time with such clusters, and when deliberately applied by skilled adults to the problem described, the contingency steadily requires that more and more time be filled by such clusters before a reinforcing cluster will be delivered.[3]

If the basic behavioral unit is always available for construction by the environmental contingency that modifies the behavior, then in this case the unit is any cluster of topographies from the response class in question that fills enough time to be responded to with a cluster of topographies from the other response class in question.

Interestingly, in applied behavior analysis, the most frequent measurement technique is continuous time-sampling, now often referred to as continuous interval recording, which is essentially an approximate measure of the time filled by a topography (or, more likely, a cluster of topographies, at least one of which is a topography specified for recording). Continuous time-sampling divides ongoing time into a succession of continuous intervals, typically of 10 seconds duration, sometimes of 5, 15, 20, or 30 seconds, and occasionally of even longer durations. In each successive interval, a single record of the occurrence of each topography

---

[3]Fifteen years ago, such experimental analyses made exciting research. Today, in behaviorally sophisticated professional-training programs, they constitute exercises for students likely to confront such problems in their subsequent professional practice.

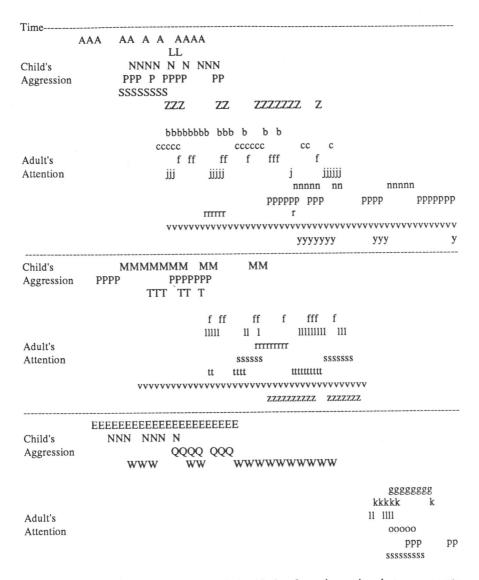

Fig. 1. Three graphic examples of the kinds of contingencies that can operate between the clusters of topography subsets, sequences, inter-response times, and concurrencies that make up both a child's "aggression" and an adult's "attention." Time flows steadily from left to right. Each topography of the child's "aggressive" class is represented by upper-case letters, and of the adult's "attention" class by lower-case letters. Each topography's duration is indicated by the unspaced repetition of its symbol letter (e.g., AAAA represents twice as long a duration as AA). Spaces between symbol letters indicate inter-response times.

under study is made if that topography occurred at any time, for any duration, during that interval. Typically, no further record is made during that interval, despite any variable-duration recurrences of that topography in the interval.[4] Time filled is thus measured no more precisely than plus or minus about 9 seconds of every 10 seconds. That practice has been shaped in many applied researchers, despite its wide margin for error, primarily because the onsets and offsets of the topographies that they observe are rarely clear and precise: With considerable reliability, observers usually can see that the topography did or did not occur sometime within the interval; but if they are asked to record more precisely how much of the interval was filled by that topography, too often their recording becomes unacceptably unreliable. (When topographies' onsets and offsets allow, of course more precise variations of continuous time-sampling can be and are employed.) That the method often works despite its apparently remarkable margin for error can be judged by scanning the studies of successful problem solutions based on it, and published in the Journal of Applied Behavior Analysis, Behavior Therapy, Behavior Modification, Behavioral Assessment, and some 25 other journals of the day.

Applied behavior analysis *is* largely characterized by fundamental units representing clusters of topographies filling time, but not directly *because* the contingencies used in applied behavior analysis recommend exactly that kind of unit. Instead, it probably has been the necessity of achieving reliable measurement through the medium of observer agreement that directly shaped and still maintains so much reliance on continuous time-sampling and its variants: Ongoing

---

[4]A potentially valuable variation of continuous time-sampling has been developed by Powell (in press). In his technique, any initiation of a topography under study is recorded in each interval, and if the topography is still ongoing at exactly the end of the interval that too is recorded (distinctively from the recording of its initiation). Powell has shown that when this technique is applied to computer-simulated visual fixations by a child on an adult, its recordings of fixation initiations represent the known rate of that behavior rather accurately, and its end-of-interval recordings represent the known durations of those fixations rather accurately. However, visual fixation is probably not typical of the behaviors that must be recorded in behavioral applications, in that once the observer

topographies with unclear onsets and offsets can hardly be recorded reliably and with some sensitivity in any other known and practical way, so far. Thus, it appears at first to be a happy coincidence that the units implicit in the measurement technique necessitated by these distinctive problems of reliable measurement should also appeal so clearly to the nature of the instrumental social contingencies typical of the field.

In fact, an underlying necessity makes the apparent coincidence a functional relationship: If well trained observers cannot react reliably to the onsets and offsets of the topographies in such clusters, neither can the other persons in the environment whose reactions to those clusters most likely was their origin and is their maintenance. Those persons are hardly likely to and hardly able to reinforce or punish such onsets or offsets, component by component; but they can and do readily reinforce or punish someone's filling time with clusters of such onsets and offsets, and so their problem is functionally contiguous (Sidman, 1960, pp. 37-38) with the observers' problem. Of course measurement will reflect function, in this case.

Another problem inherent in the measurement of topography clusters by human observers also reflects the kind of contingencies that characterize both natural and experimentally managed social interactions in application; it too imposes units on the study of many of those interactions. That is the problem of telling observers what clusters to record and what clusters not to record. Consider again the problem of the so-called aggressive preschool child. That child steadily emitted clusters

---

can take up an appropriate station (which is not always easy to do), the onsets and offsets of visual fixations can usually be seen as clear and precise. Most of the behaviors studied in applied behavior analysis do not have clear and precise onsets and offsets, no matter where the observer is stationed, and thus - as previously argued - their rate becomes irrelevant, since that is not what any intervention's contingency can be on. How much time they fill is probably what the contingency will be on. But Powell's method of estimating durations more accurately is exactly appropriate to the concept of time filled by a topography, and should be studied further with the unclear and imprecise onsets and offsets typical of topographies seen in behavioral application. The problem in doing so of course will be to know the *true* duration of the behavior being observed.

of behavior in the preschool environment; some of those clusters were reacted to with complaints and the label "aggressive," some were not. Those were the clusters that caused children to cry and teachers to intervene. When teachers remediated that problem by discontinuing their attention to those clusters and enriching their schedule of attention to other clusters called *positive peer interaction* (defined both positively and also by the absence in the cluster of any topographies defined as "aggressive"), it was essential that the teachers reliably discriminate what clusters were to be ignored and what clusters were to be reinforced. To the extent that they were complainers about those clusters, the teachers already knew how to do that, and could have conducted a private study satisfactory to themselves. But if the process was to be *proven* effective to the rest of us, it was also essential that the observers discriminate reliably and independently what clusters the teachers considered aggressive and what clusters they considered positive peer interactions. If the observers could do that, they would establish the extent to which the teachers discontinued their attention to the complained-about clusters and increased their attention to the approved-of clusters, and the extent to which those clusters then changed in the amount of time that they filled. Otherwise, there would be no way of establishing either set of facts for the rest of us.

Obviously, some clusters had stimulus control for complaints and crying in both teachers and the other children; the problem was to establish the *same* stimulus control over the observers' recording behaviors. That was done with printed words, written by the teachers to establish that stimulus control in the observers who would read those words in preparation for every day of the study. The teachers chose words that had the appropriate stimulus control *for themselves*, as best they could observe in their own behavior during the few weeks that could be allotted to the development of the measurement system. They used phrases such as "forceful application of hands to the body of another person," "forceful application of feet to the body of another person," "forceful application of mouth to the body of another person," and some 30 more phrases, usually with

examples and often with everyday connotative English words.
(For example, "forceful application of mouth . . ." was
accompanied by the connotative word, "biting," and the warning
that biting would be difficult to distinguish from kissing, both of
which the child did to unconventional parts of other people's
bodies in ways that concealed the role of his teeth. Kissing, they
were told, would involve a preliminary puckering of the lips.)
Such collections of statements about topographies are usually
called *observation codes*. They are, of course, rules - intuitive
rules, not mathematical ones (cf. Marr, 1986), and they
transform observing into a class of rule-governed behaviors.
They also establish the units of behavior by which the course of
behavioral applications is known to the rest of us; and, because
adults' attempts at intervention typically are evaluated daily by
the recordings of the extent to which they did what these rules
now define as what they had planned to do, those units in fact
often become the units of intervention, whether or not they were
at first.

The question is always the extent to which code words have
the same stimulus control in observers as they do in
code-writers. That is evaluated in the obvious way: A code
about a child's aggression is used by an observer and the
code-writer as they independently observe the same child at the
same time. After the observation, their recordings are
compared interval by interval to see that extent to which they
agreed about when clusters containing any and each topography
specified by the code occurred. If they agree closely about the
occurrences of a topography, and if they agree closely about the
nonoccurrences of that topography[5], the code is said to be
reliable for that topography and for that pair of observers.

---

[5]It is important to establish both occurrence and nonoccurrence reliabilities separately.
A very low-rate behavior may easily be well enough defined so that observers typically
agree when it is not occurring, but poorly enough defined so that they disagree about
when it is occurring. Especially if the observers know that it is a low-rate behavior, then
in 100 intervals of recording, they may well agree that in 98 of those intervals, the
behavior did not occur; but they may also disagree completely on the two intervals when
it did occur. An *overall* reliability evaluation will note 98 agreements in 100
observations, express that as 98% agreement, and convey an evaluation of highly similar

(Close agreement is generally taken to mean 85% agreement or higher.) But during the recording, the code-writer is also noting how often the code currently fails to capture clusters that the code-writer complains about as "aggressive," and how often the code captures clusters about which the code-writer after all has no complaint. That process evaluates the validity of the code; more important, it leads to amendments in the code by the code-writer such that its validity is maximized - for that code-writer, of course. Clearly, the only meaning of reliability and validity here is that what is written in the code has the same stimulus control for both observers when they record or do not record each episode of the child's behavior, and that they are recording what the code-writer wishes to record.

Thus, the units of stimulus control that govern the code-writer's reaction to the child's behavior as "aggressive" are the units that the code-writer attempts to transfer to the code, and thereby to all the observers who read the code and record by it. Furthermore, the teachers who have planned to ignore "aggressive" behaviors by the child will every day be told that on this day, they achieved their goal on, say, 87% of the relevant occasions. Typically, they will ask how that can be; typically, the observer will have made a note of the teachers' errors and can specify the occasions. Teachers then may agree that the error is an error, and their future behavior is usually modified accordingly; or they may dispute the observers'

---

stimulus control. But what is called an *occurrence* reliability evaluation will be restricted to those intervals in which at least one observer recorded an occurrence of the behavior. In this example, there are two such intervals, say the 5th and the 33rd. The question is how many of those two intervals showed observer agreement, and the answer is 0. An occurrence reliability of 0% will quite correctly convey an evaluation of highly dissimilar stimulus controls over the observers' recording of what the behavior is. A parallel argument shows that a *nonoccurrence* reliability is the more appropriate evaluation of the similarity of stimulus control for a high-rate behavior: With high-rate behaviors (especially high-rate behaviors that the observers know are high-rate behaviors), it is their similarities of stimulus control over recording what is *not* the behavior that is critical. If occurrence reliabilities are emphasized in evaluating the recording of behaviors that typically fill less than 50% of the time observed, and nonoccurrence reliabilities are emphasized in evaluating the recording of behaviors that typically fill more than 50% of the time observed,chance agreement levels (25% at most) will never approach acceptable agreement levels.

interpretation, arguing that the child behavior in question was not "aggressive." In that case, the observer reviews the code words with the teacher; often enough on such occasions, teachers will finally agree, and their future behavior is usually modified accordingly. Sometimes, teachers will continue to disagree, and perhaps the observer will agree that it was a recording error rather than a teacher error. However, if the observer has been well trained, this is unlikely: Observers should be trained to record only the topographies that the code words specify, and especially to refrain from interpreting the child's or the teacher's "intent." Thus, the units of stimulus control that governed the code-writer's reaction to the child's behavior as "aggressive" and complainable, when they are transferred to a code found to be reliable between code-writer and observer(s), tend to become very powerful in determining what will happen throughout the following intervention, and probably will become the units of the teachers' behavior, if they were not at the outset.

In part, the code is capable of imposing its units on everyone else's behavior because the code is ensconced as inviolate, as it needs to be if the measurement system is to be useful and informative throughout the study. In larger part, it is because the code is reliable - its reliability should be the essence of the observer's ability to defend its literal use when that use is questioned in specific future instances. To the extent that an observer's training was to achieve and maintain reliability in frequent checks throughout the study, to that extent the observer should be in the tight stimulus control of the phrases of the code and little else, and thus should be difficult to modify by mere protests, unless the protests are couched in the very words of the code. But that is unlikely, because it is exactly in the very words of the code, and only in the very words of the code, that the observer should have been trained - and trained more than any one else involved in the study, preferably in a promised double contingency that implies: (a) that our collective reinforcers include the child's future and what we call the truth, and that neither the child's future nor the truth will be served unless reliability can be achieved and maintained; and (b) that the observer's job will be lost unless reliability can be achieved and maintained.

Notice that the code, even when made reliable across a very wide range of observers by the necessary choice of words to accomplish its intuitive rules, need not have much validity for the next complainer. The next complainer may not complain about the same topographies; there is rarely anything universally complainable-about in topographies, especially children's. To the extent that complainers are alike in terms of the stimuli that control their complaints, to that extent their codes have generality across cases. That extent may be better explainable by the cultural and sociological factors that control conformity than by any necessities of behavioral structure.

In application, then, the operative behavioral units tend to be the code-writer's stimulus controls - the code-writer's units of response to the clusters of topographies presented and agreed to as "the problem." These are the units of stimulus control that are likely to be imposed on the behavior of the people involved - subjects and interveners alike. Ideally, the units of the code-writer's reaction to the problem presented will be identical to the units of the people involved in the problem. It would be remarkable if that happened very often. More often, the code-writer's units will to some extent have to be imposed on the behavior of the people involved. If their behavior is constrained by the units and structures already operative within it, it may well prove impossible to impose these new units and structures on that behavior. On the other hand, if their behavior is open to the imposition of new units and structures, then the application may well succeed.

Success, of course, is defined according to the code, which is the code-writer's reaction to the stimulus controls inherent in the clusters of topographies that are presented as "the problem." It is impressive how often that kind of success is achieved, sufficient to be printed in one or another of the 30 or so journals that present such work at least occasionally. Perhaps Postulate 1 is a realistic postulate in this realm.

But perhaps it is not, on at least two grounds:

(a) There is an obvious sampling problem: Where can we

read about the failures of attempts to impose code-writers' units on other people's behavior? Application failures are rarely considered informative; there are so many ways to fail other than fundamentally that it is difficult to know when failure might be due to an incompatibility of the imposed units and the units and constraints already characterizing the target behavior.

(b) Another reason to doubt that the literature of the applied field testifies to a general realism of Postulate 1 is that in most of that literature, the *only* criterion of success is the code-writer's criterion: Success is appropriate change in how much time is filled by the topographies specified by the code. But the essence of applied behavior analysis is that changing those topographies was supposed to solve the presenting problem, such that there are no longer complaints about it. Then it is not enough to show that the topographies supposed to be the analysis of the problem have changed; there should also be some measure of whether the complaints have stopped, and especially whether they have stopped in all settings and at all times when complaints would be appropriate if the problem still existed.

It is only in the last five years that applied behavior analysis has formally recommended asking its subjects and everyone else relevant whether they have stopped complaining, after the supposedly functional topographies are changed. It has taken the field that long to see that the subjective evaluations that subjects and relevant others can offer are not a substitute for hard data about topography changes (for which there is no substitute), but instead are only the token that the *correct* topographies were changed. Collecting that token is called *social validity* (Kazdin, 1977; Wolf, 1978); it is just begining to appear as a standard entry in new codes. It appears there not as a topography to modify, but as a topography to be assessed, to see if it changes when the target topographies have been changed. If it does not change from complaints about the problem to statements of satisfaction about the new topographies, about the people who caused the new topographies, and about the methods that they used to do that, then the topographies that were changed may not have been the correct ones to change, or enough of the correct ones, because the fundamental problem still exists.

Social validity is verbal behavior. It would be easy to modify it directly when the other target topographies were modified, if that change needed no generality outside of its assessment setting. But if that were done, the result would no longer be social validity, of course, and would no longer be valuable. Indeed, it would be counter-productive: It could shield the intervener from discovering that the complainers are still complaining elsewhere, or that they are mounting a counter-control movement elsewhere that soon may put the intervener out of business.

The necessities of assessing social validity validly will compel applied behavior analysts to learn what sociology and social psychology began to learn long ago about collecting valid verbal behavior. So far, not much of that has happened. Even so, the logic of social validity is so compelling for applied behavior analysis, that whatever *its* units may turn out to be, they will inevitably control the procedures of interventions necessary to achieve not only topography changes but social-validity maximization as well. These are not the units that characterize changing verbal behavior in its assessment setting; those are well known and are essentially identical to the units that characterize changing bar-pressing and key-pecking. These are the units that characterize the kind of verbal-behavior changes that mediate widely generalized other changes (cf. Skinner, 1957). In particular, those other changes should take the form of clients asking that you similarly solve another of their problems, recommending your intervention to their friends and politicians, declaring that it is worth more than it costs, writing positive letters to editors about it, voting for it at the next election, defending it against criticism, urging school boards to add your discipline to their curriculum, and the like. A social validity that can be assessed readily, yet has that kind of consequences, will be characterized by units that can allow analysis of the range of interaction possible both within verbal behavior, and between verbal behavior and all other behavior. That kind of analysis has just begun (cf. Catania, 1986). The units that will characterize it are not yet settled, perhaps, but they may have relatively little resemblance to the rate measures that served so well in the analyses of the free operant with which the experimental analysis of behavior began. Instead, they may depend on the best functional description of how to establish, maintain, and generalize stimulus equivalencies for the responses in question. That description may hinge on the quickness and correctness of single responses to a constantly changing set of what are essentially conditional match-to-sample problems, each one of them significant in its own right rather than as an element in a reinforceable chain (cf. Sidman,1986). And the unit most significant in *that* description may be the level of the conditional stimuli controlling the subsequent match to sample: Is this a three-term, four-term, or five-term contingency? As Sidman has shown, in logic, the number of terms in the match-to-sample contingency can analyze the level of meaning inherent in verbal behavior, perhaps especially in the analysis of those conversational flows that Harzem (1986) recommends as one of our next best strategic targets.

Applied behavior analysis developed out of the basic experimental analysis of behavior. In its last decade, it has pursued its applications quite independently of its basic antecedents, using behavior-analytic but distinctively laboratory-free terms. However, in its next decades, it may well discover that its emerging necessity to accomplish a valid applied analysis of social validity will return it to the now quickly developing basic experimental analyses of verbal behavior, and will confront basic researchers in that area with one of its most complex cases - the analysis of how a society's verbal behavior can mediate that society's acceptance of a scientific and applied discipline that by then had better understand social acceptance well enough to program its own.

ACKNOWLEDGMENT

This chapter is affectionately dedicated to my wife, Jacqui Baer, who asked me to show her applied behavior analysis in the context of her already exceptional skills in basic theory and research, and thereby taught me that there was much more of it than I knew. We shall pursue the question further.

REFERENCES

Baer, D. M. (1982). Applied behavior analysis. In C. M. Franks & G. T. Wilson (Eds.), *Contemporary behavior therapy* (pp. 277-309). New York: Builford.

Baer, D. M. (1985). Applied behavior analysis as a conceptually conservative view of childhood disorders. In R. J. MacMahon & R. V. Peters (Eds.), *Childhood disorders: Behavioral-developmental approaches* (pp. 17-35). New York: Brunner/Mazel.

Collier, G.H. (1981). Determinants of choice. In D.J. Bernstein (Ed.), *Response structure and organization, Nebraska symposium on motivation, 1981* (pp. 69-127). Lincoln/London: University of Nebraska Press.

Ferster, C. B. (1953). The use of the free operant in the analysis of behavior. *Psychological Bulletin, 50,* 263-274.

Johnston, J. M., & Pennypacker, H. S. (1982). *Strategies and tactics of human behavioral research.* Hillsdale, New Jersey: Lawrence Erlbaum Associates.

Kazdin, A. E. (1977). Assessing the clinical or applied importance of behavior change through social validation. *Behavior Assessment, 1,* 427-452.

Killeen, P.R. (1981). Incentive theory. In D.J. Bernstein (Ed.), *Response structure and organization, Nebraska symposium on motivation, 1981* (pp. 169-216). Lincoln/London: University of Nebraska Press.

Pinkston, E. M., Reese, N. M., LeBlanc, J. M., & Baer, D. M. (1973). Independent control of a preschool child's aggression and peer interaction by contingent teacher attention. *Journal of Applied Behavior Analysis, 6,* 115-124.

Powell, J. (in press). Some empirical justification for a modest proposal regarding data acquisition via intermittent direct observation. *Journal of Behavioral Assessment.*

Sidman, M. (1960). *Tactics of scientific research.* New York: Basic Books.

Skinner, B. F. (1953). *Science and human behavior.* New York: MacMillan.

Skinner, B. F. (1957). *Verbal behavior.* New York: Appleton-Century-Crofts.

Staddon, J. E. R. (1983). "As a sculptor shapes a lump of clay . . ." [Review of *Nebraska Symposium on Motivation, 1981*]. *Contemporary Psychology, 28,* No. 10, 795-797.

Wolf, M. M. (1978). Social validity: The case for subjective assessment, or how applied behavior analysis is finding its heart. *Journal of Applied Behavior Analysis, 11,* 203-214.

CHAPTER 8

Pharmacological Contributions to Experimental Analysis of Behavior

PETER B. DEWS

Almost every well-conceived and well-completed study of drug effects on behavior contributes something to the understanding of the behavior itself. It would not be helpful to simply catalogue as many examples as possible. So a few specific examples will be given in some detail with the hope that general conclusions will be able to be reached by the reader. Much of the work described originated in our Laboratory of Psychobiology. Only by talking about work that I have been close to can I give you background and context, the sorts of materials distinguishing a symposium contribution from just a review. Also, as a contribution cannot be recognized for sure until some considerable time after the event, I shall be dealing with old work in historical perspective.

RATES OF RESPONDING
AND SCHEDULE CONTROL

In the 1930's B. F. Skinner almost single handedly developed an approach to the experimental analysis of behavioral phenomena through the study of patterns in time of repetitive occurrence of units of behavior. It was a great achievement, one of the greatest scientific contributions of the century and, in my opinion, the greatest contribution ever made to psychology as a science. In *Behavior of Organisms*, published in 1938 while he was at the University of Minnesota, Skinner described patterns of responding in relation to the deliberate scheduling of environmental events. It was not until the 1950's, however, that schedule effects on patterns of responding were explicitly and extensively explored starting at Harvard with a fruitful collaboration between Skinner and the late C. B. Ferster (Ferster & Skinner, 1957) and by Keller and his colleagues at Columbia. Both groups were joined shortly by an extraordinary series of gifted students.

By the mid 1950's, no one could deny that the schedule of reinforcement powerfully influenced the pattern of repetitive responding of rats or pigeons. The differences between the patterns of performance maintained under, say, FI and FR patterns were too gross to be denied. But the developments were largely ignored by mainstream psychology. For example, in Kimble's 1961 version of Hilgard and Marquis' *Conditioning and Learning* (Kimble, 1961), schedules occupy a couple of pages of text out of 500 and one figure, taken from Keller and Schoenfeld (1950) who had modified it from Skinner (1938) who had conducted his experiment over a decade earlier. It shows what was well known by 1961 (but not by 1950) to be quite uncharacteristic FR responding. (It was not realized until the 50s that a large number of schedule cycles may be necessary for steady-state to be reached between schedule and pattern of responding.) Skinner's figure shows patterns of responding, perhaps early in training, perhaps with a poor rat lever, perhaps with inadequate deprivation, perhaps with any number of conditions so that the performance was not what was known in 1961 to be characteristic FR responding. The experiment was prescient, two decades ahead of the rest of the world, but it was not perfect. No blame is attributed to Kimble, whose lack of appreciation was typical rather than exceptional.

Why did not psychology recognize a dynamic and burgeoning field? First, recognition of the importance of schedules owed essentially nothing to traditional psychological theory and developed quite independently. People in the field were concerned with control of behavioral performance of individual subjects and traditional psychological theory was useless for their purposes, neither predicting results nor leading to informative experiments. Most people in experimental psychology were concerned only with experiments that purported to bear on their favorite theories. Second, there were no antecedents to schedule effects so there was no familiar language to describe the new findings; inevitably, a jargon developed, further impeding broader communication. Most experiments on schedules were conducted in rats and pigeons working a simple switch in an isolated chamber under automated control. (The terms *experiments on schedules* or *schedule effects* are being used in a loose general sense to cover most of the field sometimes called *experimental analysis of behavior*.) Other psychologists chose to dismiss the unwelcome results that did not fit at all into their conceptual framework as trivial phenomena arising from the highly contrived, artificial conditions imposed on these lower organisms. As has been pointed out by others (e.g., Thompson, 1984), in reality, the strategic and tactical approaches of the experimental analysis of behavior are more in the tradition of experimental medicine, deriving from Claude Bernard, than they are in the tradition of psychology.

Yet the study of schedule effects was still isolated from biology, even though in contrast to much of the rest of psychology, the variables were expressed in the same units as used in biology, and, indeed, the rest of science. The vectors and scalars of responses and stimuli were expressed in SI or equivalent units and the processes were followed in real time. Yet the field was isolated in the sense that it contributed (and has still contributed) little to the understanding of neurobiological processes and neurobiology has contributed almost nothing to the understanding of schedule effects. The reason for the lack of interchanges was (and is) not the lack of interest in neurobiological phenomena by students of schedules despite allegations to the contrary. It is because the problems involved in the interface have proved to be exceedingly intractable. Two examples indicate the nature of the difficulties. In the use of food as a reinforcer, regimes of partial food deprivation are usually imposed on subjects. What are the neurobiological changes in deprivation that make food presentation, properly scheduled, an effective reinforcer, and what happens in the subject when food is presented that determines, or even reflects, reinforcing efficacy? Second, when a subject generates an FI scallop, under constant external stimuli, and does so repeatedly in daily sessions over periods of months, what controls the progressive change in the rate of responding through each cycle? Each of these questions has been the subject of far more research than has been devoted to the entire field of the purely behavioral effects of schedules; yet the understanding developed is so meager that one is not sure that we have even started along the right lines. Comparable questions could be asked across the whole interface between schedule effects and neurobiology and the answers would be almost uniformly equally disappointing. Indeed, the questions seem so intractable that it is necessary to ask whether they are the right questions, and whether different formulations would be more useful heuristically. Please note this is said with sadness, not with gladness at the purity of behavioral studies in their own right, legitimate as such studies are. I have devoted a great deal of time and energy to trying to contribute to the behavioral physiology of cardiovascular functions, with very modest requital in increase in established understanding. I studied visual stimulus control in subjects with damaged visual systems: Impairment of stimulus control was roughly parallel to the impairment of transmission of relevant information from eye to occipital cortex, determined electrophysiologically. That may be a start, but what is the next step? Skinner rightly rejected neurologizing, i.e., the postulation of specious processes solely to fit the observed behavioral phenomena, but, he and his successors have had strong affinity for real behavioral physiology. Would it were not so hard.

With drugs it has been different. Let us go back to the 50's, when the potentialities of schedule effects were being first realized and documented. To people working in the field, it was perfectly clear that there was little arbitrary about the best ways to study schedule effects in pigeons and rats and other species. The pigeon keys and rat levers, and the stimuli used, were developed progressively and deliberately to work well in revealing schedule effects. In that sense, the situations were contrived. They were contrived in the same sense that, to use a hackneyed analogy, chemists or microbiologists contrived to work with pure compounds or pure cultures of organisms neither of which occur in the "real" world. The situations are not contrived in the sense of the critics: that by isolation of the subject in an environment with only one or two objects to manipulate it is possible to contrive all sorts of behavioral performances that are nonexistent or trivial in the "real" world and so have no general significance.

In fact, the isolation serves merely to protect the subject from contamination by unknown influences, as the chemist or microbiologist would say, and findings on schedule control have now been amply confirmed in "real life" situations. But in the 50's it was not so easy to refute the critics who dismissed schedule effects as contrived. From the first, however, study of drug effects showed that the drug effects were powerfully influenced by either the schedule effects directly, or by the rates of responding engendered by the schedules. Figure 1 shows in a single example that the nature of the schedule, FR or FI, incontrovertibly makes a big difference to the behavioral effects of pentobarbital. Dependence on schedule in one way or another was found for almost every drug studied. Now, the effects of drugs are, so to speak, orthogonal to subject-schedule interactions. The drugs were in the subject, with physiological and biochemical effects that could not credibly be supposed to be directly influenced reversibly and repeatedly by contrived manipulations of the environment. Yet schedule effects played a large determining role in the behavioral effects of the drugs: Therefore, schedule effects have biological as well as purely behavioral relevance: Therefore, they are not trivial manifestations of a contrived situation. Contact had been made between the study of schedule effects and an entirely independent science that could not, by its nature, be merely reflecting arbitrary choices of behavioral situations by the investigator.

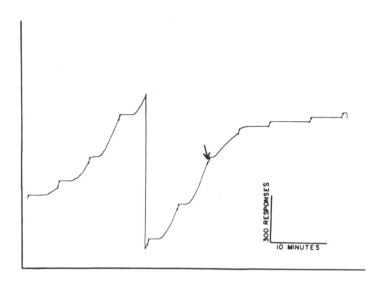

Fig. 1. Effect of pentobarbital on responding under mult FR 30 FI 300 sec. The figure shows the cumulative responding in a single session. Abscissa: time. Ordinate: cumulative responding, pen resetting partway through session. The conclusion of each component, at the delivery of food, is shown by a small hatch mark on the record. FI 300 sec components can be recognized by their 300 sec duration and by the upward concavity of the record. The FR 30 components, which alternated with the FI components, are seen as brief periods of responding at a high rate. At the arrow, 3 mg (about 7 mg/kg) pentobarbital was injected. For the rest of the session, FR responding continued more or less as before the injection, whereas FI responding was largely abolished, providing a vivid graphic picture of the dependence of the effects of pentobarbital on the nature of the ongoing schedule-controlled pattern of responding. (From Morse, 1962. Reproduced by permission of Lea and Febiger.)

STIMULUS CONTROL

Measurement of stimulus control arises naturally from studies on multiple schedules, which are compound schedules in which more than one schedule is imposed during each experimental session, each schedule component being consistently associated with a distinctive stimulus. Study of drug effects has contributed significantly to the development of better quantitative understanding of stimulus control, although much still remains to be done. It is possible that we have gone almost as far as we can with purely behavioral methods.

In the preschedule era, stimuli were considered to produce

responses: Responses were the "response" of the subject to stimuli, a formulation recognized in the term *S-R psychology*. For conditioned stimuli, increase in intensity tended to cause somewhat stronger responses, an effect that was opposed by a generalization gradient whereby the response became weaker as the intensity of the stimulus was changed from the values used in training. Emphasis was on the S-R link, and, in particular, its development; studies were conducted under the heading of "learning." While a quantitative assessment of stimulus control in such experiments is conceptually possible, for example, by measuring the probability that a response would follow a stimulus when the latter was presented many times, such an approach was little developed. The preoccupation with "learning" meant that one was perforce dealing with a shifting performance that made a stochastic approach difficult to apply. Even when a performance had been "learned," it was still susceptible to "over learning." Such a continuously changing background was not an attractive substrate for pharmacological studies, and relatively few were conducted. There was no recognition of steady-state conditions between sequences of environmental events and patterns of repetitive responding in real time.

Early drug experiments on stimulus control assessed drug effects on "discriminations" (Dews, 1955). It became clear, however, that what was being affected by drugs was not just the "discrimination" of red from green by a pigeon or of light from dark by a rat. The difference between performances under an identical pair of discriminative stimuli could or could not be attenuated by a given dose of a drug depending on factors other than the stimuli themselves. A clear early example of this phenomenon were the experiments of Terrace on effects of imipramine (Terrace, 1963). Terrace trained pigeons so that they pecked regularly when a red key light was present but did not peck and never had pecked, because of the training method, when a green key light was present. The procedure was called *errorless discrimination*. Other pigeons were trained so that they too were now pecking regularly when the red light was present and never when a green light was present but they had, because of the training method, pecked in the presence of green in the past. Imipramine caused an increase in responding in the presence of the green light when the discrimination had been developed with "errors" but not when it had been developed without "errors." Terrace implied that it was the manner of development of the discriminative performances that determined the susceptibility to imipramine, but it is still not established that the difference was not simply a matter of the greater power of the stimulus control, that could have been developed by other regimens involving "errors" in training. But either way, imipramine did, or did not attenuate "discriminative" control of identical stimuli on identical behavior depending on schedule of training.

Differences in performance controlled by a pair of stimuli can or cannot be attenuated by a given dose of drug depending on the intensity of the difference between the stimuli. One series of experiments demonstrating this phenomenon illustrates a way in which pharmacology has contributed to understanding of schedule-effects on a number of occasions viz, in a quite unpremeditated way. Studies starting from a purely pharmacological interest in an alleged selective effect of a drug have led to new insights on controls of behavior on a number of occasions. For example, from the early days of pharmacology there has been interest in the effects of drugs such as ethyl alcohol and barbiturates that have been described traditionally as having a selective effect in attenuating or "inhibiting" inhibitions. As evidence for the proposition, results were offered in which a performance suppressed by inhibition was restored towards optimum by a drug, such as amobarbital. But, invariably, the performance was different in the presence and absence of the inhibition and appropriate controls were lacking for how much that difference in performance itself determined the differential effect of the drug.

A situation was developed, therefore, in which graded differences in performance occurred in the presence and absence of an "inhibitory" stimulus (Dews, 1964). An FI performance in pigeons was repeatedly interrupted briefly by a stimulus that was, in fact, an increase in ambient illumination (by the so-called houselight). This stimulus was not present at the end of the interval when a response was promptly followed by food so it was technically an S-delta i.e., a stimulus in whose presence a response is never reinforced. Typically, S-deltas suppress responding during their presence, and did so in this instance. The effects of amobarbital were to cause a far larger proportionate increase in responding during the periods of suppression than during the nonsuppressed periods (Figure 2).

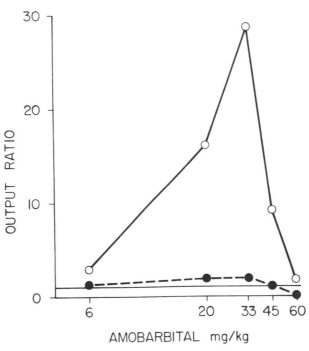

Fig. 2. Dose-effect curves of amobarbital on rate of responding of pigeons under FI 500 sec with alternating 25 sec periods with and without the houselight. As the houselight was not present when reinforcement of responding occurred, the houselight was an S-delta and inhibited responding. Abscissa: dose of amobarbital. Ordinate: rate of responding in appropriate segments of entire session following drug divided by mean rates in corresponding segments of 10 control sessions. Open circles, solid line: responding during houselight periods of entire session. Filled circles, dotted line: responding during periods without the houselight for entire session. Note the enormously greater relative increase in average inhibited rates than in noninhibited rates by amobarbital. (From Dews, 1964. Reproduced by permission of Springer-Verlag, Heidelberg.)

This was the kind of evidence that had been offered that amobarbital attenuated inhibition. In the FI experiments, however, the actual rates of responding during suppressed periods late in the FI were higher than in the nonsuppressed periods early in the FI. When the effects of amobarbital were plotted as a function of average control rates of responding for corresponding parts of the interval, it could be seen that the effect of amobarbital was systematically related to the control rate of responding, and the presence or the absence of suppression was irrelevant (Figure 3). There was, therefore, no indication of a selective effect of amobarbital in attenuating suppression. Later came unexpected results. McKearney (1970) confirmed that the effects of amobarbital were systematically related to the rate of responding, but found that the relation was different in the presence and absence of suppressing stimuli (Figure 4). To make a long story short, McKearney established in an elegant series of studies that whether the suppressed and nonsuppressed points fell on a single line or on two parallel lines depended on the intensity of the S-delta. A difference in stimulus control that could not be seen in the control performances became manifest under the influence of amobarbital just as a previously inapparent difference was revealed by imipramine in Terrace's experiments. You will remember that the argument against the inhibiting of inhibitions account of the effects of amobarbital emphasized the single relationship of rate-to-effects on both suppressed and nonsuppressed responding. Do McKearney's results showing that under some circumstances there can be a different relationship under suppressed and nonsuppressed conditions reinstate the attenuation of inhibitions hypothesis? Hardly. The effects of amobarbital are so clearly dependent on both rate of responding and on strength of stimulus control that the reintroduction of inhibition as a special kind of stimulus control is unwarranted.

The picture of stimulus control as a quantitatively graded function depending on stimulus as well as on the behavior controlled that emerged from the pharmacological studies is a contribution to understanding of behavior that has received

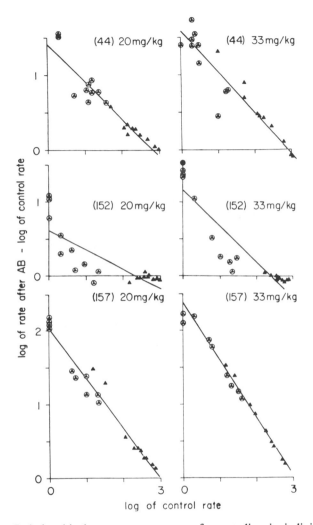

Fig. 3. Relationship between mean rates of responding in individual 25 sec periods under normal conditions and the increment in rate following amobarbital. Abscissa: log of rate as responses per session (i.e., in a total of 500 sec since each 25 sec period occured once in each of the 20 cycles). Ordinate: change in log rate following amobarbital. Since the 500 sec interval was divided for recording purpose into 20 periods of 25 sec, there are 20 points on each graph, 10 representing periods when the houselight was present, shown as circled triangles and 10 representing periods when the houselight was not present, shown as triangles. The line through them was calculated by least squares from all points. On the X = 0 ordinate are plotted all points where the mean rate of responding was 1 or less responses per 500 sec; this arbitrary assignment makes possible the logarithmic plot. Exclusion of these indeterminate points would not appreciably affect the regression line. (From Dews, 1964. Reproduced by permission of Springer-Verlag, Heidelberg.)

entirely independent support. Visual stimulus control can be attenuated not only by reducing the visual distinctiveness of stimuli but also by impairing the capacity of the receiving system. When kittens are monocularly deprived of form vision for periods in the months after birth there is a graded loss of driving of appropriate cortical units by visual stimuli through the deprived eye, the severity of loss depending on the length and timing of the deprivation (Wiesel & Hubel, 1963). There is a generally parallel loss of control of behavior by visual stimuli through the deprived eye (Dews & Wiesel, 1970). Stimulus control is again a seemingly continuously graded function. Further, Mello and Peterson (1964) showed in decisive experiments that the supposedly largely color-blind cat could be brought under the differential control of differently colored stimuli. The control was difficult to obtain and weak compared to, say, the control by color in the pigeon, but it was undeniable. Multiple cones with different spectral sensitivities, such as occur in color-sensitive humans, were not well established

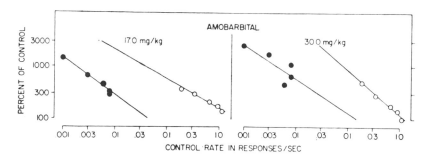

Fig. 4. Effect of amobarbital on responding during 60 sec segments of FI 600 sec with multiple S-delta periods under the Continuous Keylight procedure. Ordinate: rate after amobarbital expressed as percent of control. Abscissa: control rate during individual 60 sec segments of the FI. Ordinate and abscissa are logarithmic. Open circles: S^D. Closed circles: S-delta. Regression lines were fitted by the method of least squares. Note that the open and closed circles clearly fall on separate lines, though both sets follow a reasonably linear trend with similar negative slope, so the lines are parallel. The difference between the results shown in this figure and those in Fig. 3 is not due to the difference in FI length (600 sec vs 500 sec) nor to the number of S-delta periods in each FI (5 vs 10) because when the intensity of the houselight was reduced to the level prevailing when the experiments that led to Fig. 3 were conducted, the results of Fig. 3 were reproduced. (From McKearney, 1970. Reproduced by permission of the Society for the Experimental Analysis of Behavior, Inc.)

electrophysiologically in the cat. The suggestion was made that the color discrimination was based on the different absorption spectra of rods and cones, a differential that could certainly provide a sufficient physical basis for color discrimination (Daw & Pearlman, 1969). But color discrimination was found to persist under photopic conditions, when rods no longer contribute to visual reception, so cones alone must mediate the discrimination. A reexamination of color sensitivity of single units in the lateral geniculate showed that, although the great majority had input from a single type of cone, out of 434 units, 4 had one type of different color sensitivity and 2 had a third type (Daw & Pearlman, 1970). It is hard to avoid the conclusion that the strength of stimulus control in different species by color of stimuli is quantitatively related to the proportionate numbers of different cones. In any case, here is another example of quantitatively graded stimulus control. Although the notion of graded stimulus control was not an original contribution of pharmacological experiments, it appears that pharmacological experiments made graded stimulus control familiar as a function of far greater range and significance than had appeared previously.

SHOCK-MAINTAINED RESPONDING

Pharmacological considerations led to the discovery of the phenomenon of shock-maintained responding, but again they did so heuristically rather than directly. New types of experiments were conducted to understand more about drug effects, types of experiments that had not been previously conceived, far less performed, and the results in turn, led to new types of behavioral experiments. The story is as follows. As described earlier, experiments in the 50s had established rates and patterns of responding as powerful determinants of behavioral effects of drugs. For studies on effects of rate on drug effect, a favorite schedule has been FI (as, for example, in the previously described studies on amobarbital) because the typical pattern of responding generated by an FI schedule is a pause followed by a fairly regular continuously increasing rate within each FI cycle (Dews, 1978). Typically, responding in each FI goes from zero or very low rates at the beginning, through intermediate rates to steady fairly high rates of responding at the end. Thus effects of drugs in relation to a range of different rates of responding can be studied in single sessions, without the complication of different schedules to generate the different rates. Different schedules bring possible additional effects of their own, besides just different rates. A problem with accepting drug effects on different rates during FI as being solely related to the rate, however, is that rate of responding under FI is, at least on the average, inextricably related to the actual time in the schedule cycle: For example, the low rates occur early in the interval, temporally related to the initiation of the interval, while the higher rates occur later in the interval, in temporal proximity to the reinforcing stimuli. Kelleher and Morse (1968) conceived of the idea of trying to produce the complementary pattern of responding viz highest rates at the beginning of an interval (of constant duration in repeated cycles) and a progressive decrease to essentially no responding towards the end of the interval. Similar effects of drugs in relation to rate on such patterns as on FI patterns would be powerful evidence of the primacy of rate in determining the drug effect.

To try to produce a progressively decreasing rate through an interval, subjects were trained under a VI schedule, with food presentations as reinforcing stimuli, a schedule which alone produces steady, quite constant responding, and then for 1 min at the end of every 10 min, each response was programmed to deliver an electric shock to the subject. As the period of shocked responding approached, the rate could be expected to decrease in a manner reciprocal to the increase in rate as the time when a "positive reinforcer" is delivered under FI. But, when the experiments were conducted, there was little tendency for a graded decrease in responding through the interval. Responding could be essentially abolished, or responding could proceed at a constant rate for part of the interval and then cease, or responding could actually increase in frequency as the period of shocked responding approached (Figure 5) (Kelleher &

Morse, 1968). It was found possible to develop the increases in rate into stable patterns of responding, which, when the food schedule was eliminated, became indistinguishable, pattern-wise, from FI maintained by a food reinforcer (Figures 6,7) (Kelleher & Morse, 1968; Morse, McKearney & Kelleher, 1977). The electric shock becomes a "positive reinforcer," with

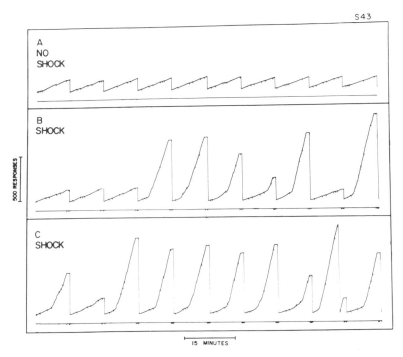

Fig. 5. Effects of scheduled electric shock on responding of squirrel monkeys. Abscissa: time. Ordinate: cumulative responding, resetting every 660 sec. A. Responding under a schedule of irregular intermittent reinforcement of steady rate of responding throughout session. Food deliveries shown by hatch marks on record. B and C. The first two consecutive sessions after a shock schedule was delivery of a shock of 12.6 ma to the tail of the monkey at the first response after 600 sec and then at every response during the next 60 sec. Notice that after only 3 shock deliveries, at start of B, there is large increase in rate of responding over that under the food schedule alone, positively accelerated up to the shock, showing the positive reinforcing properties of the shock. Thereafter, for the next 60 sec, there are very few responses, many fewer than under the food schedule alone, showing that the same shock as that showing positive reinforcing properties, can, under a different schedule, suppress responding. (From Kelleher & Morse, 1968, modified Fig. 4. Reproduced by permission of the Society for the Experimental Analysis of Behavior, Inc.)

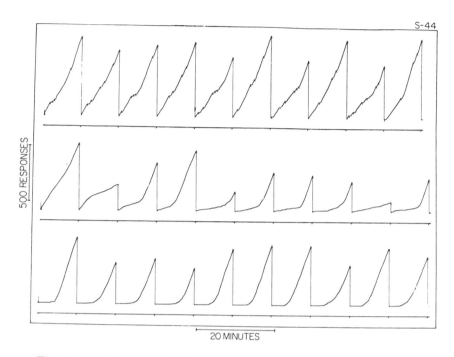

Fig. 6. Development of FI pattern of responding with electric shock as reinforcer. Abscissa: time. Ordinate: cumulative responding, resetting every 600 sec. A. Concurrent food and shock schedule. Irregular food deliveries shown by hatch marks on record (VI 120 sec), shock delivered every 600 sec at a response whereupon pen reset. Notice that responding continued throughout session but that the rate increased as the time of shock approached. B. Next session. Food schedule discontinued, so only consequence of responding is delivery of shock every 600 sec. Decline of rate of responding early in the interval is apparent already in the 3rd and 4th intervals, showing extinction of the food maintained responding, leaving the shock as the sole positive reinforcer. C. Sixty sessions later. During each of the intervening sessions the subject delivered 10 shocks at 60 sec intervals, the shock being the only consequence of the responding. The result of the total of the 100 hr of exposure to the schedule is a smoothly accelerating, highly characteristic pattern of FI responding, indistinguishable from that seen with food or other conventional positive reinforcers. (From Kelleher & Morse, 1968 from Fig. 18 and 19. Reproduced by permission of the Society for the Experimental Analysis of Behavior, Inc.)

epochal implications for our concept of reinforcers and how they control behavior, and for the whole field of motivation, with its concepts of needs and hedonism. The implications have still hardly started to be digested and incorporated into the science of analysis of behavior far less into psychology as a

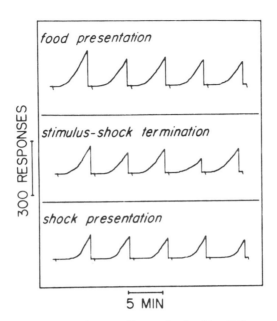

Fig. 7. Similar patterns of responding maintained by different events in squirrel monkeys under FI 300 sec. The recording pen was reset at the end of each cycle. A 30 sec time-out period separated successive FI cycles. Diagonal strokes denote the end of time-out periods. Records are segments selected from longer experimental sessions. Upper tracing: Food presentation (250 mg/cycle). Middle tracing: Termination of a stimulus-shock complex (schedule complex); brief electric shocks (10 ma) were scheduled to occur every 5 sec after 5 min had elapsed in the presence of a stimulus. A response occurring after 300 sec terminated the stimulus and instituted the time-out period. Lower tracing: Shock presentation (5 ma). Note the comparable patterns of positively accelerated responding regardless of the type of maintenance event. (From Morse, McKearney & Kelleher, 1977. Reproduced by permission of Plenum Press.)

whole and into the public's understanding (Dews, 1975).

SOME OTHER FACTORS

In the early years of behavioral pharmacology, the main emphasis was on the influence of rates and patterns of responding on the behavioral effects of drugs. Some of the emphasis was to try to counter the frequent contemporary claims of selective effects of drugs on "anxiety" or some such presumed influence on behavior; claims which were based on studies in which the rate and pattern of responding were grossly different in the presence and absence of the putative determinant of the drug effect. None of the claims was vindicated. Rates and patterns of responding seemed to be more important than any of the factors that had been supposed traditionally to determine drug effects, like states, emotions and learning status, and surprising generalizations can be based on rate alone, at least for amphetamine (Dews & Wenger, 1977). It was, however, not claimed or believed that rate and pattern were the sole behavioral determinants of drug effects on behavior. Once the importance of taking into account rate and pattern was realized

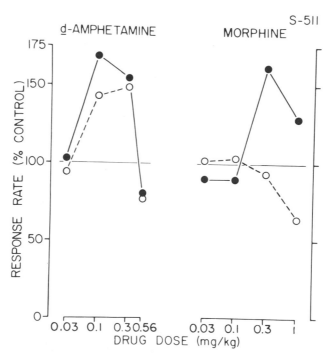

Fig. 8. Dose-effect curves of d-amphetamine sulfate and morphine sulfate on responding of a squirrel monkey (S-511) maintained under mult FI 300 sec (food) FI 300 sec (5 ma shock). Open circles, food presentation: filled circles, shock presentation. d-Amphetamine increased responding maintained by both events, whereas morphine increased responding under the shock-presentation schedule at doses that either decreased or had no effect on responding maintained by food. (From results of McKearney (1974). Figure from Morse, McKearney & Kelleher, 1977. Reproduced by permission of Plenum Press.)

and experiments conducted accordingly, it became possible to measure the effects of other factors. For example, on similar rates and patterns of FI responding maintained by food or by electric shock, some drugs have essentially the same effect while others have different effects (Figure 8) (Barrett & Katz, 1981). While it is not established that the basis of the differential effects of morphine in this example, and chlordiazepoxide and other drugs in other examples, is the specific attributes of the reinforcing events - food or shock - the near identity of both schedule and controlled pattern of responding in many examples suggests that the difference is not based on schedule or response rate. Bacotti and McKearney (1979) have shown that the effects of a drug on a pattern of responding can be influenced by temporally remote schedule factors. One of the best established findings in behavioral pharmacology is that amphetamine does not increase rates of responding that have been suppressed by response produced events such as electric shocks, appropriately scheduled. In subjects with experience of responding under a schedule of postponement of electric shocks by responses, however, amphetamine can produce substantial increases in such suppressed responding.

CONCLUSIONS

Though little has been said explicitly in this paper about behavioral units, the whole paper has been a vindication of unitary analysis of behavioral phenomena. The rates and patterns discussed are rates of repetitions of units of behavior. That so much has been learned from studying behavior as sequences of units is surely sufficient justification for the approach.

There have been few experiments seeking differences in drug effects on similarly maintained different unit responses; indeed, there have been relatively few behavioral experiments comparing directly the properties of different unit responses. Consideration of the effects of amphetamine on a variety of unit responses, in a variety of species, suggests that, for this drug at least, the nature of the unit response is not a substantial influence on the drug effect (Dews & Wenger, 1977). A comparison of effects of carbon disulfide on unit responses of running and of nose-poke in mice found no significant differences in the effect of the agent on occurrences of the two responses (Liang, Glowa, & Dews, 1983). It is hard to believe that differences based on difference in response unit will not be found, but it seems unlikely that they will be dramatic. Not only has the study of behavior as recurring units been profitable, but, so far as pharmacology is concerned, the results seem to have substantial generality for response units of different natures and topographies.

How can we epitomize pharmacological contributions to psychology? First it is well to recognize that the great majority of scientific psychologists are not much interested in the effects of drugs as such. In contrast, most scientific psychologists, including experimental analysts of behavior, are interested in the mechanisms of behavioral phenomena, mechanisms in the sense of neurobiological bases of behavioral phenomena. Enormous efforts have been devoted in pursuit of mechanism with, as previously discussed, meager success. Little if any more can be said about the mechanisms of most salient behavioral phenomena than could be said 50 years ago. The problems have proved just too difficult and may, indeed, be wrongly formulated so that the questions we are asking now may never have scientific answers. But in contrast a rich fabric of knowledge has been developed of behavioral effects of drugs. True, basic questions of physiological psychology have not been answered by pharmacological means, but new lines of experiments have been developed that may lead to the formulation of answerable questions. Francis Crick is alleged to have said: "If you are interested in function, but function is too difficult to study, study structure." Analagously, *if you are interested in neurobiological mechanisms, but the mechanisms are too difficult to study, maybe you should study pharmacological effects.* In addition to opening new lines of experiments and new formulations, the study of drugs may also help avoid waste of effort on problems wrongly formulated. Take, for example, studies on learning. Many years ago I tried to study drug effects on learning and concluded I couldn't (Dews, 1957). There has been a vogue starting in the 60's for one trial-learning paradigms as a means of studying effects on learning: Short of bringing the animal close to death immediately after the trial or giving grossly debilitating doses of inhibitors of protein synthesis throughout the body, effects that seem to be on learning as such have been unimpressive, and better appreciation of the power of schedules calls into question even some of the supposedly positive results. Pharmacological studies have not established, in my view, selective pharmacological effects on the phenomenon of learning.   I would argue that the failure to establish a pharmacology of learning, despite dedicated efforts over decades, suggest that we should reexamine our formulation of questions about learning. Thus, it behooves scientific psychologists to familiarize themselves with salient effects of drugs on behavior no matter what is their primary interest.   I think new insights into the nature of learning phenomena are more likely to come from the penetrating pharmacological analyses by people such as Harvey (Harvey, Gormezano & Cool, 1982) than from the naive incursions of molecular biologists. Time will tell.

ACKNOWLEDGMENT

It is a pleasure to honor Professor MacCorquodale and it is peculiarly appropriate to discuss pharmacological contributions to the experimental analysis of behavior in a Minnesota symposium because it was at the University of Minnesota that the first modern experiments in behavioral pharmacology were performed. The experiments were on effects of caffeine and amphetamine on responding under FI and were published by Skinner and Heron in 1937 (Skinner & Heron, 1937).

Preparation of this paper and much of the work described in it was supported by grants from the U.S. Public Health Service MH02094, MH07658, MH14275, DA00499, DA02658, and the New England Regional Primate Research Center Grant RR00168.

REFERENCES

Baccotti, A.V., & McKearney, J.W.   (1979).   Prior and ongoing experience as determinants of the effects of d-amphetamine and chlorpromazine on punished behavior. *Journal of Pharmacology and Experimental Therapeutics, 211,* 80-85.

Barrett, J.E., & Katz, J.L. (1981). Drug effects on behaviors maintained by different events. In T. Thompson, P.B. Dews, & W.A. McKim (Eds.), *Advances in Behavioral Pharmacology, Vol. 3,* (pp. 119-168). New York: Academic Press.

Daw, N.W., & Pearlman, A.L. (1969). Cat colour vision: One cone process or several? *Journal of Physiology, 201,* 745-764.

Daw, N.W., & Pearlman, A.L. (1970). Cat colour vision: Evidence for more than one cone process. *Journal of Physiology, 211,* 125-137.

Dews, P.B. (1955). Studies on behavior, II. The effects of pentobarbital, methamphetamine and scopolamine on performances in pigeons involving discriminations. *Journal of Pharmacology and Experimental Therapeutics, 115,* 380-389.

Dews, P.B. (1957). Studies on behavior, III. Effects of scopolamine on reversal of a discriminatory performance. *Journal of Pharmacology and Experimental Therapeutics, 119,* 343-353.

Dews, P.B. (1964). A behavioral effect of amobarbital. *Archiv Experimentelle Pathologie und Pharmakologie, 248,* 296-307.

Dews, P.B. (1975). Neurotransmitter balances and behavior. In E.F. Domino, & J.M. Davis (Eds.), *Neurotransmitter balances regulating behavior,* (pp. 125-133). Ann Arbor: Edwards Brothers

Dews, P.B. (1978). Studies on responding under fixed-interval schedules of reinforcement, II. The scalloped pattern of the cumulative record. *Journal of the Experimental Analysis of Behavior, 29,* 67-75.

Dews, P.B., & Wenger, G.R. (1977). Rate-dependency of the behavioral effects of amphetamine. In T. Thompson, & P.B. Dews (Eds.), *Advances in Behavioral Pharmacology, Vol. 1,* (pp. 167-227). New York: Academic Press.

Dews, P.B., & Wiesel, T.M. (1970). Consequences of monocular deprivation on visual behavior in kittens. *Journal of Physiology, 206,* 437-455.

Ferster, C.B., & Skinner, B.F. (1957). *Schedules of reinforcement.* New York: Appleton-Century-Crofts.

Harvey, I., Gormezano, I., & Cool, V.A. (1982). Effects of d-lysergic acid diethylamide, d-2-bromolysergic acid diethylamide, dl-2, 5-dimethoxy-4-methylamphetamine and d-amphetamine on classical conditioning of the rabbit nictitating membrane response. *Journal of Pharmacology and Experimental Therapeutics, 221,* 289-294.

Kelleher, R.T., & Morse, W.H. (1968). Schedules using noxious stimuli, III. Responding maintained with response-produced electric shocks. *Journal of the Experimental Analysis of Behavior, 11,* 819-838.

Keller, F.S. , & Schoenfeld, W.N. (1950). *Principles of psychology.* New York: Appleton-Century-Crofts.

Kimble, G.A. (1961). *Hilgard and Marquis' conditioning and learning.* New York: Appleton-Century-Crofts.

Liang, Y.X., Glowa, J.R., & Dews, P.B. (1983). Behavioral toxicology of volatile organic solvents, III. Acute and subacute effects of carbon disulfide exposure on the behavior of mice. *Journal of the American College of Toxicology, 2,* 379-389.

McKearney, J.W. (1970). Rate-dependent effects of drugs: Modification by discriminative stimuli of the effects of amobarbital on schedule-controlled behavior. *Journal of the Experimental Analysis of Behavior, 14,* 167-175.

McKearney, J.W. (1974). Effects of d-amphetamine, morphine and chlorpromazine on responding under fixed-interval schedules of food presentation or electric shock presentation, *Journal of Pharmacology and Experimental Therapeutics, 190,* 141-153.

Mello, N.K., & Peterson, N.J. (1964). Behavioral evidence for color discrimination in cat. *Journal of Neurophysiology, 27,* 323-333.

Morse, W.H. (1962). Use of operant conditioning techniques for evaluating the effects of barbiturates on behavior. In J.H. Nodine, & J.H. Moyer (Eds.), *Psychosomatic medicine: The first Hahnemann Symposium,* (pp. 275-281). Philadelphia: Lea & Febiger.

Morse, W.H., McKearney, J.W., & Kelleher, R.T. (1977). Control of behavior by noxious stimuli. In L.L Iverson, S.D. Iverson, & S.H. Snyder, (Eds.), *Handbook of psychopharmacology, Vol.7,* (pp. 151-180). New York: Plenum Press.

Skinner, B.F. (1938). *The behavior of organisms: An experimental analysis.* New York: Appleton-Century.

Skinner, B.F., & Heron, W.T. (1937). Effects of caffeine and benzedrine upon conditioning and extinction. *Psychological Record, 1,* 340.

Terrace, H.S. (1963). Errorless discrimination learning in the pigeon: Effects of chlorpromazine and imipramine. *Science, 140,* 318-319.

Thompson, T. (1984). The examining magistrate for nature: A retrospective review of Claude Bernard's *An introduction to the study of experimental medicine. Journal of the Experimental Analysis of Behavior, 41,* 211-216.

Wiesel, T.N., & Hubel, D.H. (1963). Single-cell responses in striate cortex of kittens deprived of vision in one eye. *Journal of Neurophysiology, 26,* 1003-1017.

PART III

LANGUAGE AND MATHEMATICS

CHAPTER 9

Mathematics and Verbal Behavior

M. JACKSON MARR

The science of behavior has given little attention to the behavior of scientists. That has been largely the province of philosophers, most of whom have avoided psychologistic speculation and even historical description in favor of rational analyses of epistemological doctrine. The implication is that somehow science stands apart from the activities of scientists. An early exception to this view was Ernst Mach, who in the introduction to *The Science of Mechanics*, discussed the origins of scientific activity, in particular, the role of *instruction*:

> When we wish to bring to the knowledge of a person any phenomena or process of nature, we have the choice of two methods: we may allow the person to observe matters for himself . . ., or, we may describe to him the phenomena in some way, so as to save him the trouble of making anew each experiment. (1960, p. 6)

Here is the first extant treatment, to my knowledge, of the significance to the development of science of rule-governed behavior (as opposed to contingency-shaped behavior), and it places proper emphasis on the role of verbal behavior in the repertoire of the scientist. Compare Mach's comment with Skinner's (1969): "The point of science . . . is to analyze the contingencies of reinforcement found in nature and to formulate rules or laws which make it unnecessary to be exposed to them in order to behave appropriately"(p. 166). Scientific behavior may be ultimately expressed by nonverbal behavior maintained by nonverbal consequences, but in large part, such behavior is *verbal*, embodying the descriptions of relatively stable environmental contingencies and "effective only through the mediation of other persons" (Skinner, 1957, p. 2). Skinner may be credited with the first attempts to treat scientific activity in the context of a larger theory of verbal behavior (Skinner, 1945, 1957, 1969, 1974). Chapter 18 of *Verbal Behavior* (Skinner, 1957) is devoted to "Logical and Scientific Verbal Behavior." The principal motif of his treatment is one of effective action or the pragmatic consequences of enhanced control of the environment. Thus, he says:

> In the history of logic and science, we can trace the development of a verbal community especially concerned with verbal behavior which contributes to successful action. (p. 418) . . .The scientific community encourages the precise stimulus control under which an object or property of an object is identified or characterized in such a way that practical action will be most effective. (p. 419) . . . Logicians and scientists have, of course, extensive repertoires of intraverbal behavior, but these are composed of items which have been found to have satisfactory practical results. (p. 421) . . . [Finally,] the test of scientific prediction is often, as the word implies, *verbal* confirmation. But the behavior of both logician and scientist leads at last to effective nonverbal action and it is here that we must find the ultimate reinforcing contingencies which maintain the logical and scientific verbal community. (p. 429)

Skinner, like Mach before him, came to emphasize the significance of rule-governed behavior to the development and maintenance of scientific practice (cf. Skinner, 1969). "Scientific knowledge . . . is a corpus of rules for effective action" (Skinner, 1974, p. 235). The rules comprising that corpus are descriptions of the contingencies confronted in Nature. The most effective form of those rules, i.e., those of the greatest generality and predictive power, are embodied in the verbal behavior we call mathematics. Mathematics, whatever else it might be, is fundamentally concerned with rules of rules, i.e., it is a corpus of rules for effective manipulation of rules, which are themselves considered to be in the domain of mathematics, though they might reflect environmental contingencies. Mathematics itself is considered by many to be a science. Perhaps the greatest mathematician of all, Karl Frederick Gauss said "Mathematics is the Queen of the Sciences . . . She often condescends to render service to astronomy and other natural sciences, but under all circumstances the first place is her due" (quoted in Bell, 1951, p. 1). Skinner provides two criteria which might lead us to label a verbal behavior as scientific. As already emphasized, first it guides effective, ultimately nonverbal action. Second, the behavior is under sharp stimulus control of relevant features of the environment including the verbal environment - control gained through the reinforcing and punishing practices of a "no-nonsense" verbal community. However, the placement of mathematics in the context of *scientific* verbal behavior is, I believe, a category decision requiring more careful treatment. The status of mathematics vis-a-vis those criteria is not, I think, straightforward.

With regard to the issue of the verbal behavior being maintained ultimately by effective nonverbal consequences, we might consider the case of so-called "pure" mathematics with its rigorous formal structure. What nonverbal consequences, effective or otherwise maintain verbal behavior of this kind? A similar question might then be raised with respect to the issue of sharp stimulus control, where again Skinner emphasizes the nonverbal circumstances responsible for the verbal behavior. Thus he says "In general, . . . practices are designed to clarify the relation between a verbal response made to a verbal stimulus and the *nonverbal* circumstances responsible for it. The community is concerned with getting back to the original state of affairs . . ." (Skinner, 1957, p. 420).

Some of the issues and concerns expressed here are similar to those of Roger Schnaitter (1980) who has provided a helpful discussion of the characteristics of and relationships between experimental and theoretical scientific behavior.

I wish to consider possible distinctive features of mathematics from the perspective of a verbal behavior account. In the process of doing this I want to consider the "grammar" of mathematics, i.e., its verbal operants and relationships between them, and the maintaining consequences and modes of justification. As Roger Schnaitter (1980) points out, the justification of scientific verbal behavior is based upon effective description, control and prediction of Nature's contingencies. ". . . the validity of such knowledge does not depend on any rational justifying processes" (p. 154). What of the justification of a mathematical argument? Is that based only upon intraverbal links or somehow is it also based upon effective description of Nature? In other words, is mathematics analytic or synthetic? To the extent to which this question is meaningful, confronting this issue is basic to an understanding of how it is possible to predict features of Nature by talking about it, particularly when there appear to be no experiential "referents" for the mathematical language. Kline (1980) has called this "the greatest paradox in mathematics" (p. 340). To treat this issue, I want to consider briefly some implications of the mathematical formalism of quantum mechanics, which provides the richest source of wonder about the relationships between Nature and mathematics. Finally, I want to discuss the processes of mathematical creation - what most mathematicians call *intuition*.

Few would argue that mathematics, in common with science, had its beginnings in our interactions with the environment where behaviors such as counting, and measurements of space and time conferred practical consequences. However, science and mathematics have evolved gradually into separate disciplines. Questions then arise as to the dimensions of that separation.

Figure 1 shows some structural and functional features of scientific and mathematical behavior. Scientific behavior is comprised of both verbal and non-verbal components, each of which may be subdivided into formal and informal categories. The distinction between these categories is not sharp but *informal activities* tend to be contingency-controlled as opposed to rule-governed. Where informal rules apply they may be "rules of thumb" rather than part of a generalized system of prescriptions as, for example, the complex set of instructions known as "experimental design"; or, as in the case of nonverbal behavior, performances under the control of the procedures of

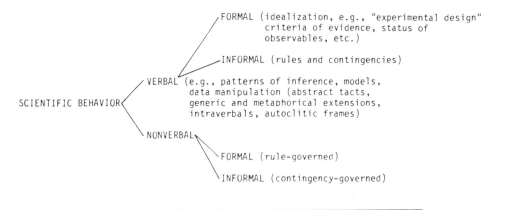

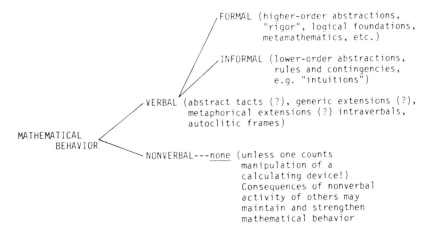

Fig. 1. A schematic indicating the formal and informal verbal and nonverbal operants comprising scientific and mathematical behavior. See text for details.

analytical   chemistry.   Scientific verbal behavior is characterized by a variety of verbal operants which, in their various combinations and interactions, yield patterns of inference, models, data manipulation, and interpretation.

Mathematical behavior appears to be exclusively verbal although that would depend upon one's tendency to extend the definition of mathematical activity. (A nonverbal organism might flee from the presence of many predators, but not from a single one - perhaps a crude form of counting.) As to the formal vs. informal aspects of mathematical (verbal) behavior, just as in scientific behavior (verbal and nonverbal) a distinction can be made on the basis of how the behavior is controlled in its "everyday" and creative context as opposed to the published, extant forms. The latter forms are subject to highly restrictive contingencies and rules.

The functional classes of verbal operants that characterize mathematical behavior are subject to debate, in that controversy has raged over the nature of mathematical entities - indeed, as I comment later, the functional classes and their origin lie at the heart of issues of mathematical foundations and philosophy.

Perspectives on the role and nature of mathematics have generated enormous debate among mathematicians and philosophers, particularly in this century (Davis & Hersh, 1981; Kline, 1980; Lakatos, 1980; Putnam, 1979). The controversies range over several dimensions, but the principal issue involves the epistemological status of mathematical operations and concepts. There are several "schools" - Platonism, Intuitionism, Formalism, Constructivism, Conventionalism, and Empiricism, with subdivisions and mixtures of each. While I believe it might be useful to analyze each of these philosophical positions from a radical behaviorist standpoint, I will focus primarily on Platonism, Formalism and Empiricism as these embody issues of particular behavioral interest.

The Platonist or realist school believes in the reality of mathematical entities as objective facts independent of human existence. The 19th century mathematician Hermite expressed the view as follows:

> I believe that the numbers and functions of analysis are not the arbitrary product of our spirits; I believe that they exist outside of us with the same character of necessity as the objects of objective reality; and we find or discover them and study them as do the physicists, chemists and zoologists. (quoted by Kline, 1980, p. 322)

Thus, mathematics is placed along side the other sciences studying the phenomena of Nature and the mathematician, by implication, is a discoverer, not a creator. As G. H. Hardy (1967) noted, "I believe that mathematical reality lies outside of us, that our function is to discover or *observe* it, and that the theorems which we prove, and which we describe grandiloquently as our 'creations' are simply our notes of our observations" (pp. 123-124).

The perspective of Platonism is compelling by any account. First, it is a view that most of us naively adopt as a result of our training in elementary mathematics. I was taught somewhere that "numbers were my friends," but the substantive nature of mathematical entities is not confined to third grade arithmetic; it is probably implicit in the activities of most practicing mathematicians. As Davis and Hersh (1981) observe: "Platonism was and is believed by (nearly) all mathematicians. But, like an underground religion, it is observed in private and rarely mentioned in public" (p. 339). We are so imbued with the reification of the integers, including fractions, that it does not seem odd to consider them as entities, but what about π or $\sqrt{2}$ or infinite-dimensional vector spaces, or "the set of all real numbers" or a function discontinuous at every point? The list of such mathematical objects is itself a nondenumerable set! What can it mean to say that there exist mathematical entities? Clearly, one is not talking about objects in the environment (other, than perhaps, marks on paper). For the Platonist, "These objects are, of course, not physical or material. They exist outside the space and time of physical existence. They are immutable - they are not created and they will not change or disappear" (David & Hersh, 1981, p. 318). René Thom, perhaps the world's leading mathematician, and a Platonist admits that ". . . mathematicians have only an incomplete view of this world of ideas" (1971, p. 697). For Kurt Gödel (1983), they are objects of a special form of perception:

> Despite their remoteness from sense experience, we do have something like a perception. . .of the objects of set theory, as seen from the fact that axioms force themselves upon us as being true. I don't see any reason why we should have less confidence in this kind of perception, i.e., mathematical intuition, than in sense perception . . . They too may represent an aspect of objective reality. (pp. 483-484)

How is the radical behaviorist to view this conceptual

Nebelheim? With regard to the general issue of object status, Willard Day (1969) has commented:

> . . . the radical behaviorist is aware that we may attribute thingness to events largely because we are accustomed to speak of the world about us as composed of objects which are felt to possess an inherent constancy or stability. He is reluctant to take for granted that all useful knowledge must be conceptualized in terms of verbal patterns of thought derived simply from our experience with material objects. Consequently, he is led to a position which is peculiarly anti-ontological. (p. 319)

Further, the notion that somehow the behavior of the mathematician is under the control of mathematical "concepts" is at variance with Skinner's account of the acquisition and control of abstraction. If we assume the status of an *abstract tact* applies to mathematical terms like "continuous function" one should be willing to consider what stimulus properties, coupled with what contingencies set up emission of the tact *continuous function*. Several levels of extension seem to be involved. First, the abstract tact *continuous* may be applied to *objects* that are smooth, unbroken, etc., then further extended to curves or surfaces bounding these objects, and then to the functions (or sets of rules) which generate these curves and surfaces. Ultimately, the extensions may be to functions generating surfaces of any dimensionality. The process of abstraction *evolves* in mathematics as indicated, for example, by changes in notions of continuity in the historical development of analysis. As Kline (1980) points out, many famous mathematicians as late as the middle of the 19th century were convinced by "proofs" that a continuous function must have a derivative at every point, a theorem today's freshman calculus student would proclaim absurd. Mathematicians now play with space-filling continuous functions that have *no* derivative at any point (Mandelbrot, 1983)!

Changes in the perspective of concepts like continuity provide support for the view of mathematics as a science and of the mathematician as scientist making new discoveries about a conceptual world existing outside of the human realm. The evolutionary growth of mathematics does not support the

Intuitional view that mathematical discoveries are essentially revelations of the structure of the human mind. That view carries with it the difficult burdens of the a priori and of infallibility (Kitcher, 1983).

Gödel's view of an alternative perception of mathematical reality might be considered as a kind of higher-order Dualism. Not only is there the real world of physical objects which engenders our distorted world of perceptual experience, there is also a world of mathematical ideas, to which we gain access (however feebly), via mathematical perceptions.

Hilary Putnam, however, an ardent realist, dismisses the notion of an independent mathematical reality:

> . . . Mathematics makes assertions that are objectively true or false, independently of the human mind, and . . . *something* answers to such mathematical notions as 'set' and 'function.' This is not to say that reality is somehow bifurcated - that there is one reality of material things, and then over and above it, a second reality of 'mathematical things' . . . Not only are these 'objects' of pure mathematics conditional upon material objects; they are in a sense merely abstract possibilities. Studying how mathematical objects behave might better be described as studying what structures are abstractly possible and what structures are not abstractly possible. (1979, p. 60, italics mine)

I cannot resist linking Putnam's "abstract possibilities" to Ryle's descriptions of mental entities as "behavioral tendencies" (Ryle, 1949). Mathematical objects are objects, not because they possess referents, but because as verbal stimuli they control certain patterns of verbal behavior with respect to other mathematical objects or to features of the environment. For Skinner (1957), most mathematical activity is intraverbal rather than tacting (e.g., p. 129, 428-429, 430-431). The "truth" or "falsity" of mathematical assertions would be assigned on the basis of tautology, i.e., internal consistency of intraverbal chains, or by effective prediction or nonverbal action with respect to the environment.

The question raised by the Platonists of the distinction between discovery vs. creation of mathematical entities is not a trivial issue from a Skinnerian perspective. In discussing the differences between the laws of government and the laws of science Skinner (1974) observes:

> ... the difference is not in the laws, but in the contingencies the laws describe. The laws of . . . governments codify contingencies of reinforcement maintained by social environments. The laws of science describe contingencies which prevail in the environment quite apart from any deliberate human action. (p. 124)

To translate this into a mathematical frame is not easy. What can it mean to say that there exist mathematical *contingencies*? I attempt to address this question later in discussing mathematical intuition, but I will say in advance that the notion of contingencies here does not imply that they exist apart from human action; in fact, they may depend upon it exclusively.

If mathematics is simply a tautology, then the issue of creation or discovery depends upon the rules which initiate the intraverbal chains. These may be discovered in the sense that they are descriptive of environmental contingencies. On the other hand, if somehow they are "arbitrary," then the use of the verb "discover" seems odd.

The doctrine of Platonism began to be challenged in the nineteenth century with the development of non-Euclidean geometry and with the advances in analysis. The search for foundations shifted away from geometric intuition toward arithmetic, and mathematicians like Cantor, Dedekind, and Weierstrass met this challenge by attempts to build a geometrical continuum by considerations of infinite sets of rational numbers. This work led in turn to a foundational structure of mathematics based upon logical operations with sets. The names of Frege, Russell, and Whitehead are associated with this approach. Platonism would seem to be saved by placing mathematics in the indubitable and incorrigible bosom of logic. But this was a failure primarily because set theory itself was rife with paradoxes. As Davis and Hersh (1981) put it:

> By the time set theory had been patched up to exclude the paradoxes, it was a complicated structure which one could hardly identify with logic in the philosophical sense of "the rules of

correct reasoning." So it became untenable to argue that mathematics is nothing but logic - that mathematics is one vast tautology. (p. 333)

An extraordinary reaction to this situation was to dispense with the infinite and to base mathematics on *finite constructions* involving the rational numbers which are taken as a priori. This viewpoint is known appropriately as constructivism and is associated with the Dutch topologist Brouwer. The consequences of constructivism are devastating to classical mathematics. Consider the following theorem: *Every real number is either zero, positive, or negative.* This theorem, known as the law of trichotomy can be proved, for example, by methods of Cantorian set theory, but Brouwer provides an example of a real number which one cannot demonstrate constructively is either positive, negative, or zero, thus showing the law of trichotomy is false. For many mathematicians, constructivism is an effort to save mathematics by destroying it. From the standpoint of epistemology, constructivism owes much to naive positivism in that it accepts the natural numbers as equivalent to basic sense impressions and builds a mathematical system with them, relying only upon "observables." Thus π does not exist as an infinite sequence of digits; it has existence only as it is represented by a finite sequence, for that is all that can be constructed. To talk about the expansion of π already existing is meaningless. An "operational definition" of π is a finite procedure used to construct it.

The parallels between the various attempts to establish a foundation for mathematics and the conflicts over the status of mental entities as bases for behavior are vivid. The Intuitionist believes that mathematics manifests the structure of the mind. So, the introspectionists held that self-knowledge was incorrigible and revealed by looking inward. J. B. Watson and the methodological behaviorists who followed him were basically constructivists, admitting only the "observable" and attempting to define mental entities by sets of operations. "Overt behavior" corresponds with "finite construction." The parallel can be extended to include certain forms of modern cognitive psychology whose views bear comparison with traditional mathematical Platonism in its structural emphasis and its assertion of the reality of immaterial entities. To conceive of the unit interval [0,1] (for example, the 0-1 inch space on a ruler) as a structure comprised of real (no pun intended) denumerable and nondenumerable sets of objects called, respectively, rational and irrational numbers may be looked upon as not unlike the cognitivist who observes behavior under the control of past events and postulates a store - a semantic or episodic organizational structure, a matched image, or a cognitive map as explanatory entities or unconscious processes.

The attempts of mathematics to disengage itself from the problems of Platonism and the futile search for foundations led ultimately to *Formalism* where mathematics becomes a *game* of logical deduction. Mathematics is then the recreation of rigorous proof, beginning with undefined terms and a set of axioms about these terms. Axioms, definitions and theorems are the sole content of a formalism and in themselves are not *about* anything more than a move in chess is about anything. Saul Gorn has defined a formalist as one who cannot understand a theory unless it is meaningless (Smullyan, 1983)! The goal of a formalist development is to eliminate any appeal to pictures or to other modes of interpretation. Theorems, like the axioms from which they are derived are neither "true" nor "false," since they are not about anything. They are valid only in the logical sense of being derived through rigorous proof. Thus there are no "facts" of geometry or arithmetic. That mathematics seems to have some relationship to the world of facts is a matter of interpretation of the axioms and theorems, but interpretations have nothing to do with mathematics itself. As Davis and Hersh (1981) put it:

> . . . mathematics appears as the tool for formulating and developing . . . (physical) theory. The fundamental laws are mathematical formulas . . . Mathematics itself is seen, not as a science, but as a language for other sciences. It is not a science because it has no subject matter. (pp. 342-343)

There are aspects of Formalism which are in sympathy with

a verbal behavior perspective. Axioms establish autoclitic frames and their relationships. These are the rules from which other rules are inferred via intraverbal chains. There are no referents for the terms or rules, except other terms and rules. In other words, mathematics is itself fundamentally trivial. Yet it is one thing to talk about intraverbal links between rules to provide a tautological system, and another to consider the source of the rules. To what degree can axioms be arbitrary? If mathematics is trivial why does it work so well? As an approach toward that question from a formalistic perspective, I want to make contact with Wittgenstein.

As a philosopher of mathematics, his views lie close to formalism (although he repudiates its foundations) and he elicits comparison with Skinner. Proving parallels and antiparallels between Wittgenstein and Skinner has gotten to be a favorite occupation (or should I say pastime) of radical behaviorists and others, and I approach such a task with trepidation if only because sailing into Wittgensteinian waters one encounters a teeming, but deep and murky sea. I do no more here than skirt the shore in the safe shallows of superficiality.

Wittgenstein in his *Remarks on the Foundations of Mathematics*, provided pointed criticism of all major theories of mathematics while at the same time adopting some features of each (Fogelin, 1980; Klenk, 1976; Wittgenstein, 1978). Wittgenstein denies the existence of any mathematical entities and, in turn, denies that mathematics is some kind of natural science. What mathematics provides is a linguistic structure for formulating and manipulating rules. Thus he says: "The proposition proved by means of a proof serves as a rule - and so as a paradigm" (p. 163). The process of inference is itself an expression of a rule: "There is nothing occult about this process, it is a derivation of one sentence from another according to a rule; a comparison of both with some paradigm or other, which represents the schema of the transition, or something of the kind" (p. 39). Mathematics consists then of rules of rules. However, Wittgenstein parts company with the Formalist in at least two important respects. First, the process of inference is not automatic. To quote Klenk (1976): ". . .

inferring is a human activity in which one proposition is uttered or written down after another, and whether the inference is correct is a matter of how people in general use these signs, what they call 'correct.' The mere *pattern* of signs in itself will not constitute a proof, but must be *accepted* as a proof, taken as a proof by a human agent" (p. 30). Wittgenstein (1978) says it this way: "The proof is the pattern of proof employed in a particular way" (p. 298). Doing mathematics then is not referring, but speaking in a certain way according to conventional accepted views.

Second, mathematics is not simply a game.

> If mathematics is a game, then playing some game is doing mathematics, and in that case why is not dancing mathematics too? (p. 258) . . . What I want to say: it is essential to mathematics that its signs are also employed in mufti. It is the use of outside mathematics, and so the *meaning* of the signs that makes the sign-game into mathematics. (p. 257)

Thus, it is the fact that mathematics has practical applications or reflects Nature that distinguishes it from a game. A basic function of mathematics is to provide us with forms of inference to allow us to deal effectively with the world. Thus he noted:

> It is interesting to know *how many* vibrations this note has. But it took arithmetic to teach you this question. It taught you to see this kind of fact. Mathematics - I want to say - teaches you, not just the answer to a question, but a whole language-game with questions and answers. (p. 381)

The role of a mathematical proposition is that of a rule to describe the world. "Mathematical propositions play the part of rules of description, as opposed to descriptive propositions" (p. 363). A proposition is thus *prescriptive*, not a statement of fact. Finally, systems of inference are not arbitrary but are suggested by our interaction with Nature. "There correspond to our laws of logic very general facts of daily experience" (p 82).

The notion of empirical logic is strongly advocated by Hilary Putnam (1979) in his discussion of quantum logic; and Kantor (see Schoenfeld, 1969) argued for the role of contingencies in the establishment and practice of logic.

Kantor's view is expressed by Schoenfeld in the context of the relationship between logic and language:

> . . . logic is a set of propositions couched in a constructional language system.   Since language and grammar are interbehavioral, logic in turn becomes behavioral in two senses. First, to understand either classical or modern logical systems as the end products of reacting human organisms, the language behavior, training and context established in the logician by his social environment must be known, since he necessarily draws upon those for his thought, his propositions, and his system. Kantor believes that even Aristotle saw this and commented upon it. Second, the interaction between the practitioner of science (or of logic, or of any verbal play) and his environment is determined by the actual conditions under which he is operating and by the data he is in process of obtaining; since this interaction or interplay is the "logic" we wish to understand, we can only do so by understanding the interactional behavior itself. (p. 335)

Mathematical developments in quantum physics provide perhaps the most interesting and challenging examples of the complex relationships between a mathematical function and observed and predicted features of Nature.   In part this is because quantum formalism cannot be based directly upon any "picture" of Nature, e.g., billiard balls, springs, etc.

Dirac, a leading formalist in the development of quantum mechanics has commented:

> . . . the main object of physical systems is not the provision of pictures, but the formulation of laws generating phenomena, and the application of these laws to the discovery of new phenomena. If a picture exists, so much the better; but whether a picture exists or not is a matter of only secondary importance. In the case of atomic phenomena no picture can be expected to exist in the usual sense of the word "picture," by which is meant a model functioning along classical lines. One may, however, extend the meaning of the word "picture" to include any ways of looking at the fundamental laws which makes their self-consistency obvious. (1981, p. 10)

Heisenberg in the early days of the development of quantum mechanics despaired of convincing "even leading physicists that they must abandon all attempts to construct perceptual models of atomic processes" (1971, p. 76). Thus this view states that the language of quantum processes is mathematics, and what is more, "we have . . . no simple guide for correlating the mathematical symbols with concepts of ordinary language . . ." (1962, p. 177). The mathematical formalism provides no pictures, not even metaphors; what it does provide is prediction. The formalism is the ultimate expression of the awesome fact that we may be led to new and even surprising features of nature by talking about it. How can this be? It is tempting for some perhaps to characterize atomic processes as "pure thought," implying a form of conceptual causation with its attendant subjectivism. Zukav (1980) describes the wave function as " . . . a tool for our understanding of nature . . . something in our thoughts" (p. 80) and, after Stapp, espouses an explicit Platonic dualism in which "physical reality is both idea-like and matter-like" (p. 81).

A radical behaviorist approach to the effectiveness of mathematical formalism might begin with the principle that *materia mathematica* be treated as features of the environment, i.e., discriminative stimuli, where manipulations can be maintained by effective verbal as well as nonverbal consequences. The latter are represented by the control over nature attained, in turn, through control by the verbal stimuli. The verbal behavior itself consists of manipulation of autoclitic frames and intraverbals accompanied by qualifying and quantifying autoclitics (Skinner, 1957). This is rule-governed behavior of enormous complexity, but as Skinner points out " . . . rules . . . are physical objects and they can be manipulated to produce other . . . rules" (1969, p. 144).

A deeper issue to be considered, however, is how do the rules of quantum formalism, for example, relate to environmental contingencies so that the application of these rules has effective consequences? Moore (1981) comments that: "For the radical behaviorist, a given verbal stimulus occasions effective prediction and description presumably *because the stimulus is derived from some factor in the observed situation*, not because of its subjective or logical-theoretical status" (p. 65, italics mine). Such factors seem to be missing from an abstract formalism and, indeed, it is sometimes said to be the expressed

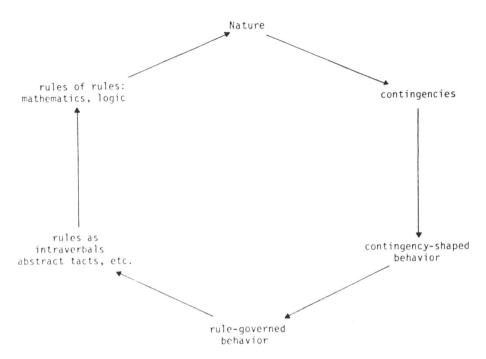

Fig. 2. An epistemological cycle. From interaction with Nature there has evolved increasingly abstract behavior, which in turn provides for the most effective desciption and control of Nature. Moreover, it may be possible in principle to link any mathematical formulation to Nature even when that formulation is deemed "pure."

goal of a mathematical scheme to achieve ultimate abstraction, in the sense that the source of control is purely verbal, and having no relationship to environmental contingencies. But the very effort required to achieve this goal tells us that, in fact, it is not possible. Verbal behavior is rooted in nature - it is acquired through interaction with a verbal community, itself subject to a long history of environmental contingencies. In a simplistic formulation we might view a hierarchy of complexity which always leads back to its source: One cannot overestimate the complexity of these relationships, however. First, it should be emphasized that the processes described here do not imply an unfolding of "ultimate truth." Mathematics is presumably a limited expression of nature and therefore limited in what it has to say about nature.

Second, the relationship between environmental

contingencies and mathematical analysis is often indeed remote, leading Kline (1980) to comment on the issue of why mathematics works:

> One might answer that the mathematical concepts and axioms are suggested by experience . . . but such an explanation is far too simplistic . . . human beings have created mathematical concepts and techniques in algebra, the calculus, differential equations and other fields that are not suggested by experience. (p. 339)

But as I have pointed out earlier, the history of mathematics reveals an extended shaping of abstraction. Consider the progression from simple counting to rational fractions, to irrational numbers, to complex numbers, to quaternions, etc. This process took thousands of years and because mathematics was originally much more closely linked to "experience," i.e., to environmental contingencies, there was often considerable controversy about the "meaning" of abstraction. Kline (1980) notes that most European mathematicians in the 16th and 17th centuries did not accept negative numbers as numbers. Presumably, negative numbers occasioned responses similar to those controlled by quantum mechanical wave functions today - e.g., "inconceivable."

Mathematics developed through effective consequences of its construction and exercise, occasioned by the solution of practical problems, but it subsequently became an endeavor substantially maintained by verbal reinforcement. Unambiguous specifications of this form of reinforcement are elusive, but achieving control over verbal stimuli can be as powerful a consequence as achieving control over a nonverbal domain, a testament perhaps to the "object" status of verbal stimuli. At any rate, as a result, mathematics has often outdistanced its applications, so when more elaborate specifications of nature's contingencies were ultimately constructed, appropriate verbal repertoires were already available, now to be further strengthened by nonverbal consequences - complex variables for electromagnetic theory and hydrodynamics, non-Euclidean geometry and tensor analysis for general relativity, Hilbert space and group theory for quantum mechanics. This is in accord with Skinner's pragmatic theory of truth (Skinner, 1953, 1972, 1974). It appears that the ultimate test for the soundness of a mathematical development is in its application (Kline, 1980) and we have come full circle.

I should like to approach the limit point of this essay by a brief consideration of mathematical intuition. Skinner has commented that "behaving intuitively in the sense of behaving as the effect of unanalyzed contingencies, is the very starting point of a behavior analysis" (Skinner, 1974, p. 132). Intuition, then, is an expression of contingency-shaped behavior. In the case of nonverbal behavior, say playing billiards, the skilled player's performance has been shaped by consequences related to the movement and relative positions of the billiard balls as generated by their interactions with the cue, the table cushion and each other. All this seems fairly straightforward. Verbal intuition, however, calls for a special analysis. The rules of mathematics seem to acquire dynamic properties which, in turn, provide for complex contingencies. The layperson's concept of the mathematician working step-by-step, one term or rule generating another in a sort of linear intraverbal chain is totally at variance with actual practice. The reality is more accurately expressed by G. H. Hardy in his description of how the great mathematician Ramanujan worked: "All his results, new or old, right or wrong, had been arrived at by a process of mingled argument, intuition, and induction of which he was entirely unable to give any coherent account" (Hardy, Seshu Aiyar, & Wilson, 1962, p. xxx).

And Feferman writes:

> The mathematician at work relies on surprisingly vague intuitions and proceeds by fumbling fits and starts with all too frequent reversals. Clearly logic as it stands fails to give a direct account of either the historical growth of mathematics or the day-to-day experience of its practitioners. It is also clear that the search for ultimate foundations via formal systems has failed to arrive at any convincing conclusion. (quoted in Davis and Hersh, 1981, p. 357)

The processes generating mathematics may thus not be basically different from those generating poetry, although the constraints and consequences might differ. As in literature, what the layperson, student (or critic) sees in the final product usually bears little resemblance to the evolving conditions of composition. Comprised of relational and manipulative autoclitics, effective compositional behavior is often under exceedingly subtle control, requiring an extensive history.

What gives mathematics its extant rigid intraverbal and abstract character is the progressive shaping by the mathematical community of the formal verbal behavior deemed "rigor." This is perhaps the ultimate expression of the sharpening of stimulus control as applied to logical and scientific verbal behavior. A premium is placed upon strict intraverbal control with a minimum number of rules, maximum generality and absolute consistency. But this is essentially a modern development and most mathematics, if not all, does not originate in that form. The development of analysis has been devoted to rigorizing essentially metaphorical intuitive notions of the calculus, for example, continuity, infinitesimal, and limit, all of which have served physicists and other scientists perfectly well without being exalted to higher orders of abstraction.

What is perhaps the most interesting aspect of mathematical intuition is that the direct source of contingencies may be *entirely* verbal. Thus Nature's contingencies may generate the basic rules, but once this occurs, the complex of rules themselves act as contingencies in the sense that their controlling features remain unspecified and, perhaps, unspecifiable. However, this situation characterizes any complex and intricate skill, verbal or nonverbal that, although initiated under control of a specified set of rules, ultimately is controlled by unspecified contingencies. Rules are important in that they allow for effective control through instruction. However, as Skinner has pointed out, the contingencies from which the rules are derived control different behaviors from the rules that describe them. One important difference is that contingency-governed behavior is likely to be more flexible, in other words, more *variable*, than rule-governed behavior. It is that variability with its resultant range in consequences that provides the *Anlage* of creative behavior in mathematics, poetry, or any other significant human activity. Finally, as to the consequences that maintain mathematical behavior, it is clear that much of this behavior is not directly maintained by practical consequences. One does not have to look far for them, however. G. H. Hardy (1967) wrote:

> The mathematician's patterns, like the painter's or the poet's must be beautiful; the ideas, like the colours or the words must fit together in a harmonious way. Beauty is the first test; there is no permanent place in the world for ugly mathematics. (p. 85)

Dirac has asserted that it is more important to have beauty in one's equations than to have them fit an experiment. Thus the reinforcers for mathematicians and poets - and I would add, scientists alike, are fundamentally aesthetic.

Finally, I should like to emphasize to an audience of behavior analysts that consideration of mathematics and verbal behavior is not simply a matter of philosophical interest. The acquisition of effective mathematical behavior may provide a productive model for language acquisition itself. Accurate development of mathematical skills occur at a later age under more explicit conditions than a "natural language" acquisition. Significant variables may be considerably easier to specify and control. As I have tried to point out, most if not all significant verbal operants and controlling relations occur in mathematical behavior. Skinner's *Verbal Behavior* gave scant attention to acquisitive processes. The careful study of mathematical behavior by behavior analysts might begin to provide a better account. There are obvious practical as well as basic reinforcers for such an effort. Recent concerns over the poor quality of education at all levels in the country emphasize basic skills in mathematics particularly. Perhaps, through appropriate behavior analysis we can make a significant contribution toward effective instruction in this most important - and beautiful - behavior.

REFERENCES

Bell, E. T. (1951). *Mathematics, queen and servant of science.* NY: McGraw-Hill Book Company.

Davis, P. J., & Hersh, R. (1981). *The mathematical experience.* Boston: Birkhauser.

Day, W. (1969). Radical behaviorism in reconciliation with phenomenology. *Journal of the Experimental Analysis of Behavior, 12,* 315-328.

Dirac, P. A. M. (1981). *Principles of quantum mechanics* (4th ed., revised). Oxford: Clarendon Press.

Fogelin, R. (1980). *Wittgenstein.* Boston: Routledge and Kegal Paul.

Gödel, K. (1983). What is Cantor's continuum problem? In P. Benacerraf, & H. Putnam (Eds.), *Philosophy of mathematics* (2nd ed.), (pp. 470-485). Cambridge: Cambridge University Press.

Hardy, G. H. (1967). *A mathematician's apology.* Cambridge: Cambridge University Press.

Hardy, G. H., Seshu Aiyar, P. V., & Wilson, B. M. (1962). *Collected papers of Srinivasa Ramanujan.* New York: Chelsea Publishing Company.

Heisenberg, W. (1962). *Physics and philosophy.* New York: Harper and Row.

Heisenberg, W. (1971). *Physics and beyond.* New York: Harper and Row.

Kitcher, P. (1983). *The nature of mathematical knowledge.* New York: Oxford University Press.

Klenk, V. H. (1976). *Wittgenstein's philosophy of mathematics.* The Hague: Martinus Nijhoff.

Kline, M. (1980). *Mathematics, the loss of certainty.* New York: Oxford University Press.

Lakatos, I. (1980). *Mathematics, science and epistemology.* Cambridge: Cambridge University Press.

Mach, E. (1960). *The science of mechanics.* (T. J. McCormack, trans., 6th ed.). LaSalle, Illinois: Open Court. (Original work published 1893.)

Mandelbrot, B. (1983). *The fractal geometry of nature.* San Francisco: W. H. Freeman and Company.

Moore, J. (1981). On mentalism, methodological behaviorism, and radical behaviorism. *Behaviorism, 9,* 55-77.

Putnam, H. (1979). *Mathematics, matter and method.* Cambridge: Cambridge University Press.

Ryle, A. (1949). *The concept of mind.* New York: Barnes and Noble Books.

Schnaitter, R. (1980). Science and verbal behavior. *Behaviorism, 8,* 153-160.

Schoenfeld, W. N. (1969). J. R. Kantor's *Objective psychology of grammar* and *Psychology and logic*: A retrospective appreciation.

Journal of the Experimental Analysis of Behavior, 12, 329-347.

Skinner, B. F. (1945). The operational analysis of psychological terms. *Psychological Review, 12,* 220-277.

Skinner, B.F. (1953). *Science and human behavior.* New York: The Macmillan Company.

Skinner, B. F. (1957). *Verbal behavior.* New York: Appleton-Century-Crofts.

Skinner, B. F. (1969). *Contingencies of reinforcement.* New York: Appleton-Century-Crofts.

Skinner, B. F. (1972). *Cumulative record* (3rd ed.). New York: Appleton-Century-Crofts.

Skinner, B. F. (1974). *About Behaviorism.* New York: Knopf.

Smullyan, R. (1983). *5000 B. C. and other philosophical fantasies.* New York: St. Martin's Press.

Thom, R. (1971). Modern mathematics: An educational and philosophical error? *American Scientist, 59,* 695-699.

Wittgenstein, L. (1978). *Remarks on the foundations of mathematics.* Cambridge: MIT Press.

Zukav, G. (1980). *The dancing wu-li masters.* New York: Bantam Books.

CHAPTER 10

Some Nonverbal Properties of Verbal Behavior

A. CHARLES CATANIA AND DANIEL T. CERUTTI

In the analysis of behavior, we often speak of a discriminative stimulus as setting the occasion on which some response will be reinforced. Strictly, however, discriminative stimuli do not occasion responses; instead, particular stimulus properties occasion particular response properties. For example, imagine an experimental setting in which the form of a stimulus determines response location whereas its color determines response rate. Suppose the stimuli presented in a standard two-key pigeon chamber consisted of green or red circles or triangles. We could reinforce left-key pecking given circles and right-key pecking given triangles and fast pecking given green and slow pecking given red. If these contingencies established correlations between stimulus forms and response locations and between stimulus colors and response rates (cf. Catania, 1973, p. 106-109), it might be simpler to speak in terms of the several stimulus and response dimensions (form controlling location and color controlling rate) than to itemize the particular combinations of response properties occasioned by particular stimuli (e.g., fast left pecking occasioned by a green circle).

This convergence of different stimulus properties in the control of the various dimensions of a response is especially relevant to verbal behavior (cf. Skinner, 1957, on multiple causation). For example, the variables that determine the noun in a simple active voice sentence (e.g., *The dog runs* or *The cats walk*) are likely to differ from those that determine the verb.

More important, such convergence may be the source of productivity in human verbal behavior (Chomsky, 1959; cf. Esper, 1933): Novel combinations of stimulus properties may produce novel behavior. The issues are in part those of where the line should be drawn between verbal and nonverbal behavior and of which features of verbal behavior are peculiarly human.

Much of the controversy over whether language can be established in primates (e.g., Terrace, Petitto, Sanders & Bever, 1979; Thompson & Church, 1980) has concentrated on the structural features, or syntax, of the behavior that has been taught. But nonverbal as well as verbal behavior can have syntactic properties (cf. Fentress, 1978). We argue here that these properties can sometimes emerge simply as the convergence of two or more dimensions of stimulus control over different dimensions of behavior. A more detailed account has been provided elsewhere (Catania, 1980); that account was concerned with some aspects of autoclitic verbal behavior (Skinner, 1957) and used a series of hypothetical pigeon demonstrations to make its points. Here we consider some experimental realizations of those hypothetical procedures.

CONTROL OF MULTIPLE RESPONSE DIMENSIONS BY MULTIPLE STIMULUS DIMENSIONS

One purpose of our first procedure was simply to establish a performance in which each of several stimulus dimensions controlled a particular response dimension (for examples of experiments on multiple stimulus dimensions controlling a single response dimension, see Blough, 1972; Butter, 1963). Because success with only a single subject is sufficient to demonstrate feasibility, we present data from only one pigeon (data from three other pigeons were consistent with those presented here, but for various reasons none of the other pigeons was exposed to all of the conditions arranged for Pigeon 95).

The demonstration used three stimulus dimensions and three response dimensions, illustrated in the apparatus diagram of Figure 1. The stimuli were presented in successive trials and consisted of one or two forms, circles or triangles, presented on a green or red background. Each trial began with the stimuli presented on all four keys. After 3 sec, a peck on any key terminated the trial. Depending on the location of that peck and the number of pecks that had preceded it during the 3 sec trial, the trial ended with a reinforcer (food delivery) or a period of timeout (darkened chamber); for economy of presentation, these sometimes will be referred to respectively as reinforced and unreinforced trials (strictly, only responses can be reinforced).

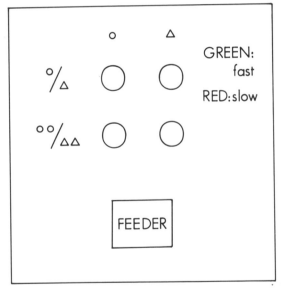

Fig. 1. Schematic view of the four-key apparatus and main procedure. Each trial began with the presentation on all four keys of a stimulus array: one or two circles or triangles on a green or a red background. The three properties of the array (one-two or singular-plural, circle-triangle, and green-red) were correlated with three properties of key pecking (top-bottom, left-right, and fast-slow): In trials with one form on each key top-row pecks were reinforced but in those with two forms on each key bottom-row pecks were reinforced; in those with circles left-column pecks were reinforced, but in those with triangles right-column pecks were reinforced; and in those with green high rates of pecking were reinforced, but in those with red low rates were reinforced. For example, with one triangle on green on each of the four keys the feeder was operated by fast pecking on the upper right key.

Fig. 2. Circle and triangle stimulus arrays. The IEE Inline Displays behind each key could project circles or triangles in any of three positions. From top to bottom, the rows show the three ways of projecting one circle, two circles, one triangle, or two triangles. With this technique, each lamp was used in both singular and plural arrays, reducing the likelihood of discriminations based on asymmetries of filaments or other idiosyncratic properties of particular lamps (cf. Gardner & Ely, 1969). Circles were about 6 mm in diameter; triangles were equilateral with sides of about 6 mm.

Stimulus number (one versus two or singular versus plural) determined whether a peck on the top or bottom row of keys was reinforced. Stimulus form (circle versus triangle) determined whether a peck on the left or right column of keys was reinforced. Stimulus color (green versus red) determined whether the peck was reinforced only after a high rate of pecking during the 3 sec trial or only after a low rate of pecking.

Colors were presented as green or red backgrounds. The singular or plural circles or triangles were presented in one of three arrangements on the key, as shown in Figure 2. This procedure was adopted to reduce the likelihood of discriminations based on idiosyncratic features of the particular lamps in each projector. We will present other procedural details later.

Data from a performance maintained by this procedure are shown in Figure 3. In general, location and rate of responding were under the control of the several properties of the stimuli that appeared on the keys. Although it may be inappropriate to speak of left-right and top-bottom as separate dimensions of the

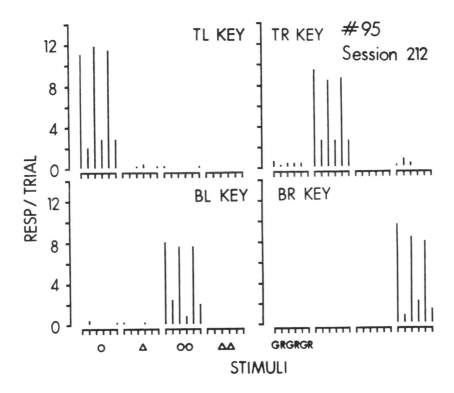

Fig. 3. The performance of Pigeon 95 on each of the four keys during Session 212. The arrangement of the graphs corresponds to that of the four keys on the panel (Figure 1); for example, the top left graph shows data from the top-left (TL) key. The 24 possible stimuli are arrayed along the x-axis: six arrangements each for singular circles, singular triangles, plural circles, and plural triangles, as indicated on the bottom-left (BL) x-axis. Within each set of six, green (G) and red (R) alternate as indicated on the bottom-right (BR) x-axis, with successive pairs corresponding to the three arrangements of forms in the three columns of Figure 2. Thus, the leftmost value on each graph presents responding during those trials with singular circle on green in which the circle was in the position shown in the first column and top row of Figure 2; the next value shows trials with the same circle stimulus but on red rather than green, and so on. The data plotted are arithmetic means over all trials with a given stimulus. In this format, stimulus control by form and number is shown by the key on which responding occurs and stimulus control by color is shown by the pattern of alternating high and low rates within the block of six stimuli correlated with reinforced pecking on a key. In this session, pecking occurred predominantly on left keys on circle trials, right keys on triangle trials, top keys on singular trials and bottom keys on plural trials, and response rates were high on trials with green and low on those with red. Although only 49% of 205 trials ended with reinforcers, 96% of 1052 responses were on the appropriate key.

response classes that generated the locations of pecks, the several configurations of forms determined the key pecked and the colors determined the rate of pecking.

In this procedure, the relations between reinforcement contingencies and particular pecks were complex. Both the location of the last peck of a trial and the number of pecks that preceded it, without regard to location, determined whether the reinforcer was delivered. Under these circumstances, it is difficult to apply consistently the characteristic language of stimulus control in trial procedures, which designates some responses as correct and others as incorrect or errors. Responding within a trial could be "correct" with respect to rate but not location or vice versa, and, on the basis of their rate, responses during the trial had their effects only on the eligibility of the final peck to produce the reinforcer. For these reasons, locutions such as responding "appropriate to a stimulus" should be understood as responding that meets one or more of the reinforcement contingencies correlated with a given stimulus property. The expansion of each case to a description of a three-term contingency (a discriminative stimulus setting the occasion on which a response has a consequence) should be evident from the context.

ESTABLISHING THE PERFORMANCES: DETAILS OF PROCEDURE

Another objective of this experiment was to establish separately control of response location by form and number and control of rate by color, and then to study transfer of these separate discriminations when the various stimulus dimensions were combined. For example, would a pigeon separately trained to peck the upper right key in the presence of singular triangles and to peck rapidly in the presence of green then peck rapidly on the upper right key given the presentation of singular triangles on green, a stimulus combination it had never seen before? Such a demonstration would constitute a simple instance of productivity in the nonverbal behavior of a nonhuman organism (this objective, however, was not attained).

In this experiment, control of location by form and number was established first. Then control of rate by color was established independently. The procedures were arranged by an APPLE II computer connected to the operant chamber by a John Bell Engineering 6522 parallel interface and solid-state switching circuitry. Each session consisted of two or more cycles of 24 stimuli, with the number of cycles adjusted from session to session to minimize supplementary feeding after the session. Because stimuli were repeated when trials ended without a reinforcer (according to a correction procedure described below), a 24-stimulus cycle could include more than 24 trials and fewer than 24 reinforcers. A new random permutation of the 24 stimuli was arranged within each cycle (in sessions with forms or colors only, permutations of 24 stimuli were generated but the irrelevant stimulus dimension was omitted in actual stimulus presentations). The reinforcer, initially a 4 sec operation of the feeder, was later reduced to 3 sec to allow an increase in trials per session.

Trials were initiated by the pigeon. First all four keys were lit white. A single peck on any key turned off the white keys and lit the houselight for 5 sec, after which the houselight was turned off and the stimuli for that trial were presented. The delay between the initiating peck and the onset of the trial stimuli was included to reduce the likelihood that subsequent pecks would be affected by the location of this peck rather than by the trial stimuli. In most conditions, a trial ended with the first peck after a fixed trial duration; this duration was reduced from 4 to 3 sec after Session 193. Depending on whether it was eligible to be reinforced, the peck at the end of the trial either operated the feeder or produced a timeout of 30 sec during which all chamber lights were off. After either of these events the keys were again lit white, enabling the pigeon to initiate the next trial with a peck.

Pigeon 95 was an experimentally naive Silver King pigeon about one year old at the start of the study. Early in the study it was maintained at 80% of its free feeding weight, but its weight was allowed to increase gradually over sessions provided it initiated trials promptly throughout a daily session; with this arrangement, Pigeon 95 typically completed four or more 24-stimulus cycles per session.

The experimental history of Pigeon 95 started with the shaping of pecks on a white key in a single-key chamber. Training with the singular and plural circles and triangles of the final procedure then began in the four-key chamber, but during the first ten sessions each stimulus appeared only on the key on which pecks were eligible to be reinforced (e.g., singular circles appeared only on the top-left key and plural triangles appeared only on the bottom-right key); pecks on dark keys produced the 30 sec timeout.

Presentation of the stimuli on all four keys, still without background colors, began in Session 11. Through Session 35, any peck on an inappropriate key produced the 30 sec timeout; thereafter, such pecks produced the timeout (thereby terminating the trial) only after the trial duration had elapsed. With this arrangement, rates of pecking given a particular stimulus could be determined in unreinforced as well as reinforced trials, because all trials were terminated only by the first peck after the trial duration had elapsed. A correction procedure also began in Session 11: The stimulus of any unreinforced trial was repeated until two reinforced trials occurred in a row, to a maximum of 10 repetitions of that stimulus.

By Session 40, accuracy exceeded 95% as measured by reinforcers per trial and 90% as measured by the proportion of responses on appropriate keys (in other words, a peck early in the trial was more likely than the peck that terminated the trial to occur on an inappropriate key). Through Session 53, accuracies at these levels or higher were maintained in all but two sessions (later in the experiment, location accuracy as a proportion of total responses exceeded 98% in some sessions).

In Sessions 54 through 58, green and red backgrounds were presented in random order on single keys; dark-key pecks produced timeout and the first peck on the lit key after the trial duration had elapsed produced a reinforcer. No appreciable rate differences occurred in the presence of green and red, and dark-key pecking was negligible. Frequency distributions of

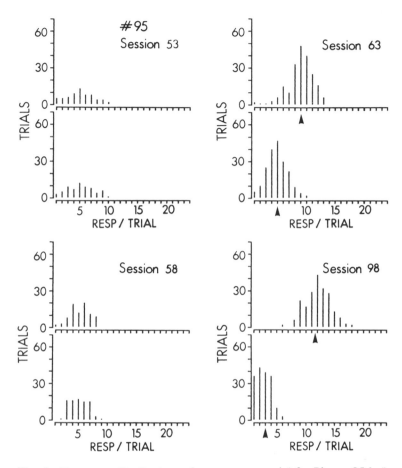

Fig. 4. Frequency distributions of responses per trial for Pigeon 95 before and during the differentiation of respective high and low response rates in the presence of green and red. Session 53 was the last session of the four-key procedure before the introduction of colors; the top graph is based on trials with stimuli to which a green background would later be added and the bottom based on those with stimuli to which a red background would be added. Session 58, the last session before rate differentiation, arranged trials of green or red on the top left key only; the distribution on green trials (top graph) was similar to that on red trials (bottom graph). Session 68 was the fifth session of rate differentiation, with the green high-rate minimum of nine responses per trial (top graph) and the red low-rate maximum of five responses per trial (bottom graph) indicated by the x-axis makers. Session 98 was the fortieth session of rate differentiation, during which the high-rate (green) minimum was increased from 11 to 12 responses per trial and the low-rate (red) maximum was three responses per trial; by this session, there was negligible overlap between the two rate distributions.

responses per trial from Sessions 53 and 58 are shown in the left column of Figure 4.

Differentiation of high and low rates began on Session 59, with green and red backgrounds presented alone in trials on the top-left key only. The procedure was designed to generate two nonoverlapping classes of responses rates, fast on green and slow on red, as measured by responses per trial. In the differentiation of high rates during green trials, a lower bound determined the minimum responses during the trial that could be followed by a reinforced peck after the trial duration had elapsed (e.g., with a lower bound of eight, the peck at the end of the trial was reinforced only if at least eight pecks had already occurred during the trial; otherwise, this peck produced timeout). Similarly, in the differentiation of low rates during red trials, an upper bound determined a response maximum (e.g., with an upper bound of three, the peck at the end of the trial was reinforced only if fewer than three pecks, including the final peck, had occurred during the trial; otherwise it produced timeout). The starting upper and lower bounds, based on median responses per trial during Sessions 54 through 58, were each set at six responses per trial; thus, reinforced trials with green included seven or more pecks and those with red included six or fewer.

In subsequent sessions, the low-rate bound was gradually reduced on the basis of inspection of data from preceding sessions. The high-rate bound began in each session at the same value with which the previous session ended, but after every two stimulus cycles it was set to the median rate over all green trials over those cycles. Frequency distributions from the fifth and fortieth sessions of rate differentiation are shown in the right column of Figure 4. By Session 98, the low-rate bound (red) was three responses per trial and the high-rate bound (green) was 12; more important, the negligible overlap between the two distributions demonstrated that two separate classes of response rates had been established (cf. Skinner, 1935).

Trials with singular and plural circles and triangles were reinstated in Sessions 99 through 102. Thereafter form and color sessions alternated, first in blocks of four sessions each and then with fewer sessions per block until single alternation between the two types of sessions began with Sessions 117 (form) and 118 (color). This alternation continued until Session 140, which was followed by the first transfer test (Session 141). In each transfer test, a color was added to only one of the four sets of form stimuli (the four rows of Figure 2); thus, eight transfer tests were conducted, four with green and four with red. During transfer tests, no rate contingency operated during trials with the test stimulus, and for the other stimuli the correction procedure was relaxed to require only one reinforced trial with a maximum of five successive unreinforced trials. Between transfer tests, sessions with color alone continued to alternate with form sessions, except that the latter included all color-form stimulus combinations for which transfer tests had already been conducted; successive tests were separated by a minimum of six sessions. The first transfer test was conducted for singular circles on red; plural triangles on green was tested next, followed by the remaining six stimulus combinations in the order: singular triangles on red, plural circles on green (completing one transfer test for each key), plural triangles on red, singular circles on green, plural circles on red, and singular triangles on green.

The outcome is easily summarized: In the transfer tests, green and red controlled appropriate response rates even when appearing in novel combinations on new keys, but the location of pecking under the control of singular and plural circles and triangles became inaccurate. In the sessions between successive transfer tests, accuracies quickly recovered with continued presentations of each form-color combination. In other words, control of response rate by color alone transferred to color stimuli to which forms had been added, but the simultaneous control of both location and rate response dimensions by the form and color stimulus dimensions did not emerge without additional training. Whether this outcome depended on idiosyncratic characteristics of these stimulus and response dimensions and their combinations (cf. Lamb & Riley, 1981) remains to be seen.

The transfer tests were completed by Session 193. In

subsequent sessions, all rate and location contingencies were maintained, trial durations were reduced from 4 to 3 sec, and the fast-slow bounds were respectively set to eight and three responses per trial. These contingencies, illustrated in Figure 3, continued through Session 221.

ABSTRACTION AND GENERALIZED CLASSES OF BEHAVIOR

When responding is under the control of a single property of stimuli, we speak of abstraction (Skinner, 1953). For example, humans respond to some common properties of certain plants, articles of clothing and currencies by calling each of them green. Abstractions may also become generalized stimulus classes, if responding continues under the control of all members of the class even though reinforcement contingencies are maintained only for some of them (cf. the generalized imitation of Baer, Peterson, & Sherman, 1967, in which children's reinforced imitations of some instances of the behavior of a model led to consistent imitations of other instances even when the latter imitations were never reinforced). The present experiment might have established abstractions or generalized classes; on the other hand, it might have established eight different classes, each under the control of a particular combination of form, number, and color. The properties of the classes that had been established by the present experiment were therefore examined by relaxing the reinforcement contingencies that operated in the presence of some of the form-number-color stimulus combinations.

In Session 222, the high-rate contingency was discontinued for the first of the three singular circles on green (Figure 2, top row and first column); on trials with this stimulus, reinforcement depended on the location of the peck at the end of the trial without regard to the number of pecks that had already occurred during the trial. This change had no obvious effect on performance, and in Session 229 the high-rate contingency was discontinued for all three arrangements of singular circles on green (Figure 2, top row). Again no effect on performance was obvious, and in Session 238 the low-rate contingency was discontinued for all plural triangles on red (Figure 2, bottom row). Response rates on trials with plural triangles on red increased slightly over the first few sessions, but thereafter rate differences with green and red stimuli remained consistent (cf. Figure 3).

Data obtained after nearly 40 sessions with these contingencies are shown at the top of Figure 5 (Session 276, with stimuli for which the rate contingencies were discontinued indicated by the x-axis markers). Through Sessions 276, high green and low red rates were maintained with all stimuli on all keys despite the fact that the rate contingencies operated only for some of them.

One possibility was that stimulus control was becoming attenuated, but only very slowly. To accelerate the attenuation if it were occurring, all rate contingencies were discontinued in Session 277: The location of the peck at the end of the trial but not the number of responses that preceded it determined whether the trial was reinforced. After about three weeks of sessions made up of these contingencies (Session 298 in Figure 5), consistent green and red rate differences remained but these differences were small relative to those when rate contingencies had operated. Over the next ten sessions (Session 308 in Figure 5), control of response rate by green and red was sufficiently reduced that several reversals (higher rates on some of the red than on some of the green trials) occurred within each session. These sessions provided a history in which relatively low response rates were reinforced on green trials and relatively high response rates were reinforced on red trials.

In Session 309, the previous rate contingencies were reinstated for all stimulus combinations except singular circles on green and plural triangles on red. Performance was at first highly variable, because only a small proportion of trials ended with reinforcers during the initial sessions. By the fifth session of the reinstated rate contingencies, however, consistent high rates on green trials and low rates on red trials were recovered for all stimulus combinations (Session 314 in Figure 6). This pattern of rates was maintained throughout the next two weeks

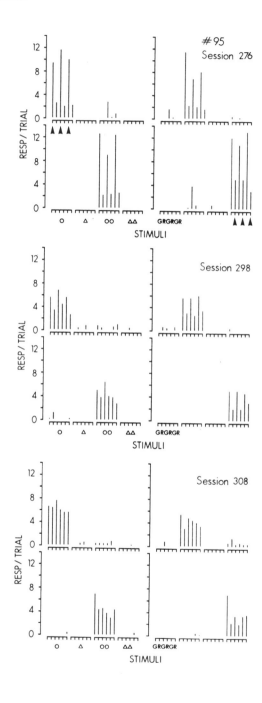

of sessions (Session 328 in Figure 6). The high rates in trials with singular circles on green and the low rates in trials with plural triangles on red returned even though a history had intervened in which other response rates had been reinforced in the presence of these stimuli and in which, during the recovery of this performance, no rate contingencies had operated in their presence. It therefore seems appropriate to refer to these two classes of discriminated response rates as instances of abstraction of generalized stimulus control.

A later attempt to repeat this demonstration with rate contingencies discontinued for all top-left key stimuli and all bottom-right key stimuli (all singular circles and all plural triangles) began to produce attenuations of control by color on those two keys after about 20 sessions; consistent high green and low red rates continued, but the rate differences for the top-left and bottom-right keys were decreasing relative to those for the other two keys. These classes were apparently not sufficiently coherent that they could withstand the discontinuation of rate contingencies for half of their members (four of the eight color-form combinations). In Session 351, rate contingencies were reinstated for all eight color-form stimulus combinations.

The data so far do not bear on whether left-right pecking under the control of form and top-bottom pecking under the control of number were also generalized classes. In Session 407, reinforcers were discontinued for singular green triangles. The question was whether those classes would be maintained even if reinforcement contingencies were discontinued for some of their members. Within ten sessions (Sessions 416 in Figure 7), responding in the presence of these stimuli had decreased substantially.

Fig. 5. (Opposite page) Performance of Pigeon 95 in Sessions 276, 298 and 308. Session 276 was the fortieth session after the removal of high-rate contingencies for singular circles on green and low-rate contingencies for plural triangles on red (x-axis markers for top-left and bottom-right keys); respective green high rates and red low rates were nevertheless maintained on all keys. The rate contingencies for the remaining stimuli included a minimum of eight responses per trial for green and a maximum of three responses per trial for red. Sessions 298 and 308 were respectively the 22nd and 32nd sessions after all rate contingencies were discontinued; location of pecking remained under the stimulus control of singular and plural circles and triangles, but red-green rate differences decreased substantially.

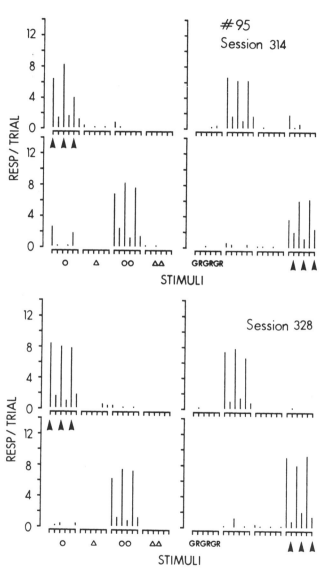

Fig. 6. Effects of reinstating rate contingencies. Sessions 314 and 328 were respectively the fifth and nineteenth session after the rate contingencies of Session 276 were reinstated: Rate contingencies operated for all stimuli but singular green circles and plural red triangles (x-axis markers as in Figure 6). The green-red rate difference emerged and was maintained for all stimuli even without differential reinforcement based on response rate for singular green circles and plural red triangles.

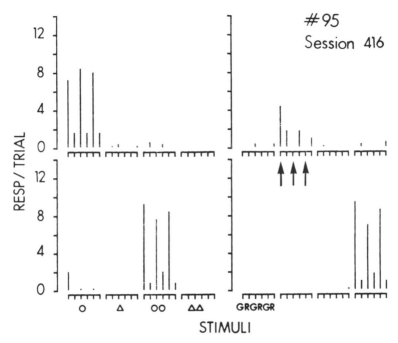

Fig. 7. Effects of removing all reinforcers for responding in the presence of singular green triangles (arrows); trials with this stimulus ended automatically without food delivery. By Session 416, the tenth session of this condition, responding in the presence of this stimulus had decreased substantially.

This effect is consistent with the assumption that responding on each key did not occur as the intersection between two discriminated response classes (left-right and top-bottom), but rather that responding on each key constituted a response class under the control of a particular form-number combination. The color procedure of Figures 5 and 6, however, involved the relaxation of reinforcement contingencies, whereas the form-number procedure of Figure 7 involved the discontinuation of reinforcers (experiments on generalized classes in human behavior have typically discontinued reinforcers instead of relaxing contingencies: e.g., Baer, Peterson, & Sherman, 1967). Perhaps stimulus control over location by form and number would have been maintained if, during trials with singular triangles on green, reinforcers had depended on the number of responses in the trial but not on the location of the peck that ended the trial. When the combination of two stimulus and response dimensions is involved, discontinuing reinforcers at some values along one dimension necessarily implies also discontinuing reinforcers at some values along the other. Thus, relaxing contingencies may be the more appropriate method for studying such classes of stimulus control.

SEQUENTIAL COORDINATIONS OF MULTIPLE STIMULUS AND RESPONSE DIMENSIONS

When a child speaks the plural of *cat*, the final *s* is unvoiced; when the child speaks the plural of *dog*, the final *s* is voiced. It is not necessary to instruct the child in these plurals. The child will voice the final *s* given that the preceding consonant is voiced even if the singular is a novel word (e.g., "one wug, two wugs": Berko, 1958); for this reason, the voicing of the plural *s* qualifies as a generalized class.

The voicing of the final consonant of the noun would probably make a difference to a listener (e.g., "cat" versus "cad"), but the voicing of a plural *s* would probably not be noticed unless a listener were attending to it carefully. Another way of saying this is that contingencies established by the verbal community presumably operate to maintain the distinction between the voicing and unvoicing of final consonants but the carrying over of voicing to a plural *s* is more likely a product of phonological or articulatory constraints than of such contingencies. In studying the phonetic or syntactic structure of verbal behavior, it may be important to determine the source of such sequential coordinations; those created and maintained by the practices of the verbal community are likely to have different properties than those arising in other ways. The voicing of a plural *s* is of interest because it seems to be a structural feature of the latter sort. The experiment that follows is a nonverbal analog of this type of sequential coordination.

The experiment was conducted in a three-key pigeon chamber (Jans & Catania, 1980) controlled by electromechanical equipment. The keys were centered at the vertices of a base-down triangle with sides of 6.5 cm; the bottom keys were 23.5 cm above the floor. Stimuli comparable to those in Figure 2 were projected by IEE In-line Digital Display units behind each key. A Gerbrands feeder was centered below the keys. During reinforcers, the feeder was lit and other lights were off; a houselight was lit during intertrial intervals. Pecks on lit keys produced feedback clicks.

We again present data from a single subject. Pigeon 8, a Silver King pigeon about two years old at the start of the experiment, was maintained at about 80% of free feeding weight. Its history began with the shaping of pecks on a white key in a single-key chamber. The experimental procedures and stimuli are summarized in the top panel of Figure 8.

The first stage of the procedure established left-right responding on the two bottom keys under the control of stimulus number. The possible stimulus configurations (all white stimuli on a dark background) are shown at the upper right; they consisted of singular or plural circles or triangles (cf. Figure 2). At the end of a 4 sec trial, a peck on the left key operated the feeder given a singular stimulus and a peck on the right key did so given a plural stimulus.

In Sessions 1 through 4, singular stimuli were presented only on the left key and plural stimuli only on the right key. Each session consisted of sixty reinforced trials, i.e., five repetitions of a recycling irregular sequence of the twelve possible stimuli. Subsequently, the sequence began at a different place in each session, and the order of stimuli was changed about once every two weeks, always with the constraint that the probabilities of a circle given a circle or of singular given singular on the preceding trial equalled .5.

Each trial consisted of a 4 sec stimulus presentation during which pecks had no scheduled consequences and which was terminated by the next peck and, depending on the key that was pecked, either a 4 sec operation of the feeder and a 28 sec intertrial interval or no feeder operation and a 32 sec intertrial interval. Except for the first 4 sec of 32 sec intertrial intervals, intertrial intervals were reset to 28 sec by pecks on dark keys.

Within trials, pecks on dark keys occurred rarely.

Discrimination training began in Session 5, with the presentation of stimuli on both bottom keys (shown schematically as I in the top panel of Figure 8). In trials with singular circles or triangles, a left but not a right peck at the end of the trial was reinforced; in those with plural circles or triangles, a right but not a left peck was reinforced. A correction procedure arranged that the stimulus of a nonreinforced trial was repeated until a reinforced trial had occurred. Over the next few sessions, the session was increased to 72 reinforced trials, the recycling stimulus sequence was increased to 24 (each of the stimuli therefore appeared twice in the sequence), and feedback clicks were added for all pecks on lit keys.

Column A of Figure 8 shows data from the last four sessions (40 through 43) of this condition. Each graph presents a relative frequency distribution of responses per trial for a given stimulus, with the rows corresponding respectively to singular circles, plural circles, singular triangles and plural triangles. Filled areas show unreinforced trials. There were no systematic differences in response rate during trials with the several stimuli.

In Session 44, the differentiation of response rates began on the top key. The procedure was similar to that illustrated for Pigeon 95 in Figure 4, except that in this procedure circles were the low-rate stimuli and triangles were the high-rate stimuli (see II in the top panel of Figure 8). The procedure started with the median response rates at the end of condition I, with the correction procedure operating for unreinforced trials. By Sessions 122 through 125, shown in Column B of Figure 8, the low-rate maximum (circles) had been reduced to four responses per trial and the high-rate minimum (triangles) had been raised to ten responses per trial, as indicated by the dashed vertical lines. There was negligible overlap between the two distributions, but some responding appropriate to the low-rate distribution was maintained during trials with singular and plural triangles.

In Session 125, the two procedures were combined, as

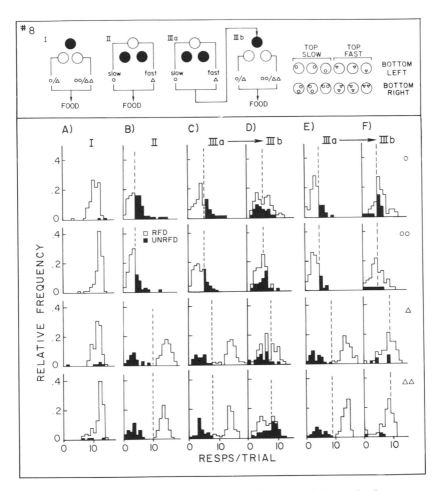

Fig. 8. Procedure and data for Pigeon 8. The top panel shows the four stages of the experiment: left-right singular-plural training on the two bottom keys (I); slow-fast circle-triangle training on the top key (II); and their combination, in which top-key responding produced bottom-key stimuli (IIIa and IIIb). Stimulus configurations are summarized on the upper right (cf. Figure 2). The graphs in the bottom panel show frequency distributions of responses per trial, with rows for each stimulus class (singular circles, plural circles, singular triangles, plural triangles, as summarized by the symbols on the right), and columns for successive conditions (I at A, II at B, and initial and later performance under III at C through F). Filled areas represent unreinforced (UNRFD) responding; boundaries for rate differentiation are shown by the dashed vertical lines. The rate difference maintained on the top key (B, C and E) emerged on the bottom keys (F) even though no contingencies were arranged for it there.

illustrated in III in the top panel of Figure 8; intertrial intervals were 4 sec shorter than those of the preceding conditions. Stimuli were first presented on the top key and trials were conducted as in II; appropriate response rates produced the same stimuli on the bottom key, the contingencies for which were the same as in I. In trials with plural triangles, for example, the reinforcer depended on a high rate of top-key pecking in the first part of the trial (IIIa) followed by a right key peck at the end of the second part of the trial (IIIb). A trial could end without a reinforcer either after the final peck on the top key given an inappropriate response rate or after the final peck on a bottom key given an inappropriate location. The question was whether the response rates established on the top key would appear on the bottom keys even though no contingencies had been arranged for them there.

Columns C and D of Figure 8 respectively show relative frequency distributions for the top key and the bottom keys during the first four sessions (125 through 128) of this condition. During these sessions, which included a total of 392 trials, the high-rate minimum was eight responses per trial and the low-rate maximum was decreased from six to five responses per trial. Because some trials terminated as a consequence of top-key response rates, the bottom-key distributions (D) are based on only 270 trials. There was a relatively high proportion of unreinforced trials in these sessions, and response rates on the bottom keys were not consistently lower in trials with circles than in those with triangles.

Ten sessions later, as shown in Columns E and F of Figure 8 (Sessions 135 through 138), the proportion of unreinforced trials was still larger than in conditions I and II, but a consistent difference in bottom-key response rates had emerged. Bottom-key rates were lower during trials with circles than in those with triangles, corresponding in direction if not in magnitude with top-key response rates, even though response rates on the bottom keys did not enter into the reinforcement contingencies.

It may be appropriate to refer to this emergence of a novel sequential coordination as an instance of productivity in the behavior of the pigeon. It differs from the transfer tests arranged for Pigeon 95 in that the criterion for transfer was not whether the novel behavior occurred on the first presentation of the combined conditions but rather whether the relevant behavior emerged even though no contingencies were arranged to generate or maintain it. Perhaps similar results would have been obtained with Pigeon 95 if the initial shape-number training had been followed immediately by the partial rate contingencies of Figure 6 instead of the several transfer tests. No doubt productivity on the basis of a single novel stimulus presentation occurs in human verbal behavior, but it is probably too much to expect in the nonverbal behavior of a pigeon.

The difference in response rates shown in column F of Figure 8 dissipated over subsequent sessions, and it was not possible to test whether the rate difference would have been observed even if the top-key segment of the trial had been omitted. Data from another pigeon from which a smaller but less transient rate difference on the bottom keys was obtained suggested that the rate difference depended only on the bottom key stimuli rather than on the persistence of the rate of responding that had been initiated on the top key (for that pigeon, the stimuli correlated with slow and fast responding on the top key had been green and red, and those correlated with left and right responding on the bottom keys had been circles and plusses). But the demonstration of sequential coordinations that emerge even though no reinforcement contingencies have been arranged to produce them is probably more important than the detailed working of particular cases. In human verbal behavior, different types of constraints presumably also operate in generating particular kinds of sequential coordinations. For example, sequential constraints of the voicing of the plural *s* differ from those producing nouns or verbs in characteristic locations within sentences.

THE NONVERBAL PROPERTIES
OF VERBAL BEHAVIOR

The rate of bottom-key responding for Pigeon 8, like the

human voicing of the plural *s*, depended on contingencies that operated on other, earlier properties of behavior. The analogy works at least to this point, and like every analogy eventually breaks down (cf. Lakoff & Johnson, 1980). Given the limited stimulus and response dimensions for which we can arrange reinforcement contingencies for the behavior of the pigeon, it is enough to have produced even partial realizations of these thought experiments in the laboratory. It may also be important to note that even the most subtle instances of productivity in human verbal behavior do not necessarily involve the simultaneity of control by different stimulus dimensions that we sought in the transfer procedures with Pigeon 95. Maybe we were asking too much. The ordering of verbal units is a critical feature of productivity (some would argue that we have not even tapped it, in that we have demonstrated nothing comparable to the rearrangements that occur in, say, a transformation from active to passive voice), and the most complex of human utterances is still a sequence in which the components are successively ordered in time.

Our first experiment could have been conducted on only two keys with only two stimulus dimensions (e.g., form controlling left-right and color controlling fast-slow). Either of the two experiments could have substituted some other stimulus property such as size for that of number. And number could have been expressed as one-two instead of singular-plural. These dimensions and the terms used to describe them were chosen primarily as continuing reminders of the relevance of these experiments to the structural properties of verbal behavior.

The experiments do not explain behavior (cf. Catania, 1983); they are demonstrations. As we have already indicated, they are to some extent nothing more than thought experiments that have been realized in practice. They needed to be done only to show to those who find the analogies unconvincing that nonverbal organisms can indeed produce such behavior. Nevertheless, some things were learned along the way, such as the importance of distinguishing between the relaxation of contingencies and the discontinuation of reinforcers in the diagnosis of generalized classes.

One other outcome of the research was the elaboration of a method for producing novel behavior (e.g., the emergence of the different botton-key response rates in Figure 8). Novel behavior can be created by the differential reinforcement of successive approximations that we call shaping. The present method also incorporates differential reinforcement, but in its combination of separate classes of discriminated responding it has properties different from shaping. As we might have expected, there is more than one way to produce novel behavior.

To the extent that we have demonstrated structural properties of nonverbal behavior analogous to structural properties of verbal behavior, we have illustrated some nonverbal properties of verbal behavior (we might as easily have called them verbal properties of nonverbal behavior). If we are interested in saying how verbal behavior differs from nonverbal behavior, part of our task is that of specifying the properties they have in common. The present experiments demonstrate that structural features of behavior often cited as defining properties of language are sometimes properties of behavior in general instead (cf. Catania, in press). If this is so, we must look elsewhere than to structure for the defining properties of language.

ACKNOWLEDGMENT

Research supported by PHS Grants MH-33086 and MH-37256 and NSF Grant BNS82-03385 to the University of Maryland Baltimore County. For their help and their critical commentary, we offer our thanks to the several colleagues and students who have been involved in various ways with this research; we must give special mention to Eliot Shimoff for Applelab, an assembly language computer program that handled timing and response inputs, and to Deisy G. de Souza for insightful comments on data analysis and interpretation.

REFERENCES

Baer, D.M., Peterson, R.F., & Sherman, J.A. (1967). The development of imitation by reinforcing behavioral similarity to a model. *Journal of the Experimental Analysis of Behavior, 10,* 405-416.

Berko, J. (1958). The child's learning of English morphology. *Word, 14,* 150-177.

Blough, D.S. (1972). Recognition by the pigeon of stimuli varying in two dimensions. *Journal of the Experimental Analysis of Behavior, 18,* 345-367.

Butter, C.M. (1963). Stimulus generalization along one and two dimensions in pigeons. *Journal of Experimental Psychology, 65,* 339-346.

Catania, A.C. (1973). The concept of the operant in the analysis of behavior. *Behaviorism, 1,* 103-116.

Catania, A.C. (1980). Autoclitic processes and the structure of behavior. *Behaviorism, 8,* 175-186.

Catania, A.C. (1983). Behavior analysis and behavior synthesis in the extrapolation from animal to human behavior. In G. Davey (Ed.), *Animal Models of Human Behavior* (pp. 51-69). Chichester, New York: Wiley.

Catania, A.C. (in press). On the differences between verbal and nonverbal behavior. In D.B. Gray & J.M. Johnston (Eds.), *Developmental behavior genetics, behavior analysis, and learning.* Hillsdale, New Jersey: Lawrence Erlbaum Associates.

Chomsky, N. (1959). Review of B.F. Skinner's *Verbal behavior. Language, 35,* 26-58.

Esper, E.A. (1933). Studies in linguistic behavior organization. *Journal of General Psychology, 8,* 346-381.

Fentress, J.C. (1978). *Mus musicus,* the experimental orchestration of selected movement patterns in mice (pp. 321-342). In G.M. Burghardt & M. Bekoff (Eds.), *The development of behavior: Comparative and evolutionary aspects.* New York: Garland.

Gardner, R.A., & Ely, D.J. (1969). A source of artifact in in-line readout projectors. *Journal of the Experimental Analysis of Behavior, 12,* 564.

Jans, J.E., & Catania, A.C. (1980). Short-term remembering of discriminative stimuli in the pigeon. *Journal of the Experimental Analysis of Behavior, 34,* 177-183.

Lakeoff, G., & Johnson, M. (1980). *Metaphors we live by.* Chicago: University of Chicago Press.

Lamb, M.R., & Riley, D.A. (1981). Effects of element arrangement on the processing of compound stimuli in pigeons (*Columba livia*). *Journal of Experimental Psychology: Animal Behavior Processes, 7,* 45-48.

Skinner, B.F. (1935). The generic nature of the concepts of stimulus and response. *Journal of General Psychology, 12,* 40-65.

Skinner, B.F. (1953). *Science and human behavior.* New York: Macmillan.

Skinner, B.F. (1957). *Verbal behavior.* New York: Appleton-Century-Crofts.

Terrace, H.S., Petitto, L.A., Sanders, R.J., & Bever, T.G. (1979). Can an ape create a sentence? *Science, 206,* 891-902.

Thompson, C.R., & Church, R.M. (1980). An explanation of the language of a chimpanzee. *Science, 208,* 313-314.

CHAPTER 11

Functional Analysis of Emergent Verbal Classes

MURRAY SIDMAN

Since Skinner's classic treatment of the reflex concept (1931), and his explication of the generic nature of stimuli and responses (1935), the identification and analysis of basic behavioral units has received only intermittent attention. At first, thoughtful psychologists examined the problem out of their concern with the systematic status of the new Behaviorism (e.g., MacCorquodale & Meehl, 1948; Meehl, 1950), and with relations between Behaviorism and other approaches to the subject matter (e.g., Estes, Koch, MacCorquodale, Meehl, Mueller, Schoenfeld, & Verplanck, 1954; Goldiamond, 1962, 1966; Schoenfeld & Cumming, 1963). As experimental and applied Behavior Analysis grew in scope and power, however, the problem of behavioral units, seemingly of no practical importance, was swept under the rug. These developing sciences were busy, devising powerful techniques for altering behavior both in and out of the laboratory, describing behavior of ever greater complexity, and advancing principles to coordinate and unify seemingly unrelated behavioral phenomena. They rarely paused to examine their own internal structure. With some exceptions (e.g., Catania, 1984; Hineline, 1980; Goldiamond, 1975; Lee, 1983; Schoenfeld, 1976), self analysis has not been a major recent preoccupation of Behavior Analysis.

Therefore, where an opposing point of view, the Cognitive Sciences, might once have provoked searching evaluations and comparisons of both approaches, behavior analysts remained instead at the mercy of reinforcement contingencies that operated within their cultural, social, and political environments. Whether they fought or joined the opposition, few based their choice on rational grounds.

BEHAVIOR, COGNITION, AND
THE PROBLEM OF ANALYTIC UNITS

After switching to cognitivism, many former behaviorists became content to leave the identification of stimuli and responses largely to the judgment of the individual experimenter or therapist. Soon, subjects and patients were even being asked to reinforce or punish themselves for their actions and thoughts (for critiques of these practices, see Catania, 1975, 1976; Goldiamond, 1976). Units of behavior no longer had to be capable of direct observation or measurement; experimenters and theorists found themselves able to "explain" the most complex behavior by appeal to representations, plans, and other mental structures, and to the innate capabilities and developmental sequences ("programs") that are supposed to give mental attributes a life of their own. Behavior analysts who became "cognitive scientists," "cognitive behavior modifiers," or "cognitive therapists" also found that they no longer had to defend themselves against the epithet, "stimulus-response psychologist."

Before taking the easy ways out - joining the opposition blindly, opposing it blindly, or ignoring it - behavior analysts might instead have gone to the trouble of examining the logic, assumptions, and research practices of both the cognitive approach and their own. If they had started with Cognitive Science, they would have found that it does not exist. There is no body of systematized principles, no unique set of data, no characteristic measurement techniques, and no typical investigative procedures to which a cognitivist can point and say, "That is my Science." The mind may possess a structure, but the Science of Mind does not.

The basic units of cognition - representations, intentions,

plans, rules, programs, and other mental structures - are linked to actual behavior only if that becomes necessary. When such necessity does arise - for example, in carrying out experiments - the logic of the linkage need not be compelling. For the cognitivist, behavior is important only as a product of mental processes, but criteria do not exist for determining whether different instances of behavior represent the same mental processes. Given an interest in some particular process, each observer is privileged to decide which behavior will provide the appropriate window into the mind.

A constructive view might be that: (a) Cognitive Science worries about important and interesting phenomena but has been too impatient, failing to accomplish the intellectually rigorous and prior task of laying a systematic foundation from which to synthesize complex processes; (b) Behavior Analysis, although it has moved swiftly even on the accelerated time scale of modern science, and has developed a systematic foundation, still has not been impatient enough to attempt all of the syntheses of which it is capable. An easy criticism has been that Behavior Analysis deals well with uninteresting behavior, but ignores everything that makes human beings superior to all other creatures. The concepts of stimulus and response have seemed impoverished, unable to capture the rich complexity of the human intellect. Behavior analysts, themselves, have not continued to examine the units of their own science in sufficient depth to appreciate whether, and how, they might be able to account for just those phenomena which concern cognitive scientists.

At this particular time, therefore, it is appropriate to honor Kenneth MacCorquodale by returning to a consideration of matters to which he and his students have made major contributions. My own recent laboratory studies, also, have made it necessary for me to reexamine the basic units of Behavior Analysis, and to evaluate how well those units might help systematize even phenomena that some hold to be nonbehavioral. I am going to attempt to describe what I believe are the basic units. For the most part, I shall merely summarize what is already known, my own contribution being, perhaps, to apply the notion that the units of analysis need not be fixed. By increasing the size and complexity of the analytic unit, step by step, we can observe new relations emerging among the elements of the unit and between units. Ever more complex behavioral phenomena fall within the systematic framework.

THE RESPONSE

For behavior analysts, the primary object of observation and measurement, behavior itself, is usually conceptualized in any particular instance as a *response*. Although the response is a most complex unit of behavior, I have nothing useful to add to existing discussions of its definition (e.g., Catania, 1973; Estes et al., 1954; Goldiamond, 1962; Notterman & Mintz, 1965; Schoenfeld & Cumming, 1963; Skinner 1935). By itself, however, the response has only limited utility as a unit of analysis. To measure behavior alone can be meaningful only in an environment that never changes. Indeed, its dictionary definition requires that a response be in reaction *to* something. Although one can *behave* in an unchanging environment, one can *respond* only to an environmental change. In the old stimulus-response Psychology, the unit of analysis was a *relation* between a response and a prior environmental event, an unconditioned or a conditioned eliciting stimulus. Functional analysis, however, has revealed and elaborated several relations between environment and behavior that go considerably beyond elicitation.

THE TWO-TERM CONTINGENCY

Skinner (1935, 1938) pointed out that an operant response is a class of organismic events that cannot be identified without reference to environmental consequences. He therefore retained the notion of a relation as the appropriate unit of analysis, but his concept of the operant turned the original stimulus-response relation around. He proposed, instead, a response-stimulus relation, the now familiar two-term reinforcement contingency, as a basic unit for the analysis and

Table 1:   The Two-Term Contingency (Reinforcement)
R = Response; C = Consequence

R1 (press) ---> C1 (coin)

R2 (other) -/-> C1 (coin)

description of operant behavior. Retention of the term, response, probably accounts in large part for the misconception that modern Behavior Analysis is constrained by a "stimulus-response formula." The consequences of behavior - events that happen subsequent to a response - determine its future probability.

Table 1 diagrams a two-term contingency. The upper line signifies that a particular item of behavior, Response 1 (R1), is followed by a particular Consequence (C1). For example, a laboratory subject receives a coin after pressing a button. The second line shows why this relation between response and consequence is a *contingency*; the coin does not come (broken arrow) if the subject does anything else (R2). The consequence follows the specified behavior, Response 1, and no other. Thus, we have: If press (and no other response), then coin. This behavior-consequence relation, modulated by many parameters (schedule, delay, amount, deprivation, alternative contingencies, etc.), will determine the future likelihood of the behavior.

Recognition of the two-term contingency as a unit of analysis, simple though it seems, must rank as a milestone in the development of behavioral analysis. Behavior that seemed controlled by future events, a puzzling scientific anomaly, could now be seen to have been generated by past contingencies. A major area of cognition, "purpose," was for the first time placed in good scientific order. It was not even necessary to invoke hypothetical "expectations," "anticipations," or "intentions" to bring future determinants back into the present or the past; one could point instead to real contingencies that had already taken place.

Because the two-term unit of analysis specifies a causal relation between behavior and environment, we might learn much about particular people simply by cataloguing their repertoire of two-term contingencies, as aptitude and personality tests attempt to do. Identifying positive and negative reinforcers, and the behavior to which these are characteristically related, should indeed help to identify a person's interests and sources of satisfaction, and how the person goes about achieving them. Applied behavior analysts, by conducting controlled observations to identify the relevant behavior-consequence relations in a client's repertoire, have achieved considerable success in defining and ameliorating problem behavior.

Useful as even a partial catalogue may be, however, it can hardly satisfy our analytic needs. If parameters local to a two-term relation completely determined the probability that it would be active at any given moment, our behavior would be chaotic. Response would succeed upon response, the sequence being determined solely by momentary reinforcement probabilities, deprivation states, energy requirements, etc. This, of course, is not what happens. Our environment not only provides consequences, but selects from our repertoires the particular two-term units that are to be active at any moment.

THE THREE-TERM CONTINGENCY

The experiments which most thoroughly and successfully clarified the basic behavior-consequence relation (e.g., Ferster & Skinner, 1957; Skinner, 1938) did so by holding the subject's environment constant except for those changes that occurred subsequent to the behavior. It then became possible to introduce variations into the subject's environment prior to or concurrently with the behavior. Behavior analysts usually conceptualize a variation in the subject's environment as a *stimulus*. Stimulus definition, like response definition, is a most complex matter, and I shall not attempt here to amplify existing discussions (e.g., Estes et al., 1954; Lawrence, 1963; Prokasy & Hall, 1963; Ray, 1972; Ray & Sidman, 1970; Schoenfeld & Cumming, 1963; Sidman, 1969; Skinner, 1935; Stoddard & Sidman, 1971; Terrace, 1966). Rather, I shall focus on the

Table 2:   The Three-Term Contingency (Discrimination)
R = Response; C = Consequence; S = Stimulus

```
                        ( R1 (press) ---> C1 (coin)
    S1 (square) ----- (
                        ( R2 (other) -/-> C1 (coin)
             ---------------------------------
                        ( R1 (press) -/-> C1 (coin)
    S2 (circle) ----- (
                        ( R2 (other) -/-> C1 (coin)
```

familiar three-term relation, the analytic unit that emerges when one considers the two-term contingency in relation to the changing environment.

Table 2 illustrates a three-term contingency. The upper half shows that the two-term contingency is now under the control of a third element, Stimulus S1. The subject can still press the button and produce the coin, but only if the button has on it a particular geometric form, for example, a square (S1). The contrast with other stimuli, S2 (in the lower half of Table 2), makes this three-term relation a contingency; the two-term relation holds true only in the presence of the square. When any other geometric form, a circle, for example, is on the button, the two-term contingency does not exist; pressing the button will not produce a coin. Thus, we have the three-term contingency: If a square (and no other form) is on the button, then, if the subject presses (no other response will do), then a coin will follow.

As Skinner (1938) pointed out, the square does not elicit the response. Rather, since it increases the likelihood that a subject will produce a coin by pressing the button, the square activates that particular two-term contingency. The two-term relation is placed under *discriminative* control. This is how the environment establishes priorities, imposing order upon behavior by selectively altering the probability of two-term relations that exist in one's repertoire. In the process, the third term, S1, becomes part of an expanded unit of analysis. The three-term contingency is the fundamental unit of *stimulus control*.

Why must we enlarge our analytic unit? Would it not

suffice to treat S1 simply as a parameter of the two-term unit? Two considerations force us to acknowledge the larger unit. First, like the two-term relation, the three-term contingency itself can come under environmental control, increasing or decreasing in probability as an entity. This point will be elaborated later. Second, to define a response requires that we take the relation between it and its controlling environment as our unit. In the case of two-term contingencies, we need consider only the behavior-consequence relation, since the consequence is the only changing aspect of the subject's environment. In three-term contingencies, however, other aspects of the environment also vary. Discriminative control introduces an additional relation between environment and behavior, and this new relation also enters into the response definition.

The problem of definition can be illustrated by reference to a familiar experimental arrangement for studying three-term contingencies, a procedure that requires only a slight reinterpretation of Table 2. Suppose a subject has two buttons available, the square appearing unpredictably on one or the other; whichever button does not have the square on it has the circle. Both S1 and S2, therefore, are present simultaneously. The subject produces a coin by pressing the button on which the square appears.

It is easy enough to distinguish pressing the button (R1) from all other responses (R2), since only R1 produces the coin. Because this response definition requires a specification of the consequence, both terms, response and consequence, must be considered together as a single relation rather than as two independent units. But now we face the problem of distinguishing between two different responses of pressing a button, one "correct," and one "incorrect" (Sidman, 1978). The common-sense differentiation is "pressing the square" and "pressing the circle." Again, however, the response definition includes a stimulus specification. To define the response in a three-term contingency therefore requires that the response be related not only to C1 but to S1. All three components of the contingency must be considered together, as a unit.

By adding a single term to its smallest analytic unit, Behavior Analysis significantly broadens its domain. For example, the three-term contingency encompasses those phenomena which have traditionally been included under "perception" (e.g., Goldiamond, 1962). Classical Psychophysics studies how quantitative and qualitative energy transformations of S1 affect the likelihood that certain three-term relations will hold true; given a history of reinforcement (C1) for saying, "Yes, I see it" (R1), in the presence of a flash of light (S1), what is the probability that flashes varying in intensity, duration, wavelength, etc. will still occasion the same behavior-consequence relation? How do stimulus characteristics determine what we see, hear, smell, etc? Modern Psychophysics (Green & Swets, 1966) takes "biasing" factors into account - variables, for example, that modulate the behavior-consequence relation (Goldiamond, 1962) - in describing how stimulus energy affects the probability of a particular three-term unit; if the payoff for saying, "Yes," is greater than for saying, "No," we are likely to report seeing the flash even when it is actually too dim to affect our visual receptors.

When the third term, S1, is added to the analytic unit, a new process, conditioned reinforcement, enters the picture. A response that produces S1 as a consequence will activate the three-term unit of which S1 is the initiating component. Such activation of a three-term unit proves, itself, to be a reinforcer. S1 can now alter the future probability of behavior that precedes it (Skinner, 1938).

This new process, derived from the expanded analytic unit, enlarges the scope of Behavior Analysis still more. First, the environmental elements that can function as effective behavioral consequences become virtually limitless, extending from the "built-in" reinforcing properties of basic biological necessities to subtly conditioned events like the sound of a cash register, the tone of a violin string, a syntactically correct verbal expression, or the blink of a listener's eye.

Second, generalized conditioned reinforcers (Skinner, 1953), each effective under many different deprivation states, support important categories of verbal behavior. Without generalized reinforcers, for example, our descriptions of the environment would be accurate only to the extent that they produced reinforcers which corresponded to our deprivation states at the moment. The three-term units in a person's repertoire would constitute demands for particular reinforcers rather than unbiased reports based solely upon S1. Generalized reinforcers make it possible for us to give accurate information no matter what our current states of deprivation may be. A special kind of three-term unit, the tact (Skinner, 1957), permits us to go beyond demands for particular reinforcers and instead, to report the environment independently of our momentary deprivations.

Third, conditioned reinforcers can support second-order schedules. These treat the completion of a first-order schedule contingency, itself, as a response. That larger response, in turn, is made part of a second-order schedule contingency, each first-order element producing a brief conditioned reinforcer until the completion of the second-order schedule produces the terminal reinforcement. The imposition of such a structure on behavior may increase to a remarkable extent the quantity of behavior that the environment can maintain at low cost (Findley & Brady, 1965; Kelleher, 1966).

Fourth, by functioning simultaneously as the consequence in one three-term unit and as the initiating element in another, conditioned reinforcers permit three-term contingencies to be chained into complex sequences (Findley, 1962). Chaining can create three-term structures of almost limitless intricacy, the elements themselves involving combinations of contingencies - alternative, conjunctive, interlocking, concurrent, and many others - and the "choice points" in the sequence providing options from which the subject can select the element which is to come next. Such structures can include many different responses, stimuli, and reinforcers, and can extend over large areas of space and long periods of time. The ability to synthesize them in the laboratory, therefore, permits direct behavioral observation and analysis of the topographical, spatial, and temporal structure of organism-environment interactions.

The three-term contingency is also the basic analytic unit of cognition. One infers *knowledge* from observations of stimulus control; we can be said to know a subject matter only if we behave differentially with respect to the materials defining that subject matter. It becomes reasonable, perhaps, to characterize individuals' knowledge repertoires by cataloguing their stimulus-control repertoires, the three-term contingencies through which their behavior has become related both to consequences and antecedents. We might assess how much a person knows by counting the number of three-term units in that individual's catalogue; we might judge the quality of the knowledge repertoire by classifying the units into categories to which we assign different values. To a large extent, that is what standard intelligence tests attempt to do.

Such a characterization would be far from complete, since the environment also sets constraints upon three-term contingencies. Alone, they do not carry a behavioral analysis far enough. An additional term is needed to describe and account for the environment's ability to select from our repertoires the particular three-term units of stimulus control that are to be active at any moment.

THE FOUR-TERM CONTINGENCY

If we allow an additional element of the experimental environment to vary, the simplest units of stimulus control, three-term contingencies, can themselves be placed under stimulus control. The upper half of Table 3 shows that the three-term relation is now under the control of a fourth element, stimulus S3. Suppose the subject still has the original two buttons available, a square on one and a circle on the other, but now we introduce a third button, which is sometimes green (S3) and sometimes red (S4). The subject can still press the square and produce a coin, but only if the new button is green.

Because other colors might also appear on the third button (as in the lower half of Table 3), this four-term relation is a contingency; the three-term relation holds true only in the

Table 3:   The Four-Term Contingency (Conditional Discrimination)
            R = Response; C = Consequence; S = Stimulus

```
                         (                    ( R1  (press) --->  C1  (coin)
                         ( S1  (square) ------ (
                         (                    ( R2  (other) -/->  C1  (coin)
S3  (green) ------       (                    --------------------------------
                         (                    ( R1  (press) -/->  C1  (coin)
                         ( S2  (circle) ------ (
                         (                    ( R2  (other) -/->  C1  (coin)
            -------------------------------------------------------------
                         (                    ( R1  (press) -/->  C1  (coin)
                         ( S1  (square) ------ (
                         (                    ( R2  (other) -/->  C1  (coin)
S4  (red) ---------      (                    --------------------------------
                         (                    ( R1  (press) -/->  C1  (coin)
                         ( S2  (circle) ------ (
                         (                    ( R2  (other) -/->  C1  (coin)
```

presence of the green button. If that button is any other color, red, for example, the three-term contingency does not exist; the subject cannot produce a coin even by pressing a button that has a square on it. The three-term relation is placed under *conditional* control (Lashley, 1938). Thus we have the four-term contingency: If the third button is green (and no other color), then, if a square (and no other form) is on one of the two original buttons, then, if the subject presses it (no other response will do), only then will a coin follow.

The structure of the four-term unit reveals that conditional and discriminative control are different stimulus functions. A discriminative stimulus (S1) can be identified only by reference to a differential response (R1); the square can be said to exert discriminative control if its presence and absence are correlated with a change in behavior - the subject learns to press the button in the presence of the square, but not in its absence. The conditional stimulus (S3) needs no additional differential behavior for its identification. The green hue can be said to exert conditional control if its presence and absence are correlated with a change in the control exerted by the square; even with a square on the button, the subject learns to press it only in the presence of the green hue. The diagram therefore shows no response intervening between S3 and S1. Even a "perceptual" response (e.g., Lawrence, 1963; Schoenfeld & Cumming, 1963), is superfluous in specifying the contingency. The stimulus-response relation gives way here to a stimulus-stimulus relation. Conditional stimuli do not control responses directly, but determine the control which other stimuli exert over responses.

To appeal to an "association" between S3 and S1 in order to account for control by the hue (S3) would be, at worst, incorrect and misleading, and at best, incomplete. Rather, since it increases the likelihood that a subject will produce a coin by pressing the square, the green hue activates that particular three-term unit. Recognizing the different roles of discriminative and conditional stimuli, Cumming and Berryman (1965) pointed out that S1, as a discriminative stimulus, sets the occasion for the reinforcement of a specific response, but that S3 functions as a "selector of discriminations, rather than of individual responses." They characterized the function of S3 as "instructional control." That is how the environment establishes higher-order priorities, selectively altering the probability of three-term relations that exist in one's repertoire. In the process, the fourth term, S3, becomes part of still another expanded unit of analysis. The four-term contingency is the fundamental unit of what we might call *conditional*, *instructional*, or, as we shall see, of *contextual* stimulus control.

Again, it does not suffice to treat S3 simply as a parameter of the three-term unit. Like the two- and three-term relations, the four-term contingency itself can come under environmental constraint (see following). Nor are we dealing simply with stimulus compounds. One might suppose, for example, that the four-term contingency shown in Table 3 could be reduced to a three-term contingency by specifying S1 as *green*-plus-*square*, and S2 as either *green*-plus-*circle* or *red*-plus-*square*-or-*circle*. Stimulus compounding would combine S3 and S1, removing any need to expand the three-term unit of analysis. Collapsing stimuli S3 and S1 into a single compound is not justifiable, however, when the two stimuli can be shown to function independently of each other (see following).

Cognitive scientists often criticize Behavior Analysis on the grounds that it cannot encompass important kinds of behavioral variability, those due to the effects of context. It is fashionable to interpret Behavior Analysis as a dogma which holds that behavior is simply a collection of reflexes; that given stimuli always elicit the same responses. The four-term analytic unit, however, contains within itself the elementary mechanism of contextual variation. Another name for conditional control might very well be contextual control. The significance of S1, for example, is no longer invariant, but depends on other circumstances. The square only sets the occasion for the subject to obtain a coin if the environmental context includes the green hue. Four-term units consist of discriminations that are under contextual control.

Contextual control is particularly evident in language, where the significance of sounds, words, phrases, etc. varies according to their context. Because the three-term unit of stimulus-control/cognition is fundamental to the analysis of all behavior, it brings general principles to bear upon the analysis of language. Contextual constraints upon a three-term contingency can therefore account for aspects of language which are themselves not linguistic in nature (Catania, 1980). The very establishment of contextual control, however, creates a potential for the emergence of a linguistic prerequisite, stimulus equivalence. Just as adding a third term to the analytic unit makes conditioned reinforcement possible, adding a fourth term also generates a new process. The formation of *equivalence relations* (Sidman, 1971) greatly extends the relevance of the four-term unit to language and other cognitive phenomena.

A small change in the four-term diagram will facilitate the exposition of equivalence relations. For an experimenter, the contingency outlined in Table 3 is unbalanced; S3 provides a context in which the subject can press the square and produce a coin, but S4 provides a context in which no behavior is effective. The arrangement in the bottom three lines of Table 4 corrects the imbalance. The subject can now obtain a coin even in the context of S4, but the appropriate button has a circle on it. Table 4 actually compresses into a single diagram two four-term contingencies of the type illustrated in Table 3, one unit having

S3 (green) as the fourth term, and the other unit having S4 (red). Whether the subject can obtain a coin by pressing a square or a circle depends on the hue of the third button.

The expanded contingencies themselves specify only conditional relations: "If *green*, then press the *square* to produce the *consequence*," and "if *red,* then press the *circle*." The conditional relations, however, will also become equivalence relations. The green hue and the square will become equivalent members of one class, while the red hue and the circle will join as equivalent members of another class.

The emergence of equivalence from conditionality has some startling implications for a behavioral analysis, beginning with the very tests that are required to document equivalence. To determine whether equivalence relations have emerged from four-term units, one must test the conditional relations for the three properties, reflexivity, symmetry, and transitivity, which define equivalence (Sidman, Kirk, & Willson-Morris, 1985; Sidman, Rauzin, Lazar, Cunningham, Tailby, & Carrigan, 1982; Sidman & Tailby, 1982).

For a relation to be reflexive, it must hold true for each individual stimulus. If the conditional relations in Table 4 between green and square, and between red and circle, are also equivalence relations, then reflexivity would require each stimulus to be conditionally related to itself. Reflexivity, therefore, translates behaviorally into generalized identity matching. If equivalence has emerged from the explicitly constructed four-term units shown in Table 4, then the units illustrated in Table 5 will also be found in the subject's repertoire *even though the subject had never experienced those contingencies before.*

Since generalized identity matching is an empirical basis for the concept of sameness, we can see that sameness is a prerequisite for equivalence. Therefore, as noted in the following, it is also a prerequisite for the emergence of simple meanings, vocabularies, or "semantic correspondences."

To help illustrate the other prerequisites for equivalence, we can set up a four-term contingency in which stimuli, although more familiar, are related to each other just as

Table 4: A Balanced Four-Term Contingency (Conditional Discrimination)
          R = Response; C = Consequence; S = Stimulus

```
                                    (                    ( R1  (press)  --->  C1  (coin)
                                    ( S1  (square)  -------- (
                                    (                    ( R2  (other)  -/->  C1  (coin)
            S3  (green)  -------  (                    --------------------------------
                                    (                    ( R1  (press)  -/->  C1  (coin)
                                    ( S2  (circle)  -------- (
                                    (                    ( R2  (other)  -/->  C1  (coin)
            -------------------------------------------------------------------
                                    (                    ( R1  (press)  -/->  C1  (coin)
                                    ( S1  (square)  -------- (
                                    (                    ( R2  (other)  -/->  C1  (coin)
            S4  (red)  ----------  (                    --------------------------------
                                    (                    ( R1  (press)  --->  C1  (coin)
                                    ( S2  (circle)  -------- (
                                    (                    ( R2  (other)  -/->  C1  (coin)
```

arbitrarily as those illustrated in Table 4. In Table 6, stimuli S1 and S2 are printed words, *two* and *six*, while stimuli S3 and S4 are printed digits, *2* and *6*. The subject can obtain a coin by pressing that button which has the word *two* on it if a third button has digit *2* on it; pressing *six* will produce the coin if the third button shows a *6*.

As with the forms and colors, conditionality is explicit both in the contingency and in the relations between behavior and environment that the contingency generates. With numbers and number names, however, one may tend to forget that four-term contingencies do not always generate stimulus equivalence. Even here, it is necessary to test the relations for reflexivity, symmetry, and transitivity in order to document equivalence.

Generalized identity matching of the digits and of the names would demonstrate reflexivity. For symmetry, the second defining property of equivalence, to be demonstrated, the conditional relation must hold true even when the sample and comparison stimuli are interchanged. The upper section of Table 7 reproduces the four-term units from Table 6. Since those relations have the subject selecting the word *two* when given digit *2* as a sample, and *six* when given *6,* symmetry would require the selection of the numbers when given the words as samples. The units illustrated in the bottom section of Table 7 will be found in the subject's repertoire, having

Table 5:   A Test for Reflexivity of the Conditional Relations in Table 4.
R = Response; C = Consequence; S = Stimulus.

```
                           (                     ( R1 (press) ---> C1 (coin)*
                           ( S1 (square) -------- (
                           (                     ( R2 (other) -/-> C1 (coin)
  S3 (square) ----- (                            -------------------------------
                           (                     ( R1 (press) -/-> C1 (coin)
                           ( S2 (circle) -------- (
                           (                     ( R2 (other) -/-> C1 (coin)
                -----------------------------------------------------------------
                           (                     ( R1 (press) -/-> C1 (coin)
                           ( S1 (square) -------- (
                           (                     ( R2 (other) -/-> C1 (coin)
  S4 (circle) ----- (                            -------------------------------
                           (                     ( R1 (press) ---> C1 (coin)*
                           ( S2 (circle) -------- (
                           (                     ( R2 (other) -/-> C1 (coin)
  -------------------------------------------------------------------------------
  -------------------------------------------------------------------------------
                           (                     ( R1 (press) ---> C1 (coin)*
                           ( S1 (green) --------- (
                           (                     ( R2 (other) -/-> C1 (coin)
  S3 (green) ------ (                             -------------------------------
                           (                     ( R1 (press) -/-> C1 (coin)
                           ( S2 (red) ----------- (
                           (                     ( R2 (other) -/-> C1 (coin)
                -----------------------------------------------------------------
                           (                     ( R1 (press) -/-> C1 (coin)
                           ( S1 (green) --------- (
                           (                     ( R2 (other) -/-> C1 (coin)
  S4 (red) ---------- (                           -------------------------------
                           (                     ( R1 (press) ---> C1 (coin)*
                           ( S2 (red) ----------- (
                           (                     ( R2 (other) -/-> C1 (coin)
  -------------------------------------------------------------------------------
```

*During reflexivity test, no coins are actually delivered.

emerged from the explicitly established four-term units shown in the upper section *even though the subject had never experienced the new contingencies before.*

Symmetry translates behaviorally into reversibility of sample and comparison roles. If, therefore, equivalence has emerged from explicitly constructed four-term units of conditional control, subjects will prove capable of additional conditional discriminations that they had never been explicitly taught.

Table 6: A Four-Term Contingency (Conditional Discrimination) Like Table 4 but with Different Stimuli.
R = Response; C = Consequence; S = Stimulus.

```
                                    (              ( R1  (press) ---> C1  (coin)
                                    ( S1  (two) ---------- (
                                    (              ( R2  (other) -/-> C1  (coin)
           S3  (2) --------- (                    -------------------------------
                                    (              ( R1  (press) -/-> C1  (coin)
                                    ( S2  (six) ---------- (
                                    (              ( R2  (other) -/-> C1  (coin)
           ----------------------------------------------------------------------
                                    (              ( R1  (press) -/-> C1  (coin)
                                    ( S1  (two) ---------- (
                                    (              ( R2  (other) -/-> C1  (coin)
           S4  (6) --------- (                    -------------------------------
                                    (              ( R1  (press) ---> C1  (coin)
                                    ( S2  (six) ---------- (
                                    (              ( R2  (other) -/-> C1  (coin)
```

In order to determine whether the conditional relations are transitive, we must first establish two more four-term units. The upper section of Table 8 shows the original contingencies, as in Table 6. The center section shows two new discriminations, between the *quantities* two and six (X's represent quantities of objects). These discriminations depend on the printed words *two* and *six*. The subject can obtain a coin by pressing the button which has a picture of *two objects* if the third button shows *two*, and by pressing the button which has *six objects* on it if the third button shows *six*.

Since the subject selects the comparison word *two* when given the number 2 as a sample, and the comparison quantity *XX* when given the word *two* as a sample, transitivity would require the subject to select the quantity *XX* when given the number 2 as a sample. Similarly, given the relations, "if 6, then *six*," and "if *six*, then *XXXXXX*," transitivity would produce, "if 6, then *XXXXXX*." Like reflexivity and symmetry, transitivity gives rise to new behavioral units - those illustrated in the bottom section of Table 8 - *even though the subject has never explicitly been taught the additional conditional discriminations.*

Table 7:   A Conditional Discrimination and Its Symmetric Counterpart.
             R = Response; C = Consequence; S = Stimulus.

```
                          (                        ( R1  (press)  --->  C1  (coin)
                          ( S1  (two)  ----------  (
                          (                        ( R2  (other)  -/->  C1  (coin)
          S3  (2) -----  (                         ------------------------------
                          (                        ( R1  (press)  -/->  C1  (coin)
                          ( S2  (six)  ----------  (
                          (                        ( R2  (other)  -/->  C1  (coin)
          -----------------------------------------------------------------
                          (                        ( R1  (press)  -/->  C1  (coin)
                          ( S1  (two)  ----------  (
                          (                        ( R2  (other)  -/->  C1  (coin)
          S4  (6) ------  (                         ------------------------------
                          (                        ( R1  (press)  --->  C1  (coin)
                          ( S2  (six)  ----------  (
                          (                        ( R2  (other)  -/->  C1  (coin)
          -----------------------------------------------------------------------
          -----------------------------------------------------------------------
                          (                        ( R1  (press)  --->  C1  (coin)*
                          ( S3  (2)  -------------  (
                          (                        ( R2  (other)  -/->  C1  (coin)
          S1  (two) ----  (                         ------------------------------
                          (                        ( R1  (press)  -/->  C1  (coin)
                          ( S4  (6)  -------------  (
                          (                        ( R2  (other)  -/->  C1  (coin)
          -----------------------------------------------------------------
                          (                        ( R1  (press)  -/->  C1  (coin)
                          ( S3  (2)  -------------  (
                          (                        ( R2  (other)  -/->  C1  (coin)
          S2  (six) ----- (                         ------------------------------
                          (                        ( R1  (press)  --->  C1  (coin)*
                          ( S4  (6)  -------------  (
                          (                        ( R2  (other)  -/->  C1  (coin)
          -----------------------------------------------------------------
```

       * During symmetry test, no coins are actually delivered.

When conditional relations possess the three defining properties of equivalence relations, the stimuli that have been related to each other become equivalent members of a class. Given equivalence, once the units in the top section of Table 8 have been constructed, 2 and *two* become equivalent members of one class, while 6 and *six* join as equivalent members of another class. The formation of such classes permits us to say that a number and a name have the same meaning, or that each is the meaning of the other. In this way, semantic correspondence

Table 8: Four-Term Contingencies and A Test for Transitivity.
R = Response; C = Consequence; S = Stimulus; X = Object.

```
                              (                    ( R1 (press) ---> C1 (coin)
                              ( S1 (two) -------- (
                              (                    ( R2 (other) -/-> C1 (coin)
         S3  (2) ------- (
                              (                    ( R1 (press) -/-> C1 (coin)
                              ( S2 (six) --------- (
                              (                    ( R2 (other) -/-> C1 (coin)
         ---------------------------------------------------------------------
                              (                    ( R1 (press) -/-> C1 (coin)
                              ( S1 (two) -------- (
                              (                    ( R2 (other) -/-> C1 (coin)
         S4  (6) ------ (
                              (                    ( R1 (press) ---> C1 (coin)
                              ( S2 (six) --------- (
                              (                    ( R2 (other) -/-> C1 (coin)
         ---------------------------------------------------------------------
                              (                    ( R1 (press) ---> C1 (coin)
                              ( S5 (XX) --------- (
                              (                    ( R2 (other) -/-> C1 (coin)
         S1 (two) ----- (
                              (                    ( R1 (press) -/-> C1 (coin)
                              ( S6 (XXXXXX) -- (
                              (                    ( R2 (other) -/-> C1 (coin)
         ---------------------------------------------------------------------
                              (                    ( R1 (press) -/-> C1 (coin)
                              ( S5 (XX) --------- (
                              (                    ( R2 (other) -/-> C1 (coin)
         S2 (six) ----- (
                              (                    ( R1 (press) ---> C1 (coin)
                              ( S6 (XXXXXX) -- (
                              (                    ( R2 (other) -/-> C1 (coin)
         ---------------------------------------------------------------------
         ---------------------------------------------------------------------
                              (                    ( R1 (press) ---> C1 (coin)*
                              ( S5 (XX) --------- (
                              (                    ( R2 (other) -/-> C1 (coin)
         S3  (2) ------- (
                              (                    ( R1 (press) -/-> C1 (coin)
                              ( S6 (XXXXXX) -- (
                              (                    ( R2 (other) -/-> C1 (coin)
         ---------------------------------------------------------------------
                              (                    ( R1 (press) -/-> C1 (coin)
                              ( S5 (XX) -------- (
                              (                    ( R2 (other) -/-> C1 (coin)
         S4  (6) -------- (
                              (                    ( R1 (press) ---> C1 (coin)*
                              ( S4 (XXXXXX) -- (
                              (                    ( R2 (other) -/-> C1 (coin)
         ---------------------------------------------------------------------
```

*During transitivity test, no coins are actually delivered.

emerges from nonlinguistic "if . . . then" relations. Expanding the analytic unit from three to four terms establishes the potential for verbal classes to emerge.

Four-term contingencies, however, do not always generate stimulus equivalence. For example, semantic correspondences have not yet been observed to emerge from conditional discriminations taught to pigeons, Rhesus monkeys, or baboons (Sidman, Rauzin, Lazar, Cunningham, Tailby, & Carrigan, 1982). Independent tests are necessary, therefore, to determine whether four-term units involve more than is immediately apparent - for example, to ascertain whether the numbers are indeed the meanings of the words.

The construction of four-term analytic units may accomplish still more than meets the eye. If, in addition to their conditional relations, the number and the word are equivalent members of a stimulus class, and the word and quantity are equivalent within the same class, then all three stimuli will be equivalent. Given equivalence within all of the conditional relations diagrammed in Table 8, the result will be two 3-member stimulus classes, one containing the equivalent elements, *2*, *two*, and *XX*, and the other containing *6*, *six*, and *XXXXXX*.

A consequence of such class formation is that a subject, when tested, will match any member of a class to any other, even without ever having encountered the tested relation before. The subject will be capable of more new performances than those we have noted so far. Table 9 illustrates what is actually a more global test for equivalence, eliminating the need to test separately for symmetry and transitivity. The upper and center sections of Table 9 are the same as those in Table 8. Again, we can ask whether more is happening here than the contingencies specify. In addition to the immediately observable conditional relations, is it also possible that the quantities are the meanings of the digits and the printed words?

Let us assume, on the basis of many experiments with human subjects, that equivalence relations hold among the conditionally related stimuli in the upper two sections of Table 9. As a consequence, the subject will be capable of the new conditional

Table 9:   Four-Term Contingencies and A Test For Stimulus Equivalence.
            R = Response; C = Consequence; S = Stimulus; X = Object.

```
                        (                    ( R1 (press) ---> C1 (coin)
                        ( S1 (two) -------- (
                        (                    ( R2 (other) -/-> C1 (coin)
        S3 (2) ----------- (                 ------------------------------
                        (                    ( R1 (press) -/-> C1 (coin)
                        ( S2 (six) --------- (
                        (                    ( R2 (other) -/-> C1 (coin)
        ------------------------------------------------------------------
                        (                    ( R1 (press) -/-> C1 (coin)
                        ( S1 (two) -------- (
                        (                    ( R2 (other) -/-> C1 (coin)
        S4 (6) ----------- (                 ------------------------------
                        (                    ( R1 (press) ---> C1 (coin)
                        ( S2 (six) -------- (
                        (                    ( R2 (other) -/-> C1 (coin)
        ------------------------------------------------------------------
                        (                    ( R1 (press) ---> C1 (coin)
                        ( S5 (XX) --------- (
                        (                    ( R2 (other) -/-> C1 (coin)
        S1 (two) -------- (                  ------------------------------
                        (                    ( R1 (press) -/-> C1 (coin)
                        ( S6 (XXXXXX) -- (
                        (                    ( R2 (other) -/-> C1 (coin)
        ------------------------------------------------------------------
                        (                    ( R1 (press) ---> C1 (coin)
                        ( S5 (XX) --------- (
                        (                    ( R2 (other) -/-> C1 (coin)
        S2 (six) --------- (                 ------------------------------
                        (                    ( R1 (press) ---> C1 (coin)
                        ( S6 (XXXXXX) -- (
                        (                    ( R2 (other) -/-> C1 (coin)
        ------------------------------------------------------------------
        ------------------------------------------------------------------
                        (                    ( R1 (press) ---> C1 (coin)
                        ( S3 (2) ----------- (
                        (                    ( R2 (other) -/-> C1 (coin)
        S5 (XX) --------- (                  ------------------------------
                        (                    ( R1 (press) -/-> C1 (coin)
                        ( S4 (6) ----------- (
                        (                    ( R2 (other) -/-> C1 (coin)
        ------------------------------------------------------------------
                        (                    ( R1 (press) -/-> C1 (coin)
                        ( S3 (2) ----------- (
                        (                    ( R2 (other) -/-> C1 (coin)
        S6 (XXXXXX) -- (                     ------------------------------
                        (                    ( R1 (press) ---> C1 (coin)
                        ( S4 (6) ----------- (
                        (                    ( R2 (other) -/-> C1 (coin)
        ------------------------------------------------------------------
```

*During equivalence test, no coins are actually delivered.

discrimination shown in the bottom section even without having ever encountered the new contingencies before. Why? First, if the explicitly constructed relation in the center, "if *two* then *XX*" is symmetric, the subject's repertoire will automatically contain "if *XX* then *two*." Second, symmetry of the other explicitly constructed relation, "if *2* then *two*" (top section), will automatically place "if *two* then *2*" in the subject's repertoire. Given the two conditional discriminations generated by symmetry, "if *XX* then *two*" and "if *two* then *2*," transitivity will automatically place the new conditional discrimination, "if *XX* then *2*" (bottom section) in the subject's repertoire. A similar derivation is possible for "if *XXXXXX* then *6*."

Furthermore, the subject will conform to the new contingencies even though the indicated consequences never actually occur. During the test, the subject receives no indication of what he or she is "supposed to do." Because *2*, *two*, and *XX* have become equivalent members of a class, a subject who has never experienced relations between digits and quantities, and who is given no "feedback" during the test, will nevertheless press *2* rather than *6* if the third button has a picture of two objects on it. Also, because *6*, *six*, and *XXXXXX* have become equivalent members of another class, the subject will press *6* if the third button depicts six objects.

Thus, we see meaning emerging from structures built out of four-term units. It is, indeed, an elementary form of meaning, yet it is a special property of language. Our subject can represent a quantity by a numerical symbol, and can react to the symbol as if it were a quantity, without having been taught explicitly to relate the two. Emergence of the new four-term units in the test justifies the assertion that the contingencies not only generated conditional discriminations, but that they also taught the subject a meaningful two-word vocabulary. The procedures diagrammed in Table 9 have successfully taught severely retarded students visual and auditory comprehension of 20 simple nouns, thereby starting them off with a 20-word vocabulary (Sidman, 1971; Sidman & Cresson, 1973). With normal children and adults, the procedures have built stimulus classes containing as many as six equivalent elements (Sidman,

Kirk, & Willson-Morris, 1985). A start has even been made in the direction of accounting for correct first-time occurrences of syntactic relations (Lazar, 1977; Lazar & Kotlarchyk, in press).

Note also that once two stimuli have been explicitly related as sample and comparison in a four-term unit, they can then function individually, one without the other. In tests for reflexivity, symmetry, and transitivity, and in the global test for equivalence, each stimulus serves its new function effectively in the derived units without ever before having been paired with the other stimulus component of the new unit. This observation documents the earlier assertion that it can be incorrect to treat sample and comparison stimuli as a unitary compound.

By reacting to a word as to an equivalent stimulus - the meaning of the word - a person can behave adaptively in an environment without having previously been exposed to it. The emergence of equivalence from conditionality permits Behavior Analysis to account for the establishment at least of simple semantic correspondences without having to postulate a direct reinforcement history for every instance. Instead of appealing to cognitions, representations, and stored correspondences to explain the initial occurrence of appropriate new behavior, one can find a complete explanation in the four-term units that are the prerequisites for the emergent behavior.

Their lack of success in providing a useful account of contextual control has prevented cognitivists from programming computers to comprehend the English language. One could begin to solve that particular context problem by programming a computer to acquire a repertoire of four-term contingencies. The programmer would, of course, have to give the computer nonlinguistic capacities that would enable it to develop and maintain the two- and three-term units from which to synthesize four-term units. The computer would therefore have to be made sensitive to consequences, some "hard-wired" into two-term contingencies, and others derivable from three-term contingencies. Having first established these nonlinguistic prerequisites, a computer program for language comprehension would then have to give the machine a capacity for generating equivalence relations from four-term contingencies.

The emergence of equivalence from the four-term unit of conditional control sets the stage for the analysis of the contextual determination of meaning. By itself, the four-term contingency provides only a unit for describing the contextual control of three-term contingencies, a level of analysis that does not encompass the role of context in determining semantic correspondences. We might, for example, attempt to characterize people by constructing catalogues of the four-term units in their repertoires. Such catalogues would be of restricted utility because the environment also sets constraints upon four-term contingencies. We would find ourselves able to account for only a limited number of instances in which people display language comprehension in the absence of direct experience with a particular linguistic unit. By placing four-term contingencies themselves under environmental constraint, however, we can bring the emergence of meaning itself under contextual control.

Our computer program, too, if it were endowed only with the capacity to generate equivalence relations from four-term units, would be unable to cope with contextual constraints upon conditional control or upon the verbal classes that emerge from conditional control. The computer would be unable, for example, to handle the distinction between "soldier" and "sailor" as equivalent members of one class - "military forces" - and as nonequivalent members of other classes - e.g., "army" and "navy." Only by making the computer sensitive to the contextual determination of equivalence relations can one expect it to comprehend language effectively.

Four-term units, therefore, still do not carry a behavioral analysis far enough. A fifth term is needed to describe the environment's ability to select conditional discriminations from our repertoire, and to influence the meanings that are derived from conditional relations.

Table 10:   The Five-Term Contingency (Second-Order Conditional
Discrimination)   R = Response; C =Consequence; S = Stimulus

```
                  (                    (                ( R1 (press) ---> C1 (coin)
                  (                    ( S1 (square) --- (
                  (                    (                ( R2 (other) -/-> C1 (coin)
                  ( S3 (green) -- (                     -----------------------------
                  (                    (                ( R1 (press) -/-> C1 (coin)
                  (                    ( S2 (circle) --- (
                  (                    (                ( R2 (other) -/-> C1 (coin)
 S5  (tone 1)-- (                      -----------------------------------------------
                  (                    (                ( R1 (press) -/-> C1 (coin)
                  (                    ( S1 (square) --- (
                  (                    (                ( R2 (other) -/-> C1 (coin)
                  ( S4 (red) ------(                    -----------------------------
                  (                    (                ( R1 (press) ---> C1 (coin)
                  (                    ( S2 (circle) --- (
                  (                    (                ( R2 (other) -/-> C1 (coin)
 ------------------------------------------------------------------------------------
                  (                    (                ( R1 (press) -/-> C1 (coin)
                  (                    ( S1 (square) --- (
                  (                    (                ( R2 (other) -/-> C1 (coin)
                  ( S3 (green) ---(                     -----------------------------
                  (                    (                ( R1 (press) ---> C1 (coin)
                  (                    ( S2 (circle) --- (
                  (                    (                ( R2 (other) -/-> C1 (coin)
 S6  (tone 2)-- (                      -----------------------------------------------
                  (                    (                ( R1 (press) ---> C1 (coin)
                  (                    ( S1 (square) --- (
                  (                    (                ( R2 (other) -/-> C1 (coin)
                  ( S4 (red) ----- (                    -----------------------------
                  (                    (                ( R1 (press) -/-> C1 (coin)
                  (                    ( S2 (circle) --- (
                  (                    (                ( R2 (other) -/-> C1 (coin)
```

THE FIVE-TERM CONTINGENCY

If, then, an additional element of the experimental
environment is allowed to vary, four-term contingencies, the
simplest units of conditional control, can themselves be placed
under conditional control. The upper half of Table 10 shows
that the four-term relation which Table 4 outlined is now
controlled by a fifth element, stimulus S5. The subject can still
obtain a coin by pressing the square in the presence of a green
hue or by pressing the circle in the presence of red, but only if
tone 1 is sounding. The bottom half of Table 10 shows that if

tone 2 (S6) is on, the significance of the hues is reversed. The subject can now obtain a coin by pressing the square in the presence of red, or by pressing the circle in the presence of green. Because the tones assume conditional control over the original conditional discrimination, the five-term contingency is the unit of *second-order conditional control*.

The five-term unit describes the influence which the environment exerts over conditional discriminations; conditional control by the hues over the form discriminations is itself conditional upon the tones. Four-term contingencies account for variations in the control which discriminative stimuli exert over response-consequence relations. Five-term contingencies, which leave discriminative control untouched, account for variations in the relations between conditional and discriminative stimuli. The four-term unit makes the stimulus control of behavior flexible; the five-term unit makes the conditional control of stimulus control flexible. Enlarging the unit of analysis step by step provides analytic tools that permit us to synthesize and account for any degree of breadth and complexity of behavioral variation that may be required.

The five-term analytic unit also describes a more powerful type of contextual control than does the four-term unit. If our original four-term unit generates equivalence relations, we can say, "*Green* means *square*, and *red* means *circle*." Second-order conditional control - the five-term unit - now provides a mechanism which accounts for the contextual determination of these meanings.

With the five-term unit, we can still say, "*Green* means *square* and *red* means *circle*," but only in the context of *tone 1*. When the context changes to *tone 2*, the meanings also change; now, *green* means *circle* and *red* means *square*. Sometimes, then, *square* and *green* are equivalent members of one class, and *circle* and *red* of another. At different times, however, one class includes *square* and *red* as equivalent members, while the other includes *circle* and *green*. The context, represented by stimuli S5 and S6, shifts elements of the environment from class to class. Stimuli may therefore have multiple class memberships, changing in meaning from occasion to occasion.

Without contextual control by tones 1 and 2, the common elements in each of the four small classes (*square* and *green*, *square* and *red*, *circle* and *red*, *circle* and *green*) would cause all of the hues and forms to combine into a single large class, for all practical purposes, meaningless. For example, mercury can be classified both as a metal and a liquid. Contextual control, e.g., "Today's topic is oxidation (or flow patterns)," prevents other members of the class, "metal," from entering into equivalence relations with members of the class, "liquid." Mercury can therefore sometimes be equivalent to iron and sometimes to water without making those two elements equivalent to each other. Any program for making our language comprehensible to a computer will not only recognize verbal classes that conditional control generates, but will take advantage of the contextual constraints that second-order conditional control imposes upon those verbal classes.

Only two behavior-analytic studies have so far explicitly explored or made use of contextual control over classes of equivalent stimuli (Fucini, 1982; Lazar & Kotlarchyk, in press). Behavior Analysis has not yet proceeded beyond this point. Many questions remain. For example, what is the relation between the second-order conditional stimuli - the tones - and the other stimuli - the hues and geometric forms?

The question can be clarified by following the two paths from S5 to C1 in the upper segment of Table 10. These paths suggest that *tone 1* could become a common element of two 3-member classes, one including *tone 1*, *green*, and *square*, and the other, *tone 1*, *red*, and *circle*. If these 3-member classes did form, however, the common element would combine the two classes, hues and geometric forms all becoming equivalent to tone 1 and to each other. Conditional control by *green* and *red* would be wiped out, as would discriminative control by *square* and *circle*, since all stimuli would have become equivalent, and the two-term contingency would be left uncontrolled; the five-term unit would "self destruct."

Similarly, *tone 2* would create and enter into a single class containing the hues and forms. With both tones now equivalent members of the large class, the whole contingency would be destroyed. Contextual control over classes of equivalent stimuli would be impossible.

Also, the paradigm illustrated in Table 10 for increasing class size from two to three members would not be feasible. There, however, may lie the solution to the problem. If the second-order conditional stimuli did *not* enter into equivalence relations with the other stimuli, maintaining only their conditional relations, then contextual control over meaning could be maintained without destroying the units from which meaning is derived. Different techniques than the one suggested by Table 10 would then be required to increase the number of equivalent stimuli that a class encompasses (see, for example, Fields, Verhave, & Fath, 1984; Lazar, Davis-Lang, & Sanchez, 1984; Sidman, Kirk, & Willson-Morris, 1985).

It is, of course, only conjectural that second-order conditional relations do not possess the properties of equivalence relations, since it is by no means clear why equivalence should be precluded, but the experiments which are needed to provide the relevant data can be done. Even nonhuman subjects have demonstrated the existence of five-term units (Nevin & Liebold, 1966; Santi, 1978; Weigl, 1941); what remains is only to apply an equivalence-test paradigm that is slightly more complex than the one illustrated in Table 9.

Other questions, too, are amenable to experimental analysis: Why does equivalence sometimes fail to emerge from four-term units? Third-order conditional control has yet even to be demonstrated; is it possible? Does the size of a stimulus class, or the amount of overlap between classes, affect the likelihood that contextual control will itself enlarge or merge the classes? Does the level of conditional control that one can attain, or the number of equivalent stimuli that one can encompass within a single class constitute an intellectual marker? How does *stimulus equivalence*, as defined by the present analysis, interact with *functional equivalence*, defined as discriminative control exerted by two or more stimuli over a single response? And a more theoretical question, less obviously open to an experimental answer, concerns the new process that might be exposed by the five-term unit of analysis.

Discriminative control makes conditioned reinforcement possible; conditional control generates stimulus equivalence; what new complexity does second-order conditional control bring within the purview of Behavior Analysis?

Along with the ever more complex interactions between environmental structures and behavior that become accessible as the analytic unit expands, the very exposure of questions, conundrums, and paradoxes may be regarded as an additional virtue of the analytic procedures. The delineation of "obvious" next steps, and the clear exposure of lacunae in a systematic structure, are characteristics of the most advanced sciences. As a consequence of its reluctance to analyze its own structure, Behavior Analysis has, perhaps, been overly reticent in establishing its position among the sciences.

REFERENCES

Catania, A. C. (1973). The concept of the operant in the analysis of behavior. *Behaviorism, 1, 103-116.*

Catania, A. C. (1975). The myth of self-reinforcement. *Behaviorism, 3,* 192-199.

Catania, A. C. (1976). Self-reinforcement revisited. *Behaviorism, 4,* 157-162.

Catania, A. C. (1980). Autoclitic processes and the structure of behavior. *Behaviorism, 8,* 175-186.

Catania, A. C. (1984). *Learning* (2nd ed.). Englewood Cliffs, New Jersey: Prentice Hall.

Cumming, W. W., & Berryman, R. (1965). The complex discriminated operant: Studies on matching-to-sample and related problems. In D. I. Mostofsky (Ed.), *Stimulus Generalization* (pp. 284-330). Stanford, CA: Stanford University Press.

Estes, W. K., Koch, S., MacCorquodale, K., Meehl, P. E., Mueller, C. G., Schoenfeld, W. N., & Verplanck, W. S. (1954). *Modern learning theory.* New York: Appleton-Century-Crofts.

Ferster, C. B., & Skinner, B. F. (1957). *Schedules of reinforcement.* New York: Appleton-Century-Crofts.

Fields, L., Verhave, T., & Fath, S. (1984). Stimulus equivalence and transitive associations: A methodological analysis. *Journal of the Experimental Analysis of Behavior, 42,* 143-157.

Findley, J. D. (1962). An experimental outline for building and exploring multi-operant behavior repertoires. *Journal of the Experimental Analysis of Behavior, 5,* 113-166.

Findley, J. D., & Brady, J. V. (1965). Facilitation of large ratio performance by use of conditioned reinforcement. *Journal of the Experimental Analysis of Behavior, 8,* 125-129.

Fucini, A. (1982). *Stimulus control of class membership.* Unpublished doctoral dissertation, Northeastern University, Boston, MA.

Goldiamond, I. (1962). Perception. In A. J. Bachrach (Ed.), *Experimental foundations of clinical psychology* (pp. 280-340). New York: Basic Books.

Goldiamond, I. (1966). Perception, language, and conceptualization rules. In B. Kleinmuntz (Ed.), *Problem solving* (pp. 183-224). New York: Wiley.

Goldiamond, I. (1975). Alternative sets as a framework for behavioral formulations and research. *Behaviorism, 3,* 49-86.

Goldiamond, I. (1976). Self-reinforcement. *Journal of Applied Behavior Analysis, 9,* 509-514.

Green, D. M., & Swets, J. A. (1966). *Signal detection theory and psychophysics.* New York: Wiley.

Hineline, P. N. (1980). The language of behavior analysis: Its community, its functions, and its limitations. *Behaviorism, 8,* 67-86.

Kelleher, R. T. (1966). Conditioned reinforcement in second-order schedules. *Journal of the Experimental Analysis of Behavior, 9,* 475-485.

Lashley, K. S. (1938). Conditional reactions in the rat. *Journal of Psychology, 6,* 311-324.

Lawrence, D. H. (1963). The nature of a stimulus: Some relationships between learning and perception. In S. Koch (Ed.), *Psychology: A study of a science, Vol. 5* (pp. 179-212). New York: McGraw-Hill.

Lazar, R. (1977). Extending sequence-class membership with matching to sample. *Journal of the Experimental Analysis of Behavior, 27,* 381-392.

Lazar, R. M., Davis-Lang, D., & Sanchez L. (1984). The formation of stimulus equivalences in children. *Journal of the Experimental Analysis of Behavior, 41,* 251-266.

Lazar, R. M., & Kotlarchyk, B. J. (in press). Second-order control of sequence-class equivalences in children. *Behaviour Processes.*

Lee, V. L. (1983). Behavior as a constituent of conduct. *Behaviorism, 11,* 199-224.

MacCorquodale, K., & Meehl, P. E. (1948). On a distinction between hypothetical constructs and intervening variables. *Psychological Review, 55,* 95-107.

Meehl, P. E. (1950). On the circularity of the Law of Effect. *Psychological Bulletin, 47,* 52-75.

Nevin, J. A., & Liebold, K. (1966). Stimulus control of matching and oddity in a pigeon. *Psychonomic Science, 5,* 351-352.

Notterman, J. M., & Mintz, D. E. (1965). *Dynamics of response.* New York: Wiley.

Prokasy, W. F., & Hall, J. F. (1963). Primary stimulus generalization. *Psychological Review, 70,* 310-322.

Ray, B. A. (1972). Strategy in studies of attention: A commentary on D.

I. Mostofsky's *Attention: Contemporary theory and analysis. Journal of the Experimental Analysis of Behavior, 17,* 293-297.

Ray, B. A., & Sidman, M. (1970). Reinforcement schedules and stimulus control. In W. N. Schoenfeld (Ed.), *The Theory of reinforcement schedules* (pp. 187-214). New York: Appleton-Century-Crofts.

Santi, A. (1978). The role of physical identity of the sample and the correct comparison stimulus in matching-to-sample paradigms. *Journal of the Experimental Analysis of Behavior, 29,* 511-516.

Schoenfeld, W. N. (1976). The "response" in behavior theory. *Pavlovian Journal of Biological Science, 11,* 129-149.

Schoenfeld, W. N., & Cumming, W. W. (1963). Behavior and perception. In S. Koch (Ed.), *Psychology: A study of a science, Vol. 5* (pp. 213-252). New York: McGraw-Hill.

Sidman, M. (1969). Generalization gradients and stimulus control in delayed matching to sample. *Journal of the Experimental Analysis of Behavior, 12,* 745-757.

Sidman, M. (1971). Reading and auditory-visual equivalences. *Journal of Speech and Hearing Research, 14,* 5-13.

Sidman, M. (1978). Remarks. *Behaviorism, 6,* 265-268.

Sidman, M., & Cresson, O. (1973). Reading and transfer of crossmodal stimulus equivalences in severe retardation. *American Journal of Mental Defiency, 77,* 515-523.

Sidman, M., Kirk, B., & Willson-Morris, M. (1985). Six-member stimulus classes generated by conditional-discrimination procedures. *Journal of the Experimental Analysis of Behavior, 43,* 21-42.

Sidman, M., Rauzin, R., Lazar, R., Cunningham, S., Tailby, W., & Carrigan, P. (1982). A search for symmetry in the conditional discriminations of Rhesus monkeys, baboons, and children. *Journal of the Experimental Analysis of Behavior, 37,* 23-44.

Sidman, M., & Tailby, W. (1982). Conditional discrimination vs. matching to sample: An expansion of the testing paradigm. *Journal of the Experimental Analysis of Behavior, 37,* 5-22.

Skinner, B. F. (1931). The concept of the reflex in the description of behavior. *Journal of General Psychology, 5,* 427-458.

Skinner, B. F. (1935). The generic nature of the concepts of stimulus and response. *Journal of General Psychology, 12,* 40-65.

Skinner, B. F. (1938). *The Behavior of organisms: An experimental analysis.* New York: Appleton-Century.

Skinner, B. F. (1953). *Science and human behavior.* New York: Macmillan.

Skinner, B. F. (1957). *Verbal behavior.* New York: Appleton-Century-Crofts.

Stoddard, L. T., & Sidman, M. (1971). The removal and restoration of stimulus control. *Journal of the Experimental Analysis of Behavior, 16,* 143-154.

Terrace, H. S. (1966). Stimulus control. In W. K. Honig (Ed.), *Operant behavior: Areas of research and application* (pp. 271-344). New York: Appleton-Century-Crofts.

Weigl, E. (1941). On the psychology of so-called processes of abstraction. *Journal of Abnormal and Social Psychology, 36*, 3-9.

CHAPTER 12

Behavior as a Function of Inner States and Outer Circumstances

ROGER SCHNAITTER

Taxonomy concerns the problem of classification, and the taxonomy of behavior, the subject of this symposium, concerns the problem of the classification of behavior into its types. My goal in this paper is to consider two broad strategies through which such a classification can be developed, and to evaluate the relative strengths and weaknesses of these two strategies. I want to introduce the two strategies by extending an illustration that has been used by Hilary Putnam (1975). In this example, Putnam's concern was to illustrate clearly and simply his contention that psychological explanations are not necessarily reductive. His illustration was not psychological at all; it was a simple physical system with a mechanical property that can't be accounted for through recourse to reductive physical explanation. If you are unfamiliar with the example, it goes like this: Suppose that we have a simple physical system consisting of a board with two holes in it. One is square, one inch on a side, and the other is round, one inch in diameter. The problem is to explain why a square peg, just short of one inch on the side, will pass through the square hole but not through the round hole.

The point Putnam draws from this example is that the standard reductionist line doesn't lead to a satisfactory explanation. Nothing about the material micro-structure of the board or the peg gets at the reason the peg goes through the square but not the round hole. Putnam concludes that " . . . the ultimate constituents don't matter . . . only the higher level structure matters . . ." (1975, p. 137). That is, what the board or the peg are *made* of doesn't matter - it might be wood or aluminum or even ice, perhaps. The only thing that matters is the relative geometrical structure of the components of the system. So reductive explanation fails here. Putnam's purpose in presenting this example is to draw the further conclusion that roughly the same situation is faced by psychological explanation. Lots of psychological problems (perhaps *all* problems that are fundamentally psychological) have the same explanatory property, to wit: The "stuff" of which psychological mechanisms are made is not particularly relevant to analyzing their workings, because *any* mechanism can do a job of mentation if its structure is right for that particular job.

This example is of special interest because it offers additional features relevant to psychology that Putnam left unexplored. So I will push the example a bit further before going on to the messier kind of example that is more characteristic of psychology. First, let us simplify Putnam's plank (as I will call it) by putting a single hole in it, just the one inch square hole. Second, we will employ Putnam's plank to sort objects into the two categories of "plank-accepted pieces," and "plank-rejected pieces." The plank, then, is a taxonomizer of objects into two classes.   With the problem thusly reconstructed, now consider the problem of explaining the sorting capacity of the plank. To begin with, if Putnam's argument against reductionism holds for his version of the example, then it surely must hold here. Consequently, I will not even explore that issue. What I want to do with the example is to suggest that there are two different strategies whereby nonreductive explanations of the sorting capacity of Putnam's plank can be developed. If that is so, then by implication there are two different strategies through which nonreductive psychological explanations can be developed as well.

Systematic Features of Mechanism: The obvious approach to this problem would be to measure the hole in the plank. Any object whose dimensions exceed those of the hole will not pass through it, and any object below the dimensions of the hole *will* pass through it. Nothing could be more simple or direct. In fact, it might be *so* obvious that this is the way to approach explaining the sorting capacity of the plank that some people would find it hard to believe that there might be any other way to go about it. I might also note a not insignificant virtue of this strategy: One can do all of the relevant investigation of the practical work of Putnam's plank without, in fact, ever attempting to pass an object through it, or indeed, even without ever looking at any possible object against which to test the capacities of the plank. Obviously, such a strategy is of enormous intrinsic appeal to those with a rationalistic bent.

Systematic Assessment of Environment: As my father oft reminded me in the days of my youth, some people just seem to *insist* on doing things the hard way. In contrast to the sensible and efficient means of solving the explanatory problem outlined above, the alternative strategy looks downright perverse. It works like this: Beyond guiding things into it, one can ignore the hole in the plank completely - treat it as untrustworthy, an apparition, a spookish sort of black hole. All that is needed is to methodically push things into it. If an object passes through, retrieve it and put it in pile *A*. If it does not pass through, put it in pile *B*. When piles *A* and *B* are big enough, study all the items in each pile, and attempt to abstract their common features. After arriving at such an abstraction, one can make a prediction about the passability of any new object, and test the prediction against the hard reality of Putnam's plank. Of course, it is almost certain that a sufficient number of tests of the tentative explanatory principle will produce a counter example, or falsifying case. Then the tentative explanation will have to be revised in light of the new evidence. Satisfactory revisions may be difficult to devise. They will fail the test of parsimony, for instance, if the problem cases are just enumerated in a list appended to a rough but fallible generalization.

It is important to note that the specification of common features via this strategy, although in this instance expressible in physical dimensional terms, is necessarily functional. That is to say, the specification of the stimulus class is in terms of the relation between objects and an independent, external criterion, not in terms of projectable physical properties of individual objects taken by themselves. In this example the class will ideally be described as consisting of all objects of dimensions not exceeding those of a square, one inch on a side. A grain of sand will be a member of such a class, but a grain of sand itself has an infinite number of comparable relational properties (e.g., it is smaller than an elephant, larger than a gnat's eyebrow, etc.). Consequently, a functional property is determinable only through examination of classes of objects, not through physical measurement of single cases. That is why radical behaviorism is properly considered a functionalistic rather than a physicalistic doctrine (Schnaitter, 1984b).

In contrast to the rational flavor of the first strategy, the second strategy is empirical with a vengeance. But the irony of this second explanation is that, could it be developed to perfection, then it would converge on the first explanation. The inside and outside of the hole in the plank are the same boundary, a boundary indifferent to the mode through which it is identified. But in truth it will take an enormous amount of time and effort to achieve results from the second strategy, in contrast to the almost instantaneous results obtainable with the first strategy.

Were the problems of psychology as simple as diagnosing the powers of Putnam's plank, then most of our professional work would by now be done, and psychologists of the second sort would be considered cranks of the most iconoclastic sort. But as we know, the problems of psychology are not simple at all. So let me bring up the most compelling complication, still within the context of this illustration. Imagine that Putnam's plank, rather than lying out across a set of horses in the workshop, is embedded deep within some gloomy and impenetrable labyrinth. Objects dropped into this device rattle around a bit and eventually fall out of one or the other of two openings, one marked *A* and the other *B*. The internal mechanism responsible for the sorting, however, is simply beyond reach. That is how it is with the machinery intermediating between stimulus conditions and behavioral events in psychology.

As Rorty has suggested, " . . . if physiology were simpler and more obvious than it is, nobody would have felt the need for psychology" (1979, p. 237), but it is not simple and obvious, so there we are. The fundamental explanatory issue in psychology is what to do about this circumstance. The natural way to explain the working of a mechanism is to describe the manner in which the parts of the mechanism are organized and causally interrelated. Think of explaining how a clock works, for example (I am thinking of an old fashioned wind up alarm clock). One wants to open it up and get a look at the gears, the mainspring, the balance wheel. Most decidedly, no normal person would think to devise plots of angular rotation of the minute hand as a function of degrees rotation of the mainspring stem, for instance. But then imagine a clock that simply can't be opened up - whose works are, perhaps *in principle*, unobservable. Then perforce one must fall back on data concerning performance of the mechanism. No other information is available.

Everyone in psychology, mentalists and behaviorists alike, relies on performance data because those are the only kind of data available. That is, everyone in psychology (except the physiologists) measures the equivalent of the pegs and not the holes in Putnam's plank; everyone measures the turning of the hands, not the gearworks, of the alarm clock. At issue is the use to which these data are put. The psychology of inner state - mentalism - employs such data as the ground on which to infer the properties of inner mechanisms. Contemporary mentalism, if I understand it properly, does not propose that any substance in addition to material substance plays a role in psychological causation. What it proposes is that an abstract and systematic *type of description* of the material machinery of the body answers more psychological questions than other potential types of description. In a word, the goal of mentalism is to characterize the functional *design* features of the mechanism that accomplish the psychologically interesting work of organisms. The functional design is independent of the specific hardware instantiating the design (in our case, a nervous system with certain physico-chemical properties), just as the geometry of Putnam's plank is independent of its material composition.[1] In contrast to mentalism, the psychology of outer circumstances - behaviorism - employs performance data to characterize the behavior of intact systems. The behaviorist's interest, rather than the determination of inner mechanisms, focuses on the external adaptation of the organism taken as a whole to its environment.

Much argument has gone on over the relative merits of a psychology of inner states as against a psychology of outer circumstances. The argument really turns on the way one evaluates the idealized preferability of the first strategy - the description of mechanism - over the second strategy - the description of performance - in light of the fact that inner psychological mechanisms are not directly accessible.[2] Mentalists argue that mechanistic explanation is so desirable that the inferential risks are trivial in comparison. In contrast, behaviorists argue that the problems of inference to mechanisms are so overwhelming as to make every mentalistic explanation a vacuous illusion. All of this debate is interesting, and much of it is relevant to the issue as developed here. But it is far too extensive to summarize, let alone evaluate critically. Nonethe-

---

[1]The notion of functional design is often analogized to computer programs rather than to the functional design of computing hardware. I suppose there is some value to this analogy, but I do not like it for several reasons: Anything that can be written in a program can be hard-wired; there is hardware to the brain for sure, but I don't quite know what to make of the idea that there are programs in the brain (e.g., what would it mean to "load a program" in the brain?); and except for some of the work in AI, I have not seen any cognitive theories that look much like computer programs. Consequently, it seems appropriate to stay with the hardware/software-neutral expression, "functional design."

[2]Sometimes I am accused of taking a methodological rather than a radical behaviorist line. Remarks like this are the ones that seem to cause the trouble. Some behaviorists apparently think it illicit to acknowledge that mechanistic accounts have desirable properties. However, I am only following Skinner here.

> The physiologist of the future will tell us all that can be known about what is happening inside the behaving organism. His account will be an important advance over a behavioral analysis, because the latter is necessarily "historical" - that is to say, it is confined to functional relations showing

less, I do want to comment on two of the charges that have been made against behaviorism, and two that have been made against mentalism.

The Argument that Machine Functionalism Proves Behaviorism to be False: The biggest problem facing behaviorism is what has been called the stimulus independence of behavior (e.g., Pylyshyn, 1984, ch. 1). That is, all kinds of examples can be given where the prevailing stimulus circumstances radically underdetermine the behavior that occurs. The content of ordinary conversation is such an example. If a person is presented with the verbal stimulus context, "A penny for your thoughts," for instance, it is notoriously difficult to predict much of interest about the ensuing verbal response. (Rigorously controlling the context by, e.g., holding a gun to someone's head and demanding, "Say 'uncle' or I'll shoot," simply begs the question.) Such a fact can be of solace to the mentalist only if the situationally undetermined parts of behavior are determined by inner states, and those inner states can be known with reasonable clarity and reliability. One way in which mentalists have attempted to introduce rigor into their formulations is to propose that mental states are identical to machine-table states of universal Turing machines. Since the concept of a Turing machine state is clear and precise, the proposed identity imbues the concept of a mental state with equal clarity and precision. Furthermore, Turing machine state tables possess just the right properties to give a principled account of the stimulus independence of

---

temporal gaps. Something is done today which affects the behavior of an organism tomorrow. No matter how clearly that fact can be established, a step is missing, and we must wait for the physiologist to supply it.   (1974, pp. 236-237)

That strikes me as a significant admission. To be sure Skinner is talking about knowledge of physiological mechanisms here, knowledge about blood and meat, so to speak, rather than knowledge of something so ethereal as the 'design' of the blood and meat. If that is a correct reading of Skinner, then I think he is wrong if he believes that the integrative functioning of the 150 billion or more neurons in the human nervous system will ever be understood bloody piece by bloody piece, rather than via an abstract description of the functional operation of that system - via its design.

INTERNAL MACHINE STATE

	S_1	S_2
nickel input	Emit no output Go to S_2	Emit a Coke Go to S_1
dime input	Emit a Coke Stay in S_1	Emit a Coke & a nickel Go to S_1

INPUT

Fig. 1. Machine state table of the "Mentalistic Coke Machine."

behavior.

In order to make this point perfectly clear, mentalists have made considerable mileage with the "mentalistic Coke machine." I have run across this example in four separate sources (Nelson, 1975, where it seems to have originated; Block, 1978; Block, 1980; and Fodor, 1981). This is a Coke machine that, due to inattention from the local distributor, still dispenses a drink for ten cents. It will accept either a dime, or a nickel when another nickel has been inserted earlier. The state table for the machine appears as follows: State 2 is the interesting state so far as the problem of the stimulus independence of behavior is concerned. Since the machine will dispense a Coke for either a dime or two nickels, it is impossible to predict the behavior of the machine on observing the insertion of any single nickel. This is because the machine will fail to dispense a Coke following a nickel input if it is in State 1, but it will dispense a Coke if it is in State 2. Consequently, knowing that a nickel has been deposited leaves one at the chance level so far as predicting the behavior of the machine, while knowledge of the machine state will allow one to predict the machine's behavior with certainty. Amazingly enough, Fodor has claimed that something here demonstrates a limitation of

INPUT N-1

	dime input	nickel input
nickel input	Emit no output	Emit a Coke
dime input	Emit a Coke	Emit a Coke & a nickel

INPUT N (appears to left of table, between the two rows)

Fig. 2. Environmental state table of the "Mentalistic Coke Machine."

radical behaviorism (Fodor, 1981).

Although it belabors the obvious, let me point out the flaw in Fodor's reasoning. The environment to which behaviorists refer, includes not only the current situation, but the historical environment with which the organism has interacted prior to the current situation. Consequently, the first nickel inserted in the Coke machine alters the *environmental* history of the machine relative to insertion of the second nickel. One can construct an environmental state table that is a precise analog of the machine state table of Figure 1, and I offer such a table as Figure 2. It is really the machine table with a slight relabeling. Or perhaps the machine table is the environmental state table, relabelled! Earlier I suggested that, in at least some cases and under idealized circumstances, analysis of systematic features of mechanism will converge with the analysis of environmental circumstances. I take this to be another demonstration of that claim. Certainly there is no basis here on which to reject radical behaviorism, although the view that Fodor has invoked, the version disallowing consideration of historical variables, is unworkable. Apparently, finite-automata equivalent versions of S-R learning theory do have this characteristic (e.g., Suppes, 1969). What Fodor has done, then, is to take a criticism that is appropriate to S-R theory, and attempt to apply it to radical behaviorism. That cannot work, however, as Skinner's causal model of selection by consequences is not even remotely similar to the mechanistic S-R model.

In fact, I think it plausible to argue that radical behaviorism is quite as much a functional-state position as any cognitive theory. Let me clarify that. Nelson makes the following point about the concept of a state:

> In sum no learning model would be adequate . . . without incorporating the internal state concept. It is important to see that this conclusion does not depend on any special interpretations of "internal" or "external" beyond those already suggested by the model. A *state* is simply an element of a *state-space*, which is characterizable purely mathematically in set theory . . . Our argument does not require and has not used any concept of "mental" or "inside the skin" or the like. (1975, pp. 257-258)

I have just given an analysis of the Coke machine in terms of environmental states, an analysis that I take to be quite congenial with the behavioristic outlook (if it is coherent to entertain a behavioristics of Coke machines!). This analysis is formally equivalent to the inner-state analysis, and the formal properties, not the geographical interpretation, are all that count so far as my claim. Furthermore, it is uncontroversial among radical behaviorists that environmental contingencies encountered in the past affect current behavior by having worked some kind of change on the organism. The behaviorist, however, takes the position of dealing directly with the environmental interactions on which such inner states depend rather than dealing inferentially with the inner states.[3]

---

[3]Those who remain unconvinced on this point might benefit from consideration of the following:

a. Skinner is well known for a position called the "mental way-station" argument (e.g., Skinner, 1953, p. 35). If environmental antecedents are lawfully related to an inner state, and the inner state is lawfully related to behavior, then one ought to be able to establish a lawful relation between environmental antecedents and behavior, without any direct reference to inner states. Clearly such a position does not deny the existence of inner states; instead, it relies on their existence and dependability so far as intermediating the environment-behavior regularity. The argument is methodological in character, and

In all candor, that project is not free of hazards. Bringing the necessary elements of environmental history to bear on accounts of complex behavior is potentially an insurmountable task. Consequently, it is of some comfort to find the occasional mentalist who comes out robustly on the side of the environment. For instance, one finds no less a luminary than Herbert Simon saying, "A man, viewed as a behaving system, is quite simple. The apparent complexity of his behavior over time is largely a reflection of the complexity of the environment in which he finds himself" (Simon, 1982, p. 65). Since that is the way behaviorists tend to see things, it is surprising to find a cognitive scientist making the same point. To adopt a bit of the computer scientist's own lingo, our experience has shown that organisms are relatively "user friendly" to behavior analysis. In light of the potentially immense practical problems of sorting out the relevance of past history to current behavior, perhaps organisms are a good deal more user friendly than we have any right to expect them to be.

---

depends for its force on the relative epistemic accessibility of environmental circumstances as contrasted with inner states.

   b. Far from denying inner states, Skinner has suggested that behavioral analysis *sets the program* for the investigator of inner states (1938, ch. 12). It identifies the properties of inner states at least so far as significant aspects of their input-output functions. The task of the neurophysiologist (true enough, Skinner is highly skeptical of the value of characterizing inner states under mentalistic descriptions) is to map out the physical nature of these states and their related mechanisms. While it might be doubted that this is a realistic description of the actual working relationship between radical behaviorism and neurophysiology, the important point here is that Skinner's understanding of the relation between behaviorism and psychology has to do with the determination of inner states.

   c. Under radical behaviorist description, environmental events are characterized *functionally* (Schnaitter, 1984b). This means that the behaviorally significant aspects of the environment are defined *relative to an organism,* not via their projectable physical properties. A given aspect of the environment is a "reinforcer" not because it has some particular physical property but because, when contingent on a response of an organism, the future probability of that response is altered in a given way. In short, a reinforcer is known by its functional effects rather than by its physical properties. That is an environmental way of stating a set of relations that can also be formulated in terms of inner states: An aspect of the environment is a reinforcer just in case the organism is in a state such that the event in question alters the future probability of responses on which it is contingent (other things equal). The organism can be moved in and out of that state by

The Argument that the Failure of Associationism Invalidates Behaviorism: At least since the publication of Lashley's famous paper on the problem of serial order in behavior (Lashley, 1951), it has been clear that associationism, as an explanatory account of serial order, has serious problems. These limitations were put in sharpest focus by linguists and psycholinguists during the decade of the sixties (e.g., Chomsky, 1963; Bever, Fodor, & Garrett, 1968). Mentalists have assumed, for reasons on which I will elaborate in a moment, that behaviorism - anyone's behaviorism - is intrinsically associationistic. Consequently, if associationism is defective as an account of serial order, then behaviorism must be defective. So behaviorism must be rejected, according to this argument.

Although the case against association is by now an old and oft-told story, a bit of it is worth repeating under present circumstances. Roughly, associationism consists of the following features: (a) a set of elements among which associations are formed; (b) an associative relation holding among the elements; (c) a set of principles by which the elements become associated; and (d) a set of parameters of the elements, associative principles, and resulting structures (this characterization has been adapted from Fodor, 1983, p. 27). In classical associationism, the elements consist of ideas, and the principles of association consist of such features as contiguity,

---

manipulating other environmental conditions, e.g., the prior accessibility of the reinforcer, etc. Behaviorists are not inclined to make much of this point as they think there is good reason to prefer environmental over inner state description; but it is true, nonetheless.

    d. Scattered through Skinner's work are many remarks of the following sort: "A person is changed by the contingencies of reinforcement under which he behaves; he does not store the contingencies" (1974, p. 84). "What an organism does will eventually be seen to be due to what it is, at the moment it behaves . . ." (1974, p. 249). "Something is done today which affects the behavior of an organism tomorrow. No matter how clearly that fact can be established, a step is missing, and we must wait for the physiologist to supply it" (Skinner, 1974, p. 215). These remarks must be taken at face value so far as acknowledging the reality of functionally relevant inner states.

    e. For more on the contrast between the mechanistic, push-pull causal model of S-R theory and the historical and selective, consequential model of radical behaviorism, see Skinner (1981), Staddon (1973), Ringen (1976), Hineline (1980), and Schnaitter (1984a).

similarity, and contrast. In behavioristic associationism, the elements consist of stimulus and response, and the principle of association consists of reinforcement by contiguity or contingency. So under this description it is true that there is a sense in which even Skinnerian behaviorism is associationistic. I will establish an important sense in which it is not associationistic in a moment.

A number of problems with associationism have been pointed out. Lashley gave several definitive illustrations. It cannot be the case, for instance, that the individual finger movements emitted in typing or playing the piano can be causally linked as stimulus to response because the speed with which such responses can be performed exceeds the operating characteristics of the relevant neurophysiology. A powerful linguistically motivated counter example to associationism is behavioral recursiveness. Much verbal as well as nonverbal behavior is subject to the following kind of expansion: a, aba, abcba, abcdcba, etc. For example, I may be walking across the quad from the parking lot to my office (a). While normally I make a continuous transit, one day I must return a book and detour to the library before continuing on to my office (aba). Then on the way to the library I encounter a colleague and stop for a brief conversation, after which I complete the library detour and then head for my office (abcba). And finally, while talking to my colleague, I am momentarily distracted by something (an attractive coed, a berserk squirrel) before completing my conversation, and so on and so forth (abcdcba). The argument against associationism here is that a serial ordering mechanism that operates exclusively among the terminal ordered elements isn't powerful enough to generate just the well-ordered forms and not additional aberrant concatenations. What is needed, so it is said, is a relatively more abstract mechanism which operates on the categories which are populated by the terminal elements (e.g., Chomsky, 1963; Bever, Fodor, & Garrett, 1968).

The radical behaviorist can make at least two replies to these charges against associationism. Pretty clearly, the anti-associationistic argument assumes that the operative associations are from *behavioral* element to behavioral element. Radical behaviorists, however, would normally propose that controlling relations hold between the extra-organismal *environment* and behavior. In the example of the professorial walk, the office and related historical variables (e.g., an office hour or an appointment scheduled for 9 a.m.) remain effective throughout the episode, even though they are contravened by temporarily more powerful environmental events. New and temporarily more effective environmental variables do not 'erase' historically prior environmental variables, although the effectiveness of those historical variables may temporarily be suspended. That is true, and cascades down, through the entire recursive series. Such an analysis of recursiveness is a good deal more problematic in the case of linguistic recursions (e.g., "The old lady swallowed the cat to swallow the bird to swallow the spider to swallow the fly"), because, unlike the situation in the professorial walk, the extrabehavioral environment can remain unchanged in all salient respects throughout a verbal episode. Furthermore, the radical behaviorist account of linguistic structure is so hazy that it is hard for me to reconstruct just how Skinner might analyze recursive verbal sequences. At least some aspects of linguistic structure may fall under one of the limiting cases I will discuss shortly.

I think the most important reason the associationistic charge does not hold up against radical behaviorism, however, is that radical behaviorism does not make use of the version of associationism that has been the subject of criticism. Associationism runs into trouble when it is advanced as a mechanistic hypothesis concerning the linkage of S-R elements. As such, it is one possible answer to the inner design question, although it is the minimal limiting case in that only direct, mechanical linkages are posited, on the order of the way that the keys of a piano are linked to the sounding of the strings. But radical behaviorism explicitly rejects such an approach. Radical behaviorists do not posit any mechanistic hypotheses concerning inner mechanisms at all. Instead, they seek only to describe the observable relations between environmental circumstances and behavior. True, in a purely descriptive sense some of these relations can be considered associative. But once again, the kind of associationism that has been pretty thoroughly repudiated is not association as a description of spatio-temporal relations but association as the operative principle of a hypothesized mechanism. So the criticism just doesn't apply.[4]

Skinner and other behaviorists have also made a number of criticisms of mentalistic explanation which, if valid, vitiate the mentalistic program. I will briefly consider the two.

The Argument that Mentalistic Explanations Go Beyond the Facts: Skinner has suggested that certain sorts of characterization of inner process and structure go beyond the facts, or are metaphorical, or worst of all, are fictional (e.g., Skinner, 1977). Certainly it is the case that mentalistic explanations go beyond the facts; that is a feature of scientific theory in general, including behavioristic theory. On the other hand, to say that an explanation is certifiably fictional is to say that it is false, and I doubt if any mentalists would argue for an explanation in light of clearcut falsification. If we can agree that going beyond the facts is intrinsic to a useful explanation but that fictionalism is fatal, then the problem is to establish a usable line of demarcation. The trouble when you get right down to it, however, is that behaviorism provides no effective criterion for evaluating when a given instance of scientific verbal behavior has wandered too far from the facts. When a neurophysiologist,

---

[4]One has to search diligently through Skinner's work to find the term "association" at all. On the few occasions where it does turn up, it is disparaged and disavowed, e.g.:

> The conditioned reflex is a simple principle of limited scope describing certain simple facts, but many internal states and activities, comparable with the driving force of instincts, have been invented to explain it. The runner's heart is said to beat fast before the start of the race because he 'associates' the situation with the exertion which follows. But it is the environment, not the runner, that 'associates' the two features, in the etymological sense of joining or uniting them. Nor does the runner 'form a connection' between the two things; the connection is made in the external world. (1974, p. 39)

In such material, it is pretty clear that Skinner takes associationism to be a hypothesis concerning inner mechanism, a hypothesis which he rejects. In Skinner's view, no mechanism of "association" operates in the person's head. Association is just a descriptive feature of spatio-temporal relations among aspects of the environment, or between environment and behavior.

as distinct from a mentalist, gives a computational information-processing description of a given piece of neural circuitry, where is the line to be drawn for claiming that the facts have been excessively transgressed? When computational language is used to describe the interaction of excitatory and inhibitory post-synaptic potentials that produce a net change in membrane potential? When the inhibition of a precursor neuron by a recurrent interneuron is described as a negative feedback loop? When a sensory system is analyzed as an organized hierarchy of converging and diverging pathways of excitation and inhibition, the net outcome of which is the extraction of an abstract feature from the original stimulus array? Or is it that neurophysiologists are at liberty to go beyond the facts but that mentalists are not, for some as yet unarticulated reason? If the behaviorist wants to claim something is wrong here, then vague handwaving will have to be supplanted by a specific and usable criterion.[5]

The Argument that Mentalistic Explanations are Circular and Hence Vacuous: Another behavioristic argument against mentalism is that such explanations are circular and hence vacuous; e.g., "A conceptual nervous system cannot, of course, be used to explain the behavior from which it is inferred" (Skinner, 1974, p. 213). Applied to a more practical case, the argument would seem to go like this: If I put a hand in my pocket and withdraw a coin, I might use this

----

[5]I know of only two suggestions along this line, and neither of them works particularly well. The first might be called the 'criterion of intraverbal distance.' As the amount of verbal behavior intermediating between the world and a conclusion about the world increases, the opportunity for a faulty inference increases. The trouble with this criterion is that just because the opportunity for error may increase as a function of the amount of reasoning on which a conclusion is based, there is no *necessary* connection between opportunity for error and the commission of error. Furthermore, it is not at all clear that this criterion would single out mentalism over behaviorism as more error-prone (see Skinner, 1974, p. 208 on the complexity of behavioristic interpretation relative to the simplicity of mentalistic accounts).

The second approach that one hears discussed from time to time could be called the "criterion of metaphoric contamination." Skinner has the notion that metaphor invariably leads to misdirection and conceptual error in science and, indeed, supporting illustrations can be found in the history of science and medicine. A case can be made,

occurrence as evidence from which to infer that a coin had been in my pocket. Then if asked for an explanation as to how I was able to produce a coin, I well might say, "You see, I had one in my pocket." (an inference that the inner state of my trouser pocket was coin-containing, if you will). The explanation would be illicit, according to Skinner's position, because the *explanans* was inferred from the *explanandum*. But rejecting such an explanation seems an odd thing to do. Simply put, true explanations are not vacuous even when of questionable logical parentage. Of course the problems of mentalistic explanation are a good deal more subtle than this illustration. Rather than such problems turning on Skinner's point of logic, however, it seems to me that the problems of mentalistic explanation are a good deal more pragmatic: How do you sort out the true explanations from all the false ones that fit the available data? I realize that the brief treatment of these two antimentalistic arguments that behaviorists hold dear is unlikely to shake anyone's faith. I believe it important, however, to at least sketch out the grounds on which some psychologists find these arguments less than completely persuasive.

Summarizing to this point, I have claimed that there are two nonreductive strategies that can be pursued in attempting to explain the behavior of organisms. One strategy is to characterize the design of the inner mechanisms responsible for behavior. The other is to describe the outer circumstances to which occurrences of behavior are related. In point of fact it is

---

however, that the most important way in which we move conceptually from the known into the unknown is to cautiously extend out concepts from areas of established use into areas of investigation and conceptual uncertainty. It is impossible to know, a priori, whether the conceptual extension will ultimately prove to be metaphoric or generic. (My hunch is that conceptual extensions that start out looking generic almost always prove to be metaphoric; then either a new name for the concept is devised or a new lexigraphic convention is established for the existing term. In either case, established usage will finally settle down into a pattern that is no longer treated as metaphor. Skinner gives countless examples of this process occurring in ordinary language: we don't consider talk of "sharp" or "dull" pains to be poetic metaphor, but straightforward description, even though such expressions are extensions from the kind of stimulation causing pains of various sorts.) Behavior analysis itself is built on such extensions: "reinforce" and "reinforcer," response "strength," stimulus "control," "extinction," and so on.

impossible to describe inner mechanisms directly, as they are inaccessible, and the kind of description sought is abstract anyway. Consequently, from a methodological perspective the two strategies begin on relatively common ground. In regard to most phenomena of interest to psychologists the two strategies each are capable of providing an account, and in some idealized cases, the two strategies will arrive at formally equivalent formulations. Two standard arguments against the behavioristic strategy were evaluated and found lacking, as were two standard arguments against mentalism.

With all that said, it is important to point out that indeed there are some limitations on what can be accounted for by pursuing the strategy of analysis of external circumstances; and in parallel there are limitations on what can be accounted for by pursuing the strategy of analysis of inner states. In other words, although the domains over which each strategy can be applied overlap considerably, they are not completely coextensive. The remainder of this paper reviews some general forms of boundary limitation on these domains of application, and illustrates them with examples I hope to be reasonably accessible. In what follows, I assume that nothing is incoherent about explanations via reference to inner states, and that it is possible to adequately characterize internal states. I make the latter assumption while maintaining a degree of skepticism about its general correctness.

FORMAL LIMITS OF TWO STRATEGIES OF EXPLANATION

The truth of behaviorism is that life is a roisterous dialogue between persons and their world, not a silent soliloquy in a moonlit garret. But the truth of mentalism is that stones, toads, and other lumpish things will never humanly think, talk, or cognize no matter what the context within which they are situated, for the right inner structure must be present to make use of such contexts. These are different truths, though not inconsistent. Yet a focus on one tends to obscure the other, to the point that it *seems* as if both cannot be true. The politics of psychology, not unlike the politics of everything else, thrives on polarization, withers in reconciliation. So we have behaviorists on the one hand, mentalists on the other, each camp believing the other to be naive, stupid, and occasionally downright evil. Few if any psychologists are willing to entertain the possibility that there is a place for both the psychologies of internal structure and of external adaptation. I would like to contribute to that possibility becoming a reality by suggesting several formal limitations to the explanatory capacities of each approach.[6]

Consider a simple model of the conditions that must hold for a limitation to exist. There is already an extensive literature on limitations that is developed from a logico-mathematical perspective (I have already cited Chomsky, 1963; Bever, Fodor, & Garrett, 1968; Nelson, 1975; and Fodor, 1981). Rather than making a foray into this domain of formalisms, however, the limitations I see are those that would occur to an experimentalist whose concern is the establishment of determinate relations between initial conditions and consequent events. The model works like this: The occurrence of any behavior is antedated both by an environmental context and by an internal state. Behaviorists analyze behavior as a function of environment, whereas mentalists analyze behavior as a function of internal state. A limitation exists in those cases where behavior (or some property of behavior) covaries with one, but not with the other, of the two antecedent conditions. There are actually four relevant kinds of case, and these are depicted in Figure 3. The situation is actually a bit messier than it looks here, because there are at least three distinct kinds of description of internal state, and they are not necessarily intertranslatable. Least controversially, inner states can be described in physiological terms. Then there is the more abstract systematic description of the design of the physiological mechanism that characterizes mentalism. And finally, there is the descriptive level of ordinary-language intentional expressions. While I

---

[6]Most of my own recent work has been directed at various aspects of this relation between behaviorism and mentalism. In addition to the present paper, see Schnaitter (1984a, 1984b, 1985a, 1985b, and in press).

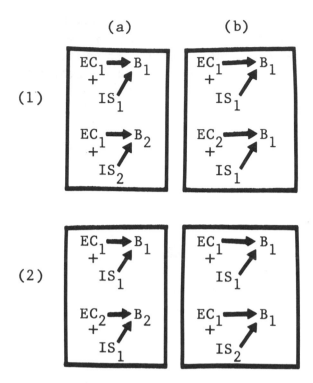

Fig. 3. A model of formal limitations on two strategies of explanation. EC = environmental context; IS = internal state; B = behavior. See text for details.

make occasional reference to the other two levels, my main concern here is with the mentalistic level of description.

(1-a). The top two cells of Figure 3, labeled 1-a and 1-b, indicate limiting conditions on explanations articulated exclusively in terms of external circumstances. That is, they indicate limitations on behavioral analysis. Take 1-a first. Consider the notation, EC, to stand for the complete behavioristic recipe for a given behavior, or aspect of behavior; a recipe of sufficient conditions for behavior. Thus, EC will include reference to the evolutionary history of the organism, as manifested in species membership; relevant past history; and aspects of the current situation, in whatever combination is sufficient to constrain the current behavior. IS designates the collateral internal state, and B the ensuing behavior. What 1-a

suggests is that cases are conceivable when the most effectively determinate environmental conditions still won't restrain some aspect of behavior from varying as a function of variations in internal state. That is the problem described earlier as the stimulus independence of behavior. There are a number of possibilities.

First, some internal mechanisms may function at least in part on a random basis. A computer that generates random numbers does so independently of current environmental conditions. Allen Neuringer (1981) also claims to be able to generate numbers that meet any statistical test of randomness, and if he can do that then so could you and I, given the appropriate training. While the training may be a necessary antecedent to Neuringer's behavior, it is not a sufficient basis on which to account for what he actually does: From perfect knowledge of the training one cannot predict the numbers that Neuringer or a similarly trained person can emit. It is almost certain that random elements enter into behavioral determination, and in some cases this may be due to evolutionary selection rather than unavoidable noise in the system.

Second, in some cases behavior may covary both with variations in external circumstances and internal state, but the former covariation is correlational while the latter is causal. This is typically true of circadian rhythms, for example. The activity level of an organism covaries in an orderly way with the normal light-dark cycle, but the covariation is shown to be correlational when the light-dark cycle is eliminated experimentally although the behavioral rhythmicity continues. Apparently what goes on in these cases is that the internal pacemaking mechanism is entrained to the period of the external cycle, but once entrained it continues to operate relatively independently.

A third case can be called complexity indeterminacy. Crudely put, does the old tin bucket no longer hold water because of the detailed history of its use and abuse, or because it has a hole in it? A lot of behavior might be traceable to the evolutionary history of the species, interacting with salient aspects of the life history of the individual, interacting with the external circumstances currently at work. In some sense, it might be possible to construct the relevant environmental state table for much behavior that appears to be stimulus independent, as suggested earlier in the vastly more simple example of the mentalistic Coke machine. Yet the majority of the relevant environmental history is unknowable. Consequently, although in fact the environmental circumstances may functionally covary with behavior, from our limited epistemological perspective the relevant environmental details are opaque. It is common to see this kind of limitation advanced in regard to the occurrence of verbal behavior in ordinary contexts. Chomsky (1959) made good use of it in his review of *Verbal Behavior* (Skinner, 1957). When a person looks at a painting in a museum, for instance, does he say "Dutch," "Rembrandt," "masterpiece," or what? Like the hole in the bucket, there is an immediate, proximal story behind every utterance, and in some respects it must be immensely simpler than the environmental story. What remains to be seen, however, is whether or not that story is in fact any more accessible than the environmental version.

Finally, it may be the case that an inner mechanism operates on a nonrandom, fully determinate basis, but in principle its outputs can neither be fully predicted nor controlled by reference to environmental circumstances. The random number generators in computers tend to be of this sort: In fact they are not truly random in operation, but operate on a determinate basis such that the output simulates a truly random process. More structured outputs can be generated in similar ways, and it has been contended that significant aspects of linguistic structure exhibit this kind of independence from environmental control. Of course, any of these four cases might apply in combination, enhancing the problems for behavioral analysis.

(1-b). The second form of limitation on explanation via external circumstances, in the upper right of Figure 3, is more easily illustrated. This is the case where a behavior or some aspect of a behavior fails to covary with variations in external

circumstances. If it doesn't covary then it can't be a function of those circumstances, and consequently it must be a function of a constant internal state. A clearcut illustration comes from Premack's *Nebraska symposium* paper (Premack, 1965), where he made the point that rats lick on drinking tubes at an invariant rate of seven licks per second. Variation in external environment can result in initiation or termination of drinking, but cannot alter its molecular rate. The internal lick-regulating mechanism can be turned on and off by environmental events, but once operating it runs at an invariant speed. Consequently, molar lick-rate is a responsive behavioral variable, but molecular lick-rate is not. Molecular lick-rate can be accounted for only by reference to the operating characteristics of internal mechanism.

(2-a). Consider now the first of the two forms of limitation on mentalistic explanation. To begin with, it is worth pointing out that in practice mentalism has an advantage relative to behaviorism. (Some, following Russell, might be inclined to call it the advantage of theft over honest toil.) First, although the mentalist has no direct access to mental mechanisms, and consequently cannot describe them directly, he is not hesitant to conjecture on the nature of these modest realities. But second, once the mentalist has conceived of the design of a mental mechanism, he has to have information on its inputs - the environmental circumstances in which it operates - in order to say anything about what it does. So mentalists would seem to have the best of two possible worlds, all the information available to the behaviorist, plus all the potential explanatory power of internal mechanism.

One limiting case for mentalistic explanation occurs when internal state remains constant while behavior changes as a function of external circumstances. While this is formally true, it is awfully hard to demonstrate because, since internal mechanism is known only inferentially, any time behavior changes it can be inferred that internal state must have changed as well. But I think we can even get around *that* possibility in a number of cases. For example, there is a range of cases in which the factors that cause a behavior to be a behavior of one type, rather than a behavior of another type, are environmental rather than organismal factors. Consider a track runner at the Olympics, a Mary Decker or a Valery Brisco-Hooks, for example. She runs a heat one day and wins. The next day, in another heat, she is in the relevantly identical mental state and runs exactly the same race so far as her physical performance. The first day she wins, but the second day she comes in second, however, because on the first day her competitors are all slower than is she, whereas on the second day someone is faster. If we categorize her behavior as 'winning a race' on the first day, and as 'placing second' in a race on the second day, we cannot do so by reference to internal states. Her placing is due to the external circumstances in which she performs mechanically identical actions.

Interestingly enough, something close to this argument was made by Fodor in his 1968 book, *Psychological Explanation.* I have changed one word throughout the following quotation, to make Fodor's usage consistent with my own. When Fodor says "psychological," he means "mental." Consequently, I have made this change.

> . . . the fact that some actions cannot be identified with motions does not *by itself* show that the causal explanation of those actions is impossible. For it leaves open the possibility that they may be identifiable with motions performed in states for which sufficient conditions can be formulated in appropriate causal language. The argument does show, however, that actions cannot, in principle, be provided with causal mental explanations in certain cases in which the background required for performance of the action constrains states of the environment rather than states of the organism. What must legally be the case for a certain motion to count as signing a deed, for example, cannot be stated in terms of the states or motions of the signer. . . If, then, mentalism is a *causal* science, and if causes cause only motions, such actions as signing a deed do not fall within its competence. . . Hence some of the states for which sufficient conditions would need to be provided to causally explain the signing of a deed are not *mental* states. (1968, pp. 46-47)

When mentalists support your best antimentalistic arguments, they are bound to hold up!

(2-b). In contrast to the relatively crisp applications of the

second and third limitations, the first and fourth are somewhat soft and conjectural. The reason seems to be that for both of these cases the causally relevant variation occurs internally. In 2-b, behavior and its external conditions remain constant while internal state varies. Such a case is hard to deal with conclusively because the internal states we are talking about here are mental, not physical, states, which is to say that they are states that abstractly characterize the design of physical states. Because of their abstractness they are rarely if ever firmly established, and hence remain in the realm of the hypothetical. In consequence, to say that the internal states vary while the circumstances within which they are embedded remain constant is to say that on some grounds the states are *hypothesized* to vary. If the states are hypothesized to vary, and they are supposed to be causally effective states, then it will normally be predicted that the resulting behavior will vary, and this limiting condition is actually identical with falsification in a hypothesis test. On the other hand, different mentalistic theorists may hypothesize different mental mechanisms to be operative and causally equivalent in the same context. Here, the fact that two designs predict the same behavior is likely to be a manifestation of that truism from automata theory that any given output is capable of being generated by multiple mechanisms. Because most psychologists would tend to think the design story should eventuate in a single master plan rather than a set of inconsistent and conflicting design overlays, this kind of situation shows that further investigation is needed to differentiate between the adequacy of the two hypothetical designs.

We can get beyond the hypothetical in at least some cases, where inner states are given a folk-psychological intentional description. Suppose a man stammers badly whenever he must talk to his boss. On a weekend just before an important Monday meeting he evaluates his plight. He decides it is silly and immature to stammer, and that he simply will not do it next time. But Monday morning when he sees his boss he stammers as much as usual. Here the putative variation in mental state, though substantial, is causally inert and thus irrelevant in accounting for the behavior.

Conclusion: So those are several limitations that can be identified formally that apply to behaviorism in some cases and to mentalism in others. It is hard to determine the overall significance of these limitations for the explanatory programs of behaviorism and mentalism, as there is no a priori means through which to determine the relative number of applications of each limitation and the significance of each to the understanding of behavior. Probably the implication of most general interest to behaviorists has to do with the analysis of action, and the limitation of mentalism in that regard, as discussed in 2-a. It may be more than an accident that the problem of action has received scant attention from cognitive psychologists, while at the same time the analysis of action as a function of its external circumstances is the central concern of behaviorism (Zuriff, 1975; Lee, 1983). Yet it is not the case that mentalism necessarily fails to provide a causal account of all action, only those actions whose individuation is solely a function of external circumstances.

But however that issue comes out, it is my view that the kind of inner mechanism whose operation serves as the proximal cause of behavior is a matter of little relevance to behaviorism. Behaviorism now and always has dealt with the given in this regard. While the domain of behavioral analysis may hinge to some extent on the nature of inner mechanism, it is important to understand that a behavioral analysis can be accomplished relative to *any* conceivable internal mechanism. Perhaps that mechanism is an enchanted loom; maybe a cybernetic control system; possibly an information-processing system; or conceivably some form of design not yet imagined. But whatever it may be, it is out of all our hands and no one, as a behaviorist, need spend much time worrying about that. Behaviorism does not address questions of inner mechanism. It is a perspective analyzing and taxonomizing behavior, not in terms of its proximal mechanistic causes, but in terms of its molar, phenomenal, adaptive relations to external circumstances. Not all aspects of behavior can be understood successfully from this perspective, it is true, but nor can all aspects of behavior be understood from the perspective of internal mechanism alone: The aspects that *can* be understood from the behavioral perspective seem pretty important to most of us, however. That ought to be enough.

ACKNOWLEDGMENT

This paper is dedicated to Kenneth MacCorquodale, who as my graduate advisor exemplified the standards of thought and scholarship that have been a model for me in my own professional career.

REFERENCES

Bever, T., Fodor, J., & Garrett, M. (1968). A formal limitation of association. In T. R. Dixon, & D. L. Horton (Eds.), *Verbal behavior and general behavior theory*. Englewood Cliffs, New Jersey: Prentice-Hall.

Block, N. (1978). Troubles with functionalism. In C. W. Savage (Ed.), *Perception and cognition. Issues in the foundations of psychology: Minnesota studies in the philosophy of science* (Vol. 9). Minneapolis: University of Minnesota Press.

Block, N. (1980). Introduction: What is functionalism? In N. Block (Ed.), *Readings in philosophy of psychology,Vol. 1.* Cambridge: Harvard University Press.

Chomsky, N. (1959). Review of Skinner's *Verbal behavior. Language, 35,* 26-58.

Chomsky, N. (1963). Formal properties of grammars. In R. D. Luce, R.R. Bush, & E. Galanter (Eds.), *Handbook of mathematical psychology, Vol. 2.* New York: Wiley & Sons.

Fodor, J.A. (1968). *Psychological explanation.* New York: Random House.

Fodor, J.A. (1981). The mind-body problem. *Scientific American, 244,* 124-133.

Fodor, J.A. (1983). *The modularity of mind.* Cambridge: MIT Press.

Hineline, P. N. (1980). The language of behavior analysis: Its community, its functions, and its limitations. *Behaviorism, 8,* 67-86.

Lashley, K. (1951). The problem of serial order in behavior. In L. A. Jeffress (Ed.), *Cerebral mechanisms in behavior.* New York: Wiley & Sons.

Lee, V. (1983). Behavior as a constituent of conduct. *Behaviorism, 11,* 199-224.

Nelson, R. J. (1975). Behaviorism, finite automata and stimulus-response theory. *Theory and Decision, 6,* 249-267.

Neuringer, A. (1981). *Freedom: A definition, a demonstration, and a discussion of its implications for behaviorists.* Invited address,

Association for Behavioral Analysis annual convention, Milwaukee, Wisconsin

Premack, D. (1965). Reinforcement theory. In D. Levine (Ed.), *Nebraska symposium on motivation* (Vol. 13). Lincoln: University of Nebraska Press.

Putnam, H. (1975). *Mind, language, and reality.* London: Cambridge University Press.

Pylyshyn, Z. (1984). *Computation and cognition.* Cambridge: MIT Press.

Ringen, J. D. (1976). Explanation, teleology, and operant behaviorism: A study of the experimental analysis of purposive behavior. *Philosophy of Science, 43,* 223-253.

Rorty, R. (1979). *Philosophy and the mirror of nature.* Princeton: Princeton University Press.

Schnaitter, R. (1984a). *Causality in radical behaviorism.* Paper read at the Association for Behavior Analysis annual convention, Nashville, Tennessee.

Schnaitter, R. (1984b). Skinner on the 'mental' and the 'physical'. *Behaviorism, 12,* 1-14.

Schnaitter, R. (1985a). The haunted clockwork: Reflections on Gilbert Ryle's *The concept of mind. Journal of the Experimental Analysis of Behavior, 43,* 145-153.

Schnaitter, R. (1985b). A coordination of differences. In T. Knapp, & L. Robertson (Eds.), *Approaches to cognition: contrasts and controversies.* Hillsdale, New Jersey: Lawrence Erlbaum Associates.

Schnaitter, R. (in press). Knowledge as action: The epistemology of radical behaviorism. In S. Modgil, & C. Modgil (Eds.), *B. F. Skinner: Consensus and controversy.* Barcombe, England: Falmer Press.

Simon, H. (1982). *The sciences of the artificial.* Cambridge: MIT Press.

Skinner, B. F. (1938). *The behavior of organisms.* New York: Appleton-Century.

Skinner, B. F. (1953). *Science and human behavior.* New York: Free Press.

Skinner, B. F. (1957). *Verbal behavior.* New York: Appleton-Century-Crofts.

Skinner, B. F. (1974). *About behaviorism.* New York: Knopf.

Skinner, B. F. (1977). Why I am not a cognitive psychologist. *Behaviorism, 5,* 1-10.

Skinner, B. F. (1981). Selection by consequences. *Science, 213,* 501-504.

Staddon, J. E. R. (1973). On the notion of cause, with applications to behaviorism. *Behaviorism, 1,* 25-63.

Suppes, P. (1969). Stimulus-response theory of finite automata. *Journal of Mathematical Psychology, 6,* 327-355.

Zuriff, G. (1975). Where is the agent in behavior? *Behaviorism, 3,* 1-21.

PART IV

INTEGRATION OF LARGER UNITS OF ANALYSIS

CHAPTER 13

Functional Units of Human Behavior and Their Integration: A Dispositional Analysis

DAVID LUBINSKI AND TRAVIS THOMPSON

If "Physics is experience arranged in economical order" as Ernst Mach suggested a century ago, then by comparison Psychology could be characterized as experience in profligate disarray. We find ourselves in the waning years of the 20th century unable to even agree on the fundamental subject matter of the discipline. The internecine quarreling becomes even more strident when the domain of discourse shifts from the behavior of laboratory animals to the actions of *Homo sapiens* in its natural habitat. The issues that puzzle even the most optimistic observer are basically these: (a) What are the natural units of a virtually continuous, uninterrupted stream of a person's activities, one blending smoothly into the next, with no obvious beginning or endpoints?; (b) Even if it were possible to identify units of analysis, how could one begin to understand their integration to form the elegantly articulated kinetic structures we call human behavior? Some have asserted there are no natural units for analysis of human behavior (Loevinger, 1957), while others have imposed units on the flux of human behavior a priori based on assumptions about the presumed underlying mental apparatus (Chomsky, 1965, 1968).

We thank M. Jackson Marr, Paul Meehl, Auke Tellegen and Michael Zeiler for commenting on an earlier version of this chapter.

We suggest in this paper that the problem of identifying fundamental units and then coming to an understanding of their integration to form larger units, the features of which are not at variance with our understanding of the complexities of human behavior in the natural environment, requires two sets of concepts. We first explore *fundamental behavioral units* in terms of their proximal controlling variables. Our second concern has to do with the *integration of clusters* of behavioral units to form larger classes, which we relate to the familiar dispositional trait concept. Finally, we suggest that the force responsible for integrating members of successive response classes derives from their relative response probabilities and their temporal distances.

FUNCTIONAL BEHAVIORAL COMPONENTS

Functional behavioral components of human behavior can be identified at four levels: *fundamental response classes*, i.e., elicited, emitted, and evoked responses (Branch, 1977; Zeiler, 1977), *behavioral combinations*, composites of two or more fundamental units (Thompson, 1969; Thompson & Grabowski, 1972), *traits*, or *response families* consisting of clusters of fundamental units and behavioral combinations, and *trait-clusters*, two or more traits that covary intra-individually. Behavioral components isolated at these various levels are *dispositional response class entities* (Carnap, 1956; MacCorquodale, & Meehl, 1954; Pap, 1958; Sellers, 1958; and Tellegen, 1981), i.e., a class of behavioral components which covary as a function of a class of stimulus events that regulate their probability of occurrence. We argue that all behavioral complexes are composed of fundamental units integrated temporally and/or collaterally. The extent to which complex systems of behavioral flux may be analyzed into their rudimentary constituents (or reduced to the next lowest level), varies across behavioral components (both within and between the proposed levels).

Fundamental Units

Branch (1977) has proposed that behavioral "units can be defined as such only by demonstration of functional relations between the supposed units and certain environmental events or arrangements, and the functional relations must bear a resemblance to those described for other proposed units" (p. 176). Though limited to units defined by their relation to a controlling consequence, Zeiler (1977) has used a similar approach to defining behavioral units. We have proposed elsewhere that behavior is composed of three types of such functional units (elicited, emitted and evoked responses), which can be identified by their relation to environmental controlling variables (Thompson & Lubinski, 1985). Such behavioral units refer to the functional response classes originally identified by Bechterev (1928), Pavlov (1927), Skinner (1938), and Thorndike (1911), and the derived response class first described by Falk (1961). Elicited responses include removing one's hand from a hot surface, increased heart rate when unexpectedly being asked to speak at a meeting, and tears generated by viewing an emotionally engaging art form; while opening a locked door, solving an algebra problem, and saying "Good morning" to a coworker exemplify emitted (or, operant) responses.

Laboratory research with rats, monkeys and pigeons has revealed a third functional response class, the strength of which is determined by the interval between successive stimulus events, as well as the nature of the stimulus event. Falk (1961) originally described excessive drinking by rats induced by a concurrent schedule of food reinforcement. It was subsequently found that schedule-induced polydipsia was a member of a far broader class of schedule-induced events including aggressive behavior (Cherek, Thompson & Heistad, 1973), pica (Villarreal, 1967) and wheel running (Levitsky & Collier, 1968). Though nearly all of the early research involved laboratory animals in highly controlled settings (Falk, 1971, 1977; Staddon, 1977), it has been recently discovered that such evoked behaviors occur in humans as well, including schedule-induced eating (Cantor, Smith, & Bryan, 1982), smoking (Cherek, 1982; Wallace & Singer, 1976), alcohol consumption (Lindman, 1982), aggression (Frederiksen & Peterson, 1974) and repetitive motor movements (Wieseler, Hanson, Chamberlain & Thompson, 1985). Such responses are not elicited on the first or second presentation of the evoking stimulus, but gradually emerge on repeated presentation of a given stimulus presented at a specific interstimulus interval. Moreover, rather than occurring in a circumscribed form immediately following the stimulus (as is true of elicited responses), evoked responses tend to be more diverse and are distributed over an extended interval following presentation of the evocative stimulus.

Behavioral Combinations

Whether a unit is judged basic has to do with the degree to which it is reducible with respect to a given level of analysis (Marr, 1981). We take it as given that human behavior is constructed of fundamental functional components combined in various patterns of complexity. Sometimes two concurrently strengthened responses alternate if they are topographically incompatible. We may laugh and cry in rapid alternation at a time of crisis. At other times, the concurrent strengthening of two responses creates a new emergent response class. The artist who has worked in oils and water colors suddenly finds herself confronted with acrylics, which simultaneously sets the occasion for elements of both prior responses. Suddenly a new set of behaviors seems to inexplicably emerge. These behavioral phenomena are the products of behavioral combinations (i.e., a composite response class composed of two or more minimal units integrated sequentially and/or in parallel). Such behavioral complexes may be classified into two subsets based on the nature of their constituents.

Homogeneous combinations consist of behavioral units of the same type (e.g., elicited or emitted), whereas *heterogeneous combinations* are composed of different types of units (e.g., elicited and emitted). Extended segments of human behavior (or the behavior of any adult organism, for that matter) rarely, if ever, consist of pure homogeneous constituents (Thompson & Lubinski, 1985). Ongoing streams of behavior are typically composed of several homogeneous and heterogeneous response classes operating collectively. Nevertheless, for analytical purposes, it is useful to conceptualize highly integrated behavioral complexes in terms of their rudimentary components in the same sense that chemists investigate individual elements though they rarely occur in isolation.

Response chains seen in many vocational settings and in carrying out daily routines in the home exemplify homogeneous combinations (e.g., meal preparation, replacing a washer in a faucet). These performances are composed of several sequenced operants (one occurring after the other), controlled by discriminative stimuli and natural consequences arranged by our environments. Often, imbedded in the flow of human behavior are reflexive responses elicited by specific antecedent events. The orientation response (Hinde, 1970) is a heterogeneous combination: A mother's voice not only sets the occasion for the three month old infant's head to turn in the direction of the sound (an operant), but elicits heart rate changes as well through classical conditioning. Such elicited responses often involve smooth muscles and glands and are associated with characteristic interoceptive stimulus events contemporaneous with familiar affective states that we label as "pleasure," "anxiety," or "anger."

It is one thing to show that certain aspects of behavior under controlled circumstances consist of discrete functional components (i.e., minimal functional units or behavioral combinations), but quite another to identify their contribution to human behavior in the natural environment. Consider the following behavioral events: The setting is an academic departmental colloquium reception. Jones is approached by fellow faculty member Smith, who says, "Not a bad turnout, considering the topic" (the topic of the preceding colloquium lecture having been in Jones' area of expertise). Jones frowns discernibly and replies in an irritable tone, "At least we heard something relevant for a change, instead of more pie-in-the-sky hogwash!" Smith smiles slightly, turns away and approaches the reception table where he fills a glass with wine. Smith turns to a female graduate student standing nearby and says, "Managed to tear yourself away from Greg for a few minutes, I see," as he takes a sip of his wine and studies her facial expression over the rim of his glass. (Greg is a male student friend of the young woman.) "Greg and I haven't been seeing much of each other lately," the young woman replies, awkwardly. "Well, it's good to see you on your own for a change," Smith replies with a warm smile, establishing prolonged eye contact. The young woman uncomfortably returns Smith's smile.

Such a hypothetical series of events are often said to be difficult, if not impossible for scientists operating within a behavior-analytic framework to deal with. We have no access to the histories of any of the speakers, nor are we cognizant of any of the multitude of other stimulus events which may be exercising control. What we do know is that two of Smith's remarks seemed to be aggressive (i.e., the consequence of two responses was to cause harm or discomfort to another person), though the topographies of the verbal responses were quite different, and the controlling consequences for Smith's remark to his male colleague and to the female graduate student may have been different to some degree (part of one of the controlling consequences may have been, at least in part, sexual).

Traits

We believe that response components within such episodes can be identified and functionally analyzed. To do so, however, requires adopting a broader meaning of response classes and a more molar level of analysis. As Marr (1981) has suggested, there are similarities in the conceptual problems faced by modern physics (e.g., Bohr, Heisenberg, Dirac) and those of behaviorism. Dirac (1958) argued that concepts drawn from classical mechanics were adequate to deal with interference and diffraction of light, but other phenomena, such as photoelectric emission and scattering by free electrons, indicated that light must be composed of small particles, hence a corpuscular account was also required. In the behavioral sciences, one set of concepts is already well developed to understand the moment-to-moment structure of small units of behavioral phenomena (i.e., fundamental units and behavioral combinations). Such units can be identified by their relation to proximal environmental controlling variables (Thompson & Lubinski, 1985). However, a second set of concepts is required to account for the composition and kinetics of larger, more diverse response classes.

The terms "small" and "large," when referring to response units have a disturbingly relativistic quality which may not seem rooted in objectively quantifiable reality. However, this need not be the case. Small functional response units are those whose probabilities of occurrence are controlled by a given temporally proximal class of environmental events, but a large cluster of responses making up a response class may not necessarily vary as a function of the same operation. That is, small and large functional units appear to be regulated by different mechanisms. Such response units exist in states of strength which are themselves not always observable. Such states are measured by sampling observable properties of the states (i.e., response frequency). At a broader level of analysis, classes of fundamental units and behavioral combinations are known to covary; that is, they are integrated collaterally. We argue that these aggregates of more basic response units can be analyzed as functional entities in their own right, and are similar to what psychologists have called traits. Traits are often referred to as "dispositional clusters" or "response families" because their response components often involve diverse topographical properties, but are nevertheless controlled by similar classes of variables. The collateral integrity of traits is analogous to the verbal behavior generated by word associations. When someone is confronted with a verbal discriminative stimulus, for example, "cat" (and instructed to say the first word that comes to mind) several responses concurrently rise to high strength (e.g., "rat," "mouse," "dog," etc.). But only one is emitted. The emitted response is, of course, viewed as having the highest probability, whereas those responses which collaterally increase in strength but don't reach the level of the emitted operant are characterized as *incipient responses* (MacCorquodale, 1969).

The number of constituent response classes defining a particular trait can only be determined by observing an individual over time; the breadth of the aggregate consists of the range of behavioral components that increase in probability in situations relevant to the trait in question. Since we cannot definitively determine (i.e., analyze) its strength without manipulating a controlling variable which alters its probability, it can be said that the momentary strength of each component response unit is *indeterminate* (i.e., the Heisenberg Principle) (cf. Davies, 1979). That is, although we may be able to predict the aggregate or a homogeneous subset of the aggregate's constituents (following the presentation of a relevant controlling variable), in all likelihood, we will never be able to make refined topographical predictions of particular individual components. One can only estimate the strength of individual components in a probabilistic sense, expressed as a measure of its average strength on many occasions. While we refer loosely to such individual components in terms of their "momentary probabilities," by which we mean a current response tendency (e.g., "He seems very anxious"), more often, however, we are interested in the aggregate's average level of strength over longer time intervals (e.g., "He tends to be very anxious").

The diversity of the interrelated individual functional response classes comprising a response family implies that the probabilities of individual members may not be equal. As a result, on any given observation (in the presence of relevant controlling variables) one or another response class may be observed. However, the various individual response classes would be observed according to their relative probabilities in the functional response cluster over many occasions. The intermediate character of the functional response family formed by the numerous individual constituent response classes expresses itself through the probability that a particular result for an observation is intermediate between the corresponding probabilities for the original response classes.

We indicated earlier that two sets of concepts are necessary to understand local behavioral integration. The structuring of local response probabilities are understood in terms of the arrangement of stimulus events in time (eliciting, evocative, discriminative, and reinforcing) relative to the temporal distribution of behavioral events. Collateral clustering of response classes, independent of time, is characteristic of traits. That is, clusters of responses tend to belong to the same class by virtue of their shared stimulus equivalence or response induction. These behavioral properties stem from genetic and/or historical sources, such that manipulation of the probability of one member of a given functional class (often called a trait) tends to be associated with changes in probability of other members of that class.

Assessing Diverse Response Classes

In practice, the task of assessing the nature and strength of a person's major response tendencies is formidable but, in principle, possible. If one could combine the skills and training of an especially brilliant ethnologist, with those of a behavior analyst and an ethologist, the job might take on more manageable dimensions. Suppose one were faced with the assignment of identifying the major response classes within the behavior of an adult human subject, freely moving in his/her natural environment. Let's simplify matters by assuming the subject is from a cultural background very much like our own. To begin, we might choose to observe our subject during all waking hours, 7 days a week, for a period of 2-3 months. Using a coded partial-interval time sampling procedure (Sulzer-Azaroff & Mayer, 1977), it might be possible to track up to 10 different behaviors and stimulus situations at a time with reasonable reliability. Over a quarter of a year's daily observations, one could probably construct a reasonably complete inventory of the major types of responses exhibited by the individual, the stimulus circumstances antecedent to those responses and any typical consequences that seemed to regulate their probability of recurrence.   Some behaviors would be more difficult to track adequately than others; for example, sexual behavior is less accessible to observation.   Other responses occur relatively infrequently, but when they occur, may be very significant (e.g., violent responses).   However, given enough skill (drawing on ethnological tactics) one ought to be able to construct a reasonably valid picture of the functional response classes   comprising the behavior of our single subject.

Having enumerated a vast number of responses, and drawn tentative conclusions about response class membership based on putative controlling variables (i.e., a functional classification), one could then begin to cluster responses sharing common controlling factors. For example, all operants, the probability of which are controlled by approval from other people, might be   tentatively   combined   into   one   class   (regardless   of topographical differences). It might prove useful to begin to aggregate groups of functional responses which commonly covary, as cases of naturally integrated response classes. Certain operants (regardless of differences in form) are often controlled by avoidance or onset of an aversive stimulus, and covary   with   conditioned   elicited   responses,   which   are frequently associated with characteristic interoceptive stimulus conditions (e.g., described by the person exposed to those conditions   as   "being   anxious").   These   integrated operant-elicited response combinations may comprise a functional heterogeneous response class. As this exercise is played out, the result would be an extensive enumeration of single and composite covarying response clusters controlled by the same variables. By recording enough instances of each functional behavior class over a 2-3 month period, the observers could translate their observations into a family of relative probability estimates.   By   arranging   such   probabilities ordinally, one would arrive at an hierarchy of relative response probabilities (Figure 1).

Upon scrutinizing the response tendencies derived from this exercise, we would probably find that many of these entities correspond   closely   to   traditional   trait-labels   and   may   be

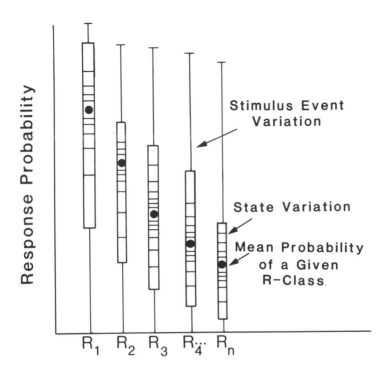

Response Classes

Fig. 1.   The hierarchy of an individual's relative response probabilities. R_1, R_2, ... R_n - the individual's dispositional profile (each "R" represents a specific disposition, the average strength of which is illustrated by a black circle). The short horizontal lines extending from each circle illustrate short-term fluctuations due to state variables (i.e., nonstructural organismic conditions that enhance or attenuate the strength of response classes, for example, fatigue, deprivation, drug, and hormonal states, etc.). Dispositions vary in the extent to which state fluctuations moderate their strength, which is highlighted by the larger variance of R_1, compared to R_n. Strength modulations due to variations in the intensity, configuration and temporal structure of exteroceptive stimulus events are shown by the narrow vertical lines extending from the bars marking variations due to state fluctuations.

classified into several functional domains. Some response classes are distinguished by their common consequences. For example, response tendencies controlled and maintained by social events might be labeled "extroverted" and the dimension along which the strength of such tendencies are measured has conventionally been called *social introversion-extroversion*. Those controlled by aversive stimuli and punishment have traditionally been called "avoidance" (or, in Freudian nomenclature, "defense mechanisms"), and the dimension along which such dispositions have been scaled has been called *neuroticism*. The maintaining events for response classes which involve pain or discomfort to others are called *aggressive*. And response tendencies directed toward inducing others to mediate reinforcers for us has been called *dominance*. These labels are descriptive devices used to characterize functional molar units, nothing more. The strength of such *preference dispositions* refers to the degree to which their respective controlling variables will function as maintaining events for instrumental responding.

A second domain of human response classes includes *response capacities*: An individual's level of strength on these dimensions refers to the ease with which certain instrumental responses can be performed. This domain consists mostly of response tendencies involving discriminative performances and generalizations to symbolic material. Examples of this class include *verbal skill* (responding discriminatively to the meaning of words and using them effectively), *spatial skill* (responding discriminatively to relationships resulting from the movement of objects in space), *clerical skill* (the tendency to respond selectively to pertinent detail in verbal or tabular material), and *finger dexterity* (facility at manipulating small objects rapidly and accurately). We refer to this domain as "response capacities" because in addition to representing an individual's response strength with respect to a normative class of controlling variables (i.e., a skill) the level of these dispositions also measures an individual's readiness to acquire subsequent response tendencies (i.e., an individual's aptitude).

A third class of response tendencies pertains to a small segment of the human population and may roughly be labeled "psychopathological" traits. We mention this class for the sake of completeness, although a thorough behavioral account of the nature of these response tendencies is difficult to characterize.

Whether the entities embraced by this class stem from systematic sources of individual differences at extreme levels or actually represent real "taxa" (Meehl, 1986) remains to be seen. Perhaps both views are correct. For example, most cases of mental retardation represent the low end of polygenetic inheritance for intelligence. However, mental retardation can also result from Mendelian inheritance (e.g., PKU and Down's syndrome) and, hence, stem from taxonic entities. The same could be true for major psychopathological disorders. For our purposes, we have chosen to place these response tendencies in a separate class.

The most salient members of this class are the psychotic response tendencies (e.g., those associated with manic-depressive disorders and schizophrenia). These traits stem from endogenous dispositions which predispose an individual toward developing abnormal (psychotic) behaviors. Individuals suffering from these disorders typically display delusions, hallucinations, and incoherent speech patterns. Often these tendencies become so debilitating that effective functioning of preference and response capacity dispositions are drastically impaired.

Like behavioral combinations, traits may be analyzed into two subsets. *Homogeneous traits* are response families composed of multiple emitted responses (e.g., response capacities). *Heterogeneous traits* consist of emitted behaviors covarying with characteristic elicited internal states (preferences and psychopathologies).

The momentary strength of heterogeneous traits can be modulated by variables controlling either the emitted or elicited components of these aggregate entities. However, the degree to which manipulating a variable controlling the probability of an elicited or emitted component will be effective in altering the strength of a heterogeneous trait depends on the response class under consideration. If, for example, the objective is to decrease the probability of psychotic behavior of a person suffering from a major affective disorder or schizophrenia, administration of a pharmacological agent (i.e., lithium or a phenothiazine derivative, respectively) would likely be the most effective. Often the internal states of people suffering from psychoses must be modulated before the contingencies of punishment and/or reinforcement are capable of making contact with behavior (Thompson, Golden & Heston, 1979).

Trait Clusters

Trait-clusters are defined as two or more traits that covary intra-individually. Like the confluence of behavioral components at more basic levels, products of these interactions may consist of brief expressions of both response tendencies in rapid alternation, a blending of response tendencies collaterally, synergistic behavior unlike either constituent response tendency when functioning in isolation, or behavior may stop. A common trait-cluster which may involve all of these integrative forms follows: Children raised in punitive households are often severely punished for engaging in sexual behavior and discussions of sexual matters. As adults, these children may develop "dysfunctional" avoidance behaviors when sexually aroused because of their past history of punishment following sexual arousal or interest. Even when these individuals are able to engage in sexual activity, they oftentimes report "feeling anxious" throughout the episode (Masters & Johnson, 1966).

In the above example, the trait plus trait covariation is due to historical factors. The *environmental mould* (Cattell, 1950) has produced a trait cluster "sexual arousal" plus "neurotic-avoidance responding" which covaries with stimuli that typically only control the former trait. Other trait clusters are composed of constituents having common biological antecedents. The cluster of traits jointly defining general intelligence (g) is, perhaps, the best known example. In complex problem solving tasks, several cognitive (numerical, spatial, verbal) skills often rise to high strength, collectively. No doubt there are specific biological antecedents for each of these traits, but their tendency to jointly covary both intra- and inter-individually probably stems from antecedents common to all of them.

Refining Time Sampling Estimates

Response tendency (including trait) estimates generated from observers' recordings over long intervals are most accurate for stimulus situations frequently encountered (e.g., work settings) and least accurate for rarely encountered situations (e.g., violent or hysterical episodes). The phrase "I've never seen that side of him before" refers to instances of the second kind; infrequent response tendencies may nevertheless be at high strength, but rarely observed because the circumstances necessary for their manifestation are infrequent. Ideally, estimates of relative response probabilities established by observing an individual over long time intervals should be complemented by observing the subject in low probability situations - to estimate the strength of infrequently observed response tendencies. Both methods estimate the strength of a particular disposition but the latter measures the strength of response tendencies that rarely have the *opportunity* to occur.

Finally, for a comprehensive account of an individual's response tendencies, behavioral data should be collected in compound stimulus situations composed of stimuli relevant to two or more response tendencies. In such circumstances, if responses are incompatible, behavior may cease or become bizarre "superstitious rituals" (Falk, 1986), responses may be integrated in a novel manner "emergent verbalizations" (Sidman, 1986), or one response tendency may emerge as temporarily dominant "regnant need" (Murray, 1938). To be sure, an adequate assessment of all possible hybrid situations can only be approximated, but to the extent that such compound situations are adequately sampled, our capacity to predict an individual's behavior in natural settings becomes more precise.

The above program, if thoroughly carried out, would generate an idiographic (intra-individual) profile of an individual's major response tendencies. However, collecting behavioral data over 3-month intervals is a formidable task, as is exposing subjects to a comprehensive array of low probability situations (and hybrid situations) such that a reasonably valid picture of an individual's response tendencies could be drawn. The opportunity to observe subjects over such long intervals is rare and inefficient. When observations are limited to more manageable intervals, the validity of our estimates of response tendencies may become suspect, because similar response forms may cut across several response classes and, conversely, disparate topographical components can be members of the same class. It is essential that a genuine functional covariation is established before a particular behavior is assigned to a specific response class.

For example, if we observe a couple dining at a fashionable restaurant and, after finishing their meal, the male diner administers a large gratuity to the waiter, we may be inclined to interpret the tipping response as a member of a larger class, say, generosity. In reality, however, someone who knows the diner well might point out that he is typically penurious, but in certain instances where the impression made on his female companion is the controlling variable, his "generosity knows no limits!" On the other hand, responses, some of which appear to have very different forms, may be controlled by the same variables and, belong to the same functional class. As a case in point, part of what it means to exhibit "authoritarian tendencies" is the manner in which superiors and subordinates function as discriminative and reinforcing stimuli for the authoritarian individual. Subordinates are addressed in a "Now hear this" tone, whereas the authoritarian responds obediently in response to orders from superiors. Some critics refer to military promotion policies as ludicrous, because officers are promoted to leadership roles based on their ability to follow orders. Although this may appear otiose, for the authoritarian the transition is often made smoothly. The apparently conflicting features of the authoritarian's behavior in work settings suggest inconsistency, however, bearing in mind that social interactions operate as conditional discriminations based on superior/subordinate social discriminative stimuli, lawful regularities emerge.

One way to circumvent the arduous task of time sampling involves exposing the subject to a variety of situations in a more efficient and standarized manner using verbal symbolic, rather than concrete discriminative stimuli - namely, psychological tests. Psychological tests are not designed to provide precise estimates of the nature and strength of specific idiographic response tendencies, but they estimate an individual's response strength relative to normative classes of controlling variables. Just as time sampling techniques generate estimates of idiographic response tendencies by abstracting commonalities across behavioral instances *within* an individual, psychological tests estimate normative response tendencies by abstracting behavioral commonalities (via an indirect medium) *across* individuals.

Both methods are concerned with assessing the strength of lawful covariations between classes of stimulus events and classes of responses, but at different levels of abstraction. To the extent that we comprehensively measure the strengths of an individual's response classes on an array of these normative response class dimensions, psychological tests can be employed to generate estimates of an individual's idiographic response tendencies.

Psychological Tests

Historically, the objectives of psychological testing have been either technological or theoretical. The technological goal is concerned with distinguishing individuals of a certain type from the general population (e.g., children likely to have difficulty learning in school, accountants, schizophrenics). This was the main purpose of the first psychometric devices.

Thus, Binet (Binet & Simon, 1905) was assigned the task (by the French Ministry of Schools) to construct an instrument to differentiate retarded children from children in general. The Strong Vocational Interest Blank (SVIB) (Strong, 1927) was constructed to identify individuals well-suited for various occupations. And, it was the success of the SVIB that set the occasion for Hathaway and McKinley (1940) to build the Minnesota Multiphasic Personality Inventory (MMPI), an instrument designed to differentiate individuals suffering from psychopathology from people in general.

These instruments are composed of verbal stimuli which provide the subject with the opportunity to tact symbolic relationships ("2 + 2 = _ "), and to estimate ("autoclitically") reinforcer preferences ("I prefer to work alone") or frequent interoceptive states ("My mind isn't working right").[1] The pattern of responses to these verbal discriminative stimuli by members of a representative criterion group (e.g., retarded children, accountants, schizophrenics, etc.) are used to determine *empirically* the items that differentiate the responses of the criterion group in contrast to the general population. This method of item selection is referred to as "empirical keying" (i.e., items are selected based on their *external structure,* or their capacity to generate contrasting response patterns between certain groups of people, and nothing else).

Although patterns of response to specific textual stimuli (test items) may distinguish groups of individuals (e.g., retarded children from children who are not, accountants from physicians, schizophrenics from people with affective disorders), they may not cast much light on the functional response classes which distinguish one criterion group from another. In later test development greater emphasis has been placed on selection of verbal stimuli based on theoretical concerns (Cronbach & Meehl, 1955; Loevinger, 1957; Messick, 1981). Verbal cues (items) are selected based on their (a) specific content, (b) internal structure (or, inter-item correlation), *and* (c) external structure in various degrees

---

[1]There is a fundamental difference between the psychometric assessment of *response capacities* (e.g., clerical, spatial, and verbal skills) and *preference* and *psychopathological* dispositions (e.g., attitudes, interests, needs, and noncognitive personality traits). In the assessment of cognitive skills, the strength of an individual's response class is estimated directly and objectively; the verbal responses emitted in this context are tacts. In the assessment of preference and psychopathology, however, individuals are asked to estimate "subjectively" the strength of certain dispositions (i.e., we ask subjects to tact the strength of certain response classes); hence, the verbal operants emitted in this context are autoclitics. This distinction may be related to the finding that the assessment of response capacities is much more reliable than the assessment of preference and psychopathological dispositions.

depending on the purpose of assessment. These additional considerations of item content and internal structure help focus scale construction toward indexing unitary response tendencies, rather than lightly tapping a variety of response tendencies which is what empirically keyed scales often do. Scales constructed in this manner may be construed as measures of reinforcer preferences (i.e., the activities and stimuli which will function as maintaining events for instrumental responding) or response capacities (i.e., the tendency to emit certain responses or the readiness to acquire certain responses). An individual's standing on these dimensions represents the strength of a given class of responses in relation to a set of controlling variables.

Numerical estimates of preference dispositions provide estimates of the reinforcing efficacy of various classes of stimuli, whereas response-capacity estimates measure the individual's capacity for gaining access to these high probability behaviors. For example, Dawis and Lofquist (1984) analyzed work adjustment by parsing the individual's work behavior and the occupational environment into two broad (and mutually corresponsive) sub-domains. An individual's work behavior is defined by their repertoire of specific *skills* and *preferences* for certain reinforcers; whereas occupations are defined in terms of their *response requirements* (skills necessary for satisfactory performance) and *reinforcer systems* (types of reinforcers typical of a given occupation). The system calls for two levels of correspondence to predict adequate work adjustment: "satisfactoriness" (i.e., correspondence between an employee's skills and the response requirements of a particular occupation) and "satisfaction" (correspondence between the employee's preferences and the reinforcer system). To the extent that these two pairs of variables correspond, the likelihood of job tenure is increased (Dawis & Lofquist, 1984). Individuals who are "satisfactory" and "satisfied" in their occupations are able to emit the required responses because of the response-capacity/skill-requirement correspondence, and stay in the occupation because of the reinforcer-preference/reinforcer-system correspondence, respectively.

Our understanding of individuals' response tendencies can

often be enhanced by increasing the comprehensiveness of our assessment program. For example, we once saw a client for vocational assessment whose response capacity estimates exceeded the minimum requirements on all occupations listed in the *Dictionary of Occupational Titles* (DOT, 1977). His assessed preferences pointed toward managerial occupations (which also corresponded to his expressed interests in-session). However, he also reported having "a hard time getting going on tasks" and spending "alot of time ruminating"; in addition, he appeared depressed. His responses to MMPI items revealed that some psychopathological dispositions were at high strength, which dramatically attenuated his instrumental effectiveness in a variety of work settings. This example serves to illustrate how estimates of an individual's hierarchy of relative response tendencies can be refined by increasing the scope of our assessment program not only in terms of indexing other classes of response tendencies, but also by adjusting other estimates. However, psychological testing is not designed to assess the way response tendencies will function in a particular setting to structure local sequences of behavioral events in time.

TEMPORAL STRUCTURE OF LOCAL RESPONSE PROBABILITIES

Stimulus events, either by elicitation, evocation or operation of the Law of Effect, structure local response probabilities. The local temporal structure of behavioral sequences depends on the relative response probabilities of successive response classes and their temporal distance. Biological state variables (qualitatively different from behavioral dispositions) modulate the degree to which a given stimulus event may exercise its effects on the probability of the response class with which it is related (i.e., either amplifying or attenuating response probability). For example, the probability that a man addicted to heroin will seek out an opiate injection will vary with time since his previous heroin self-administration and the probability of an individual's extroverted behaviors will vary as a function of fatigue. However, having been determined, the role of such a local response probability is, in all likelihood, independent of its functional class (i.e., to the extent that a behavior is highly probable it will function as a reinforcing event, regardless of whether it is elicited, emitted, evoked, or a constituent of a trait or trait cluster). Premack has shown persuasively that relative response probability relationships are at the root of the Law of Effect (Premack, 1959, 1965, 1971). The relative magnitudes of response probabilities ordered in time by stimulus events determine which response class events can serve as maintaining events for other preceding response classes. Stated more precisely, relative response probabilities can determine the access to which events can maintain other response class events.

It may initially appear that this analysis is tautological (i.e., if one response probability is higher than another, that will determine the response sequence). However, consider the situation shown in Figure 2. A given stimulus event may have discriminative, evocative and eliciting functions which regulate the probabilities of three contemporaneously overlapping response classes. At any one moment in time (e.g., t_1), only one response class will be observable, *though the probability of all three may be relatively high.* On repeated presentation of the stimulus, one might find that R_1 would be followed by R_2. On yet another occasion, R_3 would follow R_1. The casual observer would conclude they are confronted by randomness or a tangled farrago of behavioral events. In fact, which response class appeared would be determined by their relative probabilities in response to the stimulus event, though on any given occasion, the order of response instances will be unpredictable. Given enough samples of S_1R_n, the actual distributions of the relative probabilities of the three response classes would be approximated. Similarly, whether access to members of a given class (e.g., R_3) could serve as a reinforcer for a member of another response class (R_1), would be determined by their relative probabilities and temporal distance between them.

The probability of occurrence of each response class waxes

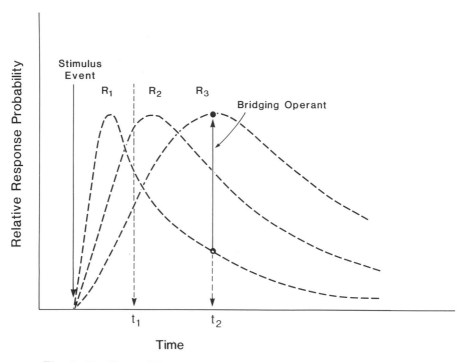

Fig. 2. R_1, R_2, and R_3 represent emitted, elicited, and evoked responses, respectively. The presentation of a stimulus event increases the probability of all three responses simultaneously, but their maximum likelihood gradients peak at different points in time. At time t_1, all three response classes are highly probable (although R_3 is least likely). The vertical line connecting R_3 with R_1 at time t_1 is intended to illustrate a "bridging operant" (i.e., a response emitted to temporally link a high probability behavior "R_3" with a low probability behavior "R_1").

and wanes in a fashion characteristic of a given class. Given the nature of those functions, and the particular points in time that controlling stimulus events occur, the times between peak probabilities of successive response classes will vary. The exact nature of the decay function characterizing the reinforcing strength of a given response class relative to a second response class is unclear, however, it is likely an exponential function describes the relationship, as is true of many biological functions. One can think of the probability relations of temporally sequenced response classes as creating a reinforcement force gradient akin to that across a semipermeable membrane separating solutions of two concentrations (Thompson & Lubinski, 1985) or two plates of a capacitor, separated by a dielectric medium. The degree to which access to members of one response class can serve as a maintaining event for members of another response class can be expressed:

$$Pr_2 \cdot s^r \cdot r_1 = f \left[\frac{1}{(t_2-t_1) \cdot (p_2-p_1)} \right]^x$$

where $Pr_2 \cdot s^r \cdot r_1$ refers to the probability access to Response 2 will reinforce emission of Response 1, t_1 and t_2 refer to modal times of Response 1 and Response 2, p_1 and p_2 refer to the relative probabilities of the two response classes (assuming $p_2>p_1$), and x is an exponential variable.

Hence, in the flow of a person's activities, r_2 will tend to follow r_1 depending on the relative differences between p_1 and p_2 and between t_1 and t_2. However, more importantly, access to r_2 will serve as a maintaining event for arbitrary operants leading from r_1 to r_2. The specific operants observed will depend on the individual's behavioral repertoire, the context and any unique response-reinforcer relations prepotent to the situation.

Consider the following exchange. A man has just emerged from a barbershop and his wife says, "What a smashing haircut!" The man's verbal acknowledgement will vary, of course, with his history, but might very well take the form, "Really, I thought it was a little short, but I'm glad you like it." After a predictable pause, the man might go on to say [unexpectedly to his spouse], "By the way, I was thinking it might be nice to go out for dinner tonight, what do you think?" In this example, the positive reinforcer (i.e., the compliment) served several purposes. It not only set the occasion for the acknowledgement, but it also increased the subsequent likelihood of another response class (approach), access to which was bridged by his verbal dinner invitation.

Punishing stimuli can have a comparable effect, and may temporally structure local response probabilities in a fashion that is often called "displaced aggression." Max (a senior faculty member) is approached in the corridor of the Psychology building by the department chair who says,"Max, you know I was expecting your report from the Executive Committee today, but I haven't received it yet . . . I thought you had understood the importance of getting it to me promptly so I can pass it on to the Dean . . . Perhaps I hadn't made myself clear." To which Max replies, "I'll see if I can get it to you first thing in the morning . . . I've really been tied up reviewing grants for the next study section." As Max walks down the corridor, he knocks on the door of Robin, a junior colleague (with whom he has frequent theoretical disagreements), and says, "Hi, how goes the battle?" Robin replies, "Not bad, how about you? . . . By the way, how's the budget report coming along?, to which Max replies, "Well, to tell you the truth, we are recommending some pretty stiff cutbacks in faculty positions . . . but I don't *think* you'll have anything to worry about." Max's increased probability of aggressing for an interval following the department chair's aversive remark is typical of the structuring of local response probabilities in time, and the tendency to seek out opportunities to emit high probability responses. His remark to Robin, designed as it was to cause discomfort over her job security, was displaced a minute or so in time from the evocative event.

In both instances, topographically arbitrary operants bridged lower and higher probability response classes. If the magnitude of the second response class had not been sufficiently high or the delay between the first and second had been too long (e.g., due to interruption or a competing response) access to the second response class would no longer reinforce the intervening operants (either verbal or motor). Hence we might observe that the spouse "failed to rise to the occasion," or that Max "dealt with his anger maturely [i.e., didn't lash out against Robin]." In such cases the expected response sequence would be interrupted. Indeed, much of what is referred to as "good timing" in interpersonal transactions (e.g., sales work, psychotherapy) and in humor, has to do with providing the opportunity for the listener to respond at exactly the most effective interval following a discriminative or evocative stimulus.

The role of such locally structured response probabilities, then, is to integrate successive higher and lower probability response classes by means of arbitrary operants that link them to one another. The foregoing proposed exponential relationship characterizes the conditions under which such linkages are likely to occur. It is this feature which gives the continuity to response sequences, providing the illusion of a continuous stream of uninterrupted activity. Groups of such concatenated response classes can be caused to covary collectively by providing major reinforcing events following entire sequences, as Findley has shown (see following discussion). The rules governing the size of units which can be organized this way are not known, nor are the algorithms by which hierarchies of response clusters become subsumed under larger and more diverse response classes.

Diverse Response Classes, Traits and Temporal Structure

That larger covarying groups of diverse response classes can be brought under the control of a maintaining event is well established. Perhaps the most persuasive example was Findley's demonstration that several complex human performances, each under the control of different stimulus and schedule events, could be regulated as a behavioral unit by the arrangement of a reinforcing event following the entire unit (Findley, 1966; Findley, Migler & Brady, 1963). Such complex responses as creating an oil painting, writing a section of a novel, and engaging in philosophical discussions with the experimenter comprised successive operant units in Findley's investigations.

In human discourse, the probability of successive response

classes also waxes and wanes. For example, in psychotherapy, the antecedent stimulus event is either a discriminative stimulus provided by another person (e.g., the therapist's asking, "Hmm . . . I wonder why she reacted that way to your suggestion?"), a previous response-produced stimulus provided by the subject (e.g., the client's own remark, "I told my boss that I thought she should refer questions like that to me.") or often in the form of a conditional discrimination (e.g., the confluence of both the previous remark by the client, and the therapist's verbal probe). The emergence of a sudden high probability response class following a sequence of verbal exchanges (e.g., the client's insightful remark, "I see . . . she wasn't angry with me . . . she thought I didn't respect her judgment!") can serve as a maintaining event for a sequence of utterances that preceded the verbal remark. In Findley's experiments, no effort was made to characterize the distinctive features of these response classes for a given individual relative to a normative frame of reference. However, the nature of the response classes making up the behavioral repertoire of a given individual, and their enduring relative response probabilities are subject to a normative analysis. In the preceding example, the client's verbal responses are part of a therapeutic exchange concerning the client's belief that she was not liked by her employer. Further exploration may reveal that this woman exhibits a wide array of responses, the probabilities of which are regulated by anticipated loss of approval by significant people in her life (e.g., her supervisor, husband, father, mother). Indeed, when her responses to specific psychological test items are investigated (e.g., "Often I cross the street in order not to meet someone I see" [True], or "I have no dread of going into a room by myself where other people have already gathered and are talking" [False]) it becomes apparent that the client's verbal responses in the therapy session were members of a larger response class. In fact, relative to the general population, the client may score two standard deviations above the mean on the dimension of relative strength of this response class. Such a response class, as we have discussed earlier, is called a *trait*. (A trait is distinguished by its diversity and topographical complexity, but otherwise operates like other response classes.) In the flow of events which set the occasion for the opportunity to engage in avoidance of loss of approval, the client in the preceding example exhibits a wide array of members of that class, given the right stimulus events. One ought not be surprised that the specific stimulus situations and particular avoidance responses are relatively content free. It is the functional controlling relation that defines members of the class, not the specific situation giving rise to a specific response form.

Moreover, the client will also display other behavior, the end product of which is the opportunity to engage in avoidance of loss of approval (i.e., a very high probability response class, or trait). If one samples the client's behavior in a narrow slice of time, it is impossible to make sense of a given motor or verbal response, since it is impossible to identify its class membership (e.g., the woman's verbally snapping at her children, when she realizes her husband is fifteen minutes later than usual). Similarly, *it is virtually impossible to predict the probability of a specific topography in time, though the probability of members of a given response class (trait) should be relatively predictable.* While there is a degree of indeterminacy vis a vis instances of a given response topography, the probability of the sequential arrangement of response classes is determined. One of the striking qualities of an astute psychotherapist is his/her ability to identify response class membership in the flow of a client's behavior with a high degree of accuracy.

Orders of Dispositions and Predispositions

In an earlier paper (Thompson & Lubinski, 1985), we argued that the minimal (i.e., elicited and/or emitted) units of several behavioral tendencies are so tightly integrated that an exhaustive analysis of many combinations may not be feasible. Thus questions naturally arise regarding the mechanisms involved in maintaining the internal consistency of such dispositional clusters.

One antecedent to formation of functional response clusters or traits is behavioral genetic endowment. An individual's genetic make-up is composed of dispositional entities (not behavioral dispositions but biological dispositions or behavioral predispositions to response tendencies). These biological antecedents integrate the elicited and emitted components of several traits (e.g., the collateral integrity of the elicited and emitted constituents of, say, extroversion and neuroticism). Moreover, these predispositions are inherited in various amounts which determine, in part, the wide range of individual differences (i.e., various quantitative levels of strength) observed across all traits. In addition, as the following discussion illustrates, the level and pattern of these biological antecedents is directly related to specific response tendencies that an individual acquires.

Biological antecedents to behavioral tendencies and behavioral tendencies can be distinguished in terms of their order (Broad, 1949; Meehl, 1972). Dispositions which are necessary for the acquisition of further dispositions are viewed as higher-order dispositions. Hence, a disposition of order "K" represents the tendency to acquire a disposition of order "K-1". For example, a three component dispositional sequence may be the following: There is evidence that (second order) behavioral components encompassed by the trait "extroversion" have (third order) biological antecedents (Gottesman, 1966; Scarr, 1969). These second order extroverted behavioral tendencies may be prerequisite for acquiring a variety of first-order dispositions, say, specific skills as a "sales person," "executive," or "politician," etc.

Individuals begin life with a host of biological dispositions relevant to the acquisition of several homogeneous and heterogeneous response classes which are inherited in various amounts (i.e., dispositions of the order "K"). The uniqueness of human individuality begins with the level and pattern of these antecedents to functional response classes. Lower-order dispositions (i.e., K-2, K-3, etc.) are acquired from these higher-order antecedents to form a truly unique dispositional hierarchy of relative response probabilities.

Biological prerequisites to functional response classes are not conceptualized as members of functional classes. Rather we consider them biochemical and physiological antecedents, akin to body build and visual acuity; they determine the extent to which certain classes of stimuli may function as reinforcers ("preferences"), the ease with which instrumental responses are acquired ("response capacities"), and, for a small subset of the population, a greater likelihood to develop abnormal behavior ("psychopathologies"). Although these biological antecedents function to channel an individual's behavioral development, the specific content of an individual's behavioral repertoire is determined by his/her experience. For example, one's standing on the biological antecedents to neuroticism determines the degree to which one's behavior is predisposed toward quick and effective control by aversive contingencies, but it takes the environment to attach the specific content of these contingencies. Just as the strength of unconditioned (second-order) reflexes determines the capacity for acquiring conditioned (first-order) reflexes, the nature of the conditioned stimuli (CS's) may vary tremendously (quantitatively and qualitatively). As Skinner (1969) has stated:

> To say that intelligence is inherited is not to say that specific forms of behavior are inherited . . . What has been selected appears to be a susceptability to ontogenic contingencies, leading particularly to a greater speed of conditioning and the capacity to maintain a larger repertoire without confusion. (p. 183)

Historically, correlational psychologists (i.e., behavior genetics, differential, personality, psychometrics, etc.) have focused primarily on higher-order (K-1) dispositions (the first dispositional order above the biological substratum), whereas experimental psychologists have tended to study lower-order dispositions. Although ostensibly these two areas of interest may appear unrelated, in reality they represent a logical progression of dispositional orders.

Response Class Composition

The homogeneity of a response class is determined by several variables, including the genetically determined tendency for certain responses to covary inter- and/or intra-individually, the uniformity of the contingency history underlying the response class, and the degree to which the same or very similar topographies contribute to other functional response classes. While the former two factors are reasonably straight forward, the latter may be less obvious. In laboratory operant situations, we are well aware of response induction, in which operants sharing common motoric elements tend to substitute for one another (formerly called response generalization). The classic experiment by Antonitis (1951) illustrated some of the dimensions along which induction occurs. In humans, two verbal utterances emitted with different intonations, accompanied by different motor responses (e.g., "body language"), and under different discriminative circumstances may be members of two very different classes. "What a lovely evening," said by the British Ambassador to the American Ambassador, on the terrace of the U.S. Embassy in London over after-dinner cigars on conclusion of an agreement, would be quite a different operant from "What a lovely evening" said by a young woman to her date as she is standing with him outside her apartment at the end of an evening together. Though the literal content of the utterances are the same, the stimulus conditions leading to them are quite different, as are their controlling consequences.

A feature of such larger and more topographically diverse response classes is that the manipulation of a variable that influences one member of the class tends to alter the probability of other members. While this is widely known for simpler response classes (e.g., lever presses), we tend not to expect this will occur with larger response classes. Much of what has often been described as "symptom substitution" refers to the phenomenon of behavioral contrast (Reynolds, 1961) within a broader response class. An extinction or suppression procedure applied to one member of a larger class of closely related educational or social responses may be associated with a temporary increase in strength of other class members. On the contrary, reinforcing one member of a class will strengthen other class members, which is usually the desired therapeutic or pedagogical outcome. For example, McConahey, Zimmerman and Thompson (1977) found that when aggressive and other disturbed behavior of retarded women was ignored (i.e., extinction) or lead to token loss in a token economy (i.e., punishment), the probability of behavior from the same or closely related classes increased during nontreatment periods (i.e., symptom substitution or behavioral contrast).

The more individual elements two response classes share, the more likely they will combine to form a larger trait cluster, though some of the members of the combined class will continue to be nonoverlapping. The response class often described as "sociopathy" includes two subresponse classes having in common very little control by aversive contingencies. Short term contingencies exercise far more control over the behavior of such people than for most of the rest of the population. In a choice situation between immediate positive reinforcement for themselves and significant aversive outcome for other people, the person whose sociopathic disposition has very high probability would reliably choose the immediate reinforcement for him or herself. The aversive consequence inflicted on others (which, for most people could carry a conditioned aversive quality) would have little suppressing effect, since sociopaths are less sensitive to conditioned aversive stimuli (cf., Lykken, 1968, pp. 157-158). People having the genetic endowment for Mania exhibit some of the same response topographies, though often under different circumstances. In addition, however, people with the Manic disposition also exhibit a variety of other behaviors, including very high rate of speech under poor social control, extremely high rate of motor activity, responding at a high rate leading to a wide variety of primary reinforcers, with limited control by conditioned negative reinforcers. Though members of the two response classes overlap, and may occur at times simultaneously in the same individual, they are in fact different response classes. The sociopathic-like person often exhibits a combination of both response classes, and generally has a very high score on both the 4(Pd) and 9(Ma) scales of the Minnesota Multiphasic Personality Inventory. However, many other individuals exhibit relatively high probability of the psychopathic disposition (Pd), or of the manic disposition (Ma), but not both.

Any aggregate response class must be viewed as the result of the confluence of two or more other response classes. The nature of their integration requires a mathematical formulation, and cannot be understood pictorially. As Dirac (1958) suggested in writing about the states of quanta,

> When a state is formed by the superposition of two other states, it will have properties that are in some vague way intermediate between those of the two original states and that approach more or less closely to those of either of them according to the greater or less "weight" attached to this state in the superposition process. The new (integrated) state is completely defined by the two original states when their relative weights in the superposition process are known, the exact meaning of weights and phases being provided in the general case by the mathematical theory. (p. 13)

However, the mathematics involved in specifying the manner in which response units and their weights and momentary fluctuating states of strength are combined to form larger response classes (i.e., traits and trait clusters) remain to be explicated. It is useful to bear in mind, however, that the indeterminate character of the response family expresses itself in a probabilistic fashion, and *it is the probability of observing a given behavioral component that is indeterminate, not the response class*. On a given occasion, one may very well sample one instance in which one of several integrated response classes is sampled, however, by repeating the observation on many occasions, the probability of each will be accurately assessed.

It should be clear that sampling a moment in time out of the ongoing flow of a person's behavior will not provide a basis for interpreting the class membership of a given response. Nor, for that matter, will it necessarily be possible to make such response class assignments by observing the individual over even a more extended period. It is necessary to assess the individual's responses to a wide sampling of situations to assess their relative response probabilities. While such measuring devices as personality and vocational assessment inventories are fallible indicators of the strength of such response classes, they are little different from any other autoclitics. To the extent that an individual is well trained to tact the strength of his/her own response tendencies, such instruments have the possibility of providing useful measures of relative response strength.

Point Predictions of Kinetic Structure

Since response tendencies are dispositional entities, i.e., they have an if "S" (stimulus situation of a given kind) then "R" (response of a given type) character (Tellegen, 1981), to the extent that our knowledge of an individual's response class tendencies is reasonably complete, predicting behavior on a moment-to-moment basis reduces to understanding state variables and predicting the environment. The problem of predicting the temporal presentation of environmental stimuli (especially in natural settings) is a formidable task by any metric, but point predictions of the kinetic structure of an individual's behavior is essentially hopeless without this knowledge. It's as if one were asked to predict the behavior of a pigeon whose behavior was under elegant stimulus control under a seven ply multiple-schedule without knowing which exteroceptive stimulus light was currently illuminated. Point predictions of the bird's behavior (assuming all lights are illuminated for equal intervals) would only be correct one in seven times. Similarly, a therapist would be hard pressed if asked to predict the behavior patterns of a client between sessions, even though they may have a comprehensive inventory of their relative response tendencies. Predictions are difficult to generate because the therapist is ignorant of the environmental events (i.e., the configuration and intensity of exteroceptive stimuli) about to confront the client during the interval in question. If these environmental events (and their temporal structure) could somehow be estimated, point predictions of the client's kinetic structure would begin to become an answerable question.

This is why most behavioral predictions are framed in terms of conditional response probabilities (i.e., given stimulus

"S" the probability of response "R" is $\hat{P}$). Because of the vast number of behavioral dispositions that an individual may possess, coupled with the infinite number of configural patterns of strength a dispositional hierarchy could reflect, perhaps our task is hopeless. At first blush, it may appear so; however, for a given individual there tends to be only a finite number of high strength dispositions within their repertoire under a given set of circumstances. Moreover, individuals tend to spend much of their time in relatively few environmental ecologies (i.e., situations relevant to only a few of their response tendencies). So the task of analyzing human behavior on a moment-to-moment basis becomes more manageable than one would initally suppose. Probably the most fruitful place to begin looking for such lawful regularities in behavior patterns is in the more circumscribed environments, such as certain educational or work settings; since these environments often contain quasi-standardized response requirements and reoccurring stimulus events, they are also environments in which individuals spend a great deal of time.

In addition to devoting more time to predicting the temporal presentation of environmental events, behavioral scientists would be well advised to conceptualize point predictions in terms of response classes, rather than the specific topographical members of a larger response class. In the preceding sections we have argued that several human response classes consist of mega-topographical response components. In fact, the overwhelming complexity of human behavior is considerably reduced by realizing that some response classes take on many forms. Nonetheless, some of our colleagues in related fields have chided practitioners of behavior analysis for failing to make topographical predictions concerning important aspects of human behavior, especially in applied settings (e.g., whether an ex-psychiatric patient will commit a particular act of violence, which verbal utterance a child will emit when confronted with a novel stimulus). While our desire to be able to make quantitative predictions of specific actions of individual subjects is understandable, it is misguided.

Focusing our attention on predicting response classes (as

opposed to the constituent components of response classes) is consistent with the manner in which other sciences operate. A chemist, for example, is able to predict with great certainty the reaction produced by mixing various solutions, provided their respective volumes are known beforehand. If, however, a specific molecule in a solution was radioactively labeled before it was mixed, and if a chemist were asked if this particular (molecular) entity will be involved in the (molar) reaction, our chemist's reply would be much less precise (i.e., the molar phenomena is quite predictable but the specific molecular constituents are indeterminate).

We sometimes forget that the very nature of the phenomenon we wish to predict logically precludes its precise topographical prediction. A given response instance (e.g., a specific violent act) is assumed to be a member of a broader functional response class of related aggressive acts, much as lever presses, chain pulls, and hurdle jumps may all be instrumental responses maintained by the same reinforcer, hence may all be members of a larger functional response class. If we were to present a discriminative stimulus for a lever press, but no lever were present, only a hurdle and a chain, where is the behavior analyst who would tell us whether the rat would emit one of the two instrumental responses, and if so, which one? A rational response would be to state a given probability based on an estimate of the likelihood of induction within the broad class of food-maintained instrumental responses and an estimate of their relative probabilities. If one knew the colors of the several training stimulus lights, and the hours of food deprivation, the adequacy of our probability estimates would increase, but nonetheless, they would be probability estimates of a class of behavior.

The violent act of the ex-psychiatric patient is even less adequately predicted because the response class is far more diverse, incorporating both respondents and operants in a very complex heterogeneous trait. As we indicated earlier, what one observes on any given occasion with respect to a specific response topography is indeterminate, but it is predictable as a class on the average across many occasions. That means, necessarily, that whether any given member of a larger class occurs on a given occasion is unpredictable - only its class probability is predictable. In the case of the would-be violent act, the probability of specific individual violent acts (e.g., verbal abuse, beating, stabbing, or shooting), would lead to a composite estimate of a probability of a violent act. Why one would expect a science of behavior to be able to make more precise predictions than chemists tracking specific molecules, is unclear.

The accuracy of predictions, and the significance of our limited ability to make such predictions depends on the homogeneity and the social importance of the response classes in question. Whether an elementary school student chooses to solve her division or multiplication problems first is less important than whether the president of the United States presses the button to initiate a nuclear attack, or picks up the telephone and dials his/her counterpart in the Soviet Union. Our confidence in predicting the latter is considerably less than most complex operants because the exact nature of the response class isn't clear, and occurrence of members of that class seem, fortunately, to be very uncommon.

In examining more circumscribed response classes, such as those involved in operating a motor vehicle, in many vocational or educational settings, or in some structured one-to-one social situations, the less diverse the behavior classes, the more manageable are predictions of the moment-to-moment flow of activities for a given individual. While limited to the humble statement of successive response probabilities, such a kinetic analysis is a reasonable step for behavioral science to take, and is consistent with the strategies of sister disciplines in the other natural sciences.

ACKNOWLEDGEMENT

Preparation of this manuscript was supported by National Institute on Drug Abuse training grant 5T32 DA07097 and an Eva O. Miller Fellowship.

REFERENCES

Antonitis, J. J. (1951). Response variability in the white rat during conditioning, extinction, and reconditioning. *Journal of Experimental Psychology, 42*, 273-281.

Bechterev, V. M. (1928). *General principles of human reflexology*, (E. Murphy, and W. Murphy (Trans.), London: Jarrolds, 1933. (Original work published 1928)

Branch, M. (1977). On the role of memory in the analysis of behavior. *Journal of the Experimental Analysis of Behavior, 28*, 171-179.

Binet, A., & Simon, T. (1905). New methods for the diagnosis of the intellectual level of subnormals. *L'Annee Psychologique, 11*, 191-244.

Broad, C. D. (1933). The 'nature' of a continuant. *Examination of McTaggart's philosophy*. Cambridge: Cambridge University Press. Reprinted in H. Feigl, & W. Sellers (Eds.), *Readings in philosophical analysis* (1949). New York: Appleton-Century-Crofts.

Cantor, M. B., Smith, S. E., & Bryan, R. B. (1982). Induced bad habits: Adjunctive ingestion and grooming in human subjects. *Appetite: Journal for Intake Research, 3*, 13-22.

Carnap, R. (1956). The methodological character of theoretical concepts. In H. Feigl, & M. Scriven (Eds.), *Minnesota studies in philosophy of science (Vol. I)*. Minneapolis: University of Minnesota Press.

Cattell, R. B. (1950). *Personality: A systematic, theoretical, and factual study*. New York: McGraw-Hill.

Cherek, D. R. (1982). Schedule-induced cigarette self-administration. *Pharmacology Biochemistry & Behavior, 17*, 523-527.

Cherek, D., Thompson, T., & Heistad, G. T. (1973). Responding maintained by the opportunity to attack during an interval food reinforcement schedule. *Journal of the Experimental Analysis of Behavior, 19*, 113-123.

Chomsky, N. (1965). *Aspects of the theory of syntax*. Cambridge, MA: MIT Press.

Chomsky, N. (1968). *Language and mind*. New York: Harcourt Brace Jovanovich.

Cronbach, L. J., & Meehl, P.E. (1955). Construct validity in psychological tests. *Psychological Bulletin, 52*, 281-302.

Davies, P.C.W. (1979). *The forces of nature*. Cambridge: Cambridge University Press.

Dawis, R. V., & Lofquist, L. H. (1984). *A psychological theory of work adjustment: An individual differences model and its applications*. University of Minnesota Press: Minneapolis.

Dirac, A. M. P. (1958). *The principles of quantum mechanics* (4th ed.). London: Oxford University Press.

Falk, J. L. (1961). Production of polydipsia in normal rats by an intermittent food schedule. *Science, 133*, 195-196.

Falk, J. L. (1971). The nature and determinants of adjunctive behavior. *Physiology and Behavior, 6*, 577-588.

Falk, J. L. (1977). The origin and functions of adjunctive behavior. *Animal Learning and Behavior, 5*, 325-335.

Falk, J. L. (1986). In T. Thompson & M. D. Zeiler (Eds.), *Analysis and integration of behavioral units*. Hillsdale, NJ: Lawrence Erlbaum Associates.

Findley, J. D. (1966). Programmed environments for the experimental analysis of human behavior. In W. K. Honig (Ed.), *Operant behavior areas of research and application*. New York: Appleton-Century-Crofts.

Findley, J. D., Migler, B.M., and Brady, J.V. (1963). A long-term study of human performance in a continuously programmed experimental environment. *Technical Report*, Space Research Laboratory, University of Maryland, submitted to the National Aeronautics and Space Administration.

Frederiksen, L. W., & Peterson, G. L. (1974). Schedule-induced aggression in nursery school children. *The Psychological Record, 24*, 343-351.

Gottesman, I. I. (1966). Genetic variance in adaptive personality traits. *Journal of Psychology, Psychiatry, and Allied Disciplines, 7*, 199-208.

Hathaway, S., & McKinley, J. C. (1940). A multiphasic personality schedule: I. Construction of the schedule. *Journal of Psychology, 10*, 249-254.

Hinde, R. (1970). *Animal behavior: A synthesis of ethological and comparative psychology* (2nd ed.). New York: McGraw-Hill.

Levitsky, D., & Collier, G. (1968). Schedule-induced wheel running. *Physiology and Behavior, 3*, 571-573.

Lindman, R. (1982). Social and solitary drinking: Effects on consumption and mood in male social drinkers. *Physiology and Behavior, 28*, 1093-1095.

Loevinger, J. (1957). Objective tests as instruments of psychological theory. *Psychological Reports, 3*, 635-694. (Monograph Supplement 9).

Lykken, D. T. (1968). Statistical significance testing in psychological research. *Psychological Bulletin, 70*, 151-159.

MacCorquodale, K. (1969). B.F. Skinner's *Verbal behavior*: A retrospective appreciation. *Journal of the Experimental Analysis of Behavior, 12*, 831-841.

MacCorquodale, K., & Meehl, P.E. (1954). Edward C. Tolman. In W.K. Estes et al., *Modern learning theory*. New York: Appleton-Century-Crofts.

Marr, M. J. (May, 1981). *Behaviorism and modern physics: Parallels and antiparallels*. Paper presented at the meeting of the Association for Behavior Analysis, Milwaukee, WI.

Masters, W. H., & Johnson, V. E. (1966). *Human sexual response*. Boston: Little, Brown.

McConahey, O.L., Thompson, T., & Zimmerman, R. (1977). A token system for retarded women: Behavior therapy, drug administration, and their combination. In T. Thompson, & J. Grabowski (Eds.), *Behavior modification of the mentally retarded* (2nd ed.). New York: Oxford

University Press.

Meehl, P. E. (1972). Specific genetic etiology, psychodynamics, and therapeutic nihilism. *International Journal of Mental Health, 1*, 10-27.

Meehl, P. E. (1986). Trait language and behaviorese. In T. Thompson & M. D. Zeiler (Eds.), *Analysis and integration of behavioral units*. Hillsdale, NJ: Lawrence Erlbaum and Associates.

Messick, S. (1981). Constructs and their vicissitudes in educational and psychological measurement. *Psychological Bulletin, 89*, 575-588.

Murray, H. A. (1938). *Explorations in personality*. New York: Oxford University Press.

Pap, A. (1958). *Semantics and necessary truth*. New Haven, CT.: Yale University Press.

Pavlov, I. P. (1927). *Conditioned reflexes: An investigation of the physiological activity of the cerebral cortex*. London: Oxford University Press.

Premack, D. (1959). Toward empirical behavior laws, I: Positive reinforcement. *Psychological Review, 66*, 219-233.

Premack, D. (1965). Reinforcement theory. In D. Levine (Ed.), *Nebraska symposium on motivation*. Lincoln: University of Nebraska Press.

Premack, D. (1971). Catching up on common sense, or two sides of a generalization: Reinforcement and punishment. In R. Glaser (Ed.), *On the nature of reinforcement*. New York: Academic Press.

Reynolds, G. S. (1961). Behavioral contrast. *Journal of the Experimental Analysis of Behavior, 4*, 107-117.

Scarr, S. (1969). Social introversion - extroversion as a heritable response. *Child Development, 40*, 823-832.

Sellers, W. (1958). Counterfactuals, dispositions, and the causal modalities. In H. Feigl, M. Scriven, & G. Maxwell (Eds.), *Minnesota studies in philosophy of science (Vol. 2)*. Minneapolis: University of Minnesota Press.

Sidman, M. (1986). Functional analysis of emergent verbal classes. In T. Thompson & M.D. Zeiler (Eds.), *Analysis and integration of behavioral units*. Hillsdale, NJ: Lawrence Erlbaum Associates.

Skinner, B. F. (1938). *Behavior of organisms*. New York: Appleton-Century.

Skinner, B. F. (1969). *Contingencies of reinforcement: A theoretical analysis*. New York: Appleton-Century-Crofts.

Staddon, J. E. R. (1977). Schedule-induced behavior. In W. K. Honig, & J. E. R. Staddon (Eds.), *Handbook of operant behavior*. Englewood Cliffs, NJ.: Prentice-Hall.

Strong, E. K., Jr., (1927). A vocational interest test. *Educational Record, 8*, 107-121.

Sulzer-Azaroff, B., & Mayer, G. R. (1977). *Applying behavior-analysis procedures with children and youth*. New York: Holt, Rinehart and Winston.

Tellegen, A. (1981). Practicing the two disciplines for relaxation and enlightenment: Comment on *Role of the feedback signal in electromyographic biofeedback: The relevance of attention*, by Qualls and Sheehan. *Journal of Experimental Psychology: General, 110,* 217-226.

Thompson, T. (1969).   Aggressive behavior of Siamese Fighting Fish: Analysis and synthesis of conditioned and unconditioned components. In S. Garatini, & E.B. Sigg (Eds.), *The biology of aggression.* Amsterdam: Excerpta Medica Foundation.

Thompson, T., Golden, R., & Heston, L. (1979). *Point-earning in a token economy as an index of lithium effects in Mania.* Paper presented at the Meeting of the Association for Behavioral Analysis, Milwaukee, WI.

Thompson, T., & Grabowski, J.G. (1972). *Reinforcement schedules and multioperant analysis.* New York: Appleton-Century-Crofts.

Thompson, T., & Lubinski, D. (1985). Units of analysis and kinetic structure of behavioral repertoires. Unpublished manuscript.

Thorndike, E. L. (1911). *Animal intelligence.* New York: MacMillian.

U. S. Department of Labor (1977). *Dictionary of occupational titles* (4th ed.), Washington, DC.: U. S. Government Printing Office.

Villarreal, J. (April, 1967). *Schedule-induced pica.* Paper presented at the meeting of the Eastern Psychological Association, Boston, MA.

Wallace, M., & Singer, G. (1976). Adjunctive behavior and smoking induced by a maze solving schedule in humans. *Physiology and Behavior, 17,* 849-852.

Wieseler, N.A., Hanson, R.H., Chamberlain, T.P. and Thompson, T. (1985). Effect of intermittent reinforcement of adaptive behavior on stereotypic behavior of mentally retarded adults.   Unpublished manuscript.

Zeiler, M.D. (1977). Schedules of reinforcement: The controlling variables. In W.K. Honig, & J.E.R. Staddon (Eds.), *Handbook of operant behavior.* Englewood Cliffs, NJ: Prentice-Hall.

CHAPTER 14

Trait Language and Behaviorese

PAUL E. MEEHL

Some twenty years ago a distinguished behavior geneticist visiting here told me at a cocktail party at Gardner Lindzey's, which my friend and research colleague MacCorquodale was unable to attend, how pleased he was at the receptiveness of Minnesota students to the idea that behavior traits were strongly influenced by genes. I told him that would be expected, since they hear a lot about the inheritance of the general intelligence factor from MacCorquodale in the big general psych section. Whereupon he said, with an expression of utter stupefaction on his face, "But, but, why, I thought MacCorquodale taught your Skinner Course," to which I replied, "Yes, and a damn good course it is, and quite orthodox Skinner." The visitor's amazement I learned was due to two firm notions based upon his previous experience with operant behaviorists responding to his lecture, that they don't like traits, and they don't like genes. This attitude has always rather amused me, since Skinner's closest academic friend at Minnesota was my mentor, the late Starke R. Hathaway, whose research career was mainly based upon assessing traits. Also, I had noticed that before accepting a graduate student as a degree candidate, Skinner always looked up his Miller Analogies score. Now the total score on the Miller Analogies Test cannot by any reasonable use of language be called a response strength; for that matter, the analysis of a correct response to a single item of that test would involve an extraordinarily complex chain of responses and discriminative stimuli, mostly covert. With these two anecdotes, and the required bow to Lee Cronbach's APA presidential address on the two disciplines of psychology (Cronbach, 1957), I set the stage for my brief discussion of a methodological conflict between operant behaviorists and clinicians like myself which I have always felt, since studying under Skinner as an undergraduate but with Hathaway as my Ph.D. advisor, was needless and confusing.

Being a clinician who constantly employs trait language in characterizing my patients, who has done research on the MMPI, whose current research is on the taxometrics of mental disorders (some of which I believe are true "disease entities") but who was greatly influenced by Skinner when he was at Minnesota, and many of whose colleagues in the Psychiatry Research Unit are operant behaviorists, I have been forced to ask myself how these two superficially so disparate ways of thinking can be put together. To get a purchase on the problem, let us begin by accepting provisionally the factor analyst R. B. Cattell's (1946,1950) division between surface traits and source traits, the latter being postulated as generating (underlying, "causing") the former. Surface traits, (e.g., hostility, dominance, social introversion) are not responses in any half way precise use of that term as employed by operant behaviorists. Trait measurements, such as a standard score on the social introversion scale of the MMPI, are therefore not response strengths. Source traits (e.g., Murray's *n Aggression*, Cattell's Surgency Factor) are postulated latent entities and hence deemed by all good Skinnerians to be methodologically objectionable.

Then what is a surface trait, since it is not a response? I daresay most of you - I suspect every one of you - when not designing an experiment or criticizing a theory, permit yourselves to make trait attributions of students and colleagues in ordinary language. Even if one has scientific purist objections to this language, it is perhaps worthwhile to ask why he nevertheless finds it useful to employ it for many purposes of daily life. If I say of somebody that he is a hostile person, and you ask me to defend this trait attribution, how do I go about it, whether speaking as a clinician or simply as an ordinary human being describing an acquaintance? Well, what we usually do, absent some kind of psychometric score believed to be a valid proxy for that surface trait, is to present in evidence a bunch of episodes that we have observed. If we do this in a more systematic way, we would present data from a randomly collected time sample, say, counting hostile episodes of a child in a playground situation, or samples of ward behavior recorded by the nursing staff. Supporting our attribution "hostile," we report that the subject snapped at a newsboy who was slow at making change; he glared at a stranger who jostled him in the elevator; he growled "damn it" when the secretary misspelled somebody's name. Perhaps we subsume these three episodes under a rough descriptive rubric "irritable." Then maybe we adduce another collection of episodes that we lump under the rubric "sarcastic." Then there are a couple of episodes where he went out of his way to harm somebody who had previously slighted him, and we call this "vindictive." And then we argue that since we have episodes instantiating the subtraits irritable, sarcastic, and vindictive, all of which we consider subdomains of the broader trait hostile, this is empirical support for the trait attribution. Note I have not said anything about alleged causal factors such as an aggressive need or drive, which would be a source trait. That surface traits are arrangeable into such hierarchies is diagrammed in Allport's classic 1937 book *Personality*.

I think this is pretty much the way it works when we attribute surface traits, whether we use ordinary language or the technical jargon of the clinician. Examples like this lead me to the following reconstruction of the concept of a surface trait: Surface traits, although not responses, are *response families*. The members of the family are related by a) empirical covariation and b) content similarity. I offer this as a stipulative definition, but not in the sense of complete arbitrariness (as the positivists thought definitions always were) but in the sense of Carnap's *explication* (Carnap, 1953), that is, by examining the way in which such trait language is employed one asks, "How do people seem to go about it?" and then offers this as a rational reconstruction of what they do when they do it effectively. As I use the term 'surface trait,' both kinds of relationship, empirical correlation and content similarity, must be present. One could call them "intrinsic surface traits," emphasizing that there is something intrinsic (inherent, contentual) about their empirical covariation, either in stimulus equivalence and topography or - more complicated - control by the same latent trait, as discussed below. If there is content similarity but not empirical covariation, the trait is not a real trait, that is, it does not exist in the subjects but only in the clinician's head, or in Webster. I believe Cattell called these "semantic traits," given by verbal or logical definition but lacking psychological reality. I call them 'semantic pseudo-traits' so as to emphasize simultaneously that their existence is in the semantic behavior of the trait-namer (the affirmative aspect) but that they lack real existence in the behavior flux of the organisms to whom they are attributed. A classic example of this problem is the Hartshorne and May investigation (1928) of the semantic trait "honesty," which most people expected to have a sizeable statistical coherence but which turns out to be remarkably specific. That is, the tendency of the child to lie, cheat, or steal [= behave "dishonestly"] over a class of situations, while not correlated zero from one context to another, was correlated much less than had been supposed. Debate continues as to the proper interpretation of the Hartshorne and May study but I don't want to go into that here. I will make so bold as to state that some current writing about this subject strikes me as partly pseudo-sophisticated and partly re-inventing the wheel. The assertion that there *are* no traits, there are only situations, seems to me almost crazy. Do those who say this really mean that they would take a bet at even odds that Jones, whose IQ on the Raven and the WAIS is 80-85, will get an A in the calculus class? Or that they would feel relaxed about taking an airplane flight whose electrical inspector had a 49" MMPI profile (Dahlstrom, et al., 1972) and 5 arrests for drunken driving? I doubt it very much.

An operant behaviorist might go along with this proposed definition of a surface trait as a correlated response family, but he would become somewhat restive about the notion of content similarity. Many of the traits employed clinically and in common life do not lend themselves readily to a characterization of the shared property of the response classes belonging to the family by reference to effector topography on the response side nor to simple, physical dimensions on the stimulus side. This is a real difficulty and of course is one reason for the low predictive power of some clinical concepts. But I would like to point out an interesting historical fact about this that some may have not reflected upon sufficiently. If you consider all of the experimental research in psychology going back to, say, Ebbinghaus, on humans or animals, I think it safe to say that 95% of the studies involve a response class falling into one of three categories, namely: words, maze turns, and lever pressings. None of these three response classes is defined (or recorded) in terms of effector topography. They are all specified by some immediate consequence (which in the case of a word is especially difficult to characterize). They are what MacCorquodale and I in our chapter on Tolman in the Dartmouth book called *achievement classes* (MacCorquodale and Meehl, 1954, p. 222). Now, as Skinner points out in the 1938 book, this does not usually present a special problem in analysis because the apparatus guarantees a correspondence between the particular disjunction of effector patterns that is necessary and sufficient to get the lever down and the delivery of the pellet. Except for his concern about the one third of rats that did not show an immediate conditioning to maximum strength on the first reinforcement, where he talks about atypical far out topographies in which there was "incomplete induction" as he then called it, the rest of his discussion is based upon the properties of a cumulative record whose jogs denote an occurrence of whatever effector event was successful in closing a mercury switch. I have nothing to complain about in all of this, as I view Skinner's section on the generic nature of the concepts of stimulus and response, based on his doctoral dissertation, as one of the most clarifying texts ever produced by a psychologist. But taking off from there, one readily recognizes that the topography of the response, and the defining properties of a discriminative or reinforcing stimulus in human social behavior, may be subtle and complex, and hence difficult to specify. Consider this far out (but not impossible) example: I am at a loss to understand why a certain person sometimes speaks louder and with more definite language when I watch him interact with a series of people in their offices, until somebody more discerning points out that he always spoke softer and moderately if the other person had a teak or oak desk than if he had a steel desk. In this individual's life history, steel desks went with lower status. ("Lower status" is a terribly complicated attribute of a social stimulus object, and although the correlated desk properties are "physical" even they are not simple, as is seen when we ask how our subject will respond in the presence of a *pine desk*. Is it "closer" on the relevant dimension to oak and teak, merely because it's wood, than to steel?) The reason I didn't notice this on my own is that I am an army officer and I'm accustomed to seeing steel desks even in the offices of Major Generals. I daresay I needn't argue with you that examples of this kind are all over the place when the subject matter is the interaction of human beings, and from my slight acquaintance with the ethology of primates I think it fair to say that the characterization of responses, and the description of their controlling stimulus conditions (e.g., what constitutes, for an Alpha Baboon, a reinforcing state of affairs when he "successfully dominates" a younger male) is a lot more complicated than whether a rat turns right at the choice point, or a lever is depressed, or shock is turned off.

Some years ago I was engaged in a large scale clinical research project (Meehl et al., 1962; Meehl et al., 1971) aiming at the development of a better descriptive language for both surface and source traits, and we spent many hours, in aiming to improve the writing of our descriptors, trying to get clear about how the clinician - or, for that matter, the ordinary person in making a trait attribution - goes about colligating what he thinks to be the relevant episodes that bear evidentially upon the trait's magnitude. We finally decided that in defending a trait attribution, as when we say "Jones is terribly shy" or "Smith is highly dominant," there seem to be three kinds of considerations in evaluating the episodes presented in evidence, namely, *frequency*, *intensity*, and *pervasity*. Frequency is the most obvious, and probably the most acceptable to operant behaviorists, because it is, if not exactly a rate, at least closely related to the concept of rate. Suppose, in a random sample of intervals in a person's conduct over a month's period, or the time sampling that developmental psychologists do on the playground, or that some more scientific personnel psychologists do in the plant (as superior to a mere impressionistic rating), we tally episodes classified as "hostile." Then the more hostile episodes tallied per extended time sample, the stronger the trait hostility.

However, special weight seems given, both in ordinary life and in clinical work, to even a small number, perhaps even a single episode, of extreme intensity. So that punching a policeman in the nose for saying, "You going to a fire?" would get more weight in attributing hostility to an individual than ten episodes of the "irritable" or "sarcastic" kind that I discussed previously.

Pervasity refers to the extent to which the trait seems to pervade many different behavior domains including those in which one would not expect such a trait to have relevance. Allport's concept of the *radix* (Allport, 1937, p. 147), or Murray's *unity thema* (Murray, 1938, p. 604), or McDougall's *master sentiment* (McDougall, 1933, p. 224) are of this sort. My favorite example here is of the old Jew who was brought by his grandchildren to hear the great Einstein lecture on cosmology, and after the lecture, during the discussion period, the old fellow got up and said, "Well, Professor Einstein, I certainly admire your intellect and I found this all very interesting, but what does it have to do with the Jewish question?"

Frequency, intensity, pervasity: We spent a lot of time trying to decide whether one could reduce one of these to the other two, or ideally two of these to one only, and never settled it. As I recall our discussions, however, if you could tolerate a little procrustean forcing, the best candidate for the basic one is intensity, provided you no longer search for high intensity episodes but simply consider intensity at all points in terms of the counter forces, and the competing responses that we would normally expect in that situation. In other words, a trait of high intensity "beats out the other traits" more often than not, and consequently its episodes are frequent, and its sufficiently high intensity means that even when weakened by some gradient of remoteness, as in our Zionist example, it still comes through.

What about a candidate surface trait when there is an empirical covariation but we cannot come up with a plausible basis of content similarity? Here we say again that there is not a surface trait, because it lacks one of the two requirements of our definition. Since, despite their lack of "intrinsic" content, they do exhibit an important part feature of surface traits by being empirically correlated, and in that sense are rather trait-like, I call them 'surface quasi-traits.' These surface quasi-traits present an interesting theoretical problem, which is one way source traits enter the picture. Example: Freud's anal triad of orderliness, parsimony, and obstinacy was proposed as a typological concept and Freud never said, or implied, that these three traits would be strongly correlated over the whole range of "normal individual differences" variation (Freud, 1908/ 1959). Setting that misinterpretation aside, psychologists have done studies correlating these three members of the anal triad and in most studies it has received empirical support, quite apart from Freud's theoretical interpretation of it in terms of anal libido and toilet training, which I reject. For three consecutive years I asked students in my clinical psychology course whether they could come up with a plausible common content between orderliness, parsimony and stubbornness, and nobody ever managed it. So "anality," despite some statistical covariation among members of the family, does not constitute a surface trait by my definition. How then are we to account for these three things tending to go together?

The most obvious source of covariation of *non*-content-similar response classes, and one which I think no operant behaviorist would have trouble accepting, is what Cattell calls an *environmental mould*. Here the source of covariation among response classes lacking common content is simply that the collection of social Skinner Boxes that made up subjects' environments were so scheduled that a person who learns one kind of thing also learns, in most cases, another kind of thing, however little the two kinds may resemble each other. An extreme case of environmental mould is a *trade test*, where the industrial psychologist can ask as few as 7 or 8 questions about the parts of a lathe and what you do with them that will discriminate lathe operators from the rest of us with almost 100% accuracy. Now defining the word 'chuck' (the only item on the lathe trade test that I could pass) doesn't have any topographical resemblance to one's skill in lathe manipulation, or defining some other term about lathes. The point is simply that somebody who was trained as a lathe operator can do all of these things, so that the distribution of scores on this type of test is not only not normal but tends to be U-shaped, most people getting either perfect scores or scores of 0.

One of the most bothersome kinds of environmental mould is social class, a "variable" that Skinner tends to denigrate because it is (a) a hodge podge variable, and (b) a cross-sectional rather than functional dynamic variable, but that can't be helped when one of the most powerful environmental moulds is social class. Here we have correlations which are utterly baffling in any other terms. For example, one could do a much better than chance job predicting a person's preference for Bach over Roy Acuff and acceptance of oral sex in marriage, from knowing his preference for martinis over beer and football over baseball. There is no conceivable way to relate these four in terms of content, and the sizeable correlations are solely attributable to the environmental mould of social class. It would be as if for some strange administrative reason those animal laboratories whose researchers had a liking for chain pulling as an operant also were particularly interested in the properties of bright light as an aversive stimulus, as a result of which a random sampling of white rats over the U.S. would show this puzzling environmental mould coherence.

The problem of understanding surface trait correlations that seem to lack content similarity gives rise to the postulation of various causal sources that are, in one of several senses, *latent*. Some of these latent causal sources are traits (more or less stable dispositions, manifesting sizeable individual differences) while others are not trait-like at all, either because they are not considered as existing within the individual organisms, or because they are not dispositions but rather *events* or *states*. I can think of four main categories of latent sources: First, we have historical events that have to be inferred because we were not there at the time, and nobody else made the observations. Suppose Freud's theory (1896/1962) of the etiology of hysteria versus obsessional neurosis had been correct, namely, that the future hysteric experienced a prepubertal sexual trauma involving genital friction, was passive and experienced mainly fear and disgust; whereas the future obsessional neurotic had a prepubescent sexual experience where he (more often than she) was the aggressor, and in which the dominant affect was pleasure. This would be a perfectly respectable behavioral learning sequence, and the only thing that makes it "latent" is its not having been observed but having to be inferred from the patient's productions in the therapy session. It is a causal source, but not a source trait, since it is an event rather than a disposition (or variable attribute of structure?).

A second kind of latent source is current schedules of discriminative and reinforcing stimuli that are particularly hard to discern because they are complex and socially defined. Most of them are, again, not within the clinician's ken. If he had an army of social workers and video tape recorders present everywhere his patient went, they would not be latent in the sense of not observed, but they might still be latent in the sense of it being hard to identify the relevant properties. In my experience, the most successful behavior modifiers are people who have a good clinical eye and ear for that particular kind of latency in the patient's current Social Skinner Box.

Thirdly, the mathematical parameters of various drive, reinforcement and discriminative control functions are not themselves measures of strength, or stimulus intensity, or hours deprivation, or level of conditioned anxiety. Rather they are mathematical characteristics of the functions that connect these sorts of dimensions. They are, in that respect, rather like the *factors* that are identified in a factor analysis of a correlation matrix of psychological tests.   They are trait-like to an intermediate degree, being more so than a historical or current event but less trait-like than something like anxiety-proneness or average level of sex drive.   They are perhaps the purest cases of true intervening variables (as distinguished from hypothetical constructs à la MacCorquodale and Meehl, 1948).

Now despite the great difficulties both of detecting and measuring them, I can see no reason why a good Skinnerian should find any of these three kinds of "latent sources" inherently objectionable.   He might not think it a fruitful strategy at a given point in time or in a given kind of context, where he has insufficient means of getting the observations, to pursue them.   That might in turn mean that he would have to abandon researching a certain domain because of the importance within it of these particular kinds of latency.   But my point is that there is no reason why a methodological behaviorist should find any of them inherently objectionable.

There is, however, a fourth kind of latent factor which is objectionable to one of Skinnerian persuasion, and that is *postulated internal entities*, such as an unconscious fantasy, holes in the super ego, damned up libido, a strong preference for repression as a defense mechanism, or a personality dominated by intense reaction formations against oral dependent wishes. Since I have no hope of making this kind of audience relaxed about those kinds of entities, I shall not here pursue that matter further.   I don't see anything inherently objectionable about them, because I don't accept strict operationism as a philosophy of science; but that is quite compatible with saying that an operational policy has shown itself to be a more powerful strategy, especially for technological aims.   I grant that as regards Skinner's program freely and happily.

When psychometrician Cattell introduced the phrase "source traits," what he had in mind was *factors*, those strange mathematical entities alleged to be discovered (some would say invented) by the statistical methods of Spearman, Kelly, Thurstone and Co.   Psychometric factors are in Skinner's standard list of nonfunctional - even mythical - variables, and I have the impression that most operant behaviorists go along with him in this. Ironically, the first major breakthrough in factor analysis since Thurstone's 1935 *Vectors of Mind*, an analytical solution to the generalized definition of simple structure, permitting a programmable algorithm, was by John B. Carroll in 1953. Carroll (Ph.D. Minnesota 1941, now Kenan Professor of Psychometrics at Chapel Hill) was Skinner's first doctoral candidate, and the dissertation was a factor analytic study of verbal behavior traits. If one conceives factors merely as parameters parsimoniously representing the cross-sectional correlations among surface traits, the operant behaviorist should have no problem accepting them. But if one conducts factor analytic studies with a theoretical interest, aiming to discover source traits that are explanatory, *causal* entities, the interpretative problem is muddy. Having worried about the reality-status of factors for some 45 years (meanwhile using it sparingly in my research with a fairly clear conscience) I will not be so foolish as to engage *that* terrible problem here. Whether the recent work on confirmatory factor analysis contributes to its solution is unclear to me, but I incline to doubt it. On a realist view of scientific constructs, such as I, like MacCorquodale, hold, the interpretation of statistical factors is provided by the embedding text, not the mathematics. (Skinner by the way, is a scientific realist and *materialist*, although some misinterpret him to be an instrumentalist, perhaps because of his technological side and his emphasis on control). It seems rather obvious that no mathematical reduction of cross-sectional trait correlations could warrant giving *causal* meaning to a factor in the interpretative text. I am not saying that psychometric factors never represent a kind of physical reality. Sometimes they do, for example, the heritable component of g must correspond to some quasi-fungible properties of brain microstructure or, if you prefer entities we know more about, the set of polygenes involved. The data are cross-sectional (e.g., MZ/DZ and adoption correlations) but of course the causal interpretative text is warranted here by our general knowledge of genetics. Thus, for example, we may safely assume that a foster child's IQ does not causally influence his biological mother's IQ taken before he was born. It's not that factors can't be real, or even that they usually aren't; it's that we don't have a good set of criteria for when they are real and when not.

To the strict "purist" operant behaviorist who is uncomfortable with the clinician's constant use of trait language to characterize patients' dispositions, it is adding insult to injury when the clinician talks of *types* - of which "disease entities" in psychiatry are the objectionable exemplar. Traits, while suggesting too much by way of hypothetical explanatory entities, have at least the merit of being, like familiar behavioral variables, quantitative things that exist in varying degrees. American psychology in general (quite apart from behaviorism) has had a distaste for types or taxa whether within the individual differences-psychometric or experimental tradition. The word 'taxon' is, I think, suitably neutral as to theoretical or causal commitments, and I advocate the noncommital word 'taxometrics' for that branch of applied mathematics that deals with development of formalized methods (ideally, algorithms) for identifying taxa and for sorting individuals into them (Meehl, 1973; Meehl and Golden, 1982). To speak dogmatically, there simply is no valid objection to the introduction of taxa in the description of behavior. The importance of quantitative measurement of the operationally defined variables is not inconsistent with a theoretical conjecture as to the taxonic character of the domain. To think so would be to say that because the operational variables of chemistry are almost wholly quantitative (and even the old fashioned qualitative ones, like saying a metal is "bright," are replaced in more rigorous treatments), *therefore* there are no such taxa as chemical elements. Whether or not the causal structure, or even the descriptor distribution, of a certain behavior domain has taxonic features is an empirical question, to be solved by mathematical data analysis and not by tendentious pronouncements imposing one's own research strategy upon other people. For my part, I think that there are some powerful taxa in psychopathology, that such entities as schizophrenia and manic depression and unipolar depression and hard core sociopathy are real entities, not mere fictions arbitrarily imposed by careless thinkers, and furthermore that the major psychoses are "diseases" in something so close to the so called medical model as to be not importantly distinguishable from it (cf., Meehl, 1972, 1973, 1977, 1985; Gottesman and Shields, 1972, 1982).

It is unfortunate that the mathematics of taxonomic analysis has lagged behind that of, say, confirmatory factor analysis or multi-dimensional scaling, since a satisfactory algorithm for objective identification of taxa, and subsequent taxonomic diagnosis of individuals, should satisfy even the most skeptical behaviorist that what is being done is scientifically respectable. Furthermore, empirical testing of some psychodynamic notions depends upon a taxometrics that has been satisfactorily worked out, both as to the mathematics and the general conceptual methodology. Going back to our Freud example about the anal triad, the first sentence of Freud's classic paper (1908) says, ". . . we often come across a type of person who is marked by the possession of a certain set of character-traits." This does not say anything about the correlation over the range, although the almost universal way of studying it among academic psychologists has been to compute Pearson r's between the traits over the general population. If one adopts a taxonic model in which some relatively small proportion of the general population belongs to the anal taxon, and the correlations of the continuous variable traits outside the taxon, while not zero, are quite small, it is easy to show that even if a clear taxon existed and showed large average differences between its members and the general population, (separations of, say, two sigma) the size of the Pearson correlation over the whole population would be rather small. For reasonable estimates it would be about the size of those that are reported in the research literature, which some have thought were, while significant and in the right direction, so small as to lend little credence to Freud's conjecture.

I am fond of asking our clinical psychology students to say what is shared methodologically by Skinner, Freud, Allport, Murray, and Thurstone? This agglutination of names of persons who it's hard to imagine having enough shared principles to even have a rational conversation with one another usually stumps them. The answer, of course, is that they all take as the rock bottom basis for their views the *fact of covariation*. The reason this is so hard for students to see as a common property is that the ways of studying covariations, and the descriptor elements chosen to be studied, look so different; whereas the basic fact of covariation is so obvious that one does not readily identify it. Despite the important data-base differences and the very different analytic strategies, I would want to insist upon the covariation feature's primacy, and to say that a Thurstone factor, a psychoanalytic guiding theme in an interview, an Allportian trait, and Skinner's operant in its generic character, are inferred for fundamentally the same kind of reason. (I do not, of course, expect most of an audience like this to agree with me.) Some psychodynamic constructs are source traits (e.g., defense rigidity, strong aggressive impulse, mobile cathexes) while others are not at all "trait-like" in character (e.g., anxiety signal, the regnant theme of an analytic session). I permit myself a short digression here from my title's topic to comment on the latter as illustrating the epistemological point about covariation. When we examine the mass of verbal behavior emitted by a patient on the couch during a classical psychoanalytic hour, and one in which the analyst has kept his mouth shut, the question is whether certain interesting properties of the verbal operants - their frequency, their sequencing, their loudness, their speech-rate, their closeness or separation in time, their interruption by silences, all of which are grist for the psychoanalytic interpreter's mill - can be adequately understood with stringent avoidance of any such concepts as an overarching guiding theme. Since no operant behaviorist has to my knowledge undertaken to conduct a serious and sustained effort at this (something more than merely programmatic "what we could do if we wanted to bother"), I do not know the answer to my question. As an unrepentant 40% Freudian, I doubt very much that it can be done, and the general kinds of grounds I would have for doubting this would be similar to those that lead Chomskyites to doubt Skinner's theory of how children acquire language. Of course, the "deep structure" allegedly needed to explain how anybody can put together a grammatical sentence is a different sort of thing from the "deep structure" of a psychoanalytic hour; but from the methodological point of view I think presents precisely the same problems. I'm inclined to doubt that the mathematics of either classical psychometrics or of taxometrics is the appropriate formalism for analyzing the verbal output of a session, although simple chi-square tests would suffice for some purposes. Perhaps Freud's theory of the session is one of those whose strong testing requires both better auxiliary theories (e.g., psycholinguistics) and subtler quantitative techniques (graph theory, catastrophe theory, temporally changing taxometrics) than we presently have or are accustomed to using. But such speculations take me out of this paper's scope (cf. Meehl, 1970, 1983).

Unlike the messy problem of relating trait language to behaviorese, that of genetics is, in principle, quite simple. The essential ideas can be stated in three short sentences, thus: A mathematical expression of the functional relations holding among behavioral variables always contains parameters. These parameters exhibit individual differences over organisms. Such individual differences have a heritable component. There never should have been a problem about this. Of course, in psychopathology the aberrant behavior and experience has a *content*, and that content is *socially learned*. (As Bleuler says, you can't have a delusion about Jesuits poisoning your soup if you've never heard of Jesuits!). One cannot, strictly speaking, "inherit" a mental disease, any more than one can inherit speaking English. The genes provide what the logicians call *dispositions*, of various orders; and the dispositions of any order exist in varying *amounts*. Once we are clear about these concepts (from undergraduate philosophy), the rest is math and facts. The math and facts may be complicated and hard to unscramble, but there is no methodological difficulty involved.

The definitions and distinctions I have offered here are, alas, somewhat complicated. But I think it misleading to simplify matters that are complex, and have aimed to do justice to the "traditional" personologist's view of traits while examining it from the operant behaviorist's methodological vantage point. I believe I can understand the letter and sympathize with the spirit of both, having been educated at Minnesota by men who were masters of them. Perhaps the following outline will help to clarify what I have said:

"Semantic pseudo-traits":
Content similarity but lacking empirical covariation.
Have no physical reality as traits.

Surface traits:
Response family sharing content *and* having empirical covariation. ('Intrinsic suface traits' would be complete label)

Surface quasi-traits:
Response family showing empirical covariation but lacking content similarity (e.g., environmental mould "traits," not really traits by my two-property definition).

"Latent" sources, inferred as causative of surface traits and quasi-traits:

1. Historical events inferred

2. Current schedules hard to discern.

Non-traits, located in environment

3. Parameters of functions relating surace traits and quasi-traits, and these to schedules and state-variables

Quasi-traits, properties of organism but need not be entities located within organism.

4. Postulated internal entities

Events   (Non-traits)

States   (Non-traits)

Structures

Dispositions

Sometimes source traits

Whether some of these category distinctions would, if pressed, be seen to be matters of degree rather than kind is a deep and interesting question I shall not here discuss.

SUMMARY

Operant behaviorists often dislike trait language, but they need not. Surface traits (e.g., hostility) are not reponses, nor (hence) are trait measurements response strengths. Source traits (e.g., *n Aggression*) postulate *latent* entities sometimes deemed methodologically objectionable. Surface traits are response families, related by (a) empirical covariation and (b) content similarity. The causal sources of surface traits and quasi surface traits are often, perhaps usually, "latent" in one of four ways: (1) historical events inferred; (2) current schedules hard to discern because complex and socially defined; (3) parameters (with a heritable component) of drive, reinforcement, and discriminative control functions; (4) postulated internal entities. Some of these latent sources are trait-like, others are not. There is no reason why latent sources of kinds (1)-(2)-(3) should be methodologically objectionable to a consistent operant behaviorist, although he might temporarily opt for avoiding some of them as a matter of research strategy. Type (4) is disharmonious with an orthodox Skinnerian position, but I urge that even these latent sources are not inherently objectionable as scientific constructs, despite their history of rather low payoff in most behavioral domains.

REFERENCES

Allport, G.W. (1937). *Personality: A Psychological Interpretation*. New York: Henry Holt and Company.

Carnap, R. (1953). The two concepts of probability. In H. Feigl and M. Broadbeck (Eds.) *Readings in the philosophy of science*. New York: Appleton-Century-Crofts, p. 438, pp. 441-446.

Carroll, J.B. (1953). An analytical solution for approximating simple structure in factor analysis. *Psychometrika*, 18, 23-38.

Cattell, R.B. (1946). *Description and measurement of personality*. Yonkers on Hudson, New York: World Book Company.

Cattell, R.B. (1950). *Personality: A systematic theoretical and factual study*.

New York: McGraw-Hill Book Company.

Cronbach, L.J. (1957). The two disciplines of scientific psychology, *American Psychologist, 12*, 671-684.

Dahlstrom, W.G., Welsh, G. W., and Dahlstrom, L.E. (1972). *An MMPI Handbook I: Clinical Interpretation*. Minneapolis: University of Minnesota Press.

Freud, S. (1959). Character and anal erotism. In J. Strachey (Ed.), *Standard edition of the complete psychological works of Sigmund Freud, 9*, 167-176. London: Hogarth Press. (Original work published in 1908).

Freud, S. (1962). Further remarks on the neuropsychoses of defense (1896). In: J. Strachey (Ed.), *Standard edition of the complete psychological works of Sigmund Freud, 3*. London: Hogarth Press. (Original work published in 1896).

Gottesman, I.I. and Shields, J. (1982). *Schizophrenia: The epigenetic puzzle*. New York: Cambridge Unviersity Press.

Gottesman, I.I. and Shields, J. (1972). *Schizophrenia and genetics*. New York: Academic Press.

Hartshorne, H. and May, M.A. (1928). *Studies in Deceit*. New York: MacMillian.

MacCorquodale, K. and Meehl, P.E. (1948). On a distinction between hypothetical constructs and intervening variables. *Psychological Review, 55*, 95-107.

MacCorquodale, K. and Meehl, P.E. (1954). "Edward C. Tolman." In Estes, W.K., Koch, S., MacCorquodale, K., Meehl, P.E., Miller, C.G., Schoenfeld, W.N., and Verplanck, W.S., *Modern learning theory*. New York: Appleton- Century-Crofts.

McDougall, W. (1933). *The energies of men*. New York: Charles Scribner's Sons.

Meehl, P.E. (1970). Some methodological reflections on the difficulties of psychoanalytic research. In M. Radner and S. Winokur (Eds.), *Minnesota studies in the philosophy of science*, Volume IV. Minneapolis: University of Minnesota Press, pp. 403-416. Reprinted in *Psychological Issues*, 1973, *8*, 104-115.

Meehl, P.E. (1972). Specific genetic etiology, psychodynamics and therapeutic nihilism. *International Journal of Mental Health, 1*, 10-27.

Meehl, P.E. (1973). MAXCOV-HITMAX: A taxonomic search method for loose genetic syndromes. In *Psychodiagnosis: Selected papers*. Minneapolis: University of Minnesota Press.

Meehl, P.E. (1973). *Psychodiagnosis: Selected papers*. Minneapolis: University of Minnesota Press.

Meehl, P.E. (1977). Specific etiology and other forms of strong influence: Some quantitative meanings. *Journal of Medicine and Philosophy, 2*, 33-53.

Meehl, P.E. (1983). Subjectivity in psychoanalytic inference: The nagging persistence of Wilhelm Fliess's Achensee question. In J. Earman (Ed.), *Minnesota Studies in the Philosophy of Science*, Vol. X. Minneapolis: University of Minnesota Press.

Meehl, P.E. (1985). Diagnostic taxa as open concepts: Metatheoretical and statistical questions about reliability and construct validity in the grand strategy of nosological revision. In G. Klerman, and T. Millon (Eds.), *Contemporary issues in psychopathology.* New York: Guilford Press.

Meehl, P.E., and Golden, R. (1982). Taxometric methods. In P. Kendall and J. Butcher (Eds.), *Handbook of research methods in clinical psychology.* New York: Wiley.

Meehl, P.E., Lykken, D.T., Schofield, W., and Tellegen, A. (1971). Recaptured-item technique (RIT): A method for reducing somewhat the subjective element in factor-naming. *Journal of Experimental Reseach in Personality, 5,* 171-190.

Meehl, P.E., Schofield, W., Glueck, B.C., Jr., Studdiford, W.B., Hastings, D.W., Hathaway, S.R., and Clyde, D.J. (1962). *Minnesota-Ford Pool of Phenotypic Personality Items,* August 1962 Edition. Minneapolis: University of Minnesota Press.

Murray, J.A. (1938). *Explorations in personality.* New York: Oxford University Press.

Skinner, B.F. (1938). *The behavior of organisms.* New York: Appleton-Century Company.

Thurstone, L.L. (1935). *The vectors of mind.* Chicago: University of Chicago Press.

CHAPTER 15

The Formation and Function of Ritual Behavior

JOHN L. FALK

Adjunctive behavior is behavior that is maintained at a high probability by stimuli which derive their exaggerated reinforcing efficacy primarily as a function of schedule parameters governing the availability of another class of reinforcing events (Falk, 1971). Thus, in a familiar example, an adjunctive behavior (drinking) is maintained at a high probability (polydipsic level) by a stimulus (water) which derives its exaggerated reinforcing efficacy primarily as a function of schedule parameters (variable-interval 1-min) governing the availability of another class of reinforcing events (food pellet delivery to a food-deprived organism). Although the animals are not deprived of water, the interruptions in eating produced by making food available only intermittently induces a water intake during the feeding session that is exaggerated by a factor of 10 compared to the intake produced when the same amount of food is given all at once as a single ration and animals are allowed the same session length to drink. It is the difference between a rat drinking about 10 ml under the latter control condition and the same animal drinking 100 ml (perhaps one half its body weight) in a similar 3 hour period.

The intermittent delivery of food and other motivationally important commodities can induce various kinds of excessive behavior and physiological consequences besides polydipsia followed by diuresis: attack, escape, hyperactivity, "empty" sequences of operant behavior, drug taking with the production of physical dependence, and the development of chronic hypertension (see Falk, 1981, 1984 for recent reviews). Many of these behaviors occur in a wide variety of species including humans. Adjunctive behavior excesses can be sustained chronically for months on end as long as their inducing conditions remain in effect.

ADJUNCTIVE BEHAVIOR: ECOLOGIC AND EVOLUTIONARY ANALOGIES

On the face of it, adjunctive behavior seems to serve no function; in fact it is energetically and temporally quite costly. It is important to note that analysis of the conditions inducing adjunctive behavior has ruled out the possibility that it is incidental behavior which has been strengthened through the operation of adventitious reinforcement. In a previous publication, I have argued that although it would appear to have no immediately obvious utility, nevertheless analysis of the conditions inducing it reveal its probable adaptive significance (Falk, 1977). An analogy was made between the diversity-stability rule in ecology (the more diverse and complex the ecosystem, the more an individual species is protected from population fluctuations and possible extinction) and how an increase in the probability of an ancillary behavior (adjunctive behavior induction) can stabilize an unstable situation which contains relatively few behavioral vectors. This runs counter to what we usually intuit about behavioral situations: that strengthening an ancillary behavior would occlude, rather than stablize, some other fragile behavior. However, given too barren a behavioral situation, adjunctive behavior generation can be so intrusive that behavioral alternatives indeed are eliminated, much as a barren island or monoculture ecology is vulnerable to invasion by a colonizing species. I have applied this latter model to the generation and persistence of drug overindulgence.

A similar conclusion known as Romer's rule can be drawn with regard to evolutionary circumstances. The rule essentially states that evolutionary modifications produced by natural selection are adaptive with respect to changes in current niche constraints and are only fortuitously adaptive to any major cumulative or qualitative environmental change. For example, the natural selection of strong fins in lungfish was an adaptation allowing them to drag their bodies onto land just to reach another pool of water. Such fins were only incidentally a fortunate preadaptation for the later invasion of the land and the exploitation of a new niche. Thus, the initial changes were contextually conservative (maintenance of aquatic life); only their fortuitous implications yielded a truly innovative adaptation (getting about on land). Again, as with the diversity-stability rule, strengthening a particular feature or function can yield unexpectedly fortunate consequences for strengthening a current biologic context or species in terms of stability or survival.

In a similar vein, what appears to be an inordinate strengthening of an ancillary behavior by schedule induction may ensure the conservation of some other critically important behavior in a currently unstable environmental context. What I am suggesting is that in all three cases (the diversity-stability rule, Romer's rule, and adjunctive behavior induction) currently adaptive diversification can give rise to subsequently greater stabilities, although this occurs through a variety of mechanisms. In the case of the diversity-stability relation, an addition in diversity can stabilize and conserve the ecological context. In the kind of situation described in connection with Romer's rule, an adaptive change producing maintenance of a particular mode of life in a changing environment turns out to be preadapted for a newly-adaptive, novel mode of life. The longer-term adaptive value afforded by the direction of the evolutionary modification is fortuitously of a different order than that produced by the original selective pressure. Adjunctive behavior posesses dynamic elements evocative of both cases: Behavioral diversification produces conservation of the present behavioral context because of its permissive action in holding the organism uncommitted in the predicament allowing unstable situational vectors time to reach a reliably advantageous resolution. For this notion to be plausible, applying it should give order qualitatively and quantitatively to data available on displacement activities and schedule-induced behaviors. I have attempted this in a previous analysis (Falk, 1977) and only summarize the argument here.

ORIGIN IN DISPLACEMENT ACTIVITIES

Displacement activities occur as collateral behaviors in situations that are of crucial adaptive importance. These include agonistic, sexual, feeding, and parental contexts. Displacement activities are observed when behavior relevant to these contexts is interrupted for some reason. Fighting in an animal may be punctuated by bouts of displacement activity when its adversary begins to gain ground. Mating behavior may give way to displacement activities if the potential mate begins to act more like an adversary than a mate. Egg removal or an intrusion upon the brooding situation often results in bouts of displacement activity. In general, when important behavior gets interrupted by an approaching rival (for territory or a mate) or predator, or when the usual releasing stimuli for the behavior fail to occur, then displacement activities become probable. They do not occur if the situation calls for immediate escape or a simple increase in the appetitive behavior. Displacement activity becomes probable when it is unclear whether the best course of action is to stay or go, to remain engaged in the primary appetitive behavior or escape. In this sort of situational conflict, behavior seems to come under the control of stimuli producing neither escape, nor the primary behavior in question, but some ancillary behavior. Thus, when the behavioral vectors for the primary, crucial behavior appropriate to the situation and escape behavior are approximately equal, the conflict constitutes an unstable equilibrium. Even momentary dominance of one vector would probably occlude the other one so that, on the one hand, an animal would stay engaged with the situation, or on the other hand, escape. Since this choice could be of fateful importance to an animal, the choice had better not be a hasty one. If the situation were quite dangerous, or quite deficient in reinforcement density, then one vector (i.e., escape) would dominate and no conflict would exist. But if the vectors were approximately equal, the best course of action would be to delay the choice until the situation resolves somewhat, until it develops into something more clearly advantageous or disadvantageous. After all, if the situation is not too hazardous or depleted, the animal stands to gain important commodities: territory, food, a mate, or progeny. A conflict situation which diversifies into displacement activities or adjunctive behavior will be buffered with respect to a too precipitous resolution of its unstable equilibrium.

Animals which have evolved mechanisms that bring them under the strong control of ancillary reinforcers that hold them within unstable equilibrium, conflict situations have distinct advantages over those which commit one way or the other too precipitously. Those individuals not prone to adjunctive behavior may chance to escape too soon and lose access to crucially valuable commodities. They may lose a mate, a nest, or a suboptimal but exploitable feeding patch.

Given these determining factors, it would be predicted that schedules of reinforcement delivering reinforcing stimuli of crucial importance would not induce adjunctive behavior if they provided these commodities on either a very rich or very lean schedule. This is the case since at both extremes no conflict would exist. Under a rich delivery schedule there is little escape behavior, and under a very lean one there is a large escape vector. In both cases, this disproportion between the vector for engaging in behavior relevant to the primary commodity in question and the escape vector constitutes minimal conflict. Data on schedule-induced polydipsia and schedule-induced attack are in agreement with this prediction. Neither very rich nor very lean schedules induce adjunctive behavior. Only when the organism is in a reinforcement range that is balanced by an equivalent escape vector is the probability of adjunctive behavior strong. This is the now familiar bitonic relation between the rate of commodity attainment and the degree of adjunctive behavior.

ADJUNCTIVE BEHAVIOR AS
RITUALIZED BEHAVIOR

Ritualization, as the term is used by ethologists, is the process whereby certain acts, particularly displacement activities, have become exaggerated through natural selection as they come to serve communicative functions. The resulting signals constitute a variety of complex display behaviors known by such descriptive labels as sexual, bonding, intimidation, distraction, and cryptic displays. While this analysis of the origin of ritualized behavior is enlightening, particularly in its emphasis on the alteration and extension of discriminative stimuli controlling the behavior (known as the process of "emancipation" by ethologists), it assumes that the intensifications of behavior characteristic of rituals occurred solely under the selective pressures of communicative function. But the excessiveness of adjunctive behavior, which is displacement behavior in its laboratory manifestations, serves no communicative function. The exaggeration of displacement activities characteristic of ritualized behavior probably occurs prior to its utilization in communication. It is behavior that fortuitously provided preadapted unitary acts that required only moderate elaboration for communicative functions. But the unusual strength of adjunctive behavior is not due to the action of natural selection for the provision of unequivocal signals. Rather, it has become strengthened phylogenetically owing to its adaptive value in maintaining an organism's engagement with situations characterized by their status as unstable equilibria. Adjunctive behavior functions to conserve an unstable situational context, occluding either escape or an increased commitment to the crucial problematic vector (e.g., territorial defense, incubation, courtship sequence, feed foraging) until the relative advantages or dangers clarify. It greatly facilitates a holding action within a problematic situation. And while it is just such situations that organisms may find it valuable to communicate about, the ritualization of displacement activities into communicative display functions is a subsequent elaboration using preadapted units of behavior already serving a conservative, rather than a current expressive or operant function.

In typical laboratory situations, adjunctive behavior, of course, does not serve any discernible function. Schedule-induced polydipsia or attack does not conserve the current context in a holding action. The experimental situation does not clarify with time; it remains invariant whether or not the excessive behavioral adjunct occurs. Further, adjunctive behavior has no operant function in the sense that it is relevant to, or effects a change in, the contingencies determining the availability of the crucial commodity. The power and persistence of adjunctive behavior attests to its probable phylogenic adaptive function, not to any current useful function in laboratory situations. Needless to say, behavior analysis need not confine itself solely to the analysis of ontogenically adaptive behavior function. Adjunctive behavior may, however, serve the useful contextual conservation functions I have suggested. But given altered circumstances, it also may give rise to maladaptive behavioral excesses that occlude the introduction or strengthening of alternative, situationally adaptive behavior.

HUMAN RITUALS

The very term "ritual" evokes ambivalent reactions in us. On the one hand, the term usually makes us think of things that are boring, empty, routine, repetitious, predictable, false, stupid, quaintly artistic or expressive, formalized, traditional, habitual, devoid of current meaning, inauthentic play-acting with no real narrative or a rudimentary one. On the other hand, the term also calls to mind that which is sacred, mysterious, organic, magic, taboo, exciting, and the truthful revelation of ourselves and our society. Ritual, then carries a heavy load of contradictory connotations. Within the disciplines of anthropology and sociology, it is given a lot of work to do. Ritual is often described as generating myths, as well as fully developed religious systems. Both are commonly thought of as being carried out or "expressed" by rituals. Ritual is described as having technical efficacies within various societies: It is the activity that divines both the future and any hidden causal variable of interest. It tells where game can be found and who is the witch cursing you. It also is important in the control of status, crops, hunting, weather, enemies, and illness. This often reduces down to theoretical and behavioral presentations of ritual as functional for society in a broad, operant sense. Thus, it is thought by the performer to produce desirable consequences or just to be what ought to be done. It is often viewed as functional in some regulatory way for the society. All of the effort that gets expended in ritual behavior must surely be for something. It must have some functional use. Some view rituals as occurring because humans have deep needs to define and express their situations and predicaments. Thus, ritual often is described as serving our need to make symbols or communicate. From this perspective, it is regarded as both ornamental and highly serious. It is the means by which a culture formulates and expresses its entire world view.

The term "ritual" is used by both ethologists and anthropologists to refer to behavior that topographically is both complex in its sequential organization and rather invariant in form. Further, it is often described as composed of repetitious units. It is these elements of constancy and repetition that give to ritual behavior its reputation as an enactment of things traditional and somewhat curious, but perhaps boring in its excessive presentation of elements lacking novelty. However, it is not the repetitious topography and often out-of-place or archaic scenarios that have maintained the interest of ethologists and anthropologists in the scientific study of ritualized behavior. Rather, there has been lively speculation concerning the inception of ritualized behavior and what functions it might serve. As mentioned previously, ethologists regard ritualization as "the process by which noncommunicative behavior patterns evolve into signals" (Eibl-Eibesfeldt, 1979). Anthropologists too have viewed rituals as facilitating communication about important events, clarifying the nature and current status of such events. These include: (a) rites of passage which communicate and formalize important changes in state and status, such as birth, puberty, marriage, shamanic identity, death, war ,and peace; (b) cyclic calendrical events important to most of the members of a society: rites marking seasonal changes, astronomical events, plantings, harvests, and hunts correlated with the migratory movements of animal; and (c) therapeutic and salvation rites, such as those relating to curing, witchcraft, sorcery, taboos, identity-altering possession, and social revitalization movements.

FUNCTIONAL SIGNIFICANCE OF RITUALS

With the first grouping of rituals (rites of passage), there is a communicative component which reduces ambiguity. For example, information about how much military support can be expected in the future among groups of Maring tribesman in New Guinea is ascertained from how many visiting individuals participate in the host group's ritual festival dancing since there are no chiefs who order their men into battle (Rappaport, 1968). A more familiar example would be the formally recognized status change produced by a rite of passage transforming an adolescent into an adult (van Gennep, 1960). In the second grouping of rituals, the communicative function of calendrical celebrations seems limited to the coordination of group member behavior with regard to seasonal changes and all that implies concerning the exploitation of food resources. Here again, an ambiguous situation is resolved: A crop can now definitely be regarded as food and legitimately harvested. Summer is ritually declared to have become fall. As Jane Harrison (1913) put it: "The periodic rite may occur at any date of importance to the food supply of the community, in summer, in winter, at the coming of the annual rains, or the regular rising of a river" (p. 74). In the third grouping, the rites involving magical control and transformation worked by individuals or groups, social communication appears minimal, although the acquisition of critical information having subsequent social implications is often an important feature. For example, the Sudanese Azande reveal what is hidden by administering poison to fowl (Evans-Pritchard, 1976). An answer to an important question is revealed by whether the bird lives or dies. The poison oracle answers questions concerning matters such as the cause of failure to conceive, sickness, death, the agent of witchcraft, lengthy journeys, adultery, changing of homestead sites, warfare, and lengthy agricultural and hunting enterprises.

In passing through a consideration of the three groups of ritual progressively less in the way of communicative function seems to occur. But they all somehow lead to the stabilizing of an unstable situation by obtaining answers to important questions, or by affirming or effecting transformations in state or status. In fact, one might legitimately ask if communicative function is at all central to ritual, or whether it follows simply as a collateral product of almost any social act. Since anything produced by humans can be deemed an overt or covert act of "communication" by simply asserting that this is so, it has the status of an unfalsifiable concept.

While ritual behavior leads to a stabilizing resolution of an unstable or ambiguous situation, it should not be regarded simply as operant behavior guided directly by current contingencies of reinforcement. Ritual behavior, like adjunctive behavior, is generated by conflict situations and it can facilitate their resolution. Consider an example of magical control most people have heard about and that occurs both in Africa and the New World. Rainfall is of crucial importance to societies cultivating crops and to those that herd cattle. But there are vast regions where rain comes mainly during one or two yearly seasons. If it is delayed or sparse the harvests and herds will be lean; it is a source of great concern. Magical rainmaking rites are calendrical. These rites may be performed by the entire community or be the function of a special rainmaking man or woman. Most of these societies operate with the belief that only a deity can really make it rain. The job of the rainmaker is to engage in the correct rites, acting as an intermediary. In areas where rainfall has not been much of a problem there may be no official rainmaker, or a suitable elder may officiate at the rites (Mbiti, 1969). In parts of Africa an unsuccessful rainmaker can lose prestige as well as be threatened with death. Performing technically correct rituals is necessary, but performing them at the right time, that is, at the appropriate seasonal point, is also a requirement. No one would attempt to make it rain at the height of the dry season. The conditions of the sky and other signs of weather, as well as astronomical indications, may all determine the timing of rainmaking rites. But if the ritual seems to fail, its efficacy is not questioned. Perhaps it was not performed quite correctly, or some taboo was broken, or the particular rainmaker is a fraud.

The critical determinants for the generation of adjunctive behavior are present in the circumstances described. There is a crucial commodity (rain) and an ambiguous condition (questionable probability of the seasonal rains). But the above description of the rainmaking context makes this ritual appear more like adventitiously-reinforced operant behavior than adjunctive behavior. However, the instrumental ends attributed to ritual behavior by its performers may be rationalizations or later modifications of behavior which at its origin has no direct, functional aim. Situational exigencies, such as drought, certainly call for solutions. But the ritual response at its inception is probably adjunctive, rather than operant, behavior. The ritual no more owes its origin and strength to reinforcement by intermittent rainfall than the generation of adjunctive behavior does to reinforcement by intermittent food pellet delivery. This is not to deny that the ritual, unlike adjunctive behavior in animals, is partially sustained by seeming to deliver the crucial commodity (rain). With the proper trappings, judicious timing, and a theoretical structure that readily accommodates failure, the ritual can give the semblance of producing rain, even if it only in fact intermittently announces it. The participants claim that what they are doing is trying to produce rain and there is no reason to doubt the statement. Nor is there any reason to doubt the socially reinforcing effects that can result from participation in such a ritual. But one may question, in light of what is known about the generation of adjunctive behavior, whether the origin and intensity of ritual behavior is just a matter of the production of operant behavior by intermittent reinforcement.

From the perspective of Western science there is reason to doubt the real efficacy of rainmaking rituals to make it rain. However, the argument against efficacy is much less clear in the case of curing rites. But certain conditions apparently must be met for shamanic cures to occur. Not only do both shaman and patient firmly believe that a cure is forthcoming, but so do all interested parties. Magical cure, like voodoo death, is a consensual phenomenon. Its similarity to psychoanalytic cure has been noted, except that rather than the patient breaking through to an emotional insight into the problem's origins, it is the shaman who contests and overcomes the sickness with a vividly dramatic performance (Levi-Strauss, 1963). Most cures also take place before, and with the reactive participation of, an involved audience (St. Clair, 1971). Beside the powerful placebo effects operating as a result of the beliefs of all concerned, shamanic cures often are aimed at remedying the patient's problems by working ritually upon the person's disturbed network of interpersonal relations. Part of the Ndembu doctor's task is to "make visible" and then ritually resolve any such ill feelings (Turner, 1967). Similar considerations are brought to bear in traditional Nigerian medicine (Maclean, 1971). Shamanic cures often demand a high degree of specificity in the diagnosis. It is not sufficient to know only what type of affliction is present, but also how it came about, through which particular malevolent witch, breached taboo, personal ill will, or offended ancestor. If a cure fails to work the system of medicine is defended in much the same fashion as in instances of failed rainmaking: a technical flaw in the execution of the ritual is suspected, or a broken taboo, or perhaps a fraudulent shaman. If the ritual is executed properly the patient may simply be proclaimed cured forthwith and indeed experience an acute improvement. Sometimes the therapeutic effects last beyond such short term episodes. Whether the cure has simply been announced (health was going to return anyway), or in some deeper sense effected (treatment efficacy was present), is not always clear. Placebo-effect cures, in which the ritual enactment is an announcement effecting efficacy, are ubiquitous. The analysis presented for the generation of rainmaking rituals also can be applied to the case of affliction. Curing rituals are overtly operant behavior. Sickness is a crucial situation with the patient poised perhaps between life and death. There is an ambiguous status in terms of improvement probability. These are the elements for conceiving of curing rituals as having their origins in adjunctive behavior.

Consider van Gennep's (1960) analysis of rites of passage; rituals which concern matters lying purely within the sphere of changing social status. The analysis distinguishes three phases in such change-of-status situations as birth, puberty, marriage, and death. In the first of these phases, the individual is separated from his or her present status. The second phase is a state of transition. Finally, the third phase incorporates the person into a subsequent status. These passages are not rapid and often take a long time. In the transitional or liminal phase, status is often viewed as partaking of the sacred or taboo and as being quite a dangerous state. The individual is an ambiguous entity, neither one thing nor the other. Rites of transition are a predominant feature of this second phase until the person is safely incorporated into the new status in the third phase. The three phases, then, can comprise a process that occurs at certain important social junctures, often in connection with the life cycle. There is the initial, antecedent phase, sometimes viewed from the perspective of the new status as rather mundane. This is followed by the ambiguous state of liminality in which the person may be driven off as an outcast for a time or sequestered. It is best that the individual be isolated if the third stage is to be attained. This is because the person is in an unstable equilibrium between two statuses with everyone expecting progression. It would not facilitate attainment of the third phase if people were to observe and react to the individual oscillating uncertainly between two states. A change in the kind of behavioral reaction occasioned in others by a person is facilitated by a dramatic transition in the individual's stimulus properties. By such arrangements there is a sharp transformation, rather than a painful successive approximation, of the adolescent into an adult, the novice into the adept, or the corpse into an ancestor.

Liminal status also can occur in situations that are not life-cycle rites of passage. During a journey when a strange individual sets up camp near a local tribal population, the locals often treat the individual as a taboo foreigner and his status partakes of the liminal. In such situations, if a native and foreign group move into contact with each other, rites involving eating, drinking, smoking a pipe, etc. may occur. These rites in liminal situations are interpreted typically as operants that get the individual or group into the incorporation phase. However, they may simply occur initially as responses to liminality or ambiguity prior to any later functions they may acquire. Current functional use is often not a reliable guide to origins. Thus, the initial ritual responses to ambiguity may be adopted only later as incorporation rites. Their prior function probably serves only a holding action. Options for rejection or further commerce are kept open. As previously indicated, adjunctive behavior can be viewed as a response to an ambivalent situation that is adaptive insofar as it stabilizes that situation. This permits a later solution of the ambiguity. But the adjunctive behavior itself may be only incidently related to the form of behavioral solution which emerges.

Individuals in the liminal phase are often treated as either taboo or sacred, separated from others, or even cast out for a period of time. However, no culture really wants to totally drive away their adolescents, menstruating women, betrothed, or others as they enter liminality. Ritual behavior has the useful function of conserving these now ambiguous individuals prior to any subsequent function it has in advancing them into the third phase.

An individual, creature, or even a social situation that is liminal or difficult to categorize is viewed as either polluted or sacred, thus giving rise to contradictory behavioral vectors. Not knowing how to behave toward it because it crosses categories generates either purification or sacramental rites, depending upon whether it is considered polluted or sacred (Douglas, 1966). Both kinds of rites are often composed of dramatic and exaggerated behavior. Dynamic conflict generates ritual behavior and what ritual is about is the sacred and the reviled. They both come down to the same thing in a way: They are untouchable, except under special circumstances, and for this reason command a lot of interest. Ritual occurs when conflicting vectors intersect and escape is either undesirable, impractical or impossible. A person passing through some liminal phase at least can be isolated, but many taboo or sacred things cannot so easily be sequestered. In India there is a ritual prohibition against killing and eating cows. This taboo might seem strange particularly during droughts and famines when people are starving. However, satisfying an immediate need for food would not serve long-term needs for survival. The sacred zebu cattle are ecologically crucial in many ways: They give milk, deposit dung used for fertilizer and fuel, pull plows, and do not eat the sort of things humans do (Harris, 1966). The sacred status is a result of conflict between the short-term alleviation of deprivation and the long-term benefits of live cattle. Similarly, ecological considerations serve to explain the prohibition on eating pork for peoples of the Middle East. In a hot, arid climate the pig is difficult to raise, competes with humans for grain, and unlike the zebu cattle, provides no critically useful products or services. It is good to eat, but too costly a luxury. The conflict between the temptation to eat tasty meat and the overall ecological unwisdom of keeping pigs generates a taboo on pigs (Harris, 1974).

Often the line between ritual behavior toward the tabooed and the sacred is difficult to draw. Whether the thing or person is viewed in a positive or negative way, the attitude is often one of veneration mixed with studied avoidance and mannered deference. As Durkheim (1965) put it: "And, in fact, there is a horror in religious respect, especially when it is very intense, while the fear inspired by malign powers is generally not without a certain reverential character" (p. 456). He then continues with an example discussed previously:

> Among certain Semitic peoples, pork was forbidden, but it was not always known exactly whether this was because it was a pure or an impure thing and the same may be said of a very large number of alimentary interdictions. (p. 457)

Finally, Durkheim makes the point that "it very frequently happens that an impure thing or an evil power becomes a holy thing or a guardian power, without changing its nature, through a simple modification of external circumstances" (p. 457). For example, dead souls, at first dreadful ghosts, become guardian spirits; and the aversive corpse becomes the venerated relic. The revered and the reviled, the sacred and the tabooed, are not, then, static qualities. Behavior toward tabooed objects can change; it is strongly relational. This can be illustrated by an example of a food taboo among the Kaluli people of Papua New Guinea (Schieffelin, 1976). Single men are allowed to eat meat. But when they marry, fresh meat is taboo for them. It is taboo for their wives since they menstruate. Fresh meat is no longer taboo to the man if he becomes a widower. But the couple is permitted to eat smoked meat. This taboo has an important effect on social relations. It inhibits married men's relations with age-mates and kinsmen in the immediate community, while encouraging those with relations by marriage. The reason it has this latter effect is because smoked meat is not prepared for one's own use; it is only used as a gift. And the main source of smoked meat for the couple is as gifts from the bride's relatives. Similar gifts are made in return. Thus, meat is not taboo if it is smoked, but is available only through affinal exchange. This set of taboos and gifting relations discourages old social relations and promotes new and important ones.

Taboos function to maintain the integrity of problematic, conflict situations. They enable functioning to continue within certain kinds of difficult circumstances. We refrain from slaughtering our valuable cow even though starving; we eschew incestuous relations without having to escape from our loved ones.

The position of Mary Douglas (1975) with regard to these matters is typified by the following two quotations:

> The first essential character by which the sacred is recognizable is its dangerousness. Because of the contagion it emanates the sacred is hedged by protective rules. (p. XV)

> We would expect to find that the pollution beliefs of a culture are related to its moral values, since these form part of the structure of ideas for which pollution behavior is a protective device. (p. 54)

But there is no such thing as "the sacred" protected entity, nor is pollution behavior a protective device for moral ideas. Rather, taboo and sacramental behavior protect important but touchy situations that must remain intact. It stabilizes them. These situations do not contain entities which in themselves are tabooed or sacred. Reverence and revulsion are relational behaviors and what they protect is neither entities nor ideas, but unstable conflict situations. The protection afforded by taboo and by sanctification is often not the usual temporary holding action permitted by adjunctive behavior; rather, a dynamic conflict can be stabilized without any hope of resolution. The stabilization is itself the resolution. A particular mode of commerce with the object or person is blocked without requiring us to escape from the situation or resolve it: The cow is not used as food, but remains in use; the close relative is not mated, but remains cherished.

However, one should not overemphasize the difference between the static, stabilizing action sometimes afforded by taboo and the permissive holding action of ritual. After all, taboo is, as indicated previously, a relational behavior that can change. To illustrate this further, consider the reaction to strange stimuli. Horton (1982) describes the first reaction to whites by the Kalabari of the Eastern Niger Delta as one of horror, followed by massive purification ceremonies, a typical taboo reaction. Similarly, the Kaluli of New Guinea reacted to the first airplane in their sky by performing a ceremony usually reserved for a context of social reciprocity (Schieffelin, 1976, p. 28). Finally, Horton's (1982) analysis of religious conversion to Islam and Christianity in Africa stresses the "holding action" of both taboo and conversion. The new stimuli are viewed as "experiential challenges" that become mediated by taboo and ritual so that there is a "balance between opposing tendencies." Further, the taboo reaction is considered not as a "defense against the threat of novel experience," which is the usual interpretation, but "as a holding device that allows the theoretical system to adjust in its own good time. So the very reaction that once seemed to be purely and simply a bulwark of cognitive conservatism now looks as though it might have an additional function as part of the mechanism of adaptive innovation!" The similarity between Horton's conception of how taboo and religious conversion reactions function to adjust traditional cultures to changed circumstances, and the analysis of ritual as adjunctive behavior presented here, is striking.

CONCLUDING REMARKS

Rituals occur under conditions that are characterized as marginal, liminal, ambiguous or conflicted. There are taboos generated by conflicts having sociobiological and ecological bases (e.g., incest, cow or pig prohibitions). Others are reactions to strange, new stimuli (e.g., airplanes). There are liminalities of rites of passage and the calendrical ambiguities of environmental status (e.g., harvest readiness, rainfall probability). There are therapeutic context uncertainties (e.g., curing, witchcraft prevention). Finally, there are noncalendrical rituals produced by ecologic marginality and conflict. For example, the periodic pig-sacrificing festivals of groups of Maring are culmination points in a cyclic process that is a function of the growth of a group's pig population in relation to both the work of maintaining them and the pig-carrying capacity of territory obtained through warfare with other groups (Rappaport, 1968). The ritual is held, according to its participants for the efficacious reason of rewarding warfare allies (as well as ancestors) and cementing their future loyalty, which it does. The ritual occurs at the point at which there is maximum conflict between two ecologic factors: (a) the pig population size and (b) land and effort available for their support.

There are several distinguishable positions within anthropology and sociology concerning the nature of ritual behavior. The following four characterize the major viewpoints: (a) Rituals are instrumental acts done because they are believed to have efficacy in bringing about some altered state. (b) Rituals are expressive statements about the structure of the society generating them. They are dramas or nondiscursive presentations about a system of beliefs. (c) Ritual performance itself holds society together. It is both expressive and efficacious, although this aspect of its efficacious action often remains unacknowledged by its participants. (d) Ritual practices are an important, although unacknowledged, component of a society's ecological adaptation (e.g., the sacred cow). These various perspectives are not necessarily independent of each other, nor do they need to be excluded from the present viewpoint: Ritual evolved through the permissive function it serves in maintaining the organism's engagement with unstable-equilibrium situations until they resolve. Later, they may, in addition to their permissive action, come to directly facilitate these resolutions by efficacious social operants.

Ritual is not primarily a communicative display. A common view that ritual is mainly there because it binds the social group into a mutually communicating network, is reminiscent of the "oversocialized conception of man in modern sociology" so tellingly skewered by Dennis Wrong (1961). Just as Wrong questioned the premise that humans, unless they are deviants, are by nature socially conforming creatures, so the view of ritual as having its origin and present function in information transfer may be the "fallacy of overproclamatory man." Ritual, if placed in the context of adjunctive behavior, also can be seen to spring not from unbalanced situations or social disequilibrium, but rather from balanced, if unstable, equilibria. The ritual response does not have its inception as behavior reinforced by the stabilizing consequences it has on conflict situations. It does not resolve problems in so direct a manner. Rather, it is an adjunctive behavior. As such, it is generated by a balanced, situational ambiguity, and in its origin allows the ambiguity time to reach an advantageous, rather than a precipitous, resolution. When generated, it is not a behavior done "for the sake of" anything. It is a diversification that, in a sense, annuls all time in its holding action except that which permits the playing out of opposing situational vectors.

In this paper I have tried to present a point of view from which we can begin to apply a behavioral analysis to the diverse and puzzling set of phenomena known as ritual, taboo and ceremony. It is time for us to at least attempt to cast a larger net in the hope of catching some heavier behavioral-unit fish. Perhaps I am hoping for a revitalization movement to sweep through behavioral analysis, addressing old, large scale questions such as verbal behavior (MacCorquodale, 1969; Skinner, 1957). What we have done recently for pharmacology we can surely do for anthropology. The alternative is for our science to become precious, to become increasingly absorbed in a seemingly endless re-enactment of our past successes, in short, to turn our science into negative ritual: an activity lacking the power of either resolution or renewal.

REFERENCES

Douglas, M. (1966). *Purity and danger: An analysis of concepts of pollution and taboo.* London: Routledge and Kegan Paul.

Douglas, M. (1975). *Implicit meanings: Essays in anthropology.* London: Routledge and Kegan Paul.

Durkheim, E. (1965). *The elementary forms of the religious life.* New York: Free Press.

Eibl-Eibesfeldt, I. (1979). Ritual and ritualization from a biological perspective. In M. von Cranach, K. Foppa, W. Lepenies, & D. Ploog (Eds.), *Human ethology: Claims and limits of a new discipline* (pp. 3-55). Cambridge: Cambridge University Press.

Evans-Pritchard, E. E. (1976). *Witchcraft, oracles, and magic among the Azande* (abridged ed.). London: Oxford University Press.

Falk, J. L. (1971). The nature and determinants of adjunctive behavior. *Physiology and Behavior, 6,* 577-588.

Falk, J. L. (1977). The origin and functions of adjunctive behavior. *Animal Learning and Behavior, 5,* 325-335.

Falk, J. L. (1981). The environmental generation of excessive behavior. In S. J. Mulé (Ed.), *Behavior in excess: An examination of the volitional disorders* (pp. 313-337). New York: Free Press.

Falk, J. L. (1984). Excessive behavior and drug-taking: Environmental generation and self control. In P. L. Levison (Ed.), *Substance abuse, habitual behavior, and self-control* (pp. 81-123). Boulder: Westview Press.

Harrison, J. E. (1913). *Ancient art and ritual.* London: Oxford University Press.

Harris, M. (1966). The cultural ecology of India's sacred cattle. *Current Anthropology, 7,* 51-66.

Harris, M. (1974). *Cows, pigs, wars and witches.* New York: Random House.

Horton, R. (1982). Tradition and modernity revisited. In M. Hollis, & S.

Lukes (Eds.), *Rationality and relativism* (pp. 201-260). Cambridge, MA: MIT Press.

Levi-Strauss, C. (1963). The sorcerer and his magic. In C. Levi-Strauss, *Structural anthropology* (pp. 167-185). New York: Basic Books.

MacCorquodale, K. (1969). B. F. Skinner's *Verbal behavior*: A retrospective appreciation. *Journal of the Experimental Analysis of Behavior*, 12, 831-841.

Maclean, U. (1971). *Magical medicine: A Nigerian case-study.* New York: Penguin Books.

Mbiti, J. S. (1969). *African religions and philosophy.* Garden City, NY: Anchor Books.

Rappaport, R. A. (1968). *Pigs for the ancestors: Ritual in the ecology of a New Guinea people.* New Haven: Yale University Press.

Schieffelin, E. L. (1976). *The sorrow of the lonely and the burning of the dancers.* New York: St. Martin's Press.

Skinner, B. F. (1957). *Verbal behavior.* New York: Appleton-Century-Crofts.

St. Clair, D. (1971). *Drum and candle.* New York: Bell Publishing Co.

Turner, V. (1967). *The forest of symbols: Aspects of Ndembu ritual.* Ithaca: Cornell University Press.

van Gennep, A. (1960). *The rites of passage.* Chicago: University of Chicago Press.

Wrong, D. (1961). The oversocialized conception of man in modern sociology. *American Sociological Review, 26,* 183-193.

Author Index

Subject Index